Rising China and
Asian Democratization

EAST-WEST CENTER
SERIES ON

CONTEMPORARY ISSUES IN ASIA AND THE PACIFIC

Series Editor, Muthiah Alagappa

RISING CHINA AND
ASIAN DEMOCRATIZATION

SOCIALIZATION TO "GLOBAL CULTURE" IN
THE POLITICAL TRANSFORMATIONS OF
THAILAND, CHINA, AND TAIWAN

Daniel C. Lynch

STANFORD UNIVERSITY PRESS
STANFORD, CALIFORNIA
2006

Stanford University Press
Stanford, California
© 2006 by the Board of Trustees
of the Leland Stanford Junior University

Printed in the United States of America
on acid-free, archival-quality paper

Library of Congress Cataloging-in-Publication Data

Lynch, Daniel C.
  Rising China and Asian democratization : socialization to
"global culture" in the political transformations of Thailand,
China, and Taiwan / Daniel C. Lynch.
      p. cm. — (East-West Center series on contemporary issues
in Asia and the Pacific)
  Includes bibliographical references and index.
  ISBN 0-8047-5394-6 (cloth : alk. paper)
    1. Democratization—China.   2. Democratization—Thailand.
3. Democratization—Taiwan.   I. Title.   II. Contemporary issues
in Asia and the Pacific
JQ1516.L96 2006
320.951—dc22   2005034078

Original Printing 2006
Last figure below indicates year of this printing:
15   14   13   12   11   10   09   08   07   06

Typeset at TechBooks, New Delhi, in 10/12 Sabon

Portions of Chapter 1 first appeared in Daniel C. Lynch, "International 'Decentering'
and Democratization: The Case of Thailand," *International Studies Quarterly*, June
2004, 339–62. Portions of Chapter 6 first appeared in Daniel C. Lynch, "Taiwan's
Democratization and the Rise of Taiwanese Nationalism as Socialization to Global
Culture," *Pacific Affairs*, Winter 2002–2003, 557–74. Portions of Chapter 7 first
appeared in Daniel C. Lynch, "Taiwan's Self-Conscious Nation-Building Project,"
Asian Survey, July–August 2004, 513–33.

A Series from
Stanford University Press and the East-West Center

CONTEMPORARY ISSUES IN ASIA
AND THE PACIFIC

Muthiah Alagappa, Editor

A collaborative effort by Stanford University Press and the East-West Center, this series addresses contemporary issues of policy and scholarly concern in Asia and the Pacific. The series focuses on political, social, economic, cultural, demographic, environmental, and technological change and the problems related to such change. A select group of East-West Center senior fellows—representing the fields of political science, economic development, population, and environmental studies—serves as the advisory board for the series. The decision to publish is made by Stanford.

Preference is given to comparative or regional studies that are conceptual in orientation and emphasize underlying processes and to works on a single country that address issues in a comparative or regional context. Although concerned with policy-relevant issues and written to be accessible to a relatively broad audience, books in the series are scholarly in character. We are pleased to offer here the latest book in the series.

The East-West Center is an education and research organization established by the U.S. Congress in 1960 to strengthen relations and understanding among the peoples and nations of Asia, the Pacific, and the United States. The Center contributes to a peaceful, prosperous, and just Asia Pacific community by serving as a vigorous hub for cooperative research, education, and dialogue on critical issues of common concern to the Asia Pacific region and the United States. Funding for the Center comes from the U.S. government, with additional support provided by private agencies, individuals, foundations, and corporations and the governments of the region.

CONTENTS

PREFACE: RISING CHINA AND ASIAN DEMOCRATIZATION

The promise of the "rise of China" is that economic development based on trade and foreign investment will eventually cause China's democratization, after which the Realist nightmare of a violent US–China "power transition" can be averted. The two megapowers would work jointly together and with other states and nongovernmental organizations (NGOs) to steer humanity clear of the great dangers it faces in the areas of resource security, sustainable development, quality of life, and complex technological advance. As Chinese individuals and groups participate more extensively and meaningfully in global civil society, the bountiful heritage of Chinese civilization would enrich the worldwide culture-construction process. Respecting a democratic and advanced China, the United States would learn the wisdom of consulting with foreign partners instead of taking unilateral acts.

This promise has occasioned much speculation on prospects for China's democratization. Most observers conclude with some variation on the theme that China "may not democratize soon, but certainly it *will* democratize at some point in the future." The optimism is sometimes based on parallel assessments of democratization in Taiwan, South Korea, and Japan. Perhaps there is an "East Asian path to democratization" on whose trajectory China must inevitably be launched.

In this book, I contend that such is not the case. I explain democratization in Asia as a function of state socialization to a liberal-rational "global culture," originating in the West some two centuries ago but now transnational in its power to provide compelling constitutive norms for domestic governance. I borrow the global culture concept from the "world polity" school of international relations (IR) theory, sometimes called "the Stanford school" because its founder is Stanford Emeritus Professor of

Sociology John M. Meyer, or "sociological institutionalism," the term favored by Meyer's student, and George Washington University professor,
Martha Finnemore. World-polity theory is dazzlingly thought-provoking.
To travel through Asia doing fieldwork while armed with its insights is an
unparalleled intellectual joy. But as I explain in the pages below, I think
world-polity theory suffers from one major and one minor flaw. The major flaw is that it implicitly assumes *all* states will be socialized successfully
to liberal-rational global culture. The minor flaw is that it assumes global
culture is unitary and coherent.

To address the major flaw, I designed my study to contrast two successful cases of Asian democratization, Thailand and Taiwan, with one failed
case, the People's Republic of China (PRC). I wanted to contrast positive
cases with a negative one, because I suspected the reason world-polity
theorists overestimate the likelihood all states will be socialized successfully is that, with some exceptions, they study only successful cases of
state socialization. I discuss this problem of "selection on the dependent
variable" in Chapter 1. It strikes me as a methodological mistake com-
promising studies not only in the world-polity school, but also in many
mainstream democratization studies from comparative politics. This may
be why a number of democratization specialists also overestimate the
likelihood that all states will eventually become democratic.

I do not claim that my own design of contrasting one failed case with
two successful ones is exemplary. I seek only to maximize variation on
the dependent variable to a reasonable extent, given that my research
methodology is qualitative (and therefore time-consuming), combining
textual analysis of documents and articles with interviews of intellectuals,
government officials, and political activists. Originally, I had a 2 × 2 design
in which I contrasted China and Burma (two failed cases) with Taiwan
and Thailand (two successful cases). All entered "transitionary moments"
in the 1980s but emerged with different outcomes. I could control that
way for cultural-historical background variables, since China and Taiwan
were similar in important respects, as were Burma and Thailand. But in
the end, I had to drop the Burma case simply because its internal political
situation and the parlous state of US–Burma relations prevented me, try
as I might, from going there to do research.

I deployed my inevitably limited fieldwork resources for research in
Thailand and Taiwan. I reasoned that since they were the positive cases,
I could most likely elucidate the liberal-rational global culture's role in
democratization by going there instead of China. In both Thailand and
Taiwan, I interviewed extensively and read at libraries, especially the
Thailand Information Centre at Chulalongkorn University and the Wu
San-lien Foundation Library in Taipei. Let me here take this opportunity
to thank the staffs of those two libraries for their helpful assistance and

unfailing patience. Let me also thank my host institutions in Bangkok and Taipei. In Bangkok, I was hosted by Chulalongkorn University's Social Research Institute. Under the talented direction of Dr. Amara Pongsapich and Dr. Suwattana Thadaniti, the Institute's staff and affiliated professors were hospitable, spirited in their discussions, and generous in their guidance. The same was true of my host in Taipei, the Institute for National Policy Research, directed by the accomplished Dr. Luo Chih-cheng. I also spent time at Taiwan's National Cheng-chih University library, and I am grateful to Dr. Chien-min Chao for arranging that productive visit.

Almost all of my Taiwan research was conducted in Chinese, a language I have studied since 1985. On four occasions over the years, I have enrolled to take intensive courses at the International Chinese Language Program (ICLP) at National Taiwan University. When I returned to the ICLP from January to August 2004, I brought with me a huge stack of articles and documents from the PRC, most copied at the Universities Service Centre library in Hong Kong—which I have also visited frequently over the years, and where, in fact, I sit now (August 2005) writing this Preface.

In class in Taiwan, with the ICLP's experienced and well-educated teachers—most of Mainlander descent—I discussed the PRC articles and worked through my thoughts. It was a good environment in which to ponder China and democracy because the ICLP's teachers are almost all committed to a Chinese identity but also to democracy. They helped me internalize deeply the notion that possibilities for China's future are not exhausted by the visions of the Chinese Communist Party (CCP). They also taught me to think more critically about the Taiwan independence movement.

I researched the Thailand chapters during six months of fieldwork in Bangkok during 2000 and five additional months in 2003. I should confess that my Thai language skills are still not sufficiently advanced for reading and digesting Thai articles and documents. Research assistants helped me to read Thai materials; otherwise, I used materials translated into English. Since Thailand has long been open to the outside world—a key factor in its democratization—most government officials, NGO activists, academics, journalists, and business people speak good and often excellent English. Two of the country's most influential newspapers, *The Nation* and *The Bangkok Post*, are published in English. The Thailand Information Centre has a large collection of stellar English publications. So my inability to read Thai fluently should not, I believe, compromise the arguments in this book. Of course I defer to readers to make the ultimate judgment.

I promised the people I interviewed for this study, in both Thailand and Taiwan, that I would not identify them by name. The reason was simply so that they would feel free to speak openly about controversial issues. I *formally* interviewed thirty-six politicians, activists, government officials, academics, journalists, and independent observers in Taiwan. I stress "formally" because I also benefited from numerous less-structured conversations, at lunches and dinners, on the sidelines of public lectures, and on other such occasions. I conducted the formal Taiwan interviews and archival work during the summer of 1999, October 2000, and the summer of 2002, with a few supplementary interviews during January–August 2004.

I number the Taiwan interviews 201–236 in the text. Though in some cases allegiances are unclear, generally twenty-two of the Taiwan interview subjects leaned toward the "Green" camp in Taiwan politics, as members or supporters of the Democratic Progressive Party (DPP) or Taiwan Solidarity Union (TSU). Some thirteen interviewees leaned toward the "Blue" camp, as members or supporters of the Kuomintang (KMT), People's First Party (PFP), or New Party (NP). The thirty-sixth interviewee lived and worked in Taiwan as a foreign diplomat. Among all thirty-six, twenty were activists and politicians (including academic-politicians), six were relatively apolitical officials, four were journalists, three were relatively apolitical academics, one was a Presbyterian minister, one was a lawyer (but not politically active), and one was a foreign official. All of the interviews were conducted in Taipei and Kaohsiung.

In Thailand, I conducted a total of thirty-one formal interviews, all in Bangkok and its immediately adjacent provinces. I number the Thailand interviews 300–330 in the text. Four interviewees were government officials, including two at the ministerial level. About twenty were people I classify as "academic/activists" because they teach and conduct research at universities but also organize NGOs and participate in democratization politics. Some of the activists were (and are) radical, some relatively conservative. Seven Thailand interviewees were pure NGO activists, all, to varying degrees, radical. Many of these people invited me to public meetings and lectures, to lunches and parties, and, in a few cases, to their homes. Their hospitality was extraordinary, and I especially appreciated it because I was, after all, an "outsider" going into the study, a scholar with expertise on China and Taiwan but very little on Thailand. My hosts educated me, with patience and kindness. They taught me, most importantly, to think of Thailand and, more broadly, Southeast Asia, on its own terms, not through the prism of China, which, as a trained China specialist, I was predisposed to do.

I use as my working definition of democratization the Linz-Stepan formulation of 1996:

In a nondemocratic setting, *liberalization* may entail a mix of policy and social changes, such as less censorship of the media, somewhat greater space for the organization of autonomous working-class activities, the introduction of some legal safeguards for individuals such as *habeas corpus*, the releasing of most political prisoners, the return of exiles, perhaps measures for improving the distribution of income, and most important, the toleration of opposition.

Democratization entails liberalization but is a wider and more specifically political concept. Democratization requires open contestation over the right to win control of the government, and this in turn requires free competitive elections, the results of which determine who governs...

A democratic transition is complete when sufficient agreement has been reached about political procedures to produce an elected government, when a government comes to power that is the direct result of a free and popular vote, when this government *de facto* has the authority to generate new policies, and when the executive, legislative, and judicial power generated by the new democracy does not have to share power with other bodies *de jure*.[1]

By this definition, Thailand and Taiwan are now democratic, though perhaps the Thai transition is not yet fully complete. Both countries have problems with "democratic quality." China has barely begun liberalization, and has in fact regressed since Hu Jintao consolidated his power in 2004.

I admit that democracy is my normative preference. I consider it inherently good. Democratic political participation, free public discussion and debate, the right to organize freely, freedom from arbitrary arrest and harassment—all create the social conditions in which people become fully adult human beings. In this book I try to be as analytically objective as possible in sorting out why Thailand and Taiwan have democratized while China has not. But I am unapologetic in expressing my preference for democracy and my belief in its universal validity.

Since I will, therefore, appear critical at various points of the CCP and its elite intellectual supporters, let me make clear from the start my enormous fondness for the Chinese people and Chinese civilization. I have been studying the language, history, culture, and politics of China for twenty years. Each time I visit China or Hong Kong, I am charmed anew by the warmth, hospitality, intelligence, and humor of the people. The country's economic and scientific accomplishments herald China's rightful return to world greatness. But until it becomes democratic, China cannot realize its full potential. To criticize the CCP's dictatorship is, therefore, *not* "anti-China." It is *pro*-China.

China's democratization is also critical to the security of democracy in other Asian countries, especially Taiwan but also Thailand (and others).

---

[1] Linz and Stepan, *Problems of Democratic Transition and Consolidation*, p. 3.

I do not see how Taiwan can survive as an autonomous democratic entity if China continues to grow stronger, while the CCP insists on pursuing a nationalistic-authoritarian agenda. Even Thailand's democracy could be undercut indirectly should the CCP succeed in its proclaimed goal of establishing an alternative new "political civilization" that would be nondemocratic and form the nucleus of an alternative world Center to the West. Because I am pro-China and pro-democracy, I hope the CCP changes course. But I try to explain this course and the reasons for CCP opposition to democracy objectively.

I have incurred enormous intellectual debts in writing this book. I want first to thank Ed Friedman for, most importantly, our ongoing dialogue, since 2001, about Chinese politics and international relations. Ed shares his insights with me through e-mail on at least a weekly, sometimes daily, sometimes twice- or thrice-daily, basis. He read the entire manuscript in minute detail, making important substantive suggestions and offering tireless editorial advice. His personal and intellectual mentorship is most appreciated. But I must work harder to meet his exacting expectations.

Hayward Alker has played a similar role as my senior colleague and mentor in the University of Southern California School of International Relations (SIR). With Ann Tickner, whom I also wish to thank for her mentorship and support, Hayward helped to establish an extraordinarily rich and open intellectual environment at SIR when he and Ann first arrived in the mid-1990s. Entering this environment to begin life as a tenure-track assistant professor *enabled* me to begin transcending the limitations of hyperrationalist political science and develop the qualitative, historically grounded sociological approach I employ here.

I want to thank my colleague and friend Stan Rosen of the USC Department of Political Science. As a fellow China specialist and jazz aficionado—an unusual but, we think, exquisite combination—Stan has, day after day, shared his observations and insights, not only on this specific project but also on China studies generally, comparative politics, the ways of academia, and, of course, film.

I want to thank SIR's Abe Lowenthal for his indirect contribution to this study. Ever since my year as a Visiting Scholar at the Pacific Council on International Policy in 1996–97, when I was also a Visiting Scholar at USC's Center for International Studies, Abe has consistently encouraged me to link my interest in history and social science theory with policy concerns. This was a key factor in my originally getting interested in democratization and the related China–Taiwan dispute.

I want to thank Shelley Rigger, the leading Taiwan specialist in the United States, for reading over the entire manuscript and offering exceptionally helpful advice. Shelley made me rethink a number of important issues in ways consistent with the thinking of my teachers at ICLP and with Ed Friedman. It is a good feeling when the manuscript reviewers agree on what needs to be changed.

Dan Fineman and Apichai Shipper, published Thailand specialists, and deeply knowledgeable about the country, read the Thailand chapters completely through and offered penetrating observations and criticisms. I thank them both. I have also benefited from numerous private conversations with Dan and Apichai in recent months, with Dan at Evergreen and at some of Bangkok's many fine eating establishments, and with Apichai at the less-pleasingly-chaotic but still pleasurable Trojan Grounds coffee shop on the USC campus.

Eric Blanchard, a superb SIR Ph.D. candidate, uniquely combining expertise in IR theory and Chinese foreign policy, read through the entire manuscript, sharing his keen observations. I particularly appreciate Eric's suggestions for Chapter 1. By coincidence, as I write, Eric prepares to make his own move to the ICLP for a year, having already spent a grueling summer there. I hope he benefits as much as I did.

Other people I would like to thank for their observations over the years about issues related to this book include Jonathan Aronson, Laurie Brand, Yun-han Chu, Larry Diamond, June Dreyer, Dennis Engbarth, Robert English, Tom Gold, Bruce Jacobs, Saori Katada, Steve Lamy, Ken Lieberthal, Jonathan Mirsky, Gerry Munck, John Odell, Todd Sandler, Jeffrey Sellers, Geoffrey Wiseman, and Jack Wills.

I wish to express my deep gratitude to the institutions that funded the research: the Fulbright Foundation (for Thailand in 2000), the Chiang Ching-kuo Foundation (for Taiwan in 2000 and 2002), the Blakemore Foundation (for Taiwan in 2004), the USC Center for International Studies (for Taiwan in 1999 and Hong Kong in 2000, and for research assistance), and the USC School of International Relations (for Thailand in 2003, and for various shorter trips to all of these places during 1999–2005).

At various stages over the years, four people provided outstanding research assistance in support of this project: Lyn Boyd Judson, Kuo Ting-yu, Florence Ferguson, and Katherine Chu. Let me also express my gratitude to them.

I thank Muriel Bell, Kirsten Olsen, and John Feneron of Stanford University Press, and Vageesh Sharma of TechBooks, for their marvelous editorial work on the project.

I could not have written the book without the help and affection of Prasomsuk Panpoonnung (Annie).

Finally, I thank my parents for their endless patience, love, and support.

ABBREVIATIONS

AMLO	Anti-Money Laundering Office (Thailand)
APEC	Asia-Pacific Economic Cooperation forum
ASEAN	Association of South East Asian Nations
CCP	Chinese Communist Party
CDA	Constitution Drafting Assembly (Thailand)
CDC	Constitution Drafting Committee (Thailand)
CDP	China Democracy Party
CHRRA	China Human Rights Research Association
DDC	Democratic Development Committee (Thailand)
DPP	Democratic Progressive Party (Taiwan)
ETIM	East Turkistan Independence Movement
FDI	Foreign direct investment
GDP	Gross domestic product
IGO	International governmental organization
INGO	International nongovernmental organization
IR	International Relations
KMT	Kuomintang ("Nationalist Chinese" political party in Taiwan)
MAC	Mainland Affairs Commission (Taiwan)
NGO	Nongovernmental organization
NGO-COD	NGO Coordinating Committee on Development
NHRC	National Human Rights Commission (Thailand)
NP	New Party (Taiwan)

NPC National People's Congress (China)
NSCT National Student Center of Thailand
PFP People's First Party (Taiwan)
PLA People's Liberation Army (China)
PRC People's Republic of China
ROC Republic of China (on Taiwan)
SAR Special Administrative Region (of China)
SDCC Socialist Democracy with Chinese Characteristics
SOE State-Owned Enterprise
TAR Tibetan Autonomous Region
TRT Thai Rak Thai (political party of Thaksin Shinawatra)
TSU Taiwan Solidarity Union (political party in Taiwan)

Rising China and
Asian Democratization

DEMOCRATIZATION AS SOCIALIZATION TO "GLOBAL CULTURE"

In October 2003, Thai Prime Minister Thaksin Shinawatra was busy making preparations to host the Asia-Pacific Economic Cooperation (APEC) summit, a glittering but normally vacuous annual event whose most memorable moment comes when regional leaders gather for a group photograph wearing specially designed shirts. October 2003 also marked the thirtieth anniversary of a Thai student-led uprising that forced the collapse of a corrupt military dictatorship and inaugurated a (brief) period of genuine democracy in Thailand for the first time in history. Many of the student leaders of October 1973 were now middle-aged members of the Thai elite, including high-profile academics and leaders of the country's most visible nongovernmental organizations (NGOs). Some wanted to stage anniversary demonstrations at Sanam Luang, the oval field next to Bangkok's Grand Palace that serves as Thailand's symbolic political center. October 1973 was, after all, a watershed date in the country's history, and younger people should be educated to its significance through exhibits and speeches. Commemorations might also help to strengthen and consolidate Thai democracy, which had been crushed in a military coup of October 1976 but then reinstated following the success of another mass uprising in May 1992.

Thaksin, an elected prime minister who often mocked democratic institutions and values, seemed far more interested in making sure the APEC summit went smoothly than in facilitating what he regarded as pointless and embarrassing NGO activism. He had, in any case, already promised the NGOs he would eradicate poverty within six years. Why did they still complain, and even go mobilize landless villagers for demonstrations in Bangkok? The thought of such scruffiness spoiling the nation's capital during APEC was evidently too much for Thaksin to bear. He became visibly angry and ordered that no demonstrations of any sort be held. But he did not have the authority to issue such an order, since freedom of assembly was guaranteed under sections 39 and 44 of the 1997 "People's Constitution," the capstone to the 1990s' democratization movements. Lacking authority, Thaksin issued threats:

Prime Minister Thaksin Shinawatra warned yesterday [1 October 2003] that any villager groups holding protests during this month's APEC summit in Bangkok would fall out of favor with his administration. "You will be among the last ones to receive financial aid from the government," he said, referring to an ambitious plan to spend at least 200 billion baht [about $5 billion] to stamp out poverty . . . Thaksin also threatened to blacklist any non-governmental organization taking part in a street rally during the meeting. "Any NGO that brings them [poor villagers] for protests will no longer be able to work with me in the future," Thaksin said . . . "It won't hurt if you will think about your country and the image of your country for just a week."[1]

Thaksin then delivered the *coup de grace* against NGO activists: "These people merely need to show they are working to please their overseas sources of funding. Everybody knows that NGOs are funded by foreigners."[2]

All through the rainy season (June–October) of 2003, Thaksin had hammered away at the theme of NGOs catering to the whims of foreigners. He initiated this strategy in August 2001, after the Constitutional Court decided in a controversial 8–7 vote that the former police colonel and (still) billionaire telecommunications tycoon—who first became Prime Minister in February 2001—did not intend, in 2000, to hide millions of dollars in assets by registering them in the names of his servants.[3] After the verdict, Thaksin could rest assured that he would not be barred from politics for five years, as would have been required under the Constitution had he been found guilty. No longer would he need to tread so cautiously.

Also buoyed by high popularity ratings accompanying Thailand's booming economic growth, Thaksin and his key lieutenants in the Thai Rak Thai (TRT) party were, by the time of the APEC summit, in no mood to tolerate activists' troublemaking. The prime minister criticized NGOs by suggesting they were "un-Thai." He instructed NGO leaders and Bangkok Governor Samak Sundaravej, as they negotiated whether and how to commemorate October 1973, to "please be helpful and do not act as if you were from different nations." Samak wanted to forbid demonstrations entirely so that the grass in Sanam Luang could be kept tidy for APEC visitors.[4] Samak had been a cabinet minister in the military government forced from power in October 1973 and was associated with the right-wing paramilitary groups that rampaged through Thailand before and during the October 1976 crackdown.[5] But apparently to Thaksin, Samak represented the Thai nation, while NGO leaders represented foreign radicalism.

Democrat Party leader Banyat Bantadtan, speaking for a weak and hamstrung parliamentary opposition, countered the prime minister by arguing in a parliamentary session that "allowing peaceful protests would reflect a democratic political system, whereas the country's reputation would be damaged if [during APEC] freedom of expression were suspended." Sounding more desperate than Banyat, the head of Forum-Asia, a human rights NGO, offered that Thaksin was making "a serious mistake" and that "his actions are like those of a dictator." In the end, Thaksin and Samak did agree to permit activists to hold restricted commemorative events in a limited section of Sanam Luang. But they also allowed rumors of impending police action to flourish, with the result that only a few dozen members of the general public dared to attend.[6]

The "International Dimensions" of Asian Democratization

Throughout Asia, contemporary struggles to establish or consolidate democracy ignite passions rooted in two centuries of humiliating encounters with Western soldiers, merchants, and proselytizers. Some of the passions are genuine; some are manufactured artificially by conservative elites. Not only in Thailand, but also in the People's Republic of China (PRC) and Taiwan, Burma and Vietnam, Malaysia and Indonesia, and most other Asian countries, *international identity*—as developed through many decades of adjustment to a West-centered global society—is a powerful factor affecting propensity to democratize. When Thaksin criticizes NGO activists, he is suggesting that the human rights, community rights, wealth redistribution, and cultural pluralism they promote represent the same forces of foreign arrogance that have humiliated Thailand in the past. It does not matter that Thaksin himself agreed to make Thailand a "major non-NATO ally" of the United States in 2003 and to send troops to Iraq. It matters less that his government received far more money from foreign aid agencies than NGOs could ever hope to receive. NGO activists do disturb the social harmony and order (*khwam riaproy*) prized by Thailand's prosperous urbanites. When Thaksin criticizes NGOs for blocking roads, interfering with dam construction, and smearing his government's reputation during APEC, he is seeking to denigrate democracy itself. That the tactic works is suggested by the experience of one human rights campaigner arrested on the way to a 2002 protest near the Burma border. The arresting officer asked the campaigner: "Why do you want to protest for human rights, anyway? Human rights are just '*farang*.' "[7]

Although not contesting the close association of human rights and democratic liberties with (the best in) Western civilization, Thai democracy activists insist that their philosophical foundations are universal, and that all Asian societies have traditions and legacies on the basis of which democracy can, and should, be built.[8] But if liberalism becomes discredited in Thailand as a result of cynical associations with images of Western arrogance, Thai democracy would be in danger, possibly to be replaced by a corrupt version of the paternalistic corporatism championed in such places as Malaysia and Singapore. A similar outcome might result if the authoritarianism of economically vibrant China were to become attractive in Thailand and legitimate Thaksin-style populist authoritarianism.

Democracy is also under threat in the Republic of China (ROC) on Taiwan, which the PRC proposes to annex under the "one country, two systems" formula used for Hong Kong and Macau. "Hongkongization" would neuter Taiwan politically and transform it into a place smoldering with discontent and unable to express or act upon popular views on a wide range of subjects Beijing deems off-limits. The fear of Hongkongization prompts an extremist wing of the Taiwanese nationalist movement to seek a restructuring of ROC society through new limits on cross-Strait economic and cultural transactions and the political rights of ethnic Mainlanders. Yet this, too, would cause Taiwan's transmogrification into an entity far less liberal than it is today. The appeal of defensively illiberal Taiwanese nationalism might evaporate if China itself were to become democratic. But given the ruling Chinese Communist Party's (CCP's) crushing of the China Democracy Party in 1998, its tight restrictions on civil society development, and its heavy regulation of Internet use and other forms of public communication, prospects for the PRC's democratization seem extremely poor.

One reason the CCP can resist democratization successfully is because Party leaders use their public discourse—even more pointedly than Thaksin—to associate democratization with caving in to Western domination. This association resonates with a Chinese public taught from childhood to feel humiliated and angry at the century of Western and Japanese imperialism from the 1840s to the 1940s. CCP elites, including establishment intellectuals, link democracy and human rights with subservience to "American hegemonism" (*Mei ba*). They mock democracy as currently practiced in Japan and Taiwan as corrupt and hypocritical. In the mid-1990s, a few years after home-grown democracy activists

TABLE 1

Classifying Theories of Democratization

Domain of explanation	Level of analysis	
	Global	Domestic
Material	A. Robinson	B. Moore; political economy
Ideational	D. World-polity	C. "Civic culture"

erected a "Goddess of Democracy" statue (modeled partly on the Statue of Liberty) in Tiananmen Square, the CCP's intensive cultivation of reactive nationalism began to bear fruit, and young Chinese started expressing hostility to the US and "Western-style" democracy and human rights. The party-state succeeded in reconstructing democracy and human rights as tools designed by Washington—sometimes with the connivance of Tokyo and Taiwan independence activists—to weaken and divide a China that had finally begun a glorious "peaceful rise" to world power status, national reunification, and mass prosperity.[9]

Clearly, Asian democratization must be conceived and understood in its rich historical and international contexts.[10] But what Laurence Whitehead calls "the international dimensions" of democratization (in any region) are under-theorized in the specialist literature.[11] Democratization theories can generally be classified with the aid of the foursquare matrix in Table 1.[12] On the vertical axis, theories are classified according to whether they stress the material (usually economic) or ideational (cultural) side of social and political life; on the horizontal axis, they are classified according to whether they stress the global or domestic level of analysis. Because the systematic study of democratization emerged from political development studies in the field of comparative politics, most democratization theories explain domestic-level dynamics. Examples would include such classics in comparative politics as Moore's *Social Origins of Dictatorship and Democracy* (material domain) and Almond and Verba's *The Civic Culture* (ideational domain).[13] The domestic approach also dominates the huge corpus of contemporary work, most prominently books and articles elucidating the role of civil society in democratization.[14]

Many democratization studies "select on the dependent variable," by only focusing on like cases, usually successes.[15] Except for the special category of large-N quantitative studies,[16] democratization specialists tend to focus their analytical attention on countries that have succeeded in becoming democratic, giving far less attention to those that remain authoritarian. This is despite Gerardo Munck's important argument that continued development of democratization theory will require specialists to "dispel

a deeply-ingrained belief that only similar cases can be compared."[17]
Persistence of the case-selection bias distorts understanding by reinforcing the popular assumption that democratization is natural, normal, and
even inevitable. *The* road of political development leads to democracy.
There is no other road. Whatever barriers exist only block the eventually inevitable, and the detours are temporary. Yet as Thomas Carothers
contends, "aid practitioners and policy makers looking at politics in a
country that has recently moved away from authoritarianism should not
start by asking, 'How is its democratic transition going?' They should
instead formulate a more open-ended query, 'What is happening politically?' Insisting on the former approach leads to optimistic assumptions
that often shunt the analysis down a blind alley."[18]

Theorists working at the global level of analysis may be more likely
than country specialists to view democratization as normal. Samuel
Huntington concludes *The Third Wave* by conceding that although "new
forms of authoritarianism could emerge that are suitable for wealthy,
information-dominated, technology-based societies," in the absence of
such scenarios (which he apparently considers unlikely), "economic development should create the conditions for the progressive replacement
of authoritarian political systems by democratic ones. Time is on the side
of democracy."[19]

Whitehead describes East European democratization as a contagious
process in which "relatively neutral transmissions of information" about
democratization entered from Western Europe and interacted with
domestic situations to produce successful transitions relatively easily.
"International demonstration effects" acquired their potency from "an
almost universal wish to imitate a way of life associated with the liberal
capitalist democracies of the core regions (the wish for modernity)." This
wish "may undermine the social and institutional foundations of any
regime perceived as incompatible" with it.[20] Yet clearly in China, and
to a lesser extent in Thailand, many people are content to tolerate authoritarianism or authoritarian tendencies if the payoff is high economic
growth. They may wish for *material* modernity, but not necessarily
political modernity. Or, from another perspective, they may seek to
redefine political modernity to include certain forms of authoritarianism.

Another study at the global level of analysis exhibiting similar problems is William Robinson's *Promoting Polyarchy*. Working primarily in
the material domain of explanation (Table 1)—but, as a Gramscian, also
concerned with culture—Robinson argues that the United States and associated global elites promote conservative "political democratization,"
in contrast to social and economic democratization, for the purpose of

obfuscating material domination by a transnational capitalist elite.[21] In the 1960s and 1970s, an increasingly fine articulation of global production and distribution processes spawned resistance movements throughout the Third World. Capitalist elites in the United States and elsewhere began worrying that the entire political-economic order might soon come under threat. Robinson contends that they responded by promoting a neutralization of radicalism through political democratization, in places ranging from the Philippines and Chile to Nicaragua and Haiti.[22]

Like many of the mainstream democratization specialists whose work he criticizes, Robinson studies only cases of successful political democratization. On this basis, he concludes that democratization is the norm under US-dominated high globalization.[23] Robinson seeks to be a critical theorist, in Robert Cox's sense of "standing apart from the prevailing order of the world" and asking how that order came about:

Critical theory, unlike problem-solving theory, does not take institutions and social power relations for granted but calls them into question by concerning itself with their origins and how and whether they might be in the process of changing. It is directed toward an appraisal of the very framework for action, or problematic, which problem-solving theory accepts as its parameters.... Critical theory is theory of history in the sense of being concerned not just with the past but with the continuing process of historical change.[24]

Robinson is critical of political-economic institutions but not the post-Enlightenment Western cultural narrative. He does not analyze this narrative's reception by non-Western actors under the assumption they might reject it *fundamentally*. Robinson and most mainstream democratization specialists work *inside* the Enlightenment tradition, Robinson taking a Marxist/Gramscian approach and Huntington, Whitehead, and others a Tocquevillian or classical political economy approach. The result is to project the concerns of one particular branch of the Western Enlightenment tradition on the entire world, implicitly ruling out the possibility that people in other countries might approach political development from a radically different set of cultural assumptions.[25]

Disinclination to take Cox's strictures to heart and try to stand outside the Western narrative makes it difficult for some scholars to accept the possibility that a country such as China may *never* democratize. For example, in predicting China's certain democratization, Bruce Gilley declares that "the laws of social science grind away in China as they do elsewhere, whether people like it or not."[26] This is precisely the sort of ahistorical and decontextualized approach that Cox rejects.[27] Gilley acknowledges the (remote) possibility that the CCP's dictatorship may "survive through a deep structure of political organization that I have simply not grasped, bound as I am by the circumstances of my time and unable to perceive the radical implications of the deep social forces that keep the CCP in power."[28] This is an important concession because accepting the possible permanence of Chinese authoritarianism is crucial to breaking the trap of methodological and conceptual selection on the dependent variable. Even acknowledging that "China may not become democratic for a very long time" would be insufficient, because if the analyst is convinced that "in the end" China is *certain* to democratize, he or she will fail to comprehend its development trajectory. The same would hold for any analyst convinced that China is certain *not* to democratize.

Yet another important globe-level theory of democratization is world-polity theory (or "sociological institutionalism"), a neo-Weberian approach developed in the 1980s and 1990s by Stanford sociologist John Meyer and protégés. World-polity theory does not explain democratization per se. It explains the "considerable, and on many dimensions increasing, isomorphism among the world's diverse national states and societies," especially the fact that most countries "adopt remarkably similar constitutional frames, around stylized goals of collective progress and individual rights and equality."[29] Today, governments worldwide collect vast amounts of socioeconomic data, establish national education systems, promote science and technology development, protect the population's health and welfare, and struggle to sustain the environment while "growing" the economy.[30] No state pursued such goals 200 years ago. World-polity theorists contend that the reason for the change—and for increasing state isomorphism—is that a powerful, rationality-esteeming "global culture" (sometimes, "world culture") developed out of the European Enlightenment and diffused worldwide through imperialism and imitation.[31] Universally, global culture now socializes state elites to pursue humanitarian progress based on rationality and reason. Global culture was thus Western in origin but eventually became denationalized.[32] Today, even Westerners are incapable of resisting its constitutive power. To world-polity theorists, states become democratic through *socialization to global culture.*[33]

World-polity theorists join most democratization specialists in expressing a normative preference for democracy and the modern rational state, hoping and expecting that states will become more alike and more humane. They would be classified as "solidarists" in the parlance of English School International Relations (IR) theory.[34] This will be a useful categorization to keep in mind when considering conservative Thai and, especially, Chinese Communist responses to democratization. As Barry Buzan explains, solidarist explanations of, and hopes for, world order can be contrasted with conventional and conservative "pluralist" approaches:

> In substantive terms, pluralism describes "thin" international societies [of states] where the shared values are few, and the prime focus is on devising rules for coexistence within a framework of sovereignty and non-intervention. Solidarism is about "thick" international societies in which a wider range of values is shared, and where the rules will not only be about coexistence, but also about the pursuit of joint gains and the management of collective problems in a range of issue-areas....

> Under pluralism, ... self-interest certainly stretches to cooperation in pursuit of a livable international order, but it keeps the focus on *differences* among the states and does not require that they agree on anything beyond the basics, or that they hold any common values other than an interest in survival and the avoidance of unwanted disorder. It nevertheless needs to be noted that pluralism does not exclude the members of interstate society from sharing a degree of common identity.[35]

In a completely solidarist international society, "states might abandon the pursuit of difference and exclusivity as their main *raison d'etre* and cultivate becoming more alike as a common goal." They might develop a deep common identity, rooted in "a package of values that is associated not just with belonging to the same civilization (which was true for the states of classical pluralist Europe), but also with a substantial convergence in the norms, rules, institutions, and goals of the states concerned."[36] Ascending solidarism is the world-polity theorists' vision. They are convinced of global culture's power to reconstitute all states as liberal-rational entities. Ascending solidarism is also the vision of many democratization specialists, especially those who hope and work for a "democratic peace." But the question is whether global culture is actually powerful enough to overcome the commitment of an authoritarian superstate such as China to "world plurality" (*shijie de duoyangxing*).[37]

Like a number of democratization specialists, world-polity theorists tend to select on the dependent variable in designing their research, and thus presume and elucidate, rather than test, global culture's (re)constitutive power. For example, in *National Interests in International Society*, Martha Finnemore develops the important argument—contra Neorealism and Neoliberalism—that states are empty organizations, devoid of identity and ignorant of their interests, until socialized by global culture: "I want to explain why all states create science bureaucracies at the same time, why they all agree to new rules of war, why they agree to redefinitions of development and change policies accordingly.... [T]here is no variation in behavior (the 'dependent variable') in my study. It is precisely the similarity in behavior where none should exist that makes these cases theoretically anomalous and worthy of investigation."[38]

Using a set of meticulously drawn case studies, Finnemore demonstrates that global culture sometimes reconstitutes states in significant ways. But because she studies only successful cases of state socialization, she cannot explain *why* socialization occurs, only *how*. In effect, she brackets the question of why and assumes socialization's inevitability. As long as her only goal is to elucidate process, there is no problem. But in stating that "I want to *explain* why *all* states" undergo socialization, Finnemore makes a claim that goes beyond what her research design can support. Selecting on the dependent variable leads too easily to the conclusion that state isomorphism is inevitable.

World-polity theorists also tend to deny states and other actors genuine agency in constructing the world polity. They do assert that actors exercise agency. Finnemore writes that "actors create structures which take on a life of their own and in turn shape subsequent action. Social structures create and empower actors who may [then] act to overturn structures for reasons of their own."[39] She and other world-polity theorists devote considerable attention to the processes by which actors such as international NGOs (INGOs) participate in this structuration process by socializing (some) states to global culture.[40]

But closer inspection reveals a structuralist bias in much of this work. World-polity theorists assume implicitly that INGOs and other "agents" of socialization enjoy little or no autonomy vis-à-vis the global culture. The culture becomes like a disembodied hermeneutical force shaping and transforming all people and organizations in its path.[41] INGOs act as "agents" only in the quite different sense of "agent" to the "principal" of a reified global culture.

Boli and Thomas exemplify this structuralist bias when they write that "in the context of these constitutive [global] cultural principles and models, actors do not *act* so much as they *enact*." At best, "enactment does not entail mechanical recitation of highly-specified scripts. Rather, actors actively draw on, select from, and modify shared [global] cultural models, principles, and identities."[42] Actors can maneuver in this limited way because global culture is internally inconsistent in some respects and so cannot completely prescribe behavior. For example, it esteems both efficiency and equality, an inconsistency that allows some actors the "agency" to choose between championing economic growth and championing wealth redistribution. But no actor can choose simply to ignore the economic-development *problematique* altogether.

The structuralist bias implies that global culture became set in the West (in unspecified ways) about two centuries ago and then slowly unfolded in a self-realization process no human actor could stop. The possibility that a powerful challenger to Western hegemony, such as China, might arise and successfully contest some of global culture's most important constitutive norms eludes most of these writers. Since global culture in the world-polity theorists' sense originated in the West, the West's successive defeats of Nazism, Fascism, Japanese *bushido* militarism, and Soviet Stalinism might contribute to the sense of the culture's invincibility. But advancing world-polity theory—as advancing democratization theory— requires explicitly allowing for the possibility that the future is open-ended. Perhaps global culture is malleable or even breakable at a deep level.

World-polity theorists also systematically underestimate the domestic sources of state identity. This reinforces their sense of global culture's invincibility. Boli and Thomas claim that "worldwide constructs provide social identities, roles, and subjective selves by which individuals rationally organize to pursue their interests. . . . World-cultural conceptions also define the collective identities and interests of such entities as firms, states, and nations."[43] Indigenous sources of identity and local agency in "imagining the community" are presumed insignificant. Boli and Thomas do concede the importance of understanding "the generation and promotion of competing world-cultural models of social organization and action."[44] But they decline to study such phenomena.

Cognate problems cloud Thomas Risse and Kathryn Sikkink's important edited volume, *The Power of Human Rights: International Norms and Domestic Change*.[45] This book's purpose is to examine how human rights norms diffuse from the centers of global culture in the West to authoritarian postcolonial states. Risse and Sikkink know that selection on the dependent variable has marred previous such studies. To avoid this problem, "in addition to the well-publicized 'success stories' of international human rights like Chile, South Africa, the Philippines, Poland, and the former Czechoslovakia, we also examine a series of more obscure and apparently intractable cases of human rights violations in such places as Guatemala, Kenya, Uganda, Morocco, Tunisia, and Indonesia."[46] Reviewing the country chapters, Risse and Sikkink conclude that "the diffusion of international norms in the human rights area crucially depends on the establishment and the sustainability of networks among domestic and transnational actors who manage to link up with international regimes, to alert Western public opinion and Western governments."[47] NGOs become central to the norm-diffusion process, and they are usually successful, because "despite the geographic, cultural, and political diversity of the countries represented in our cases, we saw similar patterns and processes in very different settings."[48]

Contributors to *The Power of Human Rights* did find that human rights violations increased in a few countries, such as Tunisia and Kenya. But in their introduction, Risse and Sikkink play down these negative cases and focus on modeling the step-by-step process by which *successful* norm diffusion occurs. In this they do a laudable job—the model is carefully drawn. But with a case like China in mind, or Thailand under Thaksin, the reader is left wondering exactly *why* successful diffusion occurs, not just how. Clearly, it does not occur in every case.

Risse and Sikkink's sample selection process also remains biased, because it includes only weak states already embarked to some degree on a course of human rights improvement. All the states in their sample had agreed in principle to accept the demands of foreign governments and international aid agencies to accede to global human rights standards. Contributors to *The Power of Human Rights* take these already semisuccessful (and some quite successful) cases, examine their history of interactions with NGOs and other important actors, and then develop an abstract model of what in effect becomes "the road" to human rights improvement. A significantly more effective approach would have been to *maximize* variation on the dependent variable by including some cases of countries—such as China, North Korea, Vietnam, and Burma—not even embarked upon "the road" and apparently not planning to embark upon it any time soon. China would be especially important to include because of its growing power.[49]

That Risse and Sikkink believe in a single road and a single process of international norm diffusion is reinforced by the "phase" metaphor they use to structure their model. "Phase" language conveys a sense of inevitability about successful socialization:

Because of changes in "world time," it is possible that denial and backlash is a normative phase particular to a period in which new international norms have emerged, but when they are still strongly contested internationally. Governments, through their denial, engage in this contestation. If this is the case, we would expect the denial stage to disappear in cases of more fully institutionalized norms.... In Latin America, it is possible that the historical limits to the denial phase are being reached in the mid-1990s, but we would expect this contestation to continue much longer in Asia and Africa.[50]

If all are embarked upon "the road," Asian and African countries must eventually exit the current "denial and backlash" phase when its "historical limits" have been reached, making their proper advance to the next stage. All countries must one day be socialized successfully to global culture's human rights norms. Resistance can only be temporary. Thus, "we argue in this book that instrumental adaptation to growing international

and domestic pressures is a typical reaction of norm-violating governments in the early stages of the socialization process."[51] Yet perhaps the
unsocialized state will *always* indulge in mere instrumental adaptation,
never internalizing liberal human rights standards. Such a state armed
with sufficient levels of what John Hobson terms "international agential
power" might even take actions to change the content of global culture,
reversing the recent trend toward global solidarism and restoring a pluralist world order.[52]

"Post-*Tiyong*" Global Socialization

The liberal-rational global culture is not invincible. NGO and other activists from all parts of the world have had to struggle and sacrifice—
exercising agency—to develop the culture's democratizing potential. Since
especially the 1960s, activists' efforts have succeeded in pressuring conservative states, including some in the West, to reform politically. Partly
because historical factors have made Thailand and Taiwan comparatively open to global socialization, they have become democratic in recent
decades. But China under the CCP, while open to some forms of socialization, rigorously macromanages the process to prevent reconstitution
at the level of collective identity. This is a key reason the CCP rejects
democratization.

When Asians first encountered liberal-rational global culture in the
nineteenth century, they unavoidably associated it with Western imperialism. Many found it difficult to reconcile Enlightenment values with actual
Western behavior. The West appeared hypocritical, but it was also attractive. In this situation, Asians had to decide what of their own culture's
imagined essence (and they did essentialize) to risk sacrificing in exchange
for Western technology, institutions, and values. Even conservatives
conceded that some borrowing would be necessary to improve popular
welfare and increase military strength. But what would be a safe and
acceptable level of damage to indigenous culture and institutions? This
traumatic crucible was called in Chinese the *tiyong* dilemma, *ti* denoting
China's imagined collective essence or identity, and *yong* the foreign technology and institutions that could be used to develop, defend, and exalt
the *ti*.[53]

All Asian societies faced the equivalent of a *tiyong* dilemma, and all
resolved it by borrowing some elements from Western culture (not necessarily the liberal elements) while rejecting others. Deciding what to borrow
and what to reject was not usually a rational, controlled, or even completely conscious process. Particularly after young Asians began going to
the West (and Japan) in significant numbers to study—Siamese students in

the 1870s and Chinese in the 1900s—different groups competed to offer different solutions to the dilemma. The competitions frequently spawned violence, and through the resulting turmoil, produced fundamental changes to Asian states, societies, and cultures. In many ways, the turbulent cascades produced by the *tiyong* crises continue to roil Asia today. The problem of democratization can only be understood in this context.[54]

Importantly, Asian societies all resolved their *tiyong* dilemmas differently. They did not simply receive the good news of liberal-rational global culture and enact its prescriptions passively on the basis of a "wish for modernity." Nor did they categorically reject it in the interest of preserving premodern and essentially authoritarian "Asian values."[55] As explained in Chapter 2, nineteenth century Siamese elites were unusually receptive to transforming their society on the basis of many (but not all) of liberal-rational global culture's values. They imagined the global culture to be consistent with Siam's Buddhist essence, and as a result made it acceptable for later generations to look abroad for ideas on how to restructure the Thai state.

In contrast, nineteenth century China was torn asunder by its encounters with the global culture. To many of the scholar-gentry class, the culture seemed fundamentally incompatible with Confucianism. For this reason, Chinese solutions to the *tiyong* dilemma remained kaleidoscopically numerous and unfocused until about 1930, when the society—governed loosely by Chiang Kai-shek and warlords—settled into a new equilibrium and on a formula for all successful *tiyong* solutions down to the present: China must remain at "the Center" of the collective imagination. Even in the aftermath of radical revolution, Mao Zedong embraced this presupposition. He jettisoned the Soviet model of social and economic development in the late 1950s because he found it unsuitable for Chinese conditions. He then launched a violent assault on certain Soviet-style (and other) institutions during the Cultural Revolution of 1966–76. Overreliance on Soviet assistance and imitation of the Soviet development model implied China's decentering within the Communist world, something Mao and other Chinese leaders could not abide. The Chinese revolution and path to development must cast China at the Center.[56]

But Enlightenment modernity—even as interpreted by Marx—exalted the West as the world's Center, the primary Subject driving world history forward. How could China embrace liberal-rational global culture without at the same time accepting decentering? Chinese elites acknowledged the desirability of economic development and political renovation, but found it difficult to accept a world in which the West—especially the United States—was the cultural Center. As detailed in Chapters 4 and 5, *aversion to decentering* is one of the chief reasons the CCP resists democratization, and is why so many establishment intellectuals support the CCP's nationalistic authoritarian project. Chinese elites do not agree with the world-polity theorists that democratic global culture is genuinely transnational. They see it as Western.

The consensus on Sinocentrism as the foundation for all *tiyong* solutions emerged with Chinese nationalism during the period 1895–1935. It was confirmed in the holocaust that followed Japan's 1937 invasion. Whatever the precise content of the imagined Chinese *ti* of today, it is not the same essence as specified by Confucian scholars of the nineteenth century. As Joseph Levenson found over forty years ago, cultural clashes with the West destroyed Chinese Confucianism as a total ideological system.[57] Remnants of Confucian values remain, but not the total system. The signal date for the system's destruction was 1905, when the Imperial Qing government abolished the examination system as the gateway to elite status. This system had for centuries created a powerful incentive for intelligent boys and young men to spend years toiling to indoctrinate themselves in Confucian beliefs, which stressed loyalty to the Emperor, to patriarchy, and to social service—as well as to the idea that the Emperor's realm (not yet the Chinese nation) was qualitatively superior to all foreign societies.

As Confucianism disintegrated, China entered cultural turmoil. Decades of experimentation followed, in everything from neo-Confucian quasi-Fascism (Chiang in the 1930s), to nativistic yet nihilistic cultural revolution (Mao in the 1960s), to unabashed authoritarian capitalism (the 1990s and beyond). Today's Chinese leaders promote conspicuous consumption, breakneck economic growth, growing military budgets, and sometimes chauvinistic foreign policies, all with the aim of elevating, glorifying, and ultimately recentering the Chinese nation. The CCP also pursues construction of a "socialist spiritual civilization" but currently invests few resources in the endeavor.[58] It tolerates "patriotic" churches of various faiths and denominations, but none that might become subservient to foreigners. The Party's goal is to reduce spiritual belief to worship of the Chinese nation. Enthusiasm that cannot be satisfied through material consumption must be channeled into nationalistic Sinocentrism. Citizens are not required to express enthusiasm in their day-to-day lives. But if they do, they must express it for material consumption and/or "patriotic" endeavors such as coercing Taiwan into unification, spending billions on a space program, or resisting "Western" democracy as a front for "American hegemonism."

As elaborated in Chapters 4 and 5, the CCP uses the media and educational systems to construct the notion China is or can be an alternative Center to the West within world society. Perhaps one day it will supplant the West as *the* Center. A state that requires its people to take the national community as their primary object of worship cannot indefinitely tolerate a condition of being decentered. The CCP struggles to amass "comprehensive national power" (*zonghe guoli*) while rejecting democratization. It fears that democratization would lead to loss of control over collective identity construction, including *the power to create difference* between "China"—the twentieth century construct fashioned from the ruins of the Manchu Qing Dynasty—and all Others. Democratization would entail a loosening of restrictions on freedom of speech and debate, after which the Chinese people could begin self-consciously to reexamine their collective identity and try, should they desire, to change it. Media and telecommunications liberalization would facilitate importation of symbol systems from abroad. CCP elites worry that throwing the doors open completely to liberal-rational global culture would run the risk of society accepting the culture's perceived West-exalting narratives. Recentering China in the popular imagination would then be impossible.

The CCP views the worldwide democratization trend of recent decades as part of a US scheme to impose global hegemony. To Chinese Communists, the world is structured ontologically around national poles of comprehensive power, which cannot be dissolved through globalization. All culture, even global culture, must serve state power. Yielding to the siren song of international cosmopolitanism would only result in China becoming a "stooge" (*fuyong*) of the United States. Democratization implies submission to US domination.

In striking contrast, Thai elites—as explained in Chapters 2 and 3—are not motivated to uphold or restore Siam's imagined global centrality and are not worried about their country dissolving into a global cosmopolitan community. The premodern Siamese state was never central to anything of significance beyond the Indo-Chinese peninsula and was always open to outside influences. King Mongkut's reforms of Buddhism in the middle third of the nineteenth century allowed Siamese elites to imagine that their country's cultural essence was not fundamentally different from the modernity then developing in the West. At root, both were rationalistic; thus, global culture was genuinely transnational. As a result, Siam avoided the traumas of a full-scale, mismanaged *tiyong* crisis. This facilitated the country's eventual democratization. Taiwan, meanwhile, holds the distinction of not actually having had an "essence" or *ti* to defend until very recently—and some would say that it still lacks a coherent *ti*. As explained in Chapters 6 and 7, ROC society was left with its collective identity shattered after the Kuomintang (KMT) state lost international recognition in the 1970s as the sole legitimate government of all of China. Taiwanese began critically debating their country's history and essence as a part of the democratization processes of the 1970s, 1980s, and 1990s. Distortions of history-teaching under the KMT had made identity questions sensitive and exceedingly difficult to answer. The KMT tried to socialize Taiwanese into a Sinocentric worldview similar in important respects to the CCP's, in which the Taiwanese were cast as peripheral players in Chinese history, just as they had been cast as peripheral in Imperial Japanese history from 1895 to 1945. Breaking out of the mental vice of being some other country's peripheral, exploited, or borrowed territory thus became the central challenge facing Taiwanese intellectual and political leaders. But precisely because Taiwanese identity was uncertain and contested, few people on the island resisted liberal-rational global culture. With Taiwan lacking a clear identity and lacking international security, the Taiwanese *ti* came to *reflect* the global culture. Becoming a model world citizen was the only way for Taiwan to remain autonomous.

Some in Taiwan and Thailand are concerned about their country's "location" in the geomoral scheme and try to think of ways to achieve a kind of recentering. They do not, as elites in China do, resist decentering or object to it bitterly, but they do take pride in being "politically advanced." Some Taiwanese and Thai perceive their countries as playing important roles in the world-historic task of disseminating liberal-rational global culture to societies still under authoritarian rule. Both Taipei and Bangkok host NGOs working to advance democratization and human rights, and promote their cities as headquarters for the world's news media. Taiwanese and Thai also try directly to socialize other countries into the global culture: Taiwanese (sometimes) work to socialize China, while Thai (sometimes) work to socialize Burma. Making these efforts signals a kind of moral recentering that many find satisfying. Numerous Taiwanese and Thai were educated in the West, Japan, and other global centers, and they travel the world participating in conferences, meetings, seminars, and business activities. They feel at a deep level that they are a *part* of the modern world. When they promote democracy and human rights in China or Burma, they feel, in a sense, that their countries are "sharing Subjecthood" with the world's leading democracies.

In absolute terms, many people in the PRC also view democracy as universally valid and would like to imagine China sharing this kind of Subjecthood. But the CCP makes selective use of such global-cultural values as rationalism and science to pursue a different kind of recentering based on massively increasing Chinese comprehensive national power. CCP praxis (if not always propaganda) rejects the concepts of civil and political rights, and frequently even social and economic rights, stressing instead the right of the entire country as a collective unit to a leading role in world affairs. The collectivity matters far more than individuals, who are often treated as expendable. As detailed in Chapters 4 and 5, the

CCP seeks over time to establish an alternative global Center based on principles antithetical to democracy and human rights. The Party remains firm in its commitment to "world plurality," rejecting liberal solidarism as a cloak for US hegemony.

Global Culture(s), Singular and Plural

As adumbrated above, understanding democratization in its world-historical context requires distinguishing among those global cultures generally supportive of authoritarianism and those generally supportive of democracy—a bifurcation fundamental to the Western experience from the French Revolution down to at least 1989.[59] S. N. Eisenstadt contends that, in a world of ultimately multiple modernities, the eighteenth century project of early (Western) modernity, which conditioned all the others, "entailed a very strong emphasis on the autonomous participation of members of society in the constitution of the social and political order."[60] Bjorn Wittrock finds that modernity's foundational institutions "involved a conception of political order as constituted and legitimated in terms of not only silent tolerance but also some form of active acquiescence and participation... [P]ublic discourse should not be subject to persecution or censorship but should rather enable the expression of opinion on all aspects of political and public life."[61] Boli and Thomas take this line of thinking a substantial step further, contending that in a *unified* high modernity of the present and future, INGOs can create a single world community in which everyone possesses "world citizenship":

Everyone is an individual endowed with certain rights and subject to certain obligations; everyone is capable of voluntaristic action seeking rational solutions to social problems; everyone has the right and obligation to participate in the grand human project; everyone is, therefore, a citizen of the world polity. World citizenship is the institutional endowment of authority and agency on individuals.... Correspondingly, only fully democratic governance structures are consistent with world citizenship.... States must ensure these rights for their citizens; national citizenship is the means whereby world-citizenship principles are to be realized.[62]

World-polity theorists find a "deep structure" at the root of global culture, anchored by the foundational institutions of early (European) modernity. Yet even a cursory glance at the historical record shows there is usually more than one culture providing attractive state socialization models at any given time. The most powerful countries in material terms are not always the most liberal, and even in the West, liberal-rational global culture has at various times been far from hegemonic. In the 1920s and 1930s, Asian elites looking to global culture(s) for models of how to reconstitute their political and socioeconomic systems could choose from among Anglo-American liberal capitalism, Marxism-Leninism-Stalinism, Italian Fascism, German National Socialism, and Japanese *bushido* militarism (itself a variant of Fascism). In the 1950s and 1960s, they could choose from Soviet Stalinism, American-sponsored authoritarian developmentalism, and, later, Maoist Communism.

In civil society, Western countercultural movements of the 1960s suggested radical experimentation truer to Enlightenment values than many of the policies pursued by leading states. Today's global NGO movement—assigned a central role in world-polity theory—traces its roots partly to this 1960s' antiwar and civil rights activism as well as to indigenous struggles for democracy and justice. The countercultural and (later) NGO movements might be interpreted as struggles to force conservative states to live up to Enlightenment ideals. To this extent, world-polity theory could accommodate them. But the inspiration for many of the people leading these movements lies outside the liberal-rational tradition. Intellectual influences in the 1960s included such Third World revolutionists as Mao, Gandhi, Frantz Fanon, and Ho Chi Minh. Some African-American leaders looked to Islam for insight. Jazz musicians probed the African depths of their art and abandoned elements they felt to be "too white" or European. Popular musicians drew on Indian and North African sources. World-polity theorists might claim that counterculturalists were driven by a unified global culture's esteem for experimentation and exploration. But in self-consciously pushing the cultural limits and opening the door to non-Western values, ideas, and perspectives, counterculturalists— even in the West—were *subverting* the dominant global culture to make it more humane, democratic, and cosmopolitan.

Critical NGOs inherited this legacy. By the 1990s, advances in travel and communications allowed far-flung opponents of globalization, conspicuous consumption, technophilia, and other contemporary practices and institutions to link together.[63] NGOs used the Internet to coordinate protests and socialize members and supporters into a common oppositional worldview. They self-consciously centered their activities in the "global South." For analytical purposes, this critical NGO culture might best be conceived as an alternative or *oppositional* global culture, inheriting the Enlightenment legacy but not strictly adhering to a narrow liberal-rational agenda. World-polity theorists might contend that NGO culture is simply a part of the overarching global culture; after all, disputation is inherent in global culture's deep structure. But as subsequent chapters make clear, trying to comprehend real-world events suggests the utility of viewing the oppositional culture as, in fact, oppositional. Global culture is (at least) bifurcated. It is probably even more complex still.[64]

Within this context, the fact that China "missed" the global 1960s becomes crucial. During the violent and nativistic Cultural Revolution (1966–76), China was more tightly closed to the outside world than at any time in the previous century. This isolation was devastating for Chinese political culture because it prevented the Chinese people from patching into the global oppositional culture, or even into the mainstream liberal-rational global culture. Starting in the 1970s and 1980s, Chinese did begin patching into the mainstream global culture, and they successfully absorbed the values of authoritarian-capitalist development. But they found it difficult *critically to assess* development, state domination of society, and militaristic foreign policies. Those who tried to criticize were often exiled, imprisoned, fired from their jobs, or banned from publishing. Missing the 1960s therefore impoverished Chinese political culture because it made Chinese intellectuals less likely than those in other countries to regard capitalism, the state, and nationalism critically. Today, with political NGOs shut out of the country and the Internet tightly controlled, China has still not patched into the global oppositional culture. This is a key reason democratization forces remain weak and the CCP's nationalistic-authoritarian agenda is relatively popular.

Summary

This book explains Asian democratization by reference to ideational factors at the point of nexus between the domestic and global levels of analysis (see Table 1). Understanding democratization requires analyzing the articulation of domestic society with global society. Focusing only on global-level culture leads to presumptions of cultural determinism (people "enact"), while focusing only on domestic culture artificially rips societies from their natural context, underestimating the contribution of external factors.

Some scholars prefer explanations in the material domain, whether at the domestic or global level of analysis. Their studies can be powerful but often feel incomplete. For example, one familiar materialist explanation holds that democratization occurs when economic development produces a new middle class, whose increased wealth creates a sense of political efficacy and a stake in the system. The middle class's demand to participate in politics eventually translates into democratization.[65] This kind of explanation persists despite Przeworski and his colleagues' demonstration that economic development does not usually "generate" democratization, though it does help powerfully to *sustain* democracy.[66]

The problem is that middle classes do not always agitate for increased participation. Sometimes—as in contemporary Singapore—they seem content to let dictators rule as long as they rule effectively. Many middle-class Thai business people anxious for unelected Prime Minister Suchinda Kraprayoon to step down in May 1992 were not motivated by a desire to participate in politics so much as by a desire to see the disorder end. As a *Bangkok Post* business commentator explained at the time:

> The problem is not just General Suchinda as a person. Nor is it his legitimacy. Some people like him; some do not.... What is worrying the business community is the Government's clear lack of stability. This is not simply because four opposition parties, human rights activists, academics, students, and tens of thousands of members of the public are willing to gather repeatedly in protest.... Without stability, then growth, income redistribution, and any other economic objective can at best be short-lived.[67]

The contributions of economic development and social-structural change to democratization are best assessed in their cultural, historical, and international contexts. As explained in Chapters 2 and 3 on Thailand, and in Chapters 6 and 7 on Taiwan, when economic development and the rise of a middle class occur in settings of openness to liberal-rational global culture—and especially to the global *oppositional* culture—middle classes are more likely to demand democratization, and moderates in the ruling groups are more likely to accept it. Communication, travel, study abroad, and economic exchange all facilitate the importation of global culture(s), important because the desire for democracy does not arise automatically with economic development. People are not born rational animals who naturally demand democratization once they acquire a certain level of wealth. They must first be socialized into valuing democracy and regarding democratization as desirable. If Thai and Taiwanese people had attained contemporary levels of wealth before the Enlightenment, they might never have demanded (or received) democracy—assuming no comparable philosophical movement arose elsewhere.

There is no inherent, structural reason why societies cannot be wealthy and support vibrant middle classes yet also accept governance by authoritarian states. As explained in Chapters 4 and 5, this is precisely the goal of the CCP, and it takes successful Singapore as its model. The CCP bans the global oppositional culture and discredits "Western" democracy, betting that China's rising middle classes will be satisfied with increasing material wealth and their country's exaltation in world affairs. The CCP rejects democratization and seeks China's recentering. Its international goal is the consolidation of "world plurality."

The CCP's experiment is of world-historical importance. On its success or failure may hinge the future not only of Chinese democracy but of *all* Asian democracy, including that in Thailand and Taiwan. If the CCP succeeds in using authoritarian institutions to enrich the Chinese people while keeping them politically subjugated, aspiring authoritarians elsewhere in Asia will be heartened. Given sufficient comprehensive national power, the CCP might one day find itself in a position to reshape global culture. Liberal-rationalism must therefore be considered only one possible road to the future in Asia. Democratization and democratic consolidation are far from inevitable.

BUDDHISM AND THE
SIAMESE ALACRITY TOWARD
GLOBAL CULTURE(S)

Understanding Thailand's eventual emergence as the only democratic country in mainland Southeast Asia requires analyzing the original Siamese elite resolution of the *tiyong* dilemma. It also requires analyzing the efforts of recent democracy activists to legitimate importation of liberal-rational global culture.

Thailand's first democratic transition began on October 13, 1973, when several hundred thousand students marched in the face of bullet-fire and other violent provocations from Thammasat University to the Democracy Monument in central Bangkok, demanding the restoration of constitutional rule.[1] The students were careful to associate their movement with the official *ti* of contemporary Thailand, as first articulated by King Rama VI (Vajiravudh) in the 1910s: Nation, Religion, and King.[2] The students carried large portrait photos of King Bhumiphol, Queen Sirikit, and other members of the royal family; they placed a figure of the Buddha prominently in the center-zone of the demonstration; and some of them even took time out to perform the morning monk-feeding ritual, despite the fact they would have a busy day ahead of them.[3] Yet the students also pointedly associated their movement with the symbols of the global oppositional culture then fueling social and political change in the United States, France, and other countries. On their most important petition, the students wrote the slogan "We Shall Overcome" in English, because their hero was Martin Luther King.[4]

After a violent forty-eight hours, during which more than a hundred demonstrators and several policemen were killed, and nearly a thousand more people wounded, the autocratic team of Premier Thanom Kittikachorn and Army Chief Praphat Charausathien fled with family (including

Thanom's son—and Praphat's son-in-law—Narong Kittikachorn) and other key supporters to a sanctuary in Taipei, at the time home to Chiang Kai-shek's authoritarian Chinese Kuomintang regime.[5] The crisis thus ended and Thailand entered three tumultuous years of democratic experimentation and social turmoil, a period whose dramas were played out against the background of communist revolution in neighboring Vietnam, Cambodia, and Laos. This turbulent phase ended with a coup and brutal crackdown on student activism in October 1976, which spelled the end of democratic experimentation. But the students' October 1973 victory had established a rich and fertile democratic tradition, a reference point that activists in the 1990s and beyond used to chart Thailand's progress and motivate additional struggle.

The origins of the October 1973 revolution lay in the authoritarian developmental politics of the previous fifteen years. When Field Marshal Sarit Thanarat took autocratic power in his *pattiwat* ("revolution") of 1958, he abolished the constitution but promised that another one would be written soon. Sarit died in 1963 and his hand-picked successors, Premier Thanom and Army Chief Praphat, repeatedly delayed promulgating a constitution as they (like Sarit) happily amassed fortunes while developing a close and lucrative Cold War relationship with the United States (then busy prosecuting its war in Vietnam). Under royal pressure, Thanom finally accepted a new constitution in 1968, with the result that Parliament was restored for the first time since Sarit's *pattiwat*. The new order was conservative and military dominated, but Parliament nevertheless became obstreperous, questioning the dictators with particular zeal on the issue of the sensitive military budget. On at least one occasion, Thanom exclaimed in a fit of pique that "never in my long political career have MPs caused such trouble to government administration as in these recent times. Some of them even attacked me over my private affairs."[6] In the midst of a showdown over the military budget in November 1971, Thanom and Praphat finally decided to put their troubles to an end by staging a coup. Thanom then revoked the constitution and dissolved the Parliament.[7]

The setting for such an act was not propitious, because Thailand had changed significantly in the thirteen years since Sarit's *pattiwat*. Fueled by agricultural exports and steadily increasing foreign direct investment (FDI)—mostly from the United States and Japan—gross domestic product (GDP) more than doubled (in current prices), and of more immediate relevance, university enrollments increased from 15,000 to 100,000 as the number of Thailand's institutions of tertiary education expanded from five to seventeen.[8] In addition, by the late 1960s, more than 40,000 US military personnel were stationed on Thai territory; their presence, combined with media development and the advent of jet air travel, implied that whereas "until the late 1960s, full access to Western culture, to Western ideas, values, and fashions, was limited to a small Thai elite, . . . the Vietnam war period brought the outside world face to face with large segments of the population as never before."[9] As a result, Thai secondary and university students became increasingly exposed to the oppositional global culture flourishing in the United States and other Western countries. "American influence was extensive here," said an October 1973 activist. "It was extensive on many levels. There were returned academics who had studied in the States, soldiers visiting on R & R, pop culture—both music and films—the example of Martin Luther King, the example of the anti-war demonstrators, and so on."[10]

The US military presence was far from universally popular in the country and was especially disliked by intellectuals angry at Washington's support for the Thanom–Praphat dictatorship. One leading intellectual—a man who, as detailed below, became the most influential dissident in contemporary Thailand—was Sulak Sivaraksa, a lay Buddhist and eventual Nobel Peace Prize nominee who had studied in Britain in the 1950s and in 1963 established the pioneering quarterly of dissent, the *Social Science Review*. As Sulak later explained:

Beginning with Sarit Thanarat . . . , the long and sustained period of military dictatorship had crushed or blunted virtually all forms of intellectual honesty in the country. Speaking out—or, more precisely, speaking the truth to any concentrations of power—was a shunned practice. Individuals who thought out loud often found themselves incarcerated or forcefully exiled. For reasons of personal security, intellectuals maintained a low profile or became experts at legitimizing the crimes of the ruling class. Against the backdrop of this intellectual desert, I launched the *Social Science Review* in 1963.[11]

The *Review* survived and eventually flourished partly because it enjoyed the protection of one of Sarit's deputy prime ministers. Also important was the fact that Sulak and his editors were cautious at first not to challenge the regime frontally. Slowly, however, they chipped away at the dictatorship's legitimacy and in the process turned the *Review* into a focal point for stimulating student disenchantment and conveying elements of the global oppositional culture into Thailand.[12] Sulak recalled in a 2003 interview that, among other things, the *Review* explained to its educated readers the significance of the rise of the New Left in the West, as represented by radical theorists such as Herbert Marcuse and Noam Chomsky. Conveying New Left views into Thailand helped to puncture the myth of Western superiority then widely held. The *Review* also published articles on American cultural and political ferment submitted by Thai graduate students matriculated at US universities. The *Review* became the first Thai journal or newspaper to expose the presence of US troops on Thai soil, which it did by reprinting the text of a Washington speech by US Senator J. William Fulbright. Most of the *Review*'s articles were less directly political, discussing Thai culture or analyzing the affairs of neighboring countries (including Mao's China, which the mainstream media refused to touch). But even the few elliptically critical articles in each issue became enormously significant in Thai intellectual and political circles at the time, because as Sulak later explained: "When you're living in the dark ages, even a little light reveals a lot."[13]

In the late 1960s, increasingly agitated students began publishing their own semiclandestine journals, which were much more directly critical of government policy than the *Social Science Review*. The students' journals were far from slickly produced, and their titles changed frequently, but they nevertheless worked to knit young intellectuals together across university boundaries in an increasingly restless, semiunderground oppositional network with nationwide reach. After promulgation of the conservative constitution in 1969, students established the National Student Center of Thailand (NSCT) for the express purpose of articulating views on educational and political affairs.[14] As charismatic students such as Thammasat University's Thirayuth Boonmi rose to NSCT leadership positions in the early 1970s, the organization grew in size, strength, and boldness. Under Thirayuth's direction from August 1972, the NSCT agitated for the restoration of constitutional rule. Thirayuth then graduated but continued to direct the student groups, which began distributing leaflets in early October 1973 demanding promulgation of a new constitution.[15] The leaflets were printed at Sulak Sivaraksa's bookshop in the Saam Yaan district of Bangkok.[16]

The Thai State's Traditional Openness to Global Culture(s)

That the showdown between student demonstrators and military elites came during the wind-down period of US involvement in Vietnam underscores the historical tendency of Thai elites to structure their state on the basis of compelling models current in international society. During the 1930s and 1940s, Phibun Songkhram experimented with Italian Fascism and an admixture of elements of the Japanese *bushido* code, trying to organize, discipline, and militarize Thai society. Sarit found strong support for his developmental authoritarianism in Washington—from both the White House and the World Bank. Later, as US power reeled from blow after blow in Vietnam, and Thailand developed its own communist insurgency, even some military officers became disenchanted with

Washington's prescriptions and less inclined to support the Thanom–Praphat dictatorship. Later still, the Thai state found its way back at least to electoral democracy, as Huntington's "third wave" spread through Asia in the mid-1980s. Thai elites' historical receptivity to global culture(s) suggests that democracy *can* be consolidated in Thailand as long as democracy remains a compelling model globally. But the tradition of receptiveness also suggests that democracy could be short-lived if for any reason (such as the "rise of China") authoritarianism should again become an attractive and exalted global model.

The cosmopolitanness of Siamese Ayutthaya (dynastic capital from 1350 to 1767) partly explains the alacrity with which the later kings Mongkut (Rama IV, r. 1851–68) and Chulalongkorn (Rama V, r. 1868–1910) embraced modern science, Enlightenment rationality, and nation-state institutions—though not yet democratic institutions—in the mid-and late-nineteenth century. This early modernization is central to understanding Thailand's eventual democratization.

Ayutthaya had been a polity completely permeated by international trade. As Pasuk and Baker write: "The court sucked forest goods out of the hinterland, sold them in the junk trade to China, and with the proceeds bought the weaponry, luxuries, and status-defining goods which were the props and privileges of rule. The key institution of government was the Phra Klang, which combined the roles of foreign ministry, port authority, export warehouse, and treasury."[17]

Ayutthaya was sacked and destroyed by invading Burmese armies in 1767, but after a period of uncertainty and chaos, Siamese elites established a new capital and the Chakri dynasty at Bangkok in 1782. Bangkok was deliberately chosen because of its proximity to the rich trading networks of the South China Sea, some of which terminated in the Chaophraya river valley. Like their Ayutthayan predecessors, the Chakri kings strongly encouraged trade, in addition to foreign migration: merchants from China, India, Persia, Arabia, and even places farther afield had been coming to Siam for generations, and many had been absorbed into the noble class. The services of foreign merchants would still be needed under the new dynasty. In addition, because Siam had always been under-populated historically, the Chakri kings felt weakened by labor shortages. To address this problem, they encouraged lower-class Chinese immigration, with the result that "between 1820 and 1950, around 4 million people boarded the boats leaving the southern China ports for Siam, and around 1.5 million chose not to return."[18] Chinese immigrants came to constitute some 10 percent of Siam's population, perhaps 30 percent of the urban population, and helped to keep the country bustling with commerce and patched into global trading networks.

In this environment—and yet apart from it, cloistered as a monk—Mongkut began reforming Siamese Buddhism in the years before he ascended to the throne in 1851. Mongkut's primary motivation was to squeeze the superstition out of Siamese Buddhism and restore it to the allegedly pristine and rational form it had evinced in the original Pali-language Tripitaka. Although there had been dissatisfaction with certain elements of Siamese Buddhist practice for two or three generations,[19] it seems clear that Mongkut's principal influence was the scientific rationalism he was learning from Westerners. "A voluminous reader [in Thai, Pali, Latin, and English,] and insatiably curious, Mongkut became familiar with a considerable body of Western scientific knowledge both while in the monkhood and later as king."[20] This knowledge convinced Mongkut that the Buddhist *Traiphuum Phra Ruang*, the oldest book in the Thai language, and the masterwork of Thai culture, was loaded with irritating, embarrassing, and misleading superstitions. The book had been composed in the 1300s under the sponsorship of Sukhothai-era (1240s–1420s) King Lithai. It described a universe of thirty-one levels in which sentient beings existed based on their relative accumulation of merit or demerit. The book was enormously influential in structuring the Siamese worldview, and "even the physical layouts of the capitals of the pre-modern Thai kingdoms were grounded in religious beliefs manifested in the *Traiphuum*." Its Buddhist cosmography served to legitimate a brittle and harshly hierarchical social and political order.[21]

Mongkut had no strong objection to social hierarchy, but as an accomplished amateur astronomer, he found the *Traiphuum*'s cosmography impossible to abide. Especially after becoming king, he chafed with embarrassment when visiting Europeans ridiculed the *Traiphuum* and in every other way asserted arrogantly that their science was superior to Siamese superstition. Mongkut struck back by arguing that the rationality at the core of "Western" science was also at the core of Siamese Buddhism before it became distorted and denatured. The Pali Tripitaka is completely consistent with rationality, Mongkut argued, and says nothing about a cosmos of thirty-one levels. The reason Siamese Buddhism had gone astray was because it became polluted by Brahmanistic influences as successive Siamese dynasties absorbed the political culture of Cambodia while expanding their boundaries beyond the Chaophraya river valley. The true Siamese essence—in effect, the Siamese *ti*—was to be found not in the superstitious and unscientific *Traiphuum Phra Ruang* but instead in the original Pali Tripitaka, whose pristine Buddhist doctrines are completely consistent, Mongkut argued, with the rationality at the core of modern science.[22]

In a brilliant illustration of Mongkut's defensive but meticulous attempts to fuse the Siamese identity with liberal-rational global culture,

Thongchai Winichakul tells the story of a public exchange of letters between Mongkut and the missionary Dan Bradley, who in 1866 published
an influential Thai-language series of articles on the topography, shape,
and atmosphere of the Earth. Mongkut wrote in reply that "the Bible was
full of mistakes about the Earth and nature, particularly the belief in a
six-day Creation. If the Bible is the origin of civilization ..., why does it
not say anything at all about how to measure latitude and longitude?"[23]
In 1867, the high-ranking noble Thiphakorawong argued in support of
Mongkut's position that "one who thinks that the Earth is flat is a follower
of those who believe in God the Creator. For one who believes the Earth
is spherical is following the Buddha's words about what is natural."[24]
The Buddha had never stated explicitly that the world was spherical.
But such truth was immanent in his rationalistic epistemology, waiting
to be discovered by later generations. Brahmanistic accretions had distorted Siamese development, but now with Mongkut's reforms, Siamese
Buddhist civilization could get back on track and join the mainstream of
modern world society.[25]

Thiphakorawong's support for Mongkut's position suggests one of the
king's most important legacies for his son Chulalongkorn: the absence
of sustained and systematic *ideological* opposition to liberal-rationalism.
To be sure, Chulalongkorn faced *political and cultural* opposition to his
efforts to modernize the Siamese state in the 1870s and 1880s, by the
powerful Bunnag family and other elite clans. But this opposition could
not be legitimated by claiming that Chulalongkorn was violating orthodoxy or destroying the Siamese essence. Few people of significance believed that the Siamese essence was in any *fundamental* way inconsistent with liberal-rationalism.[26] There was nothing "anti-Buddhist" about
Chulalongkorn's reforms, for example—not least since the Buddha himself had said that religion could only thrive in a condition of prosperity and
security.[27] Many people (including Chulalongkorn himself) did reject key
aspects of liberal-rational global culture, most notably, constitutional government. They also rejected (in their praxis, if not always their discourse)
the important philosophical premise that human beings are created equal.
But the Siamese elites' rejection of these particular values appears to have
been rooted not so much in ideology as in the simple desire to cling to
privilege—and sometimes in the familiar belief that authoritarianism and
traditional values would be useful to maintaining stability during modernization. Siamese conservatives could also point to "advanced" countries in
the West championing reactionary practices in the name of modernization:
the contemporary norm. Lacking any profound ideological objections to
liberal-rational global culture—and with a long history of openness to
the world economy—the Siamese elites flung open the country's doors

to international influence, reinforcing a predisposition that continues to drive Thai political development today.

Mongkut also bequeathed to Chulalongkorn a powerful intellect and curiosity about the world and the education and other resources to satisfy them. Chulalongkorn was only fifteen-years old when he ascended to the throne in 1868. David Wyatt writes that "his experience lay entirely in a world in which European trading ships and diplomats, foreign languages and newspapers, and international affairs were commonplace."[28] The young king became proficient in English and in 1871–72 traveled to Malaya, Indonesia, Burma, and India for the purpose of studying European colonial administration to acquire new ideas for governing Siam.[29] This was surely the most concrete manifestation possible of Siamese elites enthusiastically embracing models of governance current globally and using them to restructure their state. Chulalongkorn also sent a number of his brothers, half-brothers, and cousins to Europe for longer-term study, and secured the support of the sons of other aristocratic families studying abroad. Together, Chulalongkorn, his brothers and half-brothers, and other well-educated members of the Siamese elite formed "Young Siam," dedicated to reform and opening.[30] They achieved political supremacy by the mid-1880s, and then embarked upon ambitious modernization programs, particularly in education, infrastructure, and law.[31]

Chulalongkorn's reforms did not include democratization, or even constitutional government. In January 1885, Siamese Ambassador to France Prisdang—along with three of Chulalongkorn's half-brothers, then studying in London—sent a letter to the monarch proposing constitutional government. Their proposal read partly as follows:

The present problem facing Siam is to maintain national independence and a stable government. To resolve this problem, Siam must be accepted and respected by the Western powers as a civilized nation. Hence there is no choice but to bring about a new government modeled after the Western pattern, or at least after Japan.... According to European belief, in order for a government to maintain justice it must be based on popular consensus. Cabinet ministers must be selected from the elected representatives of the people and must be responsible to all the people. No nation in Europe can believe that Siam maintains justice since everything is decided by the king.[32]

Accordingly, they called for changing the absolute monarchy to a constitutional monarchy, establishing a parliament, promoting equality under the law, and respecting freedom of speech. In April 1885, Chulalongkorn replied that constitutional government was neither necessary nor appropriate for Siam because "he was not the same oppressive monarch as those in European history and was not as short-sighted as a frog inside a coconut shell. Therefore, he was not an obstacle to the prosperity and security of the country." In fact, Chulalongkorn had only recently prevailed over aristocratic opposition and begun implementing reforms. Any limitation on his powers—such as by giving the nobles institutional voice in the form of a parliament—would at this date derail the reforms, defeating the purpose of bringing Siam up to the standards of modern world society. A constitution and a parliament would therefore have to wait.[33]

It is significant that Chulalongkorn's objections were entirely political. At no point did he say that European institutions were rooted in a philosophy profoundly foreign to Siam, or that they would in some way endanger the Siamese essence. In 1897, after returning from his first visit to Europe, Chulalongkorn famously declared—apropos the *tiyong* dilemma—that "I am convinced there exists no incompatibility between . . . acquisition [of European science and technology] and the maintenance of our individuality as an independent Asiatic nation."[34] But he still resisted adoption of European political institutions, telling an audience in 1903 that "the use of Western ideas as a basis of reform in Siam is mistaken. The prevailing conditions are completely different. It is as if one could take the European methods for growing wheat and apply them to rice-growing in this country. There would be absolutely no benefit in this whatsoever."[35] The fact that "benefit" rather than ideological concerns was of primary importance is reinforced by a crucial incident a few months before Chulalongkorn's death. He surprisingly announced that "I entrust onto my son Vajiravudh a gift for the people and that upon his accession to the throne he will give to them a parliament and constitution."[36]

Vajiravudh (r. 1910–25) failed to grant his father's wish, instead pursuing a highly nationalistic and chauvinistic agenda that delayed the arrival of constitutional government until 1932, when European-trained intellectuals and military officers overthrew Vajiravudh's successor and ended the absolute monarchy. But it can certainly be maintained that Vajiravudh faithfully upheld the tradition of the Siamese state adopting models of governance current in world society. As crown prince, Vajiravudh studied in England and traveled widely through Europe from 1893 to 1902. During this odyssey, he failed to learn the benefits and blessings of constitutional government, but *did* develop an appreciation for the state-cultivated nationalism, anti-Semitism (which he transferred to migrant Chinese), and proto-fascism flourishing on the Continent. After ascending to the throne, Vajiravudh imitated these aspects of contemporary global culture(s) with enthusiasm.[37]

It may be objected that there were surely other reasons explaining Siam's alacrity toward global culture(s) besides the history of economic openness and Mongkut's reforms of Siamese Buddhism. At least one additional important factor is worth discussing here: Siam never suffered the pain and humiliation of direct colonization at the hands of European imperialists. The importance of this fact can easily be imagined, because continuing resentment against imperialist victimization plays a cardinal role in convincing many Chinese people that "Western-style" democracy would be odious and humiliating. Thai elites have been able to boast for generations that they steered the Siamese people through the rocky shoals of imperial-era international relations without yielding to the ignominy of colonial annexation. Of course they did have to make a number of significant institutional changes to prevent annexation and in this way (and many others) implemented a kind of "self-colonization," particularly as the Bangkok-based state extended its reach into the countryside and uplands.[38] But the illusion of having made a choice is soothing for the Thai people, and creates a mindset in which it is felt that embracing liberal-rational global culture would not be embarrassing or dangerous. They resisted the West before and could do it again, if necessary. Except for the aberration of World War II, when it allied with Japan, Siam always allied with the West and in the twentieth century was always accepted into the club of nations (albeit not as an equal). What could possibly be humiliating about accepting global institutions that originated in the West?

But the fact of having escaped colonization is not sufficient to explain Siam's relative openness. Japan, too, escaped colonization and yet in the course of the 1920s and 1930s developed an extremely hostile relationship with the West on the basis of severe estrangement from liberal-rational global culture and its supportive international institutions. Moreover, Siam did not completely escape Western pressures and affronts. The British encroached on Siamese territory in the mid- and late-nineteenth century as they consolidated control over Burma and Malaya. The French pressed militarily from Cambodia and Laos. The French blockade of the Chaophraya river valley in 1893 was both humiliating and dangerous because it brought the Grand Palace to within firing range.[39] Nevertheless, Siamese elites continued to send their sons and eventually daughters to study in Paris, London, and other European cities, and they integrated more tightly into the West-centered world order. Why could they do this but not the Chinese gentry, whose sons would not go abroad in large numbers to study until the Qing Dynasty began crumbling in the 1900s? Young Chinese men only began going abroad for study *after* the beginning of serious imperial encroachments in the wake of the 1894–95 Sino-Japanese War—and they first went to Japan to study the secrets of self-strengthening. Suffering (or not) from formal imperialism is probably a factor explaining openness to global culture(s), but is not alone decisive. Siam's history of economic cosmopolitanism is also crucial as is the fact that Mongkut's reforms of Buddhism allowed for the preemptive resolution of Siam's *tiyong* crisis.

Socially Engaged Buddhism

Over the decades of the twentieth century, Mongkut's Thammayut sect of Buddhism lost the reformist spirit and became co-opted into power by the autocrats and militarists who usually ruled Thailand. Monks were subjected to state discipline and Buddhism was put into the service of nationalistic modernization, beginning with passage of the Sangha Act of 1903 (later revised).[40] Conservative authorities stressed the validity of traditional interpretations of Buddhism such as those developed in the *Traiphuum Phra Ruang*, which emphasized "the determining influence of *kamma* [karma] and religious merit and demerit on human well-being and socio-economic status."[41] If people were born poor, they probably deserved it, and trying to remedy their situation would be tantamount to going against fundamental cosmic laws. Eventually this position generated widespread dissatisfaction. "The highest goal of Buddhism is to attain spiritual liberation and be free from suffering," wrote Bhikkhu Visalo, but "as the new nation-state was forming, Buddhist teachings were interpreted and selected which fit the needs and agenda of the nation's rulers.... [T]he liberating aspect of Buddhism has been increasingly overlooked."[42] To dissident Buddhist intellectuals, things went awry in the decades after Chulalongkorn's death, beginning with the proto-fascist Vajiravudh. In a 1989 speech on "The Crisis of Siamese Identity," Sulak Sivaraksa argued that the purpose of opening to the outside world and absorbing advanced technology should have been "to preserve the essential core of Siamese identity, which was part and parcel of the spirit of Buddhism."[43] That essential core—effectively, the *ti*—was, Sulak argued, democratic and humanistic. But instead of cultivating this core, Siamese elites pursued materialistic, nationalistic, and repressive agendas, which distorted Thailand's development and turned the country into an unjust place to live for many of its citizens.

As a result, Sulak and other "socially engaged" Buddhists assert that democracy is still unfinished in Thailand. Their mission is to agitate for the country's *deepened* democratization, empowering the poor and disenfranchised to relieve their suffering in the course of creating a more just society—a society of compassion and cooperation rather than mutually exploitative competition. To socially engaged Buddhists and the NGOs they influence, the constitutional reforms of the 1990s (discussed in Chapter 3) are only the first step in a long process of political development.[44]

These activists want to move Thailand toward a new model of society more altruistic and focused on elevating citizens spiritually as well as materially—goals that they consider faithful not only to the core concerns of Buddhism, but also to the concerns of the eighteenth century European Enlightenment.[45]

Alongside political parties and liberal members of the business class, socially engaged Buddhists played a vital role in the democratization politics of the 1990s and 2000s. Indeed, it seems unlikely that democratization would have succeeded without Buddhist participation. The most obvious example—albeit a controversial one—is Chamlong Srimuang's pivotal role in leading the demonstrations of May 1992, which forced an end to General Suchinda Kraprayoon's unelected premiership and paved the way for a democratic restoration.[46] Duncan McCargo, in his brilliant biography of the mercurial Chamlong, argues that Western scholars who portray the former general as *primarily* a Buddhist politician are off the mark: "The relationship between politics and Buddhism expounded by Chamlong was almost entirely at the level of moral injunctions. He communicated little sense that Buddhism could provide the blueprint for a new social order, a new political system."[47] But Chamlong was (and remains) a socially engaged Buddhist *par excellence*, whose antistate, antimaterialist ideology was centrally important to attracting the support of nearly two-thirds of the Bangkok electorate in a successful campaign for reelection as governor in January 1990.[48] Chamlong demonstrated that Buddhist values and themes resonate in Thai society; and indeed, that they resonate with particular clarity and force in the most modern and open zone of Thai society, the cosmopolitan and wealthy Bangkok Metropolitan Area.[49]

Whatever Chamlong's ultimate commitments to democratic principles—and McCargo demonstrates convincingly that the former general governed Bangkok in an autocratic style[50]—his association of Buddhist values and themes with the democracy movement of May 1992 helped legitimize the movement for hundreds of thousands of people, many of whom had not been especially outraged by Suchinda's original February 1991 coup. Suchinda himself understood the importance of religion. On May 8, 1992, as demonstrators flooded the streets, he told a group of twenty conservative Buddhists who paid him a politically charged "courtesy call" that "the Constitution states clearly that everyone has freedom in religion, but . . . what I am very much concerned about is the use of religion as a political tool. This is because, as we all should know well, strong belief in religion may develop into fanaticism." Suchinda argued that "once a person wants to specifically concentrate in religion, he must only engage in religion. He must not use religion as a political tool or political force."[51] Given that the name of Chamlong's political party was the "Phalang Tham," or "Force of (Moral) Truth," and given Chamlong's well-known association with the Santi Asoke Buddhist sect, Suchinda's reference was unmistakable. He had already been heckled the previous day in Parliament for declaring that "I have been asked by a large number of Buddhist followers to assume the premiership in order to protect and preserve Buddhism, which has been threatened by a group of persons who have established a new religious sect."[52]

Meanwhile, Chamlong was busy putting Buddhist symbols to work against Suchinda. On April 15, he criticized the coup leader for reneging on his promise not to seek the premiership after the March 1992 elections, quoting the Buddhist aphorism that "no liar is free from sin" to construct an argument that Suchinda's volte-face "violated Buddhist teachings." Chamlong planned to wear a black shirt with "no liar is free from sin" embroidered on the back the next day in Parliament. Use of the color black was not meant to "curse" Suchinda, Chamlong explained; rather, it was designed "to mourn virtue that has been trampled on."[53] Virtue had already been raised as an issue in the unfolding saga when former MP Chalard Vorachart began a hunger strike against Suchinda's grab for power a few days earlier. "Chalard's fast was riveting because his self-deprivation was seen as a sincere sacrifice for democracy and national interest."[54] It would only be overshadowed in importance by Chamlong's own week-long "fast to the death" from May 4–11.[55] The status of hunger strikes in Buddhism is problematic, but there seems little doubt that the use of nonviolent forms of protest against military repression is a tactic that elicits the sympathy of Buddhist publics.[56]

In the end, despite his repeated caution that "Chamlong was not animated by a pluralist view of the Thai order," even a skeptical McCargo concludes that the restoration of Thai democracy would not have occurred in the absence of Chamlong's Buddhist-inspired activism: "For some critics of Chamlong, the death of unarmed protestors was in itself conclusive evidence of the failure of his leadership, testifying to recklessness or poor judgment. On balance, however, his success in forcing the military to return to barracks must be seen as a formidable achievement, whatever the associated costs. The alternative—an extended period of rule [for Suchinda and associates]—would have been politically disastrous for Thailand."[57]

Not only democratic restoration, but also the reform movements of the 1990s and beyond (discussed in Chapter 3), would have been unlikely to succeed in the absence of Chamlong's efforts. He was perhaps ultimately no democrat in spirit, and arguably not even sufficiently free of egotism to be called a good socially engaged Buddhist—though his continued work in political retirement on behalf of the disenfranchised suggests a sincerity that should not be questioned lightly. But however half-unwittingly—the way most things happen in most countries, it would appear—Chamlong as a self-proclaimed socially engaged Buddhist played a pivotal role in restoring Thai democracy and paving the way for reformist movements aimed at deepening democratization and improving the quality of governance. Simply sitting back and relying passively on the Thai state's tradition of openness to political models championed abroad to effect democratization would obviously have been a risky and probably useless course.

Socially Engaged Buddhism and the Siamese *Tiyong* Dilemma

Many socially engaged Buddhists believe idealistically that Siam in the Sukhothai era (1240s–1420s) was already democratic because it was closer in time to the Buddha. The country only became authoritarian, they assert, because of the incorporation of Brahmanistic elements into the political culture via the mediation of Cambodia during the Ayutthaya period (1351–1767).[58] Despite Mongkut's reforms, the Chakri dynasty retained many of the Brahmanistic elements that the Ayutthayan kings had adopted because they legitimated bureaucratic domination of society. More recent authoritarian figures have done the same, and those associated with the court, in particular, have insisted upon a pomp-and-circumstance idealization of the monarchy that owes much to the Brahmanistic legacy. But authoritarianism as developed in the Ayutthayan era is *un-Thai*, the socially engaged Buddhists insist. The Thai essence is completely democratic, as established during the reign (1279–98) of King Ramkhamhaeng of Sukhothai. According to this belief, Siam was at that time *already at the center* of what would become liberal-rational global culture, even predating the Europeans by several centuries. Decentering only came about because the Ayutthayan autocrats absorbed Brahmanism from Cambodia. To rejoin the center, the Thai people need only to rediscover their roots.

Sulak Sivaraksa idealizes Sukhothai and contends that "the profound roots of Thai thought are clearly manifested in the first stone inscription of King Ramkhamhaeng."[59] The inscription reads partly as follows:

In the time of King Ram Khamhaeng this land of Sukhothai is thriving. There is fish in the water and rice in the fields. The lord of the realm does not levy toll on his subjects for traveling the roads; they lead their cattle to trade or ride their horses to sell.... [The king] does not connive with thieves or favor concealers [of stolen goods]. When he sees someone's rice, he does not covet it; when he sees someone's wealth, he does not get angry.... He has hung a bell in the opening of the gate over there: if any commoner in the land has a grievance which sickens his belly and gripes his heart, and which he wants to make known to his ruler and lord, it is easy: he goes and strikes the bell which the King has hung there; King Ram Khamhaeng... hears the call; he goes and questions the man, examines the case, and decides it justly for him.[60]

Sulak writes that "this inscription is like pure gold which expresses 'Buddhist-ness' and 'Thai-ness'.... I consider it to be a proclamation of the political, economic, and cultural trends which were associated with [Sukhothai]... and which emphasized liberty, equality, and fraternity."[61] But later: "The impact of the [negative] thought expressed in the *Trai-phuum* of Sukhothai was compounded by the fact that Ayutthaya accepted supernatural beliefs from Cambodia when we [Siamese] repeatedly attacked the Cambodian capital. This led to a decline in the 'Thai-ness' of our thought, a reduction in liberty and equality."[62]

Socially engaged Buddhist Phra Phaisaan Wisaalai also idealizes Sukhothai: "It can be said that the Sukhothai form of government (which was influenced by the [Buddhist] *dhammaraja* theory) was a government for the benefit and well-being of the people, but the Ayutthayan form of government (which accepted the [Brahmanical] *devaraja* theory...) was a government for the power of the state."[63]

Therefore, people who reject democracy for Thailand by arguing in tortuous, convoluted ways that it violates "Nation, Religion, and King" are actually themselves violating the Thai *ti* by promoting alien culture. Socially engaged Buddhists use this fundamental critique to legitimate democratization movements, which Thai conservatives have attacked for everything from promoting communism to (under Thaksin) slavishly serving foreign NGOs. The Buddhists' strategy is straightforward: Assert that empowering and enfranchising the poor and broadening participation in public life are not only consistent with the Thai essence, but in fact develop and enhance the Thai essence. Explain how the Thai essence also exemplifies the "liberty, equality, and fraternity" of the French Revolution. Then castigate the dictators and oppressors who would stage coups, repress labor, keep the poor disenfranchised, and rake money in from corruption—all in the name of "Nation, Religion, and King"—as conveying alien values into Thailand and polluting the country's collective identity.[64]

Socially engaged Buddhism first took coherent shape with the rise of the NGO movement in the 1970s and 1980s.[65] Its most important inspiration was the work of reformist Buddhist philosopher Buddhadasa Bhikkhu (1906–93). "Not since... the fifth century of the Christian era has there been such a comprehensive attempt to systematically reinterpret the entirety of Theravada [Buddhist] doctrine in the light of contemporary views and expectations."[66] Buddhadasa—who spent his adult life writing and teaching at the Suan Mokh forest monastery in southern Thailand—was an especially important influence on Sulak Sivaraksa, and also an influence on Pridi Banomyong, who—as explained in Chapter 3—was the most radical leader of the 1932 revolution and "the progenitor of Siamese democracy."[67] Prawase Wasi, a key figure in the political reform movement of the 1990s, expressed his intellectual debt to Buddhadasa in 1993 by eulogizing him in *The Nation*, emotionally telling an interviewer that the great monk's teachings would never die.[68] Chamlong Srimuang regularly expressed his reverence for Buddhadasa by visiting Suan Mokh each year on the monk's birthday.[69] King Bhumiphol Adulyadej sent letters expressing concern for Buddhadasa's health as the monk deteriorated from strokes in 1991 and 1993.[70]

What, then, did this influential personage teach? In his richly detailed biography, Peter Jackson writes that Buddhadasa's main concern was to make Thai Buddhism relevant to people living in modern conditions. He quotes Buddhadasa as saying that "*Nibbana* [nirvana] must be something we can have in this life," because "Buddhism exists in order to allow everyone to live in this world victoriously."[71] "What benefit is there in the teaching that we will get *nibbana* after we have died?"[72] Jackson argues that "Buddhadasa's use of the notion of a 'benefit' as a criterion for gauging the correctness of doctrinal interpretations provides a channel for the introduction of the contemporary social expectations of Buddhadasa's lay audience into his system."[73] There are two aspects of this statement worth stressing. "Benefit" reflects the influence of modernity's human-centeredness on Buddhadasa and the importance of enduring progress. Evaluating a doctrine by the benefit it might bring also reflects modern utilitarianism, and suggests that if a doctrine fails to bring benefit, it should be changed or jettisoned. Like Mongkut's rationalist Buddhism, Buddhadasa's work fuses the Thai *ti* with values prevalent in liberal-rational global culture. But what distinguishes Buddhadasa from the mainstream modernism centered in the West is that Buddhadasa is ultimately more concerned with spiritual benefit than material benefit. Material improvements he regards as important only to the extent that they create the conditions necessary to achieve spiritual benefits.[74]

Buddhadasa was heavily influenced by Zen Buddhism, to which he attributed modern Japan's economic strength and apparent social harmony. One knotty and abstruse (but nevertheless real) problem in reconciling Theravada Buddhism with modern humanism is Theravada doctrine's insistence on emptiness or voidness as the ultimate nature of reality.[75] In its celebration of life, modern humanism abhors such doctrines, and certainly the people of contemporary Thailand find it difficult to be motivated enthusiastically by the notion that ultimate reality is empty. Faced with this conundrum, Buddhadasa seized upon Zen, which takes as its starting point the Mahayana Buddhist notion that "the 'void' is not empty but [is instead] an originating 'fullness' which forms the undifferentiated substratum of all existence."[76] Finding fullness in the emptiness might help save Theravada Buddhism from contemporary irrelevance and reinvigorate it in a Thai society grappling with the consequences of industrialization and globalization. Zen to Buddhadasa had a proven track record of facilitating Asian modernization in a way consistent with Buddhist values because he conflated the doctrine with what he imagined to be the core Japanese traits of diligence, industriousness, and refinement.[77] In effect, Buddhadasa was arguing that a cardinal component of Japanese society and culture could be imported and put to work for Thailand. But he then faced a small-scale *tiyong* crisis himself, having to argue tortuously for his Theravada Buddhist readers that "we should not regard Zen as being Mahayana" because "true Buddhism is neither Theravada nor Mahayana."[78]

Buddhadasa did not argue for the blind embrace of global modernity in its current form. In a 1984 Suan Mokh lecture, the great monk castigated the state of humanity:

Although this world is increasingly idiotic, in the area of creating crises it is increasingly clever; it is quite talented at starting more complicated and troublesome disasters. This is the sort of progress we have. So whether people go to the moon or who-knows-where, they aren't going for peace.... All of the fine things, new products, expensive goods, and magical inventions only make people more stupid than ever. They lead people to infatuation with things that bind and attach the mind. Thus, there is no dawning of wisdom, no abating of the ignorance.[79]

Buddhadasa considered two forms of infatuation to be particularly problematic: infatuation with the nation and infatuation with conspicuous consumption. Both distracted people and caused them to become selfish and uncompassionate, absorbed in delusion and unable to see the fullness behind the void. Echoing Buddhadasa, Bhikkhu Visalo more recently has argued that "science and rationalism can lead us to some levels of truth, but not to all. The Ultimate is a level of truth inaccessible to them and thus becomes one of their casualties."[80] Uncritical celebration of "fine things, new products, expensive goods, and magical inventions" only results in more suffering in the world and less happiness. Nation-worship leads to wars. Such notions might be familiar to traditional Theravada Buddhists, but Buddhadasa takes them a step further by arguing that chasing modern delusions also creates suffering for *other people*, not just the chaser. In other words, a person's degree of suffering is determined not only by his or her individual karmic inheritance—as the *Traiphuum*

Phra Ruang had contended—but also by factors over which he or she has little or no control. Therefore, lay Buddhists, at least, should not withdraw from the world and selfishly try (in vain) to save only themselves. They should instead *engage* the world to alleviate the suffering of others caused by socioeconomic injustice, political repression, corruption, crime, and other external factors.[81] Buddhadasa quotes the Buddha: "A person who only has wisdom in seeking out his own benefit is an impure human being."[82] As elaborated by Bhikkhu Visalo:

Relationships confined to one's own small circles are conducive to a narrow mind, whereas expansive (horizontal) relationships contribute to a "civic mind." Expansive engagement helps broaden one's realm of concern: from self-concern to concern for others; from concern for family to concern for community and society (and the world); from concern for people to concern for all of nature. With this attitude, one's own welfare and the public welfare are considered identical since one has developed a strong sense that one is part of society and society is part of oneself.[83]

Ironically, Buddhadasa himself remained disengaged from politics and social activism, content to publish and teach from his Suan Mokh retreat. Nor did he champion democracy as the solution to Thailand's spiritual ills; on the contrary, in a book written at the height of the disorder and violence of the mid-1970s—as Buddhist kingdoms collapsed in Cambodia and Laos, and Thailand slid toward anarchy—Buddhadasa argued that in the ideal political system, an enlightened autocrat would supply the conditions under which everyone could achieve *nibbana*. When the crisis era passed, he softened this argument, but not before Sulak Sivaraksa— speaking for others—strongly criticized the monk, noting that "dictators never possess Dharma."[84] Still, Sulak and other socially engaged Buddhists continued to revere Buddhadasa and expressed sympathy for his inability to see much of value in the corrupt and elite-centered "democracy" practiced typically at that time in Thailand.[85]

As with so many other politically significant phenomena in contemporary Thailand, the concrete praxis of socially engaged Buddhism first emerged in the months following October 1973. With the military reeling from its devastated prestige, rural protests rocked the country, and Buddhist monks debated whether they should remain in the monasteries or go out to take part in the political life of the nation. Activist monks formed the Young Monks Group and went to work on behalf of poor farmers, staging a demonstration in January 1974 that attracted 20,000 people. Conservatives fretted that the Young Monks would ally with the Communist Party of Thailand (CPT), or in other ways destroy the fabric of Thai culture. General Krit, head of the army, proclaimed in anguish that monks protesting with peasants spelled "the end of everything; . . . there is nothing more serious than this."[86] To the extent that "everything" meant authoritarianism, inequality, corruption, and injustice, he was probably right, because if Thailand's tens of thousands of monks could be mobilized on behalf of the poor—and almost every male spends at least a few months in a monastery—oppressive institutions might well collapse.

But socially engaged Buddhism did not take hold inside the *wat*; nor did it come to dominate Thailand's cultural mainstream. After the military crackdown of October 1976, most monks returned to the monastery and resumed the life of quiet contemplation they thought would lead to personal salvation. Lay Buddhists tended to busy themselves with material accumulation, trying to live a conventionally moral life while sometimes indulging in what Buddhist reformers would call superstitious practices, such as burning incense and making offerings at temples. With some exceptions (including Bhikkhu Payutto and Bhikkhu Visalo), socially engaged Buddhism became the province of a minority of outspoken and well-educated members of the urban middle class, people like Sulak Sivaraksa, Phra Phothirak (founder of the Santi Asoke movement), Chamlong Srimuang (as a Santi Asoke practitioner), and Prawase Wasi. "They are the people who want to bring modern relevance to old practices, they identify with both Buddhism and 'Thai-ness,' and they are uneasy about this identification in modern times," writes anthropologist Niels Mulder. "Most often they appear to be the same urban intellectuals and social critics who also worry about the other problems that beset Thai society."[87]

The foremost practitioner and theorist of socially engaged Buddhism is still Sulak, the septuagenarian (as of 2003) son of a Sino-Thai merchant family who has variously been called "the moral conscience of Siamese society" and the "crucial linchpin of Siamese social movements and non-governmental organizations' networks" for decades.[88] Sulak was charged by the Suchinda regime with *lese majeste* in 1991, but was acquitted in 1995.[89] He estimated in October 2003 that of Thailand's tens of thousands of monks, only about 300 are currently his active students; but thousands of other people read his books and newsletter (*Seeds of Peace*) and attend his public lectures.[90] The 300 active students and most enthusiastic of Sulak's thousands of followers are key leaders of Thailand's NGO movement: people of the urban middle class whose national identity (as in every Asian country) must be fused with the values of liberal-rational global culture if democracy is to succeed and take root. Rationalist-materialist theories of democratization stressing the importance of a rising middle class are incomplete. For democratization to succeed, people in the rising middle class must be convinced at a deep level that global culture does not threaten their society's collective identity. If the culture appears threatening because of its associations with the West, authoritarian elites—as in China—can manipulate the new middle classes into believing that collective identity must be protected from denaturing and destruction by foreigners. Protection inevitably requires social controls of the sort that vitiate democratization. But in Thailand, socially engaged Buddhism—rooted in Buddhadasa's reforms, and ultimately those of Mongkut—convinces middle-class activists that democratization is safe and good, exalting the national heritage, not poisoning it. Autocracy destroys the national heritage, just as Brahmanism destroyed the democracy of Sukhothai-era Siam.

Socially Engaged Buddhism's Influence on Thai NGOs

Boli, Risse, Sikkink, and other world-polity theorists argue that the function of internationally linked NGOs is to socialize states into the humanistic values of liberal-rational global culture.[91] NGOs probably perform this function successfully to some degree in all countries, as the world-polity theorists demonstrate. States rarely resist socialization into acceptance of common technical standards or even more intrusive norms such as the expectation that all states will have written constitutions—not yet the global norm in Chulalongkorn's day, but certainly the norm now. However, authoritarian states often *do* resist NGO pressures when NGOs demand fundamental institutional changes that would result in loss of the state's macro-managerial control over processes of collective identity construction. They certainly resist changes that would lead to sudden democratization—though sometimes they do get caught on slippery slopes.[92] In some authoritarian countries, resistance is mild and NGOs can, by chipping away, contribute to the creation of a new situation in which the authoritarian state can no longer easily prevent developments that eventually lead in unanticipated ways to democratization. Such was the case in Thailand, where NGOs first appeared in the 1970s and coalesced into an identifiable movement by the mid-1980s—on the eve of the democratic transition in 1988–92.[93] Subsequently, NGOs played an important role alongside liberal businesspeople and the more enlightened political parties in the reform movements of the mid-1990s (and beyond), aimed at deepening Thai democracy and improving its quality. World-polity theorists might argue that this was only natural because NGOs always perform this function. But if the process was natural, the question arises as to why internationally linked (political) NGOs are not accepted as legitimate in China, Burma, Vietnam, and North Korea.[94] Obviously, many factors are involved—including the state's tradition of openness (or not) to global culture(s). In Thailand, internationally linked domestic

NGOs are able to legitimate their activities by association with socially engaged Buddhism, but nothing of this nature currently seems possible in China, Burma, Vietnam, or North Korea. Foreign-linked NGOs in these countries are subject to sometimes brutal repression.

When Sulak teaches Thai NGO activists, he uses a two-pronged pedagogical approach.[95] First, he tries to cultivate the students' "sociological imagination" by explaining how "the market kills for you" and how "the government kills for you." He intends to shock his students into an awareness that gigantic, faceless institutions falsely absolve individuals of moral responsibility by committing "sins" on their behalf. Good Buddhists do not kill, but they might not see anything wrong with eating meat bought shrink-wrapped in a supermarket. They might also fail to reflect on the fact that the "public order" that benefits them is regularly purchased at the cost of other people's lives, such as victims of police brutality in up-country border towns. Sulak considers it essential in a Thai context to *discredit* the government and market, to show how they sin, because of what he contends is the cardinal fact that Thai people are socialized from childhood into blindly respecting authority. There is nothing wrong with respecting a legitimate authority constituted by democratic procedures, Sulak concedes. Every society must be governed, and just public order is inherently desirable. Nor is a market economy inherently wrong; it certainly is preferable to invasive state planning. But Thai people should learn to think *critically* about their government and economy and develop the courage to apply social and political pressure on the authorities when they commit unacceptable acts. Such doctrines would be anathema in China.

Sulak's second pedagogical technique is to expose his activist students to suffering. They take field trips to Bangkok slums; they visit refugee camps along the Burma border. While in the field, they concentrate on how the problems they are witnessing in a variety of different settings typically have common origins in government or corporate abuse, callousness, arrogance, and incompetence. Sulak wants his students to be able instinctively to put the abstract ideas they learn in lectures and from reading to immediate use when encountering situations of suffering. He wants the students' sociological imagination to be turned on at all times, because he believes that the struggle to deepen democracy and improve its quality can only result from small victories in myriad different places accumulating gradually but with momentum.[96] The one thing that Sulak does *not* want his students to learn, he says, is to hate, or to cultivate anger. It can be daunting in the face of so much visible suffering, but Sulak actively teaches his students not to hate. "When you hate people, you become depressed," he says, "and then you imitate them. If you ever take power you will become just as bad as they are."[97]

One of Sulak's most loyal and accomplished students in 2003 was the Campaign Coordinator for Forum-Asia, a Bangkok-based regional NGO whose mission is to put pressure on East and Southeast Asian governments to respect civil and political rights. Forum-Asia's origins lie in the democratic revolution of October 1973, in the wake of which Dr. Saneh Chamarik (eventually Chairman of the National Human Rights Commission) established the Union for Civil Liberties, Thailand's first human rights NGO. The Union was suppressed after the crackdown of October 1976, but became active again in the 1980s; in 1991, when the International Committee of Jurists (of which Saneh was a member) established a fund to develop an Asian regional human rights organization, Bangkok became the natural choice for the organization's headquarters. Despite Suchinda's February 1991 coup, Thailand was the most liberal and open society in Southeast Asia at the time, with the possible exception of the Philippines. The Suchinda government did not hesitate to approve Forum-Asia's registration application, primarily because Saneh and the others involved intentionally played down the likely scope of their activities.[98] The Suchinda government's decision probably also reflected the Thai state's long-standing predisposition to embrace global culture(s). If asked, Bangkok usually says "yes" to requests to host UN agencies, field offices for other intergovernmental organizations, and the offices of internationally linked NGOs.

Forum-Asia's mission is to encourage governments to establish national (and regional) human rights mechanisms and to help human rights activists and organizations increase their capacity for working with these mechanisms and challenging governments' human rights violations. By September 2003, Forum had thirty-four member organizations spread throughout East and Southeast Asia, with many countries supporting more than one—and some supporting none. Forum's funding came from a number of foreign agencies, most in Europe and North America, including the Swedish International Development Agency (the largest donor), George Soros' Open Society (a source of controversy), the US National Endowment for Democracy, and the US Asia Foundation. As a result, Forum-Asia serves as a useful illustration of how internationally linked NGOs can convey the values of liberal-rational global culture into non-Western societies. Forum focuses on civil and political rights rather than the social and economic rights typically championed by postcolonial states, and its funding comes overwhelmingly from the metropolitan centers of world society.

Unlike certain Southeast Asian nationalists, and unlike PRC nationalists, Sulak and the socially engaged Buddhists *celebrate* civil and political rights, which they see as fundamental to deepening Thai democracy. This position naturally puts them at odds with the "Asian values" movement, promoted in Singapore, Malaysia, and Beijing. In defensive response to the pressures of globalization, proponents of "Asian values" contend that "Western" civil and political rights such as freedom of speech and freedom of assembly reflect an excessive individualism and lack of community spirit inappropriate to Asian settings. They argue for restrictions on civil and political rights to be enforced by mildly authoritarian (but uncorrupt) governments rooted in authentically native collective identities.

The "Asian values" movement was never particularly popular in Thailand. Surin Maisrikrod identifies two general Thai responses to the movement: that of the "globalizers," who argued staunchly in favor of individual rights and the pursuit of self-interest, and that of the "communitarians," who—linked with socially engaged Buddhists—asserted civil and political rights as the foundation on which to build better societies that also reflect community spirit.[99] Importantly, therefore, *both* camps in Thailand supported democracy, reflecting democracy's deep integration with Thai collective identity.[100] Sulak, as can be imagined, detests the "Asian values" movement, seeing it as a tool for dictators to mask repression. He wrote in 1999 that "if there is a conflict between universal human rights and regional particularities, the former must prevail over the latter."[101]

As a result, it should not be surprising that one of Sulak's favorite students would find a home as Campaign Coordinator for Forum-Asia, working on behalf of Thai and regional democratization. "Khun X" argues that spiritual motivation is essential to becoming an effective activist.[102] Self-cultivation on the basis of Buddhist principles automatically leads to compassion for others. If a person does not care for others, Khun X explains, then that person is broken. But coming to this realization is no easy task. The kind of Buddhism that Khun X practices entails a great deal of effort, involving intensive study, discussion retreats in austere settings, and exposure to suffering. It also includes an important measure of self-denial, such as vegetarianism, a low salary, and long working hours in a society dazzling with temptations to conspicuous consumption. Most people in Thailand (and elsewhere) would be incapable of subjecting themselves to these kinds of rigors, but partly for that reason, they express a high degree of respect for people like Khun X. This respect helps to legitimate Khun X's efforts on behalf of civil and political rights, which might otherwise more easily be disparaged as alien or threatening in a Thai setting. Herein lies the core of socially engaged Buddhism's importance. Most Thai people will not become practitioners of socially engaged Buddhism and will not donate money to support the work of NGOs. They will, however, support the work of NGOs if they see virtuous people like Khun X coordinating NGO activism. In this way, the middle classes produced by economic development come to embrace democratization as inherently good and consistent with Thai values.

Khun X's motto is that "dialogue is spiritual action." By this she means that Forum activists should never confront military officers, the police, arrogant government officials, and other violators of human rights with the hostile attitude that they should be vanquished. "They have their jobs to do, too; we have to try to understand the world as they see it," she explained. Khun X believes that by taking a patient, compassionate, and yet firm approach toward human rights violators, they can be persuaded to change, through the use of reasoned argumentation. Khun X evidently imbibed "Ajarn Sulak's" dictum that socially engaged Buddhists should never hate.[103] "We do have to play games with Thaksin and people like that, but we don't see them as our enemy because they deserve compassion, too."

Pracharat

In certain contexts—perhaps *most* contexts—Khun X's moral selflessness would lead immediately to shameless exploitation by an amoral opponent. But in Thailand, a selfless position can elicit respect, as partly reflected in Forum-Asia's (and various other NGOs') institutionalized participation in governance. In Thai, this concept is called *pracharat*, or "civil-state." It emerged as a self-conscious desideratum of Thai governance in the months and years following the Asian economic meltdown of 1997–98, but had already been gelling gradually in the years following democratization in 1992. As expressed in a November 1999 Local Development Institute report:

Time has proven that the power of the state is not sufficient to solve the national crisis; it is necessary that the social or people sector consolidates its power and takes part in solving the crisis. There is no power that can solve such complicated problems besides the power of society ("social energy"). Social energy comes from the coming together to think and act—all over the Thai nation, in all places, all organizations, on all issues—as a force of the land.... This social energy should have three methods: act by oneself, work with the state, and scrutinize the state.... The state and the people must integrate as a civil-state (*pracharat*).[104]

In a series of related articles on globalization and change, Chai-Anan Samudavanija, a well-known public intellectual, argued that while the old-fashioned nation-state "had been characterized by such features as uniformity, submission, dependence, compulsion, and control, the civil-state promotes diversity, freedom, autonomy, pluralism, empowerment, and good governance (including institutionalized relations between the state and civil society)."[105] The legitimation and perhaps inspiration for the *pracharat* concept evidently came from slogans and buzzwords current in 1990s' global society, as promoted by the United Nations, the World Bank, and other international organizations. This, again, reflects Thailand's openness to global culture(s) and its elites' eagerness to adopt the most "advanced" practices from abroad. Yet Forum-Asia's participation in *pracharat* also owes much to Campaign Coordinator Khun X's socially engaged Buddhist approach to dealing with figures in government with whom she disagrees. It therefore has an indigenous aspect likely to be important in institutionalizing *pracharat* within Thai governance.

Because of its *pracharat* participation, Forum-Asia's (and some other NGOs') influence on Thai policymaking is stronger than it first appears. Forum's staffers, including Khun X, are constantly feeding information, ideas, and perspectives to parliamentarians, senators, journalists, government officials, military officers, police officers, and other NGOs behind the scenes.[106] Forum serves as a special subcommittee of the National Human Rights Commission (discussed in Chapter 3), a legacy of its role in helping to draft the 1997 Constitution.[107] Forum is also linked closely with the academic world, a constant source of new information and critical perspectives. Its interlocutors, in turn, feed information back to Forum-Asia, making it difficult, sometimes, to locate the ultimate source of policy initiatives and, therefore, the loci of power. Forum-Asia's influence does not result from accident or from its simply existing as a respected NGO. Its staff of twenty is constantly working hard actively to shape the perspectives of decision makers and the parameters of public debate, "playing games" with opponents but trying not to view them with bitterness as enemies.[108]

The news media rely on Forum-Asia as an important resource for providing context and analytical commentary to package with stories and help audiences interpret events. This is true not only for the independent newspapers, but even for the government- and Army-controlled electronic media. The media seek Forum-Asia's assistance not so much because of Khun X's socially engaged Buddhism, but instead because Forum-Asia possesses expertise that the media must tap to satisfy audiences' growing demand for information. In a climate of competition with the Internet and satellite television, Thai media must take chances to get audiences' attention and must avoid the appearance of gross bias. These constraints provide Forum-Asia with an opportunity to carve out a bit more space in the public sphere for critical commentary on government policies and politicians' behavior. Most members of the general public would not be willing to read an NGO newsletter or attend an activist's talk, but they will sit for a news story enriched by expert NGO commentary.[109]

Forum-Asia also has informal—but institutionalized—links with officials in government. There Khun X's Buddhist-inspired tactics become useful in cultivating trust and inviting inclusion. Forum enjoys direct links to the Foreign Ministry, the National Human Rights Commission, the military, the police, the National Security Council, and even the Office of the Prime Minister. Behind the glare of the media spotlight, and even in the aftermath of bouts of public sparring, Khun X holds regularly scheduled meetings with high-ranking officials from these bureaucracies to exchange information and work in a pragmatic way on solving problems. In the media spotlight, NGOs and government officials exchange ideologically charged barbs, but at the regular *pracharat* meetings, they get down to the business of governing Thailand. Forum staffers say they did enjoy better relations with the Democrats (in office November 1997–February 2001) than with Thaksin's Thai Rak Thai (TRT) party, but even with the TRT, they engage in regular exchanges characterized by displays of mutual respect. Khun X reported in 2003 that "I receive calls every day from the police, intelligence officials, the military, and the Prime Minister's Office to check information or to encourage us to postpone a demonstration— things like that."[110] As a senior Thaksin associate acknowledged, "no single individual can have a monopoly of information or wisdom."[111] "Responsible" NGOs, he said, are a valuable social resource and should be included in governance.

Nor are the issues on which Forum-Asia is asked to provide information and analysis insignificant. They are, in fact, some of the most important issues facing Thailand, especially Burma policy and the handling of Burmese refugees. When the Democrats were in power, Forum-Asia was intimately involved in crafting the "flexible engagement" policy which Foreign Minister Surin and Deputy Foreign Minister Sukhumbhand adopted: a policy of strong pressure on Burma to improve human rights and move toward democratization.[112] The Thaksin government abandoned the Democrats' progressive approach to Burma, favoring a business-oriented "constructive engagement," but still consulted regularly with Forum-Asia because its officials were under constant pressure to think of practical new ways of preventing more Burmese economic migrants and political refugees from coming to Thailand. Khun X said in September 2003 that even some high-ranking military officers had, just days earlier, visited her office secretly to discuss ways in which the military might open a "second track" toward change in Burma—because officers were dissatisfied with Thaksin's desultory and ineffectual "road map" to Burma's liberalization.[113] Khun X relished the irony of Thai military officers discussing with an NGO "the role of the military in promoting Burma's democratization," while the civilian prime minister was more interested in facilitating business deals with the junta and ridiculing NGOs. In general, Khun X contended, most of the people in government below Thaksin wanted constructive relations with NGOs. It was only Thaksin himself and a few of his closest associates who were implacably hostile.[114]

For a variety of reasons discussed in Chapter 3, Burma's democratization is of keen interest to Thailand's educated middle classes, with the implication that—in the wake of the political changes of the 1990s—successive Thai governments have been under pressure to develop Burma policies which they could claim were designed for the purpose of encouraging political change. Should any government abandon this effort, Forum-Asia and other Burma-focused NGOs could activate their connection networks throughout Thai society and apply subtle but strong pressure on the government to change tack. The resulting political struggle would not appear in the media or to outside observers to be a frontal clash, but would instead be quietly intense and significant. Even under Thaksin, power in Thailand remained far too dispersed for the government to do just whatever it liked, without consulting its civil-society partners in the *pracharat*. The government *needs* the support of NGOs to be effective. If it goes too far in alienating NGOs and activists become extremely unhappy, they can raise the costs of governing substantially by mobilizing subtle, sullen opposition, which over time would reduce the government's ability to achieve its goals. Thaksin failed to realize this important point during his first few years in office, but some NGO activists were hopeful that, with patience and cleverness, they could in future years "domesticate" Thaksin or his successor to the way *pracharat* should work.[115]

There is, however, an important bias in the *pracharat* system: not all NGOs are welcomed to join.[116] Thaksin argued repeatedly that some NGOs are "good" and some are "bad"; with the good ones being those that have information or other resources the government lacks, and the bad ones being those that, in the words of a senior Thaksin associate, "just protest for the sake of protesting; don't know what they're actually protesting against—like a lot of those opposing the WTO; or who become disruptive by blocking roads and causing disturbances."[117] As one activist from a smaller and "borderline bad" NGO explained:

The government consults bankers on finance questions, lawyers on WTO questions, and NGOs primarily on social welfare questions like women's issues, human resettlement, and things like that. Sometimes environmental NGOs [including his own] get invited to parliamentary hearings or ministerial meetings to comment on specific issues such as the draft water resources bill. But we don't have the right to go demanding that they listen to us, and they are the ones who have the power to summon us.[118]

Forum-Asia is focused on issues of human rights and Burma, which are important to the Bangkok middle class. It also enjoys high-profile international support. But the small environmental NGO on the borderline of being "bad" not only lacks high-profile foreign support, but also is associated with positions that radically question the often environmentally unfriendly developmentalist ideology that has macro-structured Thai policymaking since the 1950s. The *pracharat* system usually excludes NGOs that promote policies seriously at odds with developmentalism; as a result, its bias is to produce policies supportive of the status quo or of only moderate change. In this respect, *pracharat* reflects the interests of Thailand's attentive public, most of whose members reside in the cities (especially Bangkok) and benefit from the existing socioeconomic system. They may not benefit as much as the super-wealthy and the old hereditary elite, but they do benefit—particularly after the economy began growing rapidly again in 2000. They want democracy, respect for civil and political rights, and gradual improvement in the lives of the poor, but they strongly oppose radical socioeconomic change.

NGOs and Global Culture(s)

Does the *pracharat* system then function only to convey a limited range of global culture(s) into Thailand, perhaps along the lines Robinson suggests in *Promoting Polyarchy*?[119] The answer is probably no, because the NGOs participating in *pracharat* are still too diverse to be dismissed as simply serving a single hegemonic logic emanating from the West. Forum-Asia is "ahead" of Washington on many issues of Asian human rights, despite the fact that its brief is civil and political rights (which the US government usually champions). Focus on the Global South, another Bangkok-based regional NGO, is Forum's counterpart in focusing on social and economic rights. The Focus agenda is significantly more radical than Forum-Asia's, though activists at both NGOs work closely together to share information and coordinate tactics. Yet Focus staffers also participate in the *pracharat* system, though not, apparently, to the same degree or at the same high level as Forum.[120]

The significance of Focus on the Global South's activities in Thailand must be understood in the context of the fundamental village (*baan*)[121] versus capital city (*muang*) cleavage in Thai politics. Although modern state building began during the reign of King Chulalongkorn, many people in the countryside, especially of the Northeast—though increasingly drawn into the market economy—were not directly affected by state administration until the 1950s and 1960s. Isolated in forests, uplands, and other hard-to-access terrain, Thai villagers developed a culture and a way of life sharply distinct from that of the cosmopolitan urbanites running the country from Bangkok. Under Sarit Thanarat (r. 1957–63) and his successors, the Thai government accepted development loans and other assistance packages from the United States, the World Bank, and other international institutions, and then actively began mobilizing the villagers into national life—frequently on exploitative terms. The US Army built a highway through the Northeast to support its war in Vietnam; that highway also became the lifeline linking Thailand's poorest region with the comparatively wealthy capital, and spawning socioeconomic and culture clashes between *baan* and *muang* that continue to contribute fundamentally to the issues and tenor of Thai politics today. For example, Bangkok bureaucrats work with urban capitalists to build dams for the purpose of supplying cheap electricity to the cities. Some of these dams wreak havoc on local ecosystems, robbing communities of the resources (such as fisheries) they have used for generations to maintain their way of life. NGOs such as Focus on the Global South go to help affected communities in their struggles, attracting media attention and thereby transforming the issues from scattered local clashes into national contests over development strategies.[122]

In the early decades of state-led development, villagers tended passively to accept bureaucratic orders, both because they felt inferior and unsophisticated in the presence of educated urbanites and because the military was usually on hand, brandishing weapons to deter any resistance. In the mid-1960s, a small-scale communist insurgency began, and by 1975 "the military reckoned that 412 villages were totally under insurgent control, and another 6,000 housing almost 4 million people were subject to some degree of insurgent influence."[123] At this point, the conflict in the countryside intersected with the post-October 1973 situation of idealistic experimentation in the cities as students began going to the countryside to assist villagers. This development marked the birth of "people's organizations": community-based NGOs that frequently work with Focus on the Global South to build capacity among the rural poor. A large proportion of contemporary NGO activists began their careers in the 1970s. "At that time, Thailand was poor," said one, "so it was easier for young people to be idealistic. We didn't have all the distractions of consumption and DVDs and everything like they get in Siam Square today. For us, going to the countryside to help rural people in development was actually fun."[124] After graduating from college, a number of people of this generation—Thailand's "best and brightest"—refused to take jobs in business or government. Some chose journalism or academia, but others decided to remain lifelong activists. At first, several thousand joined the CPT in the jungle, but by the mid-1980s, after the CPT had largely crumbled, the activists either returned to the city or went elsewhere in the countryside, many to form NGOs.[125]

By 2003, some 120 community-based NGOs—including Focus on the Global South—were active members of NGO-COD, the umbrella NGO Coordinating Committee on Development. Activists with these NGOs regularly go into the local communities (rural *and* urban) to help "empower" the weak and articulate their situation so that they come to understand how their community's problems may be caused by governmental and corporate actions at higher levels, nationally and internationally. The idea is to reshape local perceptions so that poor people learn to change what they demand from the state: to demand more, and demand more sensibly—in line with their material and cultural interests.[126] For example, Focus on the Global South held a two-day workshop in February 2002 for domestic NGOs and local community leaders to convey the functional economics literacy necessary to understand the basic issues and implications of an upcoming series of UN meetings on Financing for Development. According to the 2002 Focus Annual Report, the topics discussed at the workshop ranged from mapping the flow of money within an economy, to the introduction of "community currencies," to challenges facing mainstream growth models of economic development. Focus also works with the Assembly of the Poor (a large group of landless and otherwise victimized Thai farmers) to produce concrete policy proposals on land reform.[127]

Focus thus serves as a node linking domestic Thai and international NGOs in the oppositional global culture. As a result, it would appear that NGOs do *not* "function only to convey a limited range of global culture(s) into Thailand"—the question asked above. Certainly NGO activists begin their work in local communities as outsiders, whether because they come from other countries or, as is much more frequently the case, they come from Bangkok. NGO activists inevitably bring in values from the global or national center to the locality[128]—and in fact, that is precisely their main motivation, since empowering requires cultural and attitudinal change. Moreover, many of these values find their origins in the European Enlightenment, the philosophical bedrock of liberal-rational global culture. When asked whether she considers herself to be working to implement the logic of this kind of global culture, one foreign-born Focus staffer—"Khun Y"—said "that's not way off base, though it does represent an overly 'Northern' perspective. There is actually diversity and pluralism in the values we're promoting."[129] Ideally, Khun Y suggested, activists also serve as mediators conveying the cultural traditions of Thailand and other "peripheral" societies back to the global melting pot, contributing in the process to construction of an increasingly cosmopolitan and humane global culture with multiple geographic centers.

DEEPENING THAI DEMOCRACY: THE 1990S AND BEYOND

Thailand is unique among the three countries in this study in having had a figure of unquestioned and uncompromised prestige who could—when he chose to do so—intervene effectively in politics to support democratic governance. King Bhumiphol Adulyadej, a constitutional monarch with limited formal authority but significant political influence, celebrated his sixtieth year on the throne in 2006, the year he would also turn seventy-nine years old. King Bhumiphol has not always or even usually intervened in politics to support democracy; and in fact, the only time in Bhumiphol's long career when his prestige and popularity declined was in the aftermath of the October 1976 crackdown, for which he subtly signaled support.[1] The King also signaled his support for General Suchinda's February 1991 coup, and raised no objection to the conservative constitution Suchinda forced upon the public at the end of 1991—which would have institutionalized military domination of politics.[2] Such a record leads Kevin Hewison to conclude that King Bhumiphol has stood for "stability and order, authority and tradition, developmentalism, unity and solidarity, national chauvinism, and national security and anti-communism."[3] But Bhumiphol did intervene in Thai politics in October 1973 to support democratization, and he did the same in May 1992. Perhaps, as Hewison argues, the King's primary motivation in these cases was to support order, which—given the special circumstances of the time—democratization would have been more likely to produce. But regardless of his ultimate motives, it seems likely that without Bhumiphol's subtle, carefully crafted, and dramatic interventions, Thailand would not be a democratic country today.[4]

The significance of Bhumiphol's interventions becomes especially clear when viewed in terms of the *tiyong* dilemma and the difficulties it presents

Asians seeking to legitimate democracy. In Thailand, the King not only represents the national essence, but he also *embodies* the national essence, whatever specifically the national essence is imagined to be. This is not because the Thai people are born innately adoring the King, but instead is because the notion of the monarch's personification of Thai national identity and his embodiment of *khwam pen Thai* ("Thainess") are inculcated from birth, and reinforced day after day by means of a prodigious propaganda effort that makes use of government- and Army-run television and radio stations, billboards, brilliant decorations during the season of the King's birthday, numerous other festivals and ceremonies, and more prosaic public occasions when the national anthem is played, such as before film-showings at theaters and in the Bangkok Sky Train stations twice a day during rush hour.[5] King Bhumiphol is also thought to be a genuinely hard-working, modest, charming, and even witty monarch dedicated to his job and to the Thai people, if not to radical socioeconomic change. Given his work on developmental projects ameliorating the plight of the poor, Bhumiphol can in one sense be characterized as Thailand's most visible socially engaged Buddhist (though NGO activists might argue he is insufficiently engaged and overly conservative). In any case, when King Bhumiphol—widely accepted as the embodiment of Thainess—publicly associates himself with democracy, democracy moves another step in the direction of becoming legitimately consolidated in the eyes of Thai people, particularly social conservatives who might otherwise oppose it.[6]

The King's association of himself with democracy in May 1992 was indirect and subtle. With tens or even hundreds of thousands of demonstrators marching through the streets demanding that Suchinda resign as unelected prime minister, with the Army firing indiscriminately into crowds,[7] and with motorcycle gangs destroying the symbols of public order in angry response, Bhumiphol summoned both Suchinda and Chamlong Srimuang—the main leader of the demonstrations—to an audience at Chitralada Palace. Because Chamlong, the socially engaged Buddhist who was Bangkok's former mayor and at the time a newly elected member of Parliament, had been dragged from the crowd and placed under arrest two days earlier, he had to be released from prison to answer the King's summons. Therefore, when Bhumiphol addressed the two men as jointly responsible for the mayhem, he was in effect *rescuing* Chamlong and the demonstrators from an exceedingly dicey situation. Suchinda was apparently committed completely to crushing the demonstrations with force and then ruling Thailand both directly and through proxies for many years. By summoning Suchinda and Chamlong together, and by forcing Suchinda to release Chamlong from prison, the King was signaling that he would not accept Suchinda's sanguinary solution to the political turmoil.

Nor would he, by extension, be likely to support Suchinda's continued premiership. In a stunning scene recorded and broadcast on Thai television (and CNN), Suchinda and Chamlong knelt on the floor while the King patiently but sternly delivered his rebuke:

I ask both General Suchinda and Major General Chamlong to turn to each other and refrain from confrontation, because Thailand belongs to all of us, not to any particular individual. Turn to each other to solve the current problem, which can be described as bloody and insane. People who resort to violence lose their self-control and are unaware of what they are fighting for and what problems should be solved. They only try to win. Who will win? No one wins. Every such action is dangerous. Everyone loses.[8]

The only one of these two men who could possibly have thought at the time that Thailand belonged to a "particular individual" was Suchinda, then trying to lock down his hold on power. The only one resorting to violence was also Suchinda. Therefore it seems likely that Suchinda was the King's primary target. Yet it would have been dangerous for the King to have called Suchinda alone to the palace for such a stinging rebuke. The supercilious general would have suffered an enormous loss of face and quite possibly would have ignored the monarch (or worse), precipitating a deeper crisis. The King had little choice but to sacrifice Chamlong as part of a larger strategy of driving Suchinda from politics. Probably the King also had no special fondness for Chamlong. The former Bangkok mayor was at the time enormously popular and possessed immense charisma, traits which no monarch can appreciate in any politician because they smack of potential republicanism. Chamlong also enjoyed playing politics outside of conventional boundaries, and therefore in ways likely to produce unpredictable consequences. As a result, King Bhumiphol could conveniently both destroy Suchinda and weaken Chamlong simultaneously. But the big loser would be Suchinda, because it was Suchinda's government that would fall, and it was Suchinda's dream of dominating Thai politics for a generation that would be shattered. Suchinda would instead become for many Thai people a monstrous and detested figure and a symbol of the corrupt and arrogant military domination that they had struggled against for decades.

The King's intervention paved the way for Anand Panyarachun's return to the prime ministership and, subsequently, the restoration of democracy (with the prime minister an elected member of parliament) in September 1992.[9] It might be argued that by intervening in this way, and at this time, the King was reinforcing "liberal-royalism" as the center point of the Thai political spectrum.[10] In the decades after military officers, civil servants, and radical intellectuals engineered the overthrow of the absolute monarchy in 1932, successive kings maintained a tacit alliance with people who favored cautious democratization, and they directed their alliance against two forces: (1) right-wing but sometimes populist dictators drawn from the military's ranks, who might flirt with republicanism and (2) radical democrats who might also flirt with republicanism and who would surely pursue fundamental socioeconomic changes to Thailand's highly stratified order. Certainly Suchinda had the potential to play the role of Category 1, and—albeit to a much lesser extent— Chamlong had that potential in Category 2. By undermining these two men's political positions and entrusting the esteemed and loyal Anand to restore democracy, Bhumiphol might have thought he was putting Thailand firmly back on the liberal-royalist track.

As the center point of the Thai political spectrum, liberal-royalism is in some ways analogous to the "eclectic modernizationist" position on the so-called "Chinese political spectrum," the influential concept developed in the 1970s by Michel Oksenberg and Steven Goldstein.[11] They argued that since the early twentieth century, opinion groups active in Chinese politics over successive regimes could be classified along a continuum ranging from "nativists" through "eclectic modernizers" to "total Westernizers." Nativists, from the Boxers (active 1898–1900) through the Cultural Revolution (1966–76), rejected borrowing almost anything of significance from the West, whether institutions, technology, or popular culture. They took an extremely conservative position on resolution of the *tiyong* crisis, even at the risk of undermining China's modernization. At the other extreme, total Westernizers—from Chen Duxiu and other leaders of the New Culture Movement (1915–25) to, it might be imagined, liberal intellectuals who helped inspire the Spring 1989 student demonstrations— wanted to jettison the Chinese political and even cultural legacy almost entirely. They felt that Chinese culture and traditions straitjacketed the country and locked it into recurring cycles of brutal yet ineffective authoritarian excess.[12] Effectively, the total Westernizers rejected *tiyong* as a problematique by arguing that the Chinese essence was completely unworthy of protection and that it should be replaced by a Western essence.

In the middle of the spectrum, eclectic modernizers argued for borrowing some things while still seeking to preserve core aspects of the national essence, however it might be imagined. Eclectic modernizers have been members of every effective governing "coalition" in China since the early twentieth century, sometimes in alliance with groups closer on the spectrum to the nativists, sometimes in alliance with groups closer to the total Westernizers. The point is that China has never quite entirely shut down links to the outside world and to global culture(s) (though of course it came very close during the Cultural Revolution), yet it has also never given itself up completely to an enthusiasm for total Westernization— including democratization, which those leaning toward nativism reject.

Despite rapid economic growth and unprecedented opening to the out-side world, which have contributed to profound changes in Chinese so-ciety and probably even culture, the party-state remains committed to a course of eclectic modernization—though certainly now several notches closer to the "total Westernization" end of the spectrum.[13] Analogously, King Bhumiphol perhaps believed that his political intervention in 1992 would keep Thailand firmly on the path of liberal-royalism, avoiding the extremes of right-wing proto-republicanism (Suchinda) and left-wing rad-ical Buddhist democratization (Chamlong). In fact, the May 1992 events ushered in a half-decade of sweeping political reform, culminating in pro-mulgation of the left-leaning "People's Constitution" in October 1997.[14] Subsequently, the 1997–98 economic meltdown shocked the Thai polity and impoverished much of the former middle class, creating the conditions for Thaksin Shinawatra's election as a right-wing populist (though not yet republicanist) in January 2001. Thailand thus shifted off the liberal-royal course in the years after King Bhumiphol's 1992 intervention, first left-ward and then rightward.

Background to Reform

The left wing of the Thai political spectrum was established by Pridi Banomyong (1900–83) in the 1920s and 1930s. Pridi, who studied law in Paris from 1920 to 1927, was, in the words of one analyst, "the progen-itor of Siamese democracy," the principal figure of the 1932 revolution (ending the absolute monarchy) who "wanted a meaningful as opposed to a nominal democracy: a mass-based and participatory one in contrast to a top-down democracy where the ruling class (the self-designated best and brightest) sets the agenda and 'engineers consent.'"[15] In the June 24, 1932 "Announcement of the People's Party No. 1," the manifesto of the coup against the absolute monarch, Pridi wrote:

The king's government has governed in ways that are deceiving and not straight-forward with the people. For example, it said it would improve livelihood in this way and that, but time has passed, people have waited, and nothing has hap-pened. It has never done anything seriously. Further than that, it has insulted the people—those with the grace to pay taxes for royalty to use—that the people don't know as much as those of royal blood. But this is not because the people are stupid, but because they lack the education which is reserved for royalty. They have not allowed the people to study fully, because they fear that if the people have education, they will know the evil that they do....Everyone must have employment and need not starve. Everyone will have equal rights and freedom from being serfs (*phrai*) and slaves (*that*) of royalty. The time has ended when those of royal blood farm on the backs of the people. The thing which everyone desires, the greatest happiness and progress,...will arise for everyone.[16]

Pridi had clearly absorbed radicalism from the French Revolution and the European Enlightenment goal of "the greatest happiness and progress" during his years in Paris. But his thinking was in this respect far in excess of what Siamese society was able or willing to accept in the 1930s and 1940s. As a result, the revolution was soon successfully hijacked by Gen. Phibun Songkhram, who borrowed elements of Italian Fascism and the martial Japanese *bushido* code to regiment Thai society, in the process aligning the country's foreign policy to that of Imperial Japan.[17] In 1944–45, as Japanese losses mounted, Phibun entered temporary eclipse. Pridi, meanwhile—with British and American support—reestablished his role in Thai politics by leading the "Free Thai" movement in harassment actions against the Japanese. Pridi was allied in this effort with Seni Pramoj, a leading liberal-royalist who would, after the war, found Thailand's first political party, the staid and stolid Democrats. But Pridi and Seni fell out when King Ananda Mahidol—Rama VIII—was found dead of a gunshot wound on June 9, 1946. As descendants of a minor branch of the royal family, Seni and his even more conservative brother Kukrit Pramoj resented and feared the popular Pridi for his role in the 1932 revolution, and in particular his verbal assault on the monarchy in the "Announcement of the People's Party No. 1."

Pridi had, in the intervening years, apologized for the manifesto's tone and came more earnestly to accept that the monarch must remain head of the Thai state. In fact, Pridi was serving as young King Ananda's regent when the still-unresolved shooting death occurred. Seni and Kukrit took advantage of this coincidental fact to accuse Pridi of regicide, using their prodigious influence—especially through Kukrit's newspaper—to destroy Pridi's reputation and thereby to discredit radical socioeconomic change. "This demonization served the purpose of the military dictators who were engaged in suppressing or distorting the constitution, laws, parliament, and other institutional innovations of Pridi's era. The demonization was also appealing to many old aristocrats who found it difficult to accept that their lineage might no longer convey status and privilege."[18] Even the young Sulak Sivaraksa was taken in by the hatred stirred against Pridi, and not until the bloody military repression of October 1976 did the scales fall from his eyes and Sulak began reexamining his prejudices and conclude that Pridi was not a regicide but instead the victim of a monstrously cynical smear campaign.[19]

Seni and Kukrit opposed radical socioeconomic change but did generally support constitutional democratization as long as the King could be restored to a prominent and significant position. Restoration was paramount, however, superseding democratization, and the brothers were happy to work with Sarit Thanarat after 1957 when Sarit decided his low level of legitimacy could be buttressed by bringing young King Bhumiphol into politics. Seni and Kukrit did, however, each serve as prime minister during the years of experimental democracy in the mid-1970s, helping to establish liberal-royalism as the middle position on the Thai political spectrum. With General Prem's nurturance in the 1980s, this system became institutionalized—also with the military and financial support of the United States. An aging Kukrit supported Suchinda's coup in 1991, while Seni's protégé, the Democrat Party's Chuan Leekpai, opposed Suchinda (albeit without special vigor) and became prime minister after the Democrats secured the most seats in the September 1992 elections.

As a lawyer by training, Chuan was—like his mentor Seni (also a lawyer)—conservative in his instincts, oriented toward proper form and order, and uncomfortable with popular participation in politics. He was a man somewhat out of place and time, because Thai society in the aftermath of the May 1992 uprising crackled with activism aimed at reforming politics, deepening democracy, and ensuring that the sacrifices of those killed, injured, or missing would not be in vain. During his first term in office (September 1992–July 1995), Chuan proved himself to be incapable of responding effectively to the political activism and using it to lead Thailand in the direction of significant reform. A breach soon erupted between reform activists and Chuan's government, suggesting for the first time that liberal-royalism might no longer be sustainable as the fulcrum point on the Thai political spectrum.[20] May 1992 had taught proponents of deepened democratization that Thai society had the potential to overturn the conservative consensus and push through to a new equilibrium in which systemic corruption, institutionalized inequalities, and a host of related endemic problems could seriously be addressed in a fundamental way for the first time in Thai history.

The setting was propitious for the activists to agitate because the Thai economy had been growing at a phenomenally high rate. Gross Domestic Product (GDP) doubled between 1985 and 1992, as exports increased fourfold. The total white-collar workforce increased from about 500,000 in the 1960s to 4.5 million in the late 1980s, with a plurality of these people—termed the "salariat" by Pasuk and Baker—living in Bangkok.[21] In previous decades, highly educated people would be absorbed into the government bureaucracy, but this practice became unsustainable by the 1980s. As a result, millions of intelligent and increasingly prosperous individuals with linkages to the outside world were now available to participate in politics. Many of them came eventually to detest Suchinda and the atavistic military domination for which he stood, and after May 1992 supported democratization enthusiastically. As Chamlong noted in June 1992, the result was that the early 1990s became "a monumental period where the democratic consciousness of the people has been awakened more than ever before," even more than in October 1973—because middle class participation and enthusiasm remained limited in those days.[22] At the same time, however, given their interest in continued economic growth, the middle classes would not necessarily support radical socioeconomic change: which, after all, was also not supported by mainstream global culture in the heyday of the "Washington Consensus."[23] Nevertheless, because the economy was indeed growing so fast, and society had become permeated with a general optimism in the months and years after 1992, middle-class Bangkok residents and other Thai people were willing to support movements for political reform. Rapid economic growth and victory in 1992 had many of them in a magnanimous and idealistic frame of mind.

The Reform Agenda

As with most such processes, in any country, the reform agenda came together "chaotically" in the period after May 1992: There was no single author directing the process, certainly not the cautious Prime Minister Chuan (though Anand played an important role during his interim premiership in June–September 1992).[24] The most urgent task at the time was getting the military out of politics and ensuring that no coup could ever succeed again. To this end, the Student Federation of Thailand—long active in democratization politics—distributed leaflets at the crowded and centrally located Mahbunkhrong shopping mall in June 1992 on the subject of "peacefully resisting a coup." The leaflets argued that another coup could be imminent and that, in such an event, Bangkok people should stage a general strike, should cut off water and electricity to the coup leaders' bases and headquarters, should block streets with cars and other large objects, and should withdraw their money from banks.[25] A few weeks later, Prime Minister Anand also called for passive resistance in the event of a coup, arguing that "democracy is not sent down from the heavens. It has to be earned, loved, and protected."[26] Thinking farther ahead, *The Nation* demanded establishment of "a professional military that knows its job—protecting Thailand from foreign aggressors and assisting the government in rural development," and urged academics and democracy activists to open dialogue with responsible military officers on the subject of crafting an appropriate social role for the military. *The Nation* also called for changing the curriculum at the Chulachomklao Royal Military Academy so that officers would no longer be educated to believe that they had a special guardian role to play in politics and that they might look forward to staging a coup one day at the pinnacle of their career.[27] At the same time, the Anand government took preliminary steps to end the practice of giving senior military officers special lucrative positions on the boards of directors of state-owned enterprises, including the important Telephone Organization of Thailand and Thai Airways International.[28]

The second most urgent task facing reformers was to reduce rampant vote-buying and political corruption more generally—urgent because Suchinda had used corruption in part to justify his February 1991 coup, and because extensive vote-buying in the elections to be held in September 1992 would be demoralizing and might undermine the momentum for reform ignited by the events of May. To the end of preventing vote-buying, Anand worked closely with the PollWatch organization of (primarily) domestic NGO activists, just as he had done prior to the March 1992 elections. PollWatch called explicitly in June 1992 for the establishment of an independent body to take over responsibility for managing general elections from the corrupt and powerful Interior Ministry. It also proposed reforms of the electoral system to change Thailand from a multimember to a single-member (of Parliament) district system (which would presumably reduce the efficacy of vote-buying) and to require that candidates who failed to receive 10 percent of constituency votes pay a fine.[29] Neither of these more radical proposals could be adopted and implemented in time for the September 1992 elections, but they entered the general agenda of political reform. Meanwhile, other commentators argued that to reduce vote-buying—which was far more extensive in constituencies outside of Bangkok—the government should launch a massive democracy education campaign, holding mobile Cabinet sessions in major provincial cities and circulating videotapes of the May 1992 massacre so that rural people could be "reminded of the brutality committed during the May 17–20 bloodshed and told how they can help put the country back on the right political track."[30]

Other issues mooted for public discussion in the immediate aftermath of the democratic opening included the need to promote the public's "right to information," so that institutionalized abuses could be ferreted out and exposed and future attempts to hoodwink and repress the populace prevented and thereby discouraged.[31] Promoting the "right to information" was related to a broader and deeper concern to instill general human rights consciousness among the Thai people and in other ways to force the government to respect human rights.[32] NGOs expressed concern about the bureaucracy's overweening nature and its potential to obstruct the political reforms, and for this reason called for political decentralization, which if implemented would reverse the historical trend of centralized state-building begun under Chulalongkorn. Because local leaders were all, in effect, appointed, NGOs and their supporters argued that "there is no active leader to lead the local communities away from poverty and illiteracy because government officials are mainly outsiders who have no close concerns for the local communities' well-being." Yet because the socioeconomic structure was changing and becoming more pluralistic, society's general level of education was rising, and the communist threat had long since receded, "there is no legitimate reason for the central government to maintain its tight control over local communities as before." The only effect of such domination was to turn rural residents into "ignorant subjects" who "are prevented from getting involved in local affairs."[33] In short, the summary goal of the political reform movement was "to empower the weak," according to one activist-academic. "People have to be taught that they have the right to demand from the government and not to serve government officials as if they were high and mighty. They also have the right to resist being 'bought,' whether in the form of vote-buying or through state-backed easy loans."[34]

While in the process of crafting the reform agenda, Thai activists, government officials, parliamentarians, journalists, and intellectuals all felt pressure and received inspiration from 1990s world society—especially as international organizations and NGOs promoted "democratization" and "good governance" to the point they became buzzwords. What better place to turn for models of how to reform than to the continually evolving global culture(s), whose influence and guidance Thai elites had sought with enthusiasm for more than a century? Writing in the years immediately after promulgation of the 1997 "People's Constitution," Thirayuth Boonmi, a Thammasat University sociologist who had been a key student leader in October 1973, asserted that "I have proposed the concept of *thammarat* (good governance) as a solution" to the problems caused by the 1997–98 economic meltdown. Downplaying the authorship issue—since "good governance" was already current in world society— Thirayuth wrote that "his" concept "refers to a [voluntary] collaboration between the public, social, and private sectors to create governance and administration that are transparent, legitimate, accountable, and effective. I have suggested that solution because our problem stems from the festering depravity in our political system, bureaucracy, technocracy, and the business sector, while the popular sector is weak." Thirayuth's good governance—which, his translator writes, was called *thammarat haengchat* (national good governance) in a previous draft—did include some distinctively Thai elements, with the flavor of socially engaged Buddhism. For example, Thirayuth argued that individuals throughout all institutions in Thai society must play their roles with a sense of social responsibility if good governance is to work. "Individual good governance" requires that "each individual is aware of his/her power and is able to exercise it responsibly and justly." Thirayuth also latched on to the socially engaged Buddhist concern for community development that had influenced the call for political decentralization. He argued that good governance requires "local institutions and communities to understand their own problems so that they can rely on themselves and reform themselves."[35] Community development could serve as an antidote to the problems caused by excessive economic openness, and had the additional advantage of being consistent with UN agencies' promotion of indigenous rights and local cultures.

The Constitutional Reform Movement

All of the various efforts to reform the political system coalesced into a constitutional reform movement in the mid-1990s. Constitutions have an air of sacredness about them in Thailand, a legacy of the June 1932 coup to end the absolute monarchy and begin governing Siam by means of a charter. In the 1930s and 1940s, the average educational level was far too low in Siam to popularize the significance of a constitution by making reference to constitutional governance's inherent rightness, as judged by the standards of liberal-rational global culture. Therefore, Pridi, Phibun, and the other coup leaders made use of the reverence Thai people attached to the monarchical institution—and to the state more generally—to sacralize the constitution, thereby increasing their own legitimacy. The result was that in addition to Nation, Religion, and King, "Constitution" (*rattamanoon*) became integral to Thai "civic religious consciousness."[36] The issue has obviously been important to democracy activists over the generations because constitutional governance implies channeled, institutionalized, and predictable political behavior along with constraints on the use of power; in principle if not necessarily in practice, constitutional governance implies that military forces aligned with moneyed elites cannot quite as easily exploit and brutalize the weak. In the 1960s, the initial refusal of Sarit, Thanom, and Praphat to restore constitutional rule was a major source of dissatisfaction—including King Bhumiphol's dissatisfaction. Thanom's 1971 coup and his nullification of the conservative constitution reluctantly granted in 1968 were the immediate triggering factors in the activism that culminated in October 1973.[37] Thus it was no historical surprise that the activists of the 1990s would consider Suchinda's imposed December 1991 constitution—which institutional-ized military domination—unacceptable, even though it had been revised slightly in the immediate aftermath of May 1992.

Complicated and cynical parliamentary maneuvering combined with Premier Chuan's reluctance to exercise decisive leadership to delay the constitutional reform process until Chalard Vorachart began a hunger strike on May 25, 1994. It had been Chalard's hunger strike in April 1992 against Suchinda's unelected premiership that ignited the previous polit-ical crisis; as a result, when Chalard announced his intentions in May 1994, worries of a new crisis quickly developed. Chamlong Srimuang, now much weaker politically, tried to convince Chalard to end his hunger strike, but other pro-democracy groups rallied to the former politician's support—including Dr. Prawase Wasi, a senior socially engaged Buddhist and one of the most respected figures in Thailand. Prawase proposed es-tablishing a constitutional drafting committee to defuse the crisis and end Chalard's fast, and this proposal immediately attracted the support of ranking parliamentarians and specialists in constitutional law.[38] But the Democrats balked at succumbing to what they called "political intimida-tion," a stubborn stance that triggered protests when some 5,000 people assembled outside Parliament on June 8, 1994—many of them calling Chuan a "liar" and demanding his ouster.[39] With the threat of social tur-moil rising, and the fear that military figures could use turmoil to justify a violent crackdown and general political reaction, the parliamentary presi-dent exercised special powers and ordered establishment of a twenty-one-member "Democratic Development Committee" (DDC), which would be chaired by Prawase Wasi and composed of esteemed figures in civil society and from political parties.[40] Chalard initially refused to accept the DDC's establishment as sufficient grounds for ending his hunger strike, but finally relented on June 16—whereupon he was promptly arrested on trumped-up charges of *lese majeste*. In the eyes of political activists, the Democrats were thereby exposed for obstinacy and arrogance. The *Bangkok Post* editorialized that the Democrats' "political intrigue and treachery, . . . a special craft learned, nurtured, and honed for decades," meant that they could no longer be trusted with the important responsibility of nurturing the reform legacy of May 1992.[41]

DDC Chairman Prawase Wasi personified Thai democracy's integra-tion of liberal-rational global culture with socially engaged Buddhism. Prawase wrote explicitly that "the whole spectrum of social reform may be viewed as a process of promoting good governance, or building civil society," but also that "the politics of reform should understand the signif-icance of spiritual development" because "external reform alone cannot lead to peace and sustainability."[42] McCargo writes of Prawase's intellectual background that

the thinking of Dr. Prawes [Prawase] Wasi was firmly anti-state: Prawes argued that state institutions were incapable of promoting successful development. He favoured a thorough-going process of decentralization, giving local communities control over their own affairs. Prawes advocated the creation of small consciousness-raising groups in local communities, groups which sought to build upon their own "popular wisdom" by studying "universal culture." Ultimately, these groups should be able to assume the power and responsibilities formerly carried out by the state, which would then be dissolved.[43]

Prawase would obviously not be in a position to pursue such a radical agenda as chairman of the DDC, whose "intellectual leadership," in any case, "was provided by law professor Bowornsak Uwano, a former adviser to the Chatichai government [1988–1991] and an active exponent of constitutional change."[44] But Prawase's ethos influenced the proceedings and helped set the tone for political reform—particularly insofar as it would stress the importance of decentralization and a Buddhism-inspired compassion for the poor.

The DDC issued its recommendations in April 1995. The recommendations called in an airy way for political reform and social empowerment, but more importantly, called concretely for amending Article 211 of the December 1991 Suchinda Constitution, which specified that the Constitution could be amended but not rewritten. Reflecting Bowornsak's influence but also the desires of the social activists, the DDC was in this way recommending that the government take steps to replace the Suchinda constitution with a brand-new charter.[45]

The recommendations came at a propitious time, because coalition instability forced Chuan to call new elections for July 2, 1995. The DDC understood that political reform would only succeed if public pressure could be mobilized against the government, and its members planned from an early date to work with civil society groups in educating the public and stimulating interest. After elections were announced, the Student Federation of Thailand called for all politicians running on July 2 to accept a "social contract" committing them to pursue political reform.[46] In the heat of the contest, all of the major parties committed to the concept (with varying degrees of enthusiasm), including Chart Thai's Banharn Sinlapa-archa, whose party won the most seats, giving Banharn the prime ministership. Despite his status as a "classic" conservative and patronage-dispensing provincial politician, Banharn—however reluctantly—agreed to fulfill his campaign pledge, and appointed a Political Reform Committee to study and "take into account" the DDC's proposals and report back to the government with suggestions on political reform's next phase. Liberals worried that Banharn intended in this way to shelve political reform and neutralize the activism.[47] But in constituting the Committee, the premier had no choice but to appoint high-profile social activists, and these individuals took a variety of actions in the following months to keep the public focused on reform.[48]

In October 1995, the Committee faithfully recommended amending Article 211, but Banharn hesitated because the proposal would have excluded senators and MPs from the subsequent process of drafting a new charter. This prompted the Confederation for Democracy, a leading NGO, to withdraw its members from the Committee, an act that increased the pressure on Banharn.[49] Chart Thai's coalition partners agreed in November 1995 to amend Article 211, and then finally, after several months of wrangling, the Parliament approved a Constitution Amendment Bill in May 1996 that would establish a ninety-nine-person Constitution Drafting Assembly (CDA), with one member from each of the seventy-six provinces and twenty-three others selected from the professions of public law, political science, and public administration. NGOs and institutions of higher education would nominate candidates for these positions, producing a shortlist, and then the political parties' ruffled feathers would be smoothed by allowing Parliament to choose finally from among the nominees. As Prudhisan Jumbala observes, "all sides were sufficiently satisfied; indirect election gave an appearance of popular mandate and Parliament would do the final selection."[50] The result was that the CDA enjoyed a high degree of legitimacy when it began its work at the end of 1996. Its legitimacy increased even further when Anand Panyarachun was elected chair of the CDA's Constitution Drafting Committee (CDC) in January 1997.[51]

The world-polity theorists discussed in Chapter 1 stress constitutionalism as a defining value of liberal-rational global culture. During the past century, elites worldwide have reorganized their societies on the basis of constitutions, usually written—though implementation is of course far from universally faithful. The fact that almost all societies now have written constitutions is taken as evidence of liberal-rational global culture's power to socialize postcolonial state-builders to values that there is no evidence they embraced prior to encounters with the West. Reflecting Thailand's historical enthusiasm for accepting global cultural prescriptions, members of the CDC consulted foreign constitutions for ideas on how best to address Thailand's specific problems. Particularly for the electoral system, "Germany was the model," in the words of an informant active in the process (but not as a CDC member).[52] The reason was that Germany had perfected the single-member district/party list system, which the drafters believed could help remedy the problems of vote-buying and personality-based campaigns. Strengthened parties would be more likely to impose discipline on members of Parliament and pursue issue-based campaigns.[53] The drafters also consulted the US, French, and even South African constitutions, and were influenced in particular by the US separation of powers model, which convinced them of the need to establish independent commissions to check governmental abuse.[54]

Yet another avenue of global cultural (both mainstream and oppositional) influence on the constitution-drafting process was the consulting work of internationally linked NGOs. The Asia Foundation, Friedrich Ebert Stiftung, and Canadian International Development Agency all provided assistance; according to Doneys, the Asia Foundation "even provided MPs and senators with their own staff, hoping to influence the process through their 'women in politics' program."[55] Foreign NGOs also exerted influence indirectly through their relations with domestic Thai NGOs involved in the drafting process.

Despite such foreign input and influence, one person active in linking the Asia Foundation's Women in Politics program to the drafting process argues that the massive consultation process used to maximize public participation ensured that, in the end, the document was "made in Thailand."[56] The drafters and political reform activists were well aware of the basic *baan* vs. *muang* cleavage in Thai politics,[57] and as largely Bangkok intellectuals, they wanted to make sure that rural residents would not reject the new charter as yet another unwanted imposition by an arrogant central state. As a result, CDA subcommittees were established in each of the seventy-six provinces for the purpose of relaying parts of successive drafts to interested up-country publics for comment. Joined by NGOs, the seventy-six provincial CDA members unveiled components of the draft at public hearings held in the provincial capitals and then fanned out to many of the provincial districts for the joint purpose of educating the people and soliciting feedback. Suggestions for revision were incorporated into subsequent drafts, which eventually came back for recirculation and more opinion-soliciting in several iterations during the course of the mandated eight-month drafting period. The process served an important social-mobilizational function and was vital to generating broad and deep support for the new charter. Up to one million people (out of a total population of sixty-three million) throughout Thailand either attended the public hearings or submitted suggestions in writing:[58] "Especially in the provincial towns, these meetings were intense and lively. Thousands turned up to listen. Hundreds queued at the microphones to have their say. Participation went far beyond local politicians and activists. Businessmen, professionals, community leaders, and ordinary people took part."[59]

Meanwhile, 10,000 members of the Assembly of the Poor peacefully encamped outside Government House in Bangkok from January 24 to May 2, 1997—at the height of the drafting process—to demand redress for a variety of grievances stemming from government policies on forest-clearing, infrastructure-building, and rural industrialization. Using their linkages to NGOs, Assembly members managed to convey to drafters the key demand that *community rights* be recognized in the new charter alongside individual rights, and that a human rights commission be established to ensure government protection and compliance.[60] In addition to making these specific demands, Assembly members pressured the government to accept the draft by sheer dint of their massive presence. The rules stated that when the draft constitution was finished, Parliament could only accept or reject it in toto; the politician-choked institution would have no power to tinker with the document for the purpose of gutting it. If fewer than two-thirds of parliamentarians approved the draft, the charter would be put to the public for a referendum. It was unclear what proportion of the public might support the document, and some activists predicted pessimistically that—given the generally low education and political awareness levels outside of Bangkok—it might not pass. On the other hand, the mobilizational quality of the drafting process and the evident organizational power of the Assembly of the Poor suggested that perhaps the public *would* support the new constitution, which could have caused a crisis: the public versus Parliament.

Just as the final draft was being prepared for release in July 1997, the Asian economic meltdown began with the collapse of the Thai baht.[61] A crisis atmosphere gripped Thailand immediately. On August 5, 1997, Prime Minister Chavalit Yongchaiyudh (who had replaced Banharn the previous November) was forced to apply for a $15 billion IMF loan to try to stabilize the currency, which nevertheless continued to decline in value. Chavalit was a unique Thai politician, a retired general whose efforts to quell communist insurgency in the 1970s and 1980s had convinced him of the need to seriously address the problems of the rural poor (albeit while maintaining "order"). He was in this way quite distinct from General Suchinda, a significantly more conservative and self-absorbed politician. Nevertheless, Chavalit's New Aspiration Party was peopled generally by conservatives, and certainly his coalition partners were old-style politicians. A well-known *Nation* columnist wrote in July that "politicians and other power-holders slated the draft with words like ugly, vicious, mad, absurd, dangerous, divisive, and sadistic."[62] Interior Minister Snoh Thienthong said in all seriousness that he thought "communists" were behind the new constitution. "They are here using the strategy to use towns to surround the jungle. That's their strategy. You can go and see it."[63]

But with the experience of May 1992 still fresh in everyone's minds, and the evident power of NGOs to organize mass demonstrations, momentum shifted in favor of the charter as the economic crisis deepened. Thirayuth Boonmi argued that supporting the draft was the only way to prevent a popular uprising. "All problems will take a turn for the worse by the beginning of next year," he predicted in an interview with the *Bangkok Post*. "They are likely to develop into a mass and violent protest."[64] One informant argued that "the crisis changed the definition and dynamics of the situation. If you didn't support the reforms, you were passé and maybe irresponsible—because the reforms were seen as the key to political stability and it was thought if the reforms had been in place to begin with, we wouldn't have had the crisis."[65] In the face of such pressure and logic, Chavalit and even most of the parliamentary conservatives came to the conclusion that voting down the draft charter and putting it to the required public referendum would have been a dangerously high-risk course. Consequently, Parliament voted on September 27, 1997, to approve the new Constitution by a vote of 518 to 16, with 17 abstentions. The King officially promulgated the new charter on October 11.[66] A month later, Chavalit resigned to take responsibility for the economic meltdown, and the Democrats under Chuan Leekpai returned to form a new government.

Deepening Democratization

To address the political corruption problem, the Constitution restructured the electoral system so that 400 of 500 House of Representative seats would be filled by individuals elected (on the basis of one-person, one-vote) in single-member districts. To strengthen political parties, the Constitution provided that the remaining 100 House members would be elected at large from party lists, with each voter casting a single ballot for one party's roster. Any party receiving less than 5 percent of the vote would not be allotted House seats from its list. In addition, a 200-seat Senate—joining the House in a National Assembly—would be elected directly (instead of, as in the past, appointed) in a single, nationwide constituency on the basis of one-person, one-vote. The Senate's primary responsibility would be to recommend the names of candidates to serve on new independent commissions (including the Election Commission, National Human Rights Commission (NHRC), National Counter-Corruption Commission, Constitutional Court, and State Audit Commission). The Senate would also screen legislation and interpellate ministers and bureaucrats, and was made responsible for approving emergency decrees and declarations of war and treaties. With the hope of filling Senate seats with responsible, esteemed individuals instead of selfish politicians, the drafters required that candidates for Senate seats could not be members of a political party. House members wishing to fill Senate seats would have to leave office at least one year before running. Senators could not become government ministers and would have to leave office at least one year in advance of taking a government ministership. Senators would serve for single, six-year terms while House members would serve renewable four-year terms.[67]

These changes to the parliamentary system were obviously of extreme importance in reforming Thailand's governance, though precisely what their ultimate effect will be remains to be seen. In strengthening the party system, they were crucial to Thaksin Shinawatra's rise to power. On the other hand, the Constitution deepens Thai democracy in ways that combine the values of liberal-rational global culture with indigenous Thai values. For example, Section 46 of the charter states that people assembling as "a traditional community" have the right "to conserve or restore their customs, local knowledge, arts or good culture of their community and of the nation and participate in the management, maintenance, preservation and exploitation of natural resources and the environment in a balanced fashion and persistently as provided by law." Communities are thereby recognized as legal entities with corporate rights and responsibilities vis-à-vis the state, business corporations, and individuals. The Chairman of the new NHRC, Saneh Chamarik—a history professor and veteran human rights activist—argued explicitly that in stressing community rights, the Constitution moves beyond the democratization models promoted by the West. "Individuals are assumed by Thai people, but they are against the monopoly of human rights by individuals. Even in the West, people have a sense that something is lacking in human rights; so . . . you could say that we have something to teach." On the other hand, Saneh is adamant that the community rights to which Thailand is now constitutionally committed have nothing to do with the "Asian values" championed by autocrats in Singapore, Malaysia, and China. "Human rights are natural but not universal in terms of specifics. The West has developed the human rights concept farther than anyone else so far, but now we need to consolidate those gains and build on them."[68]

The Thai Constitution is unusually progressive by global standards. For example, in the area of community rights, Section 56 requires that "any project or activity which may seriously affect the quality of the environment shall not be permitted, unless its impacts on the quality of the environment have been studied and evaluated and opinions of an independent organization . . . have been obtained." Section 59 mandates that "a person shall have the right to receive information, explanation, and

reason from a State agency, State enterprise or local government organization before permission is given for the operation of any project or activity
which may affect the quality of the environment, health and sanitary conditions, the quality of life, or any other material interest concerning him
or her or a local community." This provision was adopted explicitly with
reducing the tensions spawned by the *baan* vs. *muang* cleavage in mind.
More broadly, Section 80 requires that "the State shall protect and develop children and youth, promote equality between women and men, and
create, reinforce, and develop family integrity and the strength of communities." In this way, the Constitution requires that the government be
proactive and energetic: it must protect *and* develop children and youth,
promote gender equality rather than defend it passively, and so on.

The Constitution also empowers and mobilizes Thai citizens to defend
their hard-won democratic gains. To avoid a recrudescence of coups, Section 65 states that "a person shall have the right to resist peacefully any
act committed for the acquisition of power to rule the country by a means
which is not in accordance with the modes provided in this Constitution."
Section 66 reads that "every person shall have a duty to uphold the Nation, religions [not only Buddhism], the King, and the democratic regime
of government with the King as Head of the State." The drafters resisted
conservative demands to make Buddhism the state religion, which in particular would have antagonized southern Muslims. Section 68 states that
"every person shall have a duty to exercise his or her right to vote at an
election." Section 170: "The persons having the right to vote of not less
than fifty thousand in number shall have a right to submit a petition to the
President of the National Assembly to consider . . . [a proposed] law." The
drafters clearly wished to activate the citizenry, to involve them in politics
enthusiastically, and to create a political ecology in which not only coups
but also the demagoguery that thrives in climates of ennui and cynicism
could be precluded and neutralized. In a sense, they were trying to institutionalize the political activism of 1992–97, which may have been the
reason conservatives in Chavalit's government "sneered at the CDA draft
as the work of a gang of French-educated intellectuals who think they are
re-enacting 1789."[69]

Among the new constitutionally mandated independent commissions—inspired by the American separation of powers system—the
NHRC is most directly responsible for ensuring implementation of the
core values of liberal-rational global culture, as elaborated and developed in Thailand. Parliament passed enabling legislative for the NHRC
in August 1999 and the Commission was formally established in July
2001.[70] Its Strategic Plan outlines several focus areas and approaches, all
with the vision of "achieving human rights culture as a way of life in Thai

society." By October 2003, the NHRC had handled a few more than 600 cases, in generally five categories: denial of judicial rights, denial of environmental rights, denial of economic rights, gender discrimination, and denial of the right to privacy.

The problem is that the NHRC's actual capacity and power to redress human rights violations remain quite limited. If the Commission determines that a human rights violation has occurred, its next step is to "propose remedial measures to responsible individuals and organizations." If the offending agencies refuse to respond, the Commission "reports to the Prime Minister to command for action within 60 days." If the problem still persists, the Commission can "report to the Parliament [and/or] disseminate information to the public."[71] At a UN meeting in Pakistan in March 2003, Commissioner Pradit Chareonthaitawee criticized the excesses of Prime Minister Thaksin's sanguinary crackdown on suspected methamphetamine dealers, in which over 2,000 people were killed.[72] Thaksin's response was to brand Commissioner Pradit a "traitor" and "whistle-blower" whose comments were "sickening." Thaksin associates accused Pradit of "helping drug dealers," and unknown persons threatened to blow up the commissioner's car or burn down his house.[73] Nevertheless, NHRC commissioners and staffers remained idealistic and enthusiastic about their job, committed to using what powers they have and the *pracharat* network discussed in Chapter 2 to "domesticate" Thaksin and continue to deepen Thai democracy.

Socializing Other Countries to Liberal-Rational Global Culture

Thai democracy activists seem almost universally to consider assisting Burma's transformation into a democratic country to be central to their own struggle. The two countries are fused into a long-term dyadic relationship in which each plays the role of a highly significant "Other" for the other. Thai people are constantly reminded in government-controlled television programs, films, and in school that Burma's ferocious assault on the city of Ayutthaya in 1767 destroyed the previous dynasty, and that Burma has been Thailand's primary source of security threats for centuries. Many Thai people seem to have memorized the fact that "between 1500 and 1880, Burma and Siam fought 24 wars, and 21 times Burma started them with invasions."[74] More recently, Burma has become a source of non-traditional security threats: political refugees, economic migrants, and an annual flood of hundreds of millions of cheaply produced methamphetamine tablets (called *yaa baa* or "crazy drugs" in Thai) that prove powerfully addictive and within several months of regular use, wreck addicts for perhaps the rest of their lives.[75] "Sixty percent of Thailand's problems emanate from Burma," asserted one political scientist.[76] The military junta that controls Burma is "the great mafia in this area," said a historian.[77]

As a result, there are quite practical reasons to pursue Burma's political transformation, as even one official in Thaksin's government (which was reluctant to put pressure on the Burmese government) freely acknowledged.[78] Many people share the sentiment that if Burma would become democratic, the methamphetamine and other problems could be reduced sharply in severity and perhaps even eliminated. But the democracy activists move beyond this simple utilitarian calculus to argue that Thailand should help Burma democratize because democracy is inherently good. Activists motivated by socially engaged Buddhism assert that compassion dictates the Thai people help those suffering under the yoke next door. Others view Burma as a reflection of what Thailand would have become if the October 1973 revolution had failed, and suggest that Burma's transformation would confirm the rightness, success, and security of Thailand's democratization.[79] All of the activists—and even politically uninterested Thai people, and some conservatives—seem to believe that Thailand's transition to democracy is incomplete as long as Burma remains untransformed. Confirmation that a "late democratizer" has "arrived" and joined the mainstream of world society follows naturally from making efforts to socialize other countries to democratic values. And unlike the apparently hopeless cases of Cambodia, Laos, and Vietnam, Burma holds real promise for Thai democracy activists. The Burmese opposition is popular and well connected internationally, and the military junta's persistent failure to launch the economy on a development track implies that one day the opposition could take power. Aung San Suu Kyi remains an iconic figure both within Burma and abroad—including in Thailand. "Investing" in Burmese democratization therefore appears to offer reasonable chances of a high payoff.

All of these considerations came together with the excitement generated by promulgation of the "People's Constitution" to produce a surprising change in official Thai policy toward Burma in 1998: an effort led by Democrat Foreign Minister Surin Pitsuwan and Deputy Foreign Minister Sukhumbhand Paribatra to goad the Association of Southeast Asian Nations (ASEAN) into pressuring Burma to liberalize. Before 1998, the Thai government's policy—even during the previous Democrat administration (September 1992–July 1995)—had been to eschew the temptation to "interfere in Burma's internal affairs" and encourage the country's gradual change through "constructive engagement": placing hope in trade and investment to stimulate the Burmese economy (and, of course, make some Thai people rich), perhaps thereby cultivating the emergence of a democracy-minded middle class that would demand change. But Thai NGOs became active in pursuing Burma's democratization almost immediately after the junta's brutal crackdown on democracy demonstrators in August 1988, during which soldiers using truck-mounted machine guns shot dead some 3,000 people in the streets.[80] These NGO and other democracy activists connected to Surin and Sukhumbhand through the *pracharat* network encouraged the Democrats to adopt a forward policy, because pressuring ASEAN countries generally to become democratic would, in the words of Sukhumbhand, "be in line with the provision of Thailand's new Constitution, which gives importance to . . . the respect of people's rights and freedoms."[81]

The immediate triggering event for the NGOs and activists to press for the foreign policy change was Burma's admission to ASEAN in July 1997, at the height of the frenetic activity surrounding publication of the draft Constitution. Sulak Sivaraksa led a group of Thai and international human rights activists to Prime Minister Chavalit's office on May 14, 1997 to request that Chavalit "disengage" with the Burmese junta and reconsider his support for Rangoon's efforts to join ASEAN. Sulak contended that since Chavalit rose to power through democratic processes, he should not associate himself and therefore Thailand with "a brutal and illegitimate regime."[82] Nevertheless, ASEAN—with Thailand's support—voted to approve Rangoon's application on May 30, a decision *The Nation* editorialized as "A Triumph of Evil over Humanity" because it ignored "the burning desire of the people in all ASEAN member states to incorporate democracy and human rights as part of their national development."[83] One *Bangkok Post* columnist worried about the reaction of Thailand's Western friends: "I dare not imagine how the American and European delegates will react if they are asked to hold hands with the SLORC representative in the typical ASEAN show of solidarity."[84]

The Democrat Party also criticized the decision. Democrat MP Noppadol Pattama of the House Committee on Foreign Affairs asserted on June 1 that ASEAN should have delayed Burma's candidacy until Rangoon improved its human rights record and began making tangible progress toward democratization.[85] There was not, of course, much the Democrats could do about the decision at the time, but when Chuan Leekpai formed his second government in November 1997—just after the new Constitution was promulgated, and at darkest phase of the economic crisis—the Democrats found themselves in a position from which they could demand ASEAN focus serious efforts on democratic change. They were not yet ready frontally to challenge the hallowed ASEAN principle of mutual nonintervention in member countries' affairs, but they were willing to begin broaching the subject publicly. Deputy Foreign Minister Sukhumbhand attended a December 1997 public discussion cosponsored by Forum-Asia and several international NGOs on the subject of "Thailand's Political Reform and Its Effect on ASEAN." At the meeting, Sukhumbhand conceded that Thai people "are not entitled to lecture anybody as long as our own political system is not fully democratic"—especially in light of the nonintervention principle—but that nevertheless ASEAN countries should expand political participation because "the globalized world . . . highlights the values of democracy, human rights, environmental protection, and equality of genders, races, and religions."[86] To advance this cause concretely, the government sent Permanent Secretary for Foreign Affairs Saroj Chavanaviraj to Manila for a conference in May 1998 with regional human rights NGOs—the only government willing to send a representative. At the meeting, the Foreign Ministry announced Thailand's "strong support" for establishing an ASEAN Human Rights Commission, which would be consistent with Thailand's own planned establishment of an NHRC.[87]

But the dramatic developments occurred in June and July 1998. At a Thammasat University forum on June 12, Foreign Minister Surin announced boldly that "perhaps it is time for ASEAN's cherished nonintervention principle to be modified," since "when a matter of domestic concern poses a threat to regional stability, a dose of peer pressure or friendly advice can be helpful." Surin dubbed his concept "constructive intervention," and explained that "non-interference does not mean that we cannot espouse the values of our own society, although of course we should not try to impose them on others."[88] During the following two weeks, Surin repeatedly reaffirmed Thailand's intention to pursue "constructive intervention," and argued on June 26 that Thailand "should have the freedom and liberty to express its opinions on any matters that could possibly escalate from being internal to becoming regional problems." He explicitly denied a report that Thailand would soon back down from the policy.[89]

Nevertheless, that is exactly what Thailand was forced by its ASEAN partners to do. Even as Surin spoke on June 26, his Foreign Ministry bureaucrats were changing the name of the concept from "constructive intervention" to "constructive involvement." Within a few days, it had morphed again, becoming "flexible engagement," a term which *Nation* commentator Kavi Chongkittavorn suggested was meaningless.[90] By the time the annual ASEAN summit convened in Manila in late July, the concept had become less than a shadow of its former self, termed finally "enhanced interaction" to stave off the criticisms of ASEAN's conservative leaders.[91]

Surin sought to give the debacle a positive spin, underscoring the fusion of Thai identity (at least under the Democrats) with efforts to socialize others to democracy. He proclaimed in Manila that ASEAN must become more democratic so that its member countries would not always be "on the receiving end" of charges of violating human rights and being autocratic. "Like it or not," Surin said, "the issues of democracy and human rights are those that we have to increasingly deal with in our engagement with the outside world."[92] Speaking in Singapore the following week, Deputy Prime Minister Sukhumbhand elaborated on the philosophy behind "enhanced interaction" by contending that ASEAN must pursue "self-renewal" in the course of economic development and must strive toward "development with a human face." In remarks aimed squarely at addressing the crux of the *tiyong* problem, Sukhumbhand declared that "the direction of political, social, and economic development in the region must serve not only efforts to bring about national and regional resilience or security, but also the causes of civil society and the dignity of the human person."[93] This was of course precisely the modern Enlightenment agenda, underscored by Sukhumbhand's call for political reform, which he said requires "measures to increase accountability, to promote transparency, and to open up the political system in order to expand the processes of political participation and decision-making":

I am a Thai, and therefore, by definition, no revolutionary. I have never advocated revolutionary changes and I do not wish to do so now. But I firmly believe that, to make a full contribution to the ASEAN of the future, . . . [we] must now reappraise, modify, or discard political arrangements and policy directions which over the longer term only serve to make [our] societies less caring, less open, less generous of opportunities for the development of all citizens, and less protective of the welfare and dignity of the individual.[94]

At about the same time as Surin and Sukhumbhand were charting a bold new course in foreign policy, Mahidol University—just outside of Bangkok—was establishing an Office of Human Rights and Social Development, whose purpose would be to develop a Master of Arts (MA) program for training Southeast Asians and others in human rights philosophy and activism.[95] The program was the brainchild of Pradit Chareonthaitawee, the Human Rights Commissioner called "sickening" and "a traitor" by Prime Minister Thaksin in March 2003. Pradit was President of Mahidol in 1992. In the aftermath of the May political upheaval, he was searching for ways to help institutionalize democratization. He proposed the program to the University Council in 1993, but it took several years to secure formal approval. The program was finally established in 1998, with a mission "to develop the ways and means by which human rights are transformed into social and political realities at the community, national, and international levels," through education, workshops, and outreach programs, as "an active component of the human rights network of NGOs" and others involved in *pracharat*.[96]

The first group of the fifteen or so to be admitted annually arrived in February 1999. By 2003, several dozen students had passed through the program, not only from Thailand but also from Nepal, Bangladesh, Kenya, Cambodia, Laos, Aceh (Indonesia), the Netherlands, and the United States. The curriculum these students imbibed included a mixture of Western and non-Western materials. Sample course titles included "Philosophical, Social Scientific, and Legal Concepts in Human Rights," "International Human Rights Standards," "Human Rights Protection Mechanisms," and "Practical Skills for Human Rights Protection." Course instruction was entirely in English, though the Office planned to open a parallel Thai-language program in the future. Program directors encouraged students also to attend workshops the Office cosponsored with international NGOs. For example, a training program in April/May 2002 gave students the opportunity to interact with twenty-four activists who came to attend the program from Cambodia, Indonesia, Laos, Malaysia, the Philippines, the Burma–Thailand border, and Thailand proper. Participants attended lectures and discussions but also took field trips to a migrant workers' community and an up-country Burmese refugee camp. The hope was that students would not only learn to apply theory to practice, but also network with the NGO activists upon graduation and join them in some capacity in the regional struggle for human rights.

As a result, not only the Thai government but also groups in Thai civil society were becoming active in socializing people from other countries (especially in Southeast Asia) to the values of liberal-rational global culture. Foreign governments and NGOs assisted these efforts; for example, the Swedish International Development Cooperation Agency provided most of the Office of Human Rights and Social Development's funding. In fact, much of the curriculum for the MA program appears to have been modeled on a similar program at Sweden's Raoul Wallenberg Institute of Human Rights and Humanitarian Law. These sorts of connections and lines of influence are both a source of strength and a source of trouble for the Office. Without them the program could not exist, but with them, the Office becomes vulnerable to the charge of catering to foreigners for the purpose of making money or even being "traitorous." Yet in 2005, the program remained sufficiently strong and politically well supported that the Office's director was planning not only to establish a Thai-language MA program, but also an English-language Ph.D. program.

Reaction: Thaksin

On December 10, 2003, Prime Minister Thaksin declared explicitly that "democracy is just a tool, not our goal. The goal is to give people a good lifestyle, happiness and national progress." Thaksin was responding to the efforts of political opponents and even some members of his own governing coalition to revise the Constitution so that independent commissions could be made strong enough to check his power. "Democracy is a good and beautiful thing," Thaksin conceded, but—apropos the *tiyong* dilemma—it was ultimately just "a vehicle," a vehicle perhaps inappropriate for Thai conditions: "We can't drive a Rolls-Royce to a rural village and solve people's problems. A pickup truck or good off-road car will do. We just need to think carefully and make the right choices." Consequently, Thaksin vowed to fight democracy activists' efforts to revise the charter, a task some of his opponents considered urgent because the Thai Rak Thai (TRT) party was projected to win 350 of 500 seats in the February 2005 elections.[97]

The Thaksin phenomenon was challenging. On the one hand, as detailed in the pages below, the prime minister was contemptuous of democracy and those who promoted it. Many NGOs, and even Sulak Sivaraksa, had supported Thaksin in January 2001 because they considered him more energetic and visionary than the staid Chuan Leekpai. But soon they were at odds with the new prime minister over his autocratic tendencies and refusal to take charges of human rights violations seriously. His landslide reelection victory in February 2005 was a huge blow to the democracy activists, who failed to anticipate that the "People's Constitution" on which they worked so hard would pave the way for a populist and quasi-nationalist to take power by generally legal means (discounting the inevitable vote-buying).

Thaksin's government was energetic and bold, but not universally effective. From 2001 to 2005, Thailand's economy did grow faster in most years than that of any other Asian country except China. But Thaksin's critics argued that what the Thai people needed in their first prime minister elected under the "People's Constitution" was a leader committed to deepening democracy, to empowering the people by increasing their capacity to participate in national and community decision making. Otherwise, the cycle of desultory, corrupt politics would never end. Thaksin could often be effective but he made decisions paternalistically. He disempowered the Thai people. His high-handedness and penchant for brutality worsened the southern Muslim insurgency. Critics charged that the long-term effect of such a leadership style would be the undercutting of democratic deepening.[98]

When Thaksin called Human Rights Commissioner Pradit Chareon-thaitawee "sickening" for criticizing his methamphetamine crackdown in March 2003, the former Mahidol University president was already in trouble for having compared Thaksin with Field Marshal Sarit Thanarat, the autocratic leader from 1957 to 1963 who laid the groundwork for the Thanom–Praphat dictatorship, overthrown with such historical significance in October 1973.[99] A TRT legal adviser warned in February 2003 that Pradit's insidious comparison was "biased and against national interests" and aimed cynically at "creating political repercussions."[100] In fact, a number of people interviewed for this study thought the comparison apt, both in terms of the two leaders' particular style and the enthusiastic responses that their straight-talking, tough-guy approaches generated in Thai society.[101] To the extent that Thaksin does resemble Sarit, he may be appealing to deep-seated authoritarian cultural values that must be challenged if the quality of Thai democracy is to improve.

Similar to Sarit—who was a career military officer—Thaksin began his career in an authoritarian institution, the Royal Thai Police Department, in which he served from 1978 to 1984 after completing a master's degree in criminal justice from Eastern Kentucky University and a doctoral degree in criminal justice from Sam Houston State University in Texas. But Thaksin's Sino-Thai Chiang Mai family had been central figures in Thailand's silk business for several generations. Such a background combined with his experiences abroad made Thaksin significantly more urbane and internationally minded than the gruff Sarit, who was gauche around foreigners and unable to speak English. Thaksin, moreover, obviously developed extensive personal business experience after quitting the police force in 1984 to establish his own telecommunications company, Shin Corporation; Sarit, in contrast, never left the Army. Thaksin became fabulously wealthy through rent-taking (selling computers to his erstwhile compatriots in the Police Department); Sarit also became fabulously wealthy, but only through brazen corruption.[102] Thaksin is a dashing figure in Thai high society, but also, apparently, a committed family man. Sarit, in contrast, was said to have had eighty-one mistresses ensconced in various houses and other facilities around Bangkok.[103] As Thak Chaloemtiarana writes, Sarit was "seen as a *nakleng*, a person who was not afraid to take risks, a person who 'lived dangerously,' kind to his friends but cruel to his enemies, a compassionate person, a gambler, a heavy drinker, and a lady-killer: in short, the kind of person who represented one model of Thai masculinity."[104] Thaksin is significantly more cautious about his public image, sober-minded, and even health-conscious than the cruder Sarit. But Thaksin certainly is risk-seeking, compassionate, loyal, and cruel.

Sarit's take on the *tiyong* dilemma was similar to Thaksin's: democracy is at best a tool for development. As shaped by Luang Wichit Wathakan, Sarit's "ideology" (the term is perhaps too charitable) held that the "truly Thai political principles were political stability, proper social behavior (*khwam riaproy*), and strong executive leadership which would 'represent' the popular will and [pursue] national development."[105] This seems clearly to be Thaksin's philosophy, as well. Sarit was the prototypical Thai populist. Immediately following the 1957 coup, he lowered electricity rates, ordered a reduction in prices for iced coffee, sugar, and charcoal, experimented with the provision of free tap water to urban residents, and arranged for medicine and health care to be dispensed free to the poor.[106] Thaksin mandated in 2001 that every individual throughout the Kingdom could receive health services from state-employed physicians for only thirty baht (about US seventy-five cents) per visit; he also ordered the Government Savings Bank, the Government Housing Bank, and other state-owned financial institutions to make billions of dollars in low-interest loans to farmers, small businesspeople, families who wished to buy home computers, and even civil servants who wanted to take vacations.[107]

Both leaders were perceived to be dedicated selflessly to serving the people. Sarit was adored for his frequent forays among the masses to discover their concerns and needs; this reflected the *pattiwat* leader's compassion and concern for "development" (*phattana*)—a byword of the Sarit era. Thaksin, who on November 16, 2003, reiterated his pledge "to eradicate poverty within six years," was also adept at cultivating the image of a compassionate *phokhun* (patriarchal) leader, serving the people while guiding them sternly. Presiding over a November 2003 essay competition for poor students to obtain scholarships, Thaksin produced 150,000 baht (about US $3,850) from his own pocket to augment the winners' prizes. Moved to tears by the occasion, the prime minister declared that "if there are one million who need help out there, we'll help all of them. . . . As for the money, let me do the worrying. It's my responsibility to find the money."[108]

Like Sarit, Thaksin is deeply concerned about social order and not afraid to violate the law to maintain it. Sarit's personal peccadillo was extinguishing arsonists. It all began on November 6, 1958, when an ethnically Chinese merchant in Thonburi hired an unemployed laborer to burn down his shop for the insurance money. Within hours, the amateur arsonist was arrested and the shopkeeper thereupon apprehended. Sarit joined enthusiastically in the interrogation proceedings and concluded that the shopkeeper was guilty. Afterward, he addressed the public:

I will do anything to achieve happiness for the people, regardless of the consequences. The fire which erupted on November 6th of this year has been thoroughly investigated by me and the police. We all agree that there is no doubt that the fire was the result of a selfish individual. Therefore, I now order the execution of this person. . . .

I would like to inform my Thai brothers and sisters that decisiveness . . . is the only instrument which can help the nation achieve progress.[109]

In the years to follow, Sarit cultivated his personal interest in fire investigations. "Night or day, sick or well, Sarit always appeared at fires. Thus his reputation grew with his interest in fires, and the public appeared convinced that Sarit was a great leader."[110] He also cracked down on other kinds of criminals and explained to a group of petty hoodlums released from prison in September 1960 that the crackdowns were necessary because Thailand was like a big family, and he was the patriarch. "I have extended to all my goodwill, but if any person in this household creates trouble for the whole, it is my duty to stop this person. The reason why I had you arrested and incarcerated is to make you good people again."[111] Sarit also had little patience for more prosaic disturbers of public order. In a speech on February 10, 1960, he denounced pedicab drivers for obstructing traffic, constituting eyesores, getting addicted to opium, and generally undermining national development.[112] About the same time, and also in pursuit of *khwam riaproy*, Sarit outlawed the weekly dance at Bangkok's Lumpini Park because he believed it was destroying the morals of the young. Soon afterward, "rock and roll music was banned from government parties and the police were told to be on the lookout for illegal dancing of 'the Twist' in public places."[113]

Thaksin similarly displayed a commitment to public order. His campaign against suspected methamphetamine dealers resulted in more than 50,000 people being arrested between February and May 2003, and 2,245 shot to death in extrajudicial circumstances.[114] Among those caught literally in the crossfire was nine-year-old Chakraphan Srisa-ard, killed by gunshot wounds on February 23, as police fired wildly at the car carrying the boy and his mother. According to Asian Legal Resource Centre researcher Meryam Dabhoiwala, the boy's father—the primary suspect— was already under arrest. An uncle reported that, nevertheless, "the police kept shooting and shooting at the car. They wanted them to die. Even a child was not spared." Three days later, a sixteen-month-old baby was shot to death by dealer-hunting police while cradled in her mother's arms.[115]

The problem was that police faced special incentives to eliminate as many suspected dealers as possible during the three-month crackdown period. Police who succeeded in eliminating dealers and/or seizing methamphetamine tablets would be given bonuses; those who failed would be transferred, demoted, or fired. Under Deputy Prime Minister

Chavalit Yongchaiyudh's leadership, the National Command Centre for Combating Drugs compiled lists of suspected dealers in late 2002. But the lists were hastily prepared and they tempted people with personal grudges to file false reports against their enemies. Once the shooting began, thousands of people whose names were on the lists went to police stations to turn themselves in, but many of them were killed anyway. Respected pathologist Pornthip Rojanasunan of the Forensic Science Institute charged that in more than half the cases she investigated, "drugs appeared to have been planted on the victims after their deaths—jammed in pockets at unnatural angles."[116]

Despite criticism, Thaksin held his ground, calmly explaining that "the government's strategy is to smoke out pushers, who will [then] be eliminated by their own kind." This became the standard Thaksin line: almost all the killings were perpetrated by dealers for the purpose of silencing informers. Only forty-two were killed by "law enforcement" officers.[117] As a former police officer himself, Thaksin had little patience for critics of the campaign. He professed bewilderment at Thai and foreign liberals' apparent sympathy for the suspected dealers: "I don't understand why some people are so concerned about them while neglecting to care for the future of one million children who are being lured into becoming drug users." He mused philosophically that, in any case, "murder is not an unusual fate for wicked people."[118] A few months later, at the scholarship competition for poor children, a teary-eyed Thaksin confessed that he is a man with a bifurcated heart: "One half is for bad guys like drug dealers. With them, it is always an eye for an eye attitude. I have no sympathy for them. Their deaths, even in hundreds, can't make me flinch. The other [half] is for the helpless. I am ready to help them fight their hardships until they can stand on their own feet."[119]

Cracking down roughly on arsonists and "hooligans" earned Sarit the Thai people's support in the early 1960s; Thaksin's assault on suspected methamphetamine dealers consolidated his already high popularity ratings in 2003. Ninety percent of respondents polled in the days immediately following the start of the campaign expressed support,[120] while the prime minister's overall popularity rating remained at 70 percent.[121] People in the Thai middle class had grown enormously concerned in the years following the economic meltdown that the spread of methamphetamine addiction would eventually threaten the fabric of Thai culture and life. There is in Thailand—perhaps more than comparably in other countries— a high degree of self-conscious identification with "Thai culture" and a conviction that the culture is distinctive and precious. Because culture is constituted through interactions among society's individual members, the personality destruction caused by methamphetamine addiction would eventually cause Thai culture to corrode if addiction rates continued to increase.

Buddhism proscribes violence. But many Thai people believe that when core values are under attack, a violent response is justified. One extreme version of this argument was articulated forcefully in 1976 by the rightist monk Phra Kittivuttho. Long an outspoken critic of reformist Buddhism, Kittivuttho contended that the success of communist revolutions in Vietnam, Laos, and Cambodia implied that killing Thailand's own communists—broadly defined, evidently, to include social activists—was justified: "I think we must do this, even though we are Buddhists. Such killing is not the killing of persons (*khon*). Because whoever destroys the nation, religion, and monarchy is not a complete person but *mara* (evil). Our intention must be not to kill people but to kill the Devil. It is the duty of all Thai."[122]

In a subsequent elaboration, Kittivuttho argued that it would be legitimate "to kill some 50,000 people to secure the happiness of 42 million Thai.... The Thai must kill communists. Anyone who wants to gain merit must kill communists."[123] Apparently, Thaksin could count on the same sort of logic resonating in Thai society twenty-seven years later, just as it had apparently worked to Sarit's benefit in the 1950s and 1960s.

NGO activists criticized Thaksin's violence precisely on the grounds that it violated Buddhism. Some believe that, as a result, they succeeded in chipping away at the prime minister's prestige.[124] In the same poll in which 90 percent of respondents said they supported the crackdown, 70 percent acknowledged that they feared that they, too, might get caught in a police crossfire some day; hence, the public was primed to accept criticisms of the campaign.[125] Thaksin had instructed that the names of people killed and the specific circumstances surrounding their deaths be concealed from the public, reducing the opportunities for people to mull over the killings and reflect upon their implications. Apparently he hoped that in this way the controversy would fade and he could go about the tasks of consolidating his power and "growing" the economy in preparation for the 2005 elections—and even subsequent elections, since "as time passed, he talked of three four-year terms, and lately four, to the consternation of his critics and some analysts."[126] Democracy activists were cheered with a ray of hope in December 2003 when King Bhumiphol, in his annual birthday address, instructed that the government should launch investigations into the circumstances surrounding every killing. "If the matter is not clarified, many people will blame the prime minister," the king noted sardonically. "The findings should be made available to the public and to the international community."[127]

Bhumiphol's intervention was a rare victory for Thaksin's critics. They had been on the defensive for over two years, and growing increasingly depressed that the self-proclaimed "CEO-type premier" was wounding Thai democracy and canceling the hard-won democracy gains of the previous decade. In addition to the methamphetamine crackdown, the critics were concerned about Thaksin's attacks on NGOs and the media. When Thaksin declared that he would eliminate poverty within six years, the subtext (sometimes articulated explicitly) was that "afterwards, there won't be any need for NGOs."[128] Already Thaksin was attacking NGOs for accepting money from foreign foundations. His strategy was simple: Since community-based NGOs argue that they represent the people where business-affiliated political parties have failed, cut the connections between NGOs and citizens. Assert repeatedly and with a mocking tone that NGOs serve foreign masters, not Thailand. Even claim that NGOs have an interest in *perpetuating* Thai poverty and displaying it circus-like to the world so that foreign foundations will continue to give them money and therefore jobs. Imply, in effect, that they prostitute themselves to foreigners.[129] Who would then rescue the Thai people from degradation? Thaksin and his patriotic "Thai Rak Thai" ("Thais love Thais") party, dispensing inexpensive health care, low-interest loans, and dazzling public spectacles such as those associated with the October 2003 APEC summit—all of which have the effect of increasing Thai people's dependence on the state and the average indebtedness of Thai households.[130]

Thaksin's government also made life rough and sometimes dangerous for NGOs and human rights activists. In March 2002, the government mobilized the Anti-Money Laundering Office (AMLO) to investigate the assets of some forty NGO activists, partly to uncover putative foreign connections.[131] AMLO's envisaged function had been to investigate the sort of corruption associated with the business people, bureaucrats, and "security" officials at the core of Thaksin's support base.

In April 2002, the Cabinet passed a resolution authorizing the police to crack down "on any gatherings which violate the law, including those which block roadways."[132] Throughout Thailand, such gatherings are a frequent occurrence, as community-based NGOs and villagers protest development projects designed primarily to benefit the urban middle classes and the rich. In December 2002, police rudely repressed one such protest, at Hat Yai, by opponents of the Thai–Malaysian gas pipeline project. Protestors accused the police of using excessive force and produced a videotape to support their charges. Thaksin countered that NGO-led *agents provocateurs* were responsible for the mayhem. "NGO workers who use violence . . . live well but like making trouble," he declared in a radio address on December 21.[133] Although claiming that he believed more than 90 percent of NGO workers were "good," the rest were "bad," and "those people demanding rights but ignoring duties are anarchists."[134]

Not surprisingly, the UN Special Envoy on Human Rights, Hina Jilani, after a ten-day visit to Thailand in May 2003, reported that "I have sensed a level of insecurity among human-rights defenders which ranges from general unease to actual fear."[135] Thaksin responded by saying that Jilani was "biased and not acceptable"; that she should go home and criticize the human rights record of her own country, Pakistan; and that in any case, Thailand "has never begged the UN for food" and therefore did not need to accept its advice.[136] The prime minister had already dismissed UN criticism of the methamphetamine crackdown by noting derisively that the UN "is not my father."[137]

King Bhumiphol, however, could stake a claim to being Thaksin's symbolic "father" within the cultural universe of Thai politics. The monarch's criticisms could not be so cavalierly dismissed. Thaksin must at least give the impression of heeding them since otherwise he would lose public support. Bhumiphol had long been subtly at odds with the prime minister when he issued his criticisms in December 2003, in stark contrast to his much earlier relationship with Sarit. When Sarit seized power in 1957, King Bhumiphol was still in the political wilderness as a lingering legacy of the 1932 revolution. Sarit, not of the revolutionary generation, and generally lacking charisma, calculated that he could increase his legitimacy by restoring the monarch to an exalted, yet still symbolic, role in political life. Bhumiphol then carved out a sphere of political power significantly more substantive than that envisaged by Sarit.[138] Concerned to protect this power, the King did not appreciate Chamlong Srimuang's whiff of potentially antiroyal republicanism in 1992; a decade later, Thaksin's challenge was significantly more threatening because (1) the prime minister was wealthy and well connected globally, (2) his party was unusually well organized and disciplined (partly an intended consequence of the 1997 Constitution), and (3) he was self-absorbed and narcissistic to the point that it seemed unlikely he respected the King in any genuine and fundamental sense. As early his birthday address of December 2001, Bhumiphol had warned that "arrogance" and "intolerance for criticism" could lead Thailand to disaster. Lest anyone in attendance missed the target of his remarks, the King then noted dryly that "I can see the prime minister has a grim look on his face."[139] The audience laughed, but two years later Bhumipol would feel compelled once again to criticize Thaksin for arrogance:

I know the prime minister doesn't like to be criticized, because it always irritates him. But let me tell you this: Even when I was 40 or 50 years old, whenever the Princess Mother complimented me, she followed up with the warning that you must not forget yourself. She always told me not to be aloof.... [If] the prime minister is in charge of everything, he has to be responsible for everything, and that means he has to take criticism.... When newspapers say the government did it the wrong way, or too violently, they must be heeded. Read those newspapers. Let them write. When they criticize, listen to them. Thank them when they said the right thing, or tell them to take it easy when they give wrong criticism.[140]

The King's interventions suggested the possibility that an alliance of the Palace (liberal-royals), dissident intellectuals, NGOs, opposition parties, and what remained of the independent media might be able to check Thaksin and prevent him from destroying democracy. Thai society had changed enormously in the decades since Sarit's dictatorship. The population was significantly wealthier, better educated and informed, and—crucial for the influence of liberal-rational global culture—tightly linked into international networks, with large proportions of the elite and the middle class traveling regularly and sending their sons and daughters abroad for study.

But would the population reject Thaksin's criticism of NGOs as stooges of foreign forces? Would it become alarmed at the prime minister's attacks on critical intellectuals and the media? The shock of the 1997–98 economic meltdown had primed the public to accept limitations on democratic development for the purpose of recovering a reasonable quality of material life, and the hope for even better days. Thus a majority tolerated Thaksin's excesses so long as he continued to work effectively and with energy on the economy and problems of social order. But should the economy falter, or the social order situation worsen—as they began to do in 2005—the prime minister might find himself in trouble with a people who at several times in the past have made heroic sacrifices for democracy.

In January 2006, Thaksin's government began implementing new regulations allowing foreigners to hold up to 49 percent of Thai telecommunications properties. Three days later, regulators approved the sale of the Shinawatra family's giant Shin Corporation to the Singapore government's investment arm for US $1.85 billion. "Some nifty, dubious advice saved the family paying about US $450 million tax."[141] Many members of the general public became furious. Not only did the act seem corrupt, but it also appeared unpatriotic, since telecommunications is a strategic industry. Already a media tycoon had begun leading large demonstrations against Thaksin in October 2005, attracting diverse discontented groups. After the Shin Corp sale, the demonstrations mushroomed in size as NGOs and eventually Chamlong Srimuang himself mobilized their supporters to participate. Under mounting pressure, Thaksin dissolved Parliament on February 24 and called a snap election for April 2. Sensing blood, his opponents vowed to continue demonstrating until the prime minister resigned from politics. The main opposition parties decided to boycott the election. They worried that the TRT's deep pockets and mobilizational strength would ensure Thaksin an election victory, despite widespread popular disenchantment. The activists wanted to force a crisis that, though destabilizing, could lead to a deepening of democratic reform.

Thai elites have long structured their country's political system on the basis of models dominant in world society. Thaksin failed to articulate a systematic ideological objection to liberal-rational global culture.[142] This gives reason to think that as long as democracy remains a compelling model globally, the vibrancy of Thai civil society will ensure that Thailand remains formally democratic (though democratic quality will remain a problem). On the other hand, should alternative authoritarian models become respected in world society, a political entrepreneur of Thaksin's talents might be able to use them to legitimate populist dictatorship. The Chinese Communist Party seeks precisely to establish an alternative "political civilization" that would reject "Western" liberalism. It also seeks to lead Asia. The future of Thai democracy therefore hinges partly on prospects for Chinese democratization—the subject of Chapters 4 and 5.

4

THE CHINESE COMMUNIST PARTY'S PURSUIT OF "MULTIPOLAR MODERNITY"

China shares with Thailand (and Taiwan, as detailed in Chapters 6 and 7) the status of an Asian state under pressure from the liberal-rational global culture's socialization agents to accept democracy as the organizing principle for internal governance. Like Thailand and Taiwan, China underwent a "transitionary moment" in the late 1980s and might have emerged from that crisis democratic. But the Chinese Communist Party (CCP) crushed the Spring 1989 democracy movement and continues to deflect pressure from international NGOs and other socialization agents to accept political liberalization—though it does in the post-Mao period accept many of liberal-rational global culture's other core values and institutions, including bureaucratic management of society and continuous economic growth.[1]

This chapter and Chapter 5 explain the CCP's resistance to democracy as a function of its *aversion to decentering* within global society. Aversion to decentering is not the only reason the CCP refuses to democratize. It also refuses because of fear of the unknown; the love of power and privilege; and—for some cadres—a sincere belief that China is "not yet ready" for democracy because of its (still) relatively low level of economic and social development, and the precariousness of reform's successes. But Thai and Taiwanese leaders had similar sentiments and concerns. What distinguishes China—apart from size and other obvious factors—is *identity*, rooted in a profoundly distinctive historical experience and convincing CCP leaders and supportive intellectuals that they cannot accept socialization to the constitutive norm of democracy if that will mean China's permanent geopolitical and "geo-historical" decentering.

Chapter 1 explained how Eisenstadt and colleagues conceive of global society as consisting not of the inevitably converging units of world-polity theory but instead of "multiple modernities." CCP leaders and establishment intellectuals would approve of the multiple modernities concept to the extent it legitimates China being modern and yet not Western, but they see deeper and more abiding divisions in a world structured ontologically around "poles" of comprehensive national power.[2] They believe that even in the course of worldwide modernization, national poles of power can neither be dissolved nor denatured through absorption of a transnational culture: the basic reason China and other countries will not (and, they believe, *should* not) necessarily democratize in the course of becoming wealthy, strong, and in other ways modern. Chinese elites thus articulate a vision of what might be called "multi*polar* modernity," which differs from "multiple modernity" and the concept of a democratic peace in that the latter require and expect constituent state members eventually to become democratic and integrated into a single world community. Chinese elites link domestic political development to a Realist international power structure and set as an official goal the establishment of a distinctively Chinese "political civilization" enshrining "socialist democracy," meaning a responsive authoritarianism legitimated by nationalism. Because nations are ontologically distinct, a single "road" of political development would be unnatural and immoral.

CCP elites must impose their vision by using propaganda and force because not everyone in China believes that democratization is wrong or that China should pursue an antidemocratic course.[3] Use of phrases such as "China thinks..." and "China articulates..." in this book is only a shorthand way of saying "Chinese leaders and establishment intellectuals think...."[4] Such rhetorical conveniences should not be taken to mean that an essential and undivided China acts and thinks as an unchangeable, antidemocratic monolith. In absolute terms, many people in China champion "Western-style" democracy as universal, and certainly as relevant for contemporary Chinese conditions. But following repeated rounds of repression, Chinese liberals seem to be without significant social influence and unlikely to gain it in the years immediately ahead. Paradoxically, their prospects seem especially poor in the event rapid economic development continues, because economic success emboldens the CCP to resist democratization pressures even more stubbornly and mercilessly to silence critics.

This chapter and Chapter 5 explain the People's Republic of China's (PRC's) dominant official and intellectual positions on democratization within the international context as elites perceive it. The primary source materials used are (1) Chinese-language journals on international relations (IR) and American studies and (2) Foreign Broadcast Information Service (FBIS) translations and reprints of party-state pronunciamentos and Chinese newspaper, magazine, and journal articles. International Relations journals are used because Chinese IR scholars have the primary professional responsibility of assessing and criticizing the interface between the global realm and domestic Chinese society.[5] IR scholars are not alone in having this professional responsibility, but they, more than any other category of intellectual, regularly assess the realm of experience that *would* be "the international dimension of China's democratization," should democratization one day occur. Analyzing samples of the large corpus of work these scholars produce, as well as some of the work produced by their colleagues in American studies, is an effective and efficient means—within the context of events and official statements reported by FBIS—to probe elite-level Chinese receptions of liberal-rational global culture, especially international pressures and inducements to democratize.

Decentering

The assumption behind this method is that the Communist party-state is the primary obstacle to China's democratization, and even to significant political experimentation that could lead in democratization's direction.[6] Democratization rarely occurs unless moderates in an authoritarian regime ally with moderates in civil society.[7] Under General Secretary Hu Jintao, who consolidated his power in 2003–2004, the CCP has relentlessly repressed the shoots of civil society and has silenced moderates in its own ranks. The repression has not been completely successful, and China continues to change significantly in ways outside the party-state's control. But the leadership is evidently committed to preventing Party moderates even from assuming positions of power, let alone negotiating with moderates in a still-inchoate civil society.[8]

Sustained CCP propaganda since 1989 has also cultivated in many Chinese people a suspicion that calls for democratization are part of a foreign plot designed to weaken and divide China and deny the country its rightfully glorious place on the world stage. The discourse in Internet chat rooms—probably China's freest public sphere—conveys an overwhelming hostility to democracy as promoted particularly by the United States, and mocks such terms as "human rights" (*renquan*) as emanations of "American hegemonism" (*Mei ba*).[9]

Yet as explained in Chapter 5, Internet chat rooms have also become forums for the expression of serious political discontent, and frequent contributors to chat room discussions have developed a sense of entitlement to use cyberspace to vent their grievances and freely (if often elliptically) discuss party-state shortcomings. In this respect, cyber-dissidents reflect broader patterns of social and cultural change, since in recent years millions of people—including villagers, sometimes dismissed as politically "backward"—have evinced an important new "rights consciousness" through demonstrations, strikes, lawsuits, and other forms of agitation, suggesting precisely the sort of well-developed sense of political efficacy necessary for successful democratization.[10] Meanwhile, economic growth and structural transformation have produced a new middle class, large in absolute if not relative terms. Many of these people are wealthy enough to travel abroad, and they fill the airports of Singapore, Malaysia, Thailand, and Hong Kong on their tourist junkets. Increasingly, middle-class youngsters join members of higher-status groups in securing opportunities to study in the United States, Canada, Japan, Australia, and Europe. Some members of the new middle class now work with internationally linked Chinese NGOs active in solving environmental and (increasingly) social problems which the state has ignored. These experiences all result in changes to the fabric of culture, changes that promise—or, to conservative elites, threaten—slowly to dissolve China into the emerging new cosmopolitan global order.[11]

This is precisely the condition Chinese elites seek to avoid through strenuous efforts to resist democratization and to construct a new political civilization (alongside material and spiritual civilizations) "with Chinese characteristics." They apparently believe that democratization, with its concomitant relaxation of controls on public discourse, would combine with globalization thoroughly to denature China, down to the level of identity. This perception—accurate or not—convinces them of an imperative need to direct and guide (*yindao*) a society they can no longer tightly control. The elites do not trust the Chinese public to filter Western and especially US culture sensibly in the ongoing process of constructing Chinese culture. They do not trust the peasants in particular to make rational decisions about national economic management, public works investment, educational policy, and even foreign policy—which, ironically, they assert is likely to become even more nationalistic and hostile to foreigners in the event of democratization.

Elites in all postcolonial countries worry about such considerations to a degree. But in China the concern is profound at a level difficult for outsiders to grasp. Chinese elites perceive and portray themselves as custodians of "5,000 years of history" centered on the North China Plain. Their "central plain (*zhongyuan*) consciousness" may be artificial to a degree, and certainly is manipulated for cynical political purposes.[12]

But these facts do not make central plain consciousness any less real or motivating for those Chinese who feel genuine anguish at the prospect of China becoming permanently decentered and swamped by a US-led West which they admire and respect in important ways, but also fear as crafty and explosively dangerous, and disdain as consumeristic, hedonistic, and uncouth.

Chinese elites want wealth and power for China, but what they want to *do* with wealth and power is not transform China into a compliant citizen of some US-centered new world order. They want wealth and power for the purpose of *establishing China as an alternative and not-necessarily-democratic Center*, radiating distinctive values (which they have yet to specify convincingly), and rewriting global history so that China is exalted as playing a decisive role not only in Asian history but also in world history. They do not necessarily envision becoming hostile to the West after recentering, let alone going to war. But they do envision becoming both modern and distinct from the West and absolutely not subservient to it.[13] Certainly the elites want China to become a member in good standing of a future global community in whose construction they will participate, but which the United States will not dominate. They also want China to remain a member of the international regimes that benefit the country, especially those associated with the United Nations, in which China enjoys a special status as a veto-wielding member of the Security Council. But, as explained below, the elites want the global community and international regimes to evolve in such a way that domination by the United States and broader West ends.

Only rarely do Chinese officials and academics explicitly articulate "aversion to decentering" as a chief motivating factor behind their policies and discourse. Fear of decentering is instead *deduced* from the elites' numerous other declarations (discussed in the pages below) on such subjects as sovereignty, geopolitics, multipolarity, hegemonism, human rights, splittism, and an array of related concepts. The reason decentering is not articulated explicitly may be precisely because *it is the single, unconscious, no-need-to-be-spoken unifying theme* linking all of the elites' other concerns together. Aversion to decentering is the transcendent, presuppositional core shared assumption, the kind that usually does not need to be brought to conscious awareness in any society. The only circumstance under which these kinds of assumptions are normally brought to conscious awareness is when they are challenged fundamentally—but arguably central plain consciousness has never been challenged fundamentally in China, at least not during periods when the capital was in the north and the state strong.[14]

Westphalia as Genesis and Revelation

To Chinese IR specialists, the world effectively begins in 1648 at Westphalia, because to them, the Treaty of Westphalia marks the origins of *multipolarity*, or at least humankind's recognition of multipolarity as the natural and normal base-state of international affairs.[15] In all the recent issues of such influential Chinese journals as *Zhanlue yu Guanli* ("Strategy and Management," banned in August 2004), *Xiandai Guoji Guanxi* ("Contemporary International Relations"), and *Guoji Wenti Yanjiu* ("International Studies"), it is extremely difficult to find references to IR before Westphalia. Almost no mention is made of IR in East Asia before Westphalia, possibly because East Asian IR was dominated by the succession of mainland empires which the CCP—and, indeed, Chinese nationalists of all stripes—claim today as "Chinese." As nearly as possible in that early age, before the development of "enabling facilities" such as warships and guided missiles, the "Chinese" (actually, sometimes Turkic, Mongol, or Manchu) state exerted what today would be called hegemony over East and parts of Southeast and Central Asia.[16] Ancient East Asia was normally unipolar. Yet hegemony and unipolarity, to contemporary Chinese IR scholars, are both immoral and impossible. The world is naturally and eternally multipolar, a condition in which sovereign, independent states—poles of power—fight, trade, and manage flows of people in competitive pursuit of "comprehensive national power" (*zonghe guoli*). Sometimes overly aggressive and ambitious states *seek* hegemony and the establishment of a unipolar world order. But after years or even decades of struggle, hegemonists inevitably fail, because their quest violates what effectively amounts to mystical natural laws. Multipolarity is eternal, which is why the world must begin and end at Westphalia.[17]

Chinese scholars acknowledge that the world has witnessed important changes during recent decades, but none of these developments "has changed the fundamental nature (*benzhi*) of international relations or the fact that sovereign countries exist," in the words of Ni Shixiong and Wang Yiwei.[18] The context and phrasing of this assertion make clear that the authors view sovereign countries as the essential, irreducible elements of globe-level human interaction and multipolarity as the natural condition in which they relate to each other. Moreover, "from beginning to end, relations among countries require structuring and direction from these correct principles";[19] nothing can transcend them because they are ontological rules, rooted in the Westphalian Genesis. No amount of globalization, transnational communications development, rise of multinational corporations and international NGOs, or attempts by some countries to seek hegemony can violate the logic of these bedrock principles.[20] It therefore becomes apparent why Chinese IR specialists are reluctant to discuss pre-Westphalian East Asia: The order of affairs that existed at that time was at best impossible and at worst immoral; moreover, the predominantly immoral actor was "China."

For many Chinese writers, the essentially multipolar—and violent—nature of global society is rooted in an elemental geopolitics. States control territories that contain resources, including energy, animals, land, and people. From these territorial bases states must compete to increase comprehensive national strength, which is the ultimate point and purpose of national security policy. "The highest goal of national security is to guard the country's sovereignty, and the highest expression of guarding the country's sovereignty is to guard the country's right to existence and right to development."[21] These rights are under constant threat from other states, which will use almost any means to wage their struggle. Nothing of fundamental significance changes with globalization and technological advance—or, by extension, with the increasingly widespread diffusion of liberal-rational global culture. "International structural change has not changed the contentious essence of geopolitics," writes Zhang Yan. For example, "information is everywhere, but information space in reality becomes a new tool for technologically-powerful countries to control the physical realm. . . . The new geopolitical space encompassed by information space is still the locus of plunder for hegemonists."[22] Even in the "postterritorial era," geopolitics is "a nearly eternal main theme" (*jinsi yongheng de zhuti*) of IR, which powerfully conditions the full panoply of other social relations.[23] Indeed, widespread acceptance of the norm of state territorial integrity only shunts state competition down new avenues. Thus, Wang Zhijun writes that since states can no longer easily get away with attacking each other militarily, they wage economic wars, science and technology wars, and information wars. Even when a country as inherently dangerous as the United States is not menacing China with military deployments, it will certainly be menacing China in other ways. The fact of menacing is a constant, and no evidence of substantially altered behavior (should it arise) could possibly be interpreted as undermining this basic fact.[24]

Wang's argument concerning international norms is revealing because it suggests how Chinese IR scholars (at least in their Chinese-language publications) react to schools of thought in Western IR challenging Realism. Wang is willing to concede that international norms exist, but does not entertain the possibility that the power of norms suggests a different social ecology from the one portrayed by multipolar modernity. This point is important because, as detailed below, the same logic applies when discussing liberal-rational global culture. Almost every significant international phenomenon or new interpretation is recast and distorted to fit into the multipolar/geopolitical/Realist framework. No fundamental challenge is possible, no matter how strong the evidence, because the basic assumptions are inviolable. They even have an air of sacredness about them, which suggests that the Party has sanctified them as "correct," and therefore that it would be dangerous to think (or at least to write) in ways inconsistent with the assumptions. For example, Chinese authors completely reject the discourse of the "democratic peace" (see below). But most of them accept uncritically Samuel Huntington's categories in *The Clash of Civilizations*, if not necessarily his substantive conclusions.[25] Most Chinese writers argue that dialogue among civilizations is more likely than clashes, except for relations between the West and Islam, which they both expect and, it appears, hope will be troubled. But they completely agree that the world can be divided into seven or eight distinctive civilizations. The reason is surely because Huntington's categories are consistent in important respects with the elemental geopolitical and multipolarist assumptions that guide Chinese thinking. In this respect, the validity of a new theory is judged by the degree to which it conforms to preexisting orthodoxy.[26]

Hegemonism and Democracy-Promotion

Few Chinese IR specialists accept that a global culture could exist independent of the states comprising the international system. If there is a dominant culture "out there" globally, then by definition it is a culture that must be servicing a hegemony-seeking state. No state serves or is enacted by a free-floating global culture, as the world-polity theorists contend.[27] State-centered power poles are the pillars of world order; they are the system's primary actors, and they shape culture and manipulate ideational phenomena for the purpose of increasing comprehensive national strength and waging the great geopolitical struggles that are the essence of world politics. The strongest of these actors, the United States, uses its awesome arsenal of ideational and material power to seek hegemony, and *all significant global phenomena—including democratization—must be understood in terms of this basic fact*. Opposition to US hegemony-seeking is the central drama of the present era.[28] The great world "story" to these Chinese intellectuals is not the familiar American or broader Western story of a struggle to end the strife of history by remaking the world democratic. The story is instead the arduous effort to block the illegitimate and dangerous US scheme to defy the laws of multipolarity and dominate the world, a "tradition-transcending attempt by one country to determine universal perspectives (*ding tianxia guannian*)" and establish a "completely new geopolitical model."[29] In pursuit of hegemony, writes Song Yimin, the United States "uses military attacks, political subversion, [and] thought penetration." Its main method is to

use the "provide a model" function (*shifan zuoyong*) to make other countries will-ingly or unavoidably accept American leadership.... It takes maintaining contact and exchanges with all countries as a basic policy, seeking to divide on the basis of opponent, level, and degree, and then cause every country in the world to dis-solve together (*shijie ge guo ronghe*) in a condition with the US as the Center, and with the rules of operation chiefly determined by the US-established international system.[30]

Song's anxiety and displeasure specifically at the possibility of having to accept the United States as the Center are palpable.[31] He continues that the unjust international order the United States seeks to establish "is expressed in the US ranking and treating of other countries unequally.... The US will not tolerate any other power center (*liliang zhongxin*) strengthening to the point that it could raise challenges to the US in important regions."[32] Similarly, Zhang Minqian complains that "what the US wants is not a globalization in which all countries are equal and mutually-respectful; it wants to cause globalization to become global 'Americanization.' With this kind of globalization the US seeks to pursue its traditional goals of realizing 'liberalization' of the global economy and, politically, 'democra-tization.'" Zhang disapprovingly quotes (with uncertain accuracy) Sec-retary of State Madeleine Albright as having gloated in 1997 that "the US is at the central position of the international system." He notes in an accusatory tone that the United States "wants to establish a kind of com-munity of democratic states worldwide both because democratic states are less likely to fight wars and because they are more trustworthy." Though it seems counterintuitive, such a community would be inherently bad, Zhang argues, because it excludes the nondemocratic states and would serve hegemony.[33]

One puzzling question is exactly why the United States would seek hegemony. If multipolarity is virtually a law of nature, then why would any state try to end it, especially given the "fact" (to Chinese specialists) that the state is doomed to failure?[34] What motivates Americans to at-tack other countries and demand China's democratization? Wang Jisi, the dean of China's America specialists, addresses this question in the lead article to the special Autumn 2003 issue of *Meiguo Yanjiu* ("American Studies"), devoted entirely to explicating American hegemonism. "There are two worlds in the eyes of Americans," Wang writes. "There is the 'free world,' as represented by the United States, and the 'evil world,' as represented by America's enemies. The US mission is to safeguard the free world and annihilate the evil powers; gray areas do not exist."[35] This Manichaean orientation and the hegemonism it spawns are "rooted deeply in the soil of [US] domestic politics"—a significant statement, it bears stressing, because the US political system is democratic. (If democracy spawns hegemonism, then how can it be good?) Wang writes that there are three specific ways in which hegemonism grows vibrantly from the soil of American democracy:

1. Democratic decision-making processes legitimate hegemonism. If committed in the name of democracy, hegemonistic acts are justifiable.
2. Congress as a corporate body and individual senators and representatives frequently act independently of the Executive to promote hegemonism. The most important piece of evidence in this regard is the 1979 Taiwan Relations Act.
3. Pluralism is illusory. Despite their surface policy disagreements, US educational institutions, think tanks, philanthropic organizations, NGOs, religious groups, businesses, and the media—all American institutions, in fact—share the strategic goal of establishing hegemony.[36]

There are at least two points to Wang's assertions worth underscoring. First, the illusory nature of American pluralism rules out *a priori* not only the possibility that dissenting Americans could use democratic political institutions to alter US foreign policy and end the quest for hegemony; it rules out even the possibility that dissenting Americans could exist.[37] Using "crucial case" logic, Wang even finds Noam Chomsky, the radical linguist, to be a hegemonist.[38] He notes that Chomsky did strongly chastise America's own "terroristic behavior" after the September 11, 2001, World Trade Center attacks, yet still criticized Osama bin Laden for cruelly tormenting and injuring poor and oppressed peoples. Wang finds it ironic and revealing that Chomsky could write that "terrorists do not care about the people." Wang takes this to mean that Chomsky is unable fundamentally to criticize the United States; that, in other words, he ultimately represents US hegemonism, like every other American.[39] It is ultimately impossible for Chomsky to speak as an objective individual, or as a citizen of world society, because no one can be denationalized. The world is divided ontologically into poles, and every individual, group, or corporate body must represent and speak on behalf of some pole, or sovereign state. By extension, there is no possibility of a genuinely autonomous global civil society developing outside of state control and putting pressure on all oppressive states to end human rights violations and other abuses.[40] An international community of freethinking and critical intellectuals and activists (including NGOs) is impossible given the logic of state-based multipolarism. Transnational NGO activists working in Thailand would by extension represent US hegemony, even though they are—at least to the untutored—highly critical of American foreign policy. All such activists, and the oppositional global culture they propagate, must be resisted if China is to escape victimization by hegemonists.[41]

The second important point of Wang's argument to underscore is the apparent cultural motivations behind America's quest for world domination. His tone suggests that he believes a disembodied, hermeneutical force informs the identity and interests of the US state, in a way not dissimilar to the world-polity theorists' conception of a disembodied global culture constituting all state identities and interests.[42] In this case, however, the culture is internal, and the result is normatively unacceptable— because American culture makes the American state hegemonistic. This is why Congress cannot help itself but to enact laws that service hegemony. Individual senators and representatives compete with each other to grandstand on hegemony's behalf. People from all walks of life, representing the full range of material interests, share the hegemonistic impulse. American culture is inherently hegemonistic, and the culture shapes the state. Washington's world strategy, therefore, will not change unless (1) American culture changes or (2) outside forces stymie it through resistance. For China to accept democratization in such a situation would be disastrous because it would only reward hegemonism, strengthening American self-confidence.[43]

What specific aspects of American culture make it hegemonistic? Wang himself does not address the question—at least, not in this publication— but Lu Qichang, Zhang Yanyu, and Wang Wenfeng do, in an article in *Xiandai Guoji Guanxi*. Lu, Zhang, and Wang argue that an "Anglo-Saxon sense of superiority" convinces Americans that they have a mission from God to transform the world in America's image. "Missionary zeal" is of course a standard stereotype, but is not usually tied to the ethnic category "Anglo-Saxon." It is unclear if Lu and colleagues wish seriously to argue that genes determine culture, because they also contend that "no matter what their political persuasion or policy preference, all Americans share this sense of superiority and sense of mission; and it is deeply rooted and unshakeable."[44] Since most Americans are without Anglo-Saxon genes, Lu and colleagues presumably intend the term to denote a cultural orientation rather than an ethnic category. But even so, the problem of explaining hegemonism remains unresolved, and the new question becomes, what determines the Anglo-Saxon cultural sense of superiority?

Writing in the more popular *Liaowang* ("Outlook") magazine, one "Shan Min" (probably a pseudonym) strives to get to the bottom of this question by attacking American culture in particularly colorful terms as *abnormal*, and therefore incapable of serving as a healthy global model:

The United States is a playground for adventurers. The "spirit of America" advocated and upheld by the US ideological system is formed through a combination of the belief that "the American way of life is best" and esteem for power and the spirit of adventure. Hence, engaging in unscrupulous adventures in order to preserve its own way of life has become a basic article of faith in American society. Although this spirit has promoted economic development, it has also deposited historical and cultural filth.

In American society, therefore, it has become quite rational for an individual or organization to fabricate lies and slanders and indulge in sophistry. The series of waves of public opinion that had to be whipped up by lies—such as McCarthyism, the causes of the wars of aggression against Korea and Vietnam, the collective slaughter in Kosovo ... [are all] related to the US hegemonistic culture.[45]

Many Chinese writers contend that US promotion of democracy abroad reflects this barbaric culture. Lu and colleagues identify democracy-promotion specifically as a key component of the 1998 Pentagon geopolitical strategy report that vowed the United States would never allow any other country or group of countries to emerge as a challenger in the Asia-Pacific.[46] "Exporting democracy" (*shuchu minzhu*) is a specific subcomponent of hegemonism which numerous IR specialists (and countless propagandists) link to US efforts to "Westernize and split" China and transform the world into a society of American clones. Exporting democracy is justified in terms of democratic peace theory, which is similar in key respects to world-polity theory. Shi Aiguo of Nankai University (in 2002) dismisses democratic peace theory as yet another tool of US hegemonism. Shi criticizes the theory for establishing as an "ulterior structure" a fundamental divide between East and West, civilized and uncivilized:

In the eyes of some of those Westerners promoting "democratic peace theory," "Orientals" [*dongfangren*] are born with a proclivity for authoritarian governance and dictatorship.... Oriental authoritarian governance and "fondness for war" [*hao zhan*] are used to set off the West's "democratic peace".... When we get past the surface of "democratic peace theory," we can smell the thick odor of Western white racism.... It is a contemporary extension of the age-old Western discourse on the oriental "threat."[47]

Democratic peace theory probably does establish a divide between civilized and uncivilized, but whether it establishes a similar divide between East and West is highly debatable. The only way Shi can make such a claim is if he is willing to argue that such democratic Asian countries as

Mongolia, Japan, South Korea, Taiwan, the Philippines, Thailand, and India have become essentially "occidental" and "white." Perhaps he intends to claim that Asian democracies have surrendered in the struggle with the West and are now "passing" in an unseemly way within world society. He does not spell out the logic in sufficient detail to answer definitively. Yet he clearly believes that authoritarian China represents a purer Asia, because his argument rests on the notion that when Americans criticize China for being undemocratic, they are actually criticizing the entire (genuine) "Orient." Moreover, it bears stressing that US criticism is completely cynical, driven solely by geopolitical interests. Thus, Shi continues by arguing that democratic peace theory is "almost the same" as the China (replacing "Oriental") threat theory. In particular, those who promote the notion that rising China is a threat are sometimes influenced by democratic peace theory; therefore, Shi contends, they must be the same.[48] Should China accept democratization, it would be surrendering to these enemies.

Sometimes Chinese propagandists (though not usually IR specialists) assert that Chinese society already *is* democratic, with the implication being that US democracy-promotion can *only* be designed with hegemonistic purposes in mind. Thus, Zheng Hangsheng argued in *Renmin Ribao* ("People's Daily," the Communist Party's flagship newspaper) that there are many different forms of democracy in the world, reflecting different instantiations of the general principle. On this basis, China can claim to be democratic; after all, diversity is "normal," reflecting the logic of multipolar modernity. "What is abnormal," Zheng writes, "is that the United States treats its particular kind of parliamentary [sic] democracy as the only popular kind, and makes wild boasts about it, ... falsely accusing our socialist democratic system of being a 'totalitarian system.' " US cultural and political hegemonism "completely negates the particularity of democracy" and in doing so "steps into the old shoes of the Eurocentrism of the 19th century and follows the evil path of taking the United States as the core" of world order.[49] Evidently, this path is "evil" because with the United States at the core, China is decentered: an inherently immoral situation.

Zheng continues that when American officials and human rights activists assert their particular kind of democracy as the global norm, they actually have no greater purpose in mind than to achieve world domination. He then derives three essential features of Western democracy-promotion:

1. It is arrogant. "These self-styled 'teachers'—Western countries headed by the United States, who do not consider themselves ordinary beings— have all along regarded the special criteria of their own countries or

their own regions as international criteria, and accuse their 'students' of not blindly following their example."

2. It is hypocritical. Democracy and human rights "are clearly means in the hands of the US government to secure selfish interests, but they pretend they are defending democracy and human rights in other people's interests."

3. It is politicized. Democracy and human rights are rhetorical "weapons to wage ideological war against socialist and developing countries and weapons to achieve Westernization, division, and peaceful evolution."[50]

Zheng argues that China's resistance to US democracy-promotion is a matter of global importance because it defends the essentially "normal" multipolar system of world politics. Chinese "socialist democracy" is the "force at the core of resistance to US-centrism" worldwide, Zheng writes. Chinese views on democracy "occupy an important position in Asian views on democracy," with other Asian countries "taking an identical stand in opposing US-centered democracy." Such an argument suggests a desire not only to defend China from Western cultural and political domination, but also to promote China as an alternative global Center— in this case, leading Asian countries (and perhaps others) in a righteous resistance to American hegemony.

Many Chinese commentators portray Americans as hypocritical for demanding that China democratize even while the United States is beset with so many social problems. Its hypocritical stance makes the powerful United States a unique menace to Chinese civilization, which must be soothed, jousted with, and used, but never allowed to transform the Chinese nation at the level of identity. In this context, Jiang Zhaoyong and Li Xiaoguang argue in a discussion of "the cultural roots of the Sino-US conflict" that the only reason American politicians sometimes criticize China's human rights record is because they "fear that if China establishes a friendly, responsible, and progressive international image, it will directly threaten the world supremacy of the United States."[51] The notion that US politicians or human rights groups would criticize China on the basis of sincerity defies credibility. "The current American culture has nearly abandoned all morality and sacred things," Jiang and Li write. The only sincere Americans are those who, like an unnamed former ambassador, freely admit that "no government in human history has done so much for so many in so short a time as the Chinese government." Less effusive Americans are playing a cynical game of power politics when they call for democracy in China, indulging a lust for hegemony. In their amorality, these Americans "believe that might is the grounds for settling everything, with profit being the point of procedure for dealing with everything."[52]

Using a substantially less enflamed tone, historian Wang Xiaode of Nankai University contended in the Autumn 2003 *American Studies* that American culture includes the following essential elements: a belief in the benefits of having a market economy, celebration of individual freedoms, emphasis on the importance of citizens' rights, and a stress on the supremacy of democratic politics. These were the positive values. Negative values included a tolerance for profound social inequalities, corrosive commercialization of social life, exaltation of surface phenomena or "images" (*xingxiang de youshi*), and worship of consumption. "Even more serious," Wang writes, is the problematic American esteem for individualism, hedonism, and self-perfection (*ziwo wanshan*).[53] This list is important because it suggests what some Chinese intellectuals worry China might become if it succumbs to global decentering and gets swamped by liberal-rational global culture—which can only be a smoke screen for American culture if no culture exists independent of states.[54] Note, too, that the "opposite" of each of the negative American values Wang identifies is a positive value in Confucianism and/or Maoist Communism. Presumably this is the core value system that Wang and other intellectuals (as well as CCP leaders) want to preserve, and they worry that accepting democratization would imply accepting the entire American cultural package, destroying the Chinese essence (*ti*).

The Kosovo Crisis

All of these concerns came together in the outrage that gripped China during the Spring 1999 Kosovo crisis and accidental US bombing of the Chinese embassy in Belgrade, events which the CCP used to denigrate democratization and human rights. After reform and opening began in 1978, the CCP at first avoided expressions of open hostility toward the United States for promoting peaceful evolution, but changed tack after the Spring 1989 nationwide democracy movement (centered in Tiananmen Square) and subsequent collapse of East European, Soviet, and Mongolian communism. Many in the Chinese elite argued that Washington incited Chinese students, most notably by broadcasting pro-democracy propaganda on the Voice of America. Certainly the United States played a catalytic role in the disintegration of the Soviet empire, Chinese elites believed. As a result, following the June 4th Beijing massacre, Sino-US relations became extremely sour and generally remained troubled throughout the 1990s. Relations improved briefly during 1997–98, when President Jiang Zemin and President Bill Clinton exchanged official visits.[55] One key reason for the improvement was that China's rapid economic growth and transformation into the developing world's largest recipient of foreign direct investment convinced Clinton Administration officials that they had no choice but to work with Beijing, however odious its system. In some Chinese circles this gradual American turnabout in the face of increasing Chinese wealth and power spawned confidence in the Chinese system. Thus, *Renmin Ribao* published an article in July 1997 declaring that "the self-examination by Western ideological circles of their own civilization seems to have undergone a pilgrimage from ecstatic arrogance to doubt, anxiety, and pessimism. We must say that this is a wiser orientation of study than their past cultural arrogance."[56]

Not long after Clinton's summer 1998 visit, the relationship began deteriorating again. In August 1998, Beijing outlawed the nascent China Democracy Party (CDP) and arrested a number of its members.[57] The United States protested but decided not to let the matter become an obstacle to improved relations. This decision was in line with the Clinton Administration's commitment (after 1994) to "constructive engagement" with a China unavoidably becoming a significant player in the world economy. Pressure from the American business community to turn a blind eye to Chinese repression was enormous, and the administration's national security strategists saw a need for Beijing's support at the United Nations to manage problems in North Korea, Iraq, and other danger zones.

It was Clinton's decision in the spring of 1999 to bypass the UN Security Council and work instead with NATO in using military force to prevent butchery in Kosovo that set the stage for a crisis in Sino-US relations—a crisis linked inextricably to democratization, human rights, and China's general reception of global constitutive norms. Without Security Council authorization, NATO launched a seventy-eight-day bombing campaign in Yugoslavia on March 24, 1999, alarming and infuriating a Chinese elite who supported the Milosevic regime and probably had been smuggling arms to it.[58] Coincidentally, April 1999 also marked NATO's fiftieth anniversary, and the member states (increasing in number as former Warsaw Pact members joined) used the occasion of a politician-packed celebration in Washington to articulate a "New Strategic Concept" that would commit NATO to intervene in certain conflicts outside of the NATO region without authorization from the United Nations. By coincidence, just a few days later the Japanese Diet passed legislation to implement new US–Japan Defense Cooperation Guidelines, which increased Japan's military responsibilities and commitments and suggested vaguely that Tokyo might become involved in a future Taiwan conflict. The conjunction of these events turned Chinese commentary sharply harsher toward the United States than at any time since Deng Xiaoping's 1992 "trip to the south." A *Renmin Ribao* article proclaimed that Kosovo showed "the United States, as the sole superpower, urgently wants to dominate the world":

Since they have thrown away the classic principles of international law, the US and its allies have put forward a new principle for dealing with international relations, so-called "protecting human rights" and "preventing a humanitarian catastrophe." This war is being fought in order to realize the new principle. The principle has three key links tied together: First, a country's human rights situation should be an issue of concern to the international community; second, the US and its allies are the judges weighing up a country's human rights situation; and third, without going through the UN, the US and its allies can resort to all means, including launching a war, to "put right" the human rights situation of certain countries.[59]

Chinese commentators argued that the US action in Kosovo was driven by geostrategic ambitions, despite the fact that human rights NGOs took the lead in prodding an initially unwilling Clinton Administration to act.[60] Yao Youzhi, a "researcher and strategist" (in 1999) at the People's Liberation Army's (PLA's) Academy of Military Sciences, used a geopolitical framework in explaining to *Ta Kung Pao* that the new US strategy should be termed "one center and two basic points":

One center: This refers to using US soil as a base to vie for the position of unipolar global hegemon. Two basic points: The first one is to gain control in the direction of Europe off the Atlantic Ocean, and the second one is to gain control in the direction of Asia off the Pacific Ocean. The US intention is to start by controlling areas bordering these two directions and then proceed to completely take over the "global island" of the Eurasian Continent.[61]

Because Russia and China were the two biggest obstacles in this scenario, Washington would surely "aim the spearhead" at these two countries next. This was precisely why developing a "Sino-Russian Strategic Partnership" became a dominant theme in Chinese diplomacy during subsequent years.[62] In fact, the new US–Japan Defense Cooperation Guidelines suggested that the situation was becoming urgent because the United States had already set its plan to gain control of Eurasia in motion. The hysteria of the times prompted *Ta Kung Pao* political columnist Shih Chun-yu to ask worriedly on May 1st: "Isn't it clear where the pincer-like offensive is directed?"[63]

Paranoia and extraordinary leaps of logic generally characterized Chinese commentary during the Kosovo crisis. One writer argued in *Liaowang* that "NATO's war against Yugoslavia is a long premeditated plot" aimed at eliminating a last bastion of European communism and advancing the alliance eastward. The war had nothing to do with human rights or promoting democracy:

They stirred up ethnic contradictions within Kosovo and supported ethnic separatists, thereby causing the contradictions to evolve into a crisis. Then, under the guise of "stopping humanitarian disaster," NATO began the savage bombing against [Yugoslavia] and further created hatred between the Serbs and the Albanians in an attempt to profit from it. . . . This has not only fully exposed the state of mind of an aggressor in playing power politics but has also shown that the aggressor has reached the stage of behaving unscrupulously in trying to achieve its goals.[64]

Another writer suggested that the United States instigated ethnic conflicts for the joint purpose of (1) establishing a rationale for conquering Yugoslavia and stationing troops there permanently, and (2) setting up an alternative international mechanism to legitimate military intervention outside of UN Security Council auspices. Given China's steadying presence, this writer argued, the Security Council's preference is usually to resolve conflicts by peaceful means. In contrast, "NATO's new strategy is to conquer others by force" because the United States "is trying to make NATO its tool for world domination."[65] Other analysts contended that all of the discussion about developing norms for humanitarian intervention was simply a ruse designed to divert attention from the naked pursuit of illegitimate geopolitical interests.[66]

Yet typically, almost all Chinese writers agreed that the United States would ultimately be defeated in its evil quest, because of ontological multipolarity's inescapable logic combined with China's resolute determination grounded in absolute moral rightness. Upon being asked by his interviewer "what kind of shadow the US strategy for the 21st century will cast on mankind," the PLA's Yao Youzhi responded that although the US intention is to dominate NATO and prevent Europe from evolving into a distinctive power pole, "hegemonism will definitely end up as absolute decline and fall" as the United States falters and fails. Moreover, hegemonism's doom spells the *success* of modernity, and the attainment of the fruits (other than democracy) promised by liberal-rational global culture:

"People are hoping that economic globalization, the information society, political multipolarization, and rapid strides in new and high-tech development in the 21st century will bring peace, development, civilization, and stability to mankind. . . . The 21st century will not sink into confusion and the chaos of war if only all countries and peoples of the world boldly say "no" to the United States."[67]

Saying "no" would of course mean more than refusing to accept expanding US military influence. People of the world must also say "no" to

US demands for democratization, human rights, and self-determination for minority ethnic groups. All of these demands are, in any case, simply ruses designed to induce the countries that resist to self-destruct internally: "sugar-coated bullets" that, if swallowed, will explode inside and destroy the world's heroic champions of multipolar modernity without even the need for direct military confrontation. Washington's assertions that its military interventions are "humanitarian" are no more than obfuscations designed to divert attention from America's ultimate hegemonistic designs. There is no reasonable way to argue that the United States attacked Serbia to improve the human rights situation in Kosovo; how could the human rights situation be improved when bombing "caused the innocent deaths and injuries of thousands of common people as well as the displacement of hundreds of thousands of refugees"?[68] Simple logic puts the lie to US human rights propaganda. The people of the world must not be fooled.

If Chinese analysts already considered their country to be one of the prime targets of the "pincers movement" uniting NATO in the West and the US–Japan Security Alliance in the East—in addition to being the target of American democratization diplomacy—a US–NATO bombing of China's Belgrade Embassy on May 7, 1999, drove the point home and convinced Chinese that their country was vulnerable and despised. "The news has shocked the whole nation. The Chinese government and people are furiously indignant and strongly protest and condemn the barbaric crime of attacking our embassy and killing our compatriots."[69] Four times in this authoritative article, the *Renmin Ribao* commentator used the term "barbaric" (*yeman*) to describe the bombing: It was a "barbaric crime," a "barbaric violation of China's sovereignty," a "cold-blooded barbaric act that makes people boil with anger," and "an extremely barbaric and aggressive act." The term *yeman* has a special meaning in this context, denoting "beyond the pale" of civilized society: savage and unreasonable. The term matches "hegemonistic" (*badao*) in connoting unbridled and wildly militaristic bullying, and suggests that the international community should join China in denouncing NATO's act as a violation of the regulatory norms of global society and a reflection of the dangers of hegemonism. As *Ta Kung Pao* editorialized:

The so-called "human rights are superior to sovereignty" theory actually wants other countries to copy the Western human rights outlook and model. If any country refuses to comply, it is subject to punishment and suppression. Those who submit will prosper; those who resist shall perish. This is the logic of "might is right." If we refuse to criticize and effectively contain the theory, the existing international security order will be totally undermined. . . . If NATO is allowed to go unchecked, the world will be thrown into confusion and human rights will meet unheard-of devastation.[70]

President of the All-China Lawyers Association Gao Zongze warned that the bombing and NATO intervention generally threatened to undermine the entire modern global project. "If we let such behavior go unchecked, the whole international community will have no law to abide by; peace, progress, and development will be empty statements; the most basic norms governing and handling ties among countries will no longer exist; and the whole world will become a society where the weak are prey of the strong."[71] Even more alarmed (and alarmist) was Professor Liu Wenzong of the Foreign Affairs College. "These activities are clearly barbaric fascist savage acts," Liu fumed.

They have been crimes in a war of aggression that plainly and massively violates the law governing humanitarianism. They have been very similar to what the Axis powers did during World War II. Lies will never conceal the truth. Any wild ambition or dream of wishfully becoming the sole hegemonic power in the world or establishing a world order in which a small number of developed countries rules the broad masses of developing countries is doomed to failure.[72]

China's ambassador to the UN Human Rights Commission in Geneva, Qiao Zonghuai, charged that NATO had "launched gratuitous attacks at the Chinese diplomatic mission and savagely slaughtered Chinese citizens," under the false pretense of protecting human rights.[73] President of the Chinese Society for Human Rights Studies Zhu Muzhi was moved to call upon human rights activists worldwide to mobilize and "lay bare the hypocrisy of the US and denounce its aggression and destruction of human rights."[74]

To some extent, such commentary reflected sincere outrage at the bombing and an inability to accept the West's protestations of humanitarian motives. In fact, the Chinese general public—especially students and intellectuals—did not need to rely on government propaganda to direct their attention toward the bombing. Many people became transfixed and angered by it from the start. Within hours, news of the bombing spread China-wide and sparked protests in all cities with American consulates (and many others). Tens of thousands of angry demonstrators surrounded and stoned the US Embassy in Beijing. Ambassador James Sasser phoned CBS's "Face the Nation" program to warn that "we are hostages here in this embassy" as rocks and Molotov cocktails rained down into the embassy compound from outside. The US consulate in Chengdu was "burned and gutted," Sasser reported, and he protested that the Communist Party was organizing students and busing them to demonstration sites.[75] Meanwhile, state-controlled media initially refused to convey President Clinton's immediate apology (his first of seven) and the US explanation that the bombing was an accident.

Vice President Hu Jintao appeared on national television the night of Sunday, May 9th, to endorse the demonstrations explicitly: "China firmly supports and protects in accordance with the law all legal protest activities against the US-led NATO attack."[76] Hu's declaration prompted then senior RAND analyst Jonathan Pollack to argue in the *Los Angeles Times* that "the Chinese leadership believes it can harness public anger for political advantage," but that such manipulation was irresponsible and disturbing.[77] Chinese leaders had been worried that the tenth anniversary of the June 4th, 1989 Beijing massacre might lead to demonstrations of a different kind. Let the students demonstrate against the Americans, the CCP seems to have decided. Their sentiments concurred with official anger, and in any case efforts to repress the demonstrators might explode in Beijing's face. Support supernationalism to protect the CCP from democracy.

One group that would not be allowed to demonstrate under any circumstances was the banned CDP. It would obviously be highly damaging to the CCP's grand domestic strategy if democrats succeeded in allying with nationalists. Such a development would undermine the establishment elites' own strategy of associating democratization with American hegemonism and China's degradation. As a result, as soon as the demonstrations erupted, Chinese police detained several CDP members and warned others to stay off the streets. The Hong Kong-based Information Center on Human Rights and the Democracy Movement in China told reporters that authorities were worried the CDP might hijack the demonstrations on June 4th and direct them against the government. But this was never likely to happen, a Center spokesperson argued, because "anti-American sentiment throughout China is growing and is expected to weaken the troubled democracy movement" even further.[78] The movement had already been decimated by arrests and propaganda. Meanwhile, the CCP targeted exiled democracy activists overseas with a venomous attack when some of them publicly expressed a willingness to accept President Clinton's apologies and Washington's claim that the bombing was accidental. *Renmin Ribao* accused "the self-branded 'leaders' and 'elite' of the so-called 'patriotic pro-democracy movement' " of treasonous bootlicking:

"You take the side of the hegemonists, brazenly defend them, defile your motherland and its people, and crow over encroachment on the sovereignty of your motherland and the murder of your compatriots. Do you still have any conscience or affection towards the land where you were raised?"[79]

The editorial continued that the overseas democracy activists' recent "ugly performances" only confirmed the correctness of the 1989

Tiananmen repression. "If the attempts of those people had materialized ten years ago, China would have been 'Westernized' and 'disintegrated,' sold out by those so-called 'elite,' and turned into a dependency of the hegemonists." The point was that accepting democracy could only mean China's humiliating subjugation within a world order that privileges Western culture and traditions and decenters China and every other non-Western nation.

Some writers concluded that the embassy bombing was positive to the extent it made the scales fall from people's eyes. "People now see the hideous face of the hegemonist under its flashy overcoat and hear the rumbling of bombing by missiles behind the sweet-sounding slogans. . . . When the US and Western countries shout aloud about 'press freedom,' good and honest people must raise vigilance."[80] The bombing "made the good and honest Chinese intellectuals and students cast away their illusions. We [now] also have to say: 'Farewell, American-style human rights, humanitarianism, freedom, and democracy!' "[81]

Sovereignty, Human Rights, and Nationalism

Human rights is a concept fundamental to liberal-rational global culture and also to the rhetoric of US foreign policy. This intersection provides the CCP with an easily legitimated rationale for rejecting international criticism of China's human rights record. In conjunction with Kosovo, CCP intellectual and political elites began a new line of attack on the global human rights discourse by contending that although Westerners argue human rights should take precedence over sovereignty, secure sovereignty is the precondition for all human rights guarantees.[82] In the absence of state sovereignty, world order would crumble, and human rights would be impossible to guarantee. This is because, to Chinese elites, the notion that organizations other than the state might fill the world's basic institutional spaces is anathema. The poles of multipolar modernity are always sovereign states, rooted in national communities. All people belong to nations; national identities and interests supersede all others. Therefore, only the sovereign state can protect, develop, and elevate people and guarantee their human rights. Those who argue that human rights take precedence over sovereignty are propagating "absurd and strange theories" (*miulun he guailun*) that must be rejected and refuted.[83]

Yet it is important to stress that Chinese thinkers do *not* reject the concept of human rights out of hand. At least rhetorically, most accept the notion that people everywhere are endowed with certain inalienable rights. Li Zhimin, of the China Science and Technology University (in 2001), writes: "As everyone knows, sovereignty is the basic guarantee of human rights, and human rights are the end goal of sovereignty."[84] This is an important statement in at least two respects. First is the standard point that the necessary (but not sufficient) precondition for developing countries to guarantee human rights is that other countries respect their sovereignty. Second—and more intriguing—is that the formulation seems to accept liberal-rational global culture's norm that pursuing human rights and related *desiderata* is the primary *function* of states, the basic reason they exist. By implication, even the Chinese state must be informed by liberal-rational global culture and seek the goal of human rights protection if it is to count as legitimate. The Chinese state does not exist as a timeless, fundamental entity, a pre-Enlightenment power center in a multipolar ecology that structures culture but is not structured by it. The Chinese state only exists legitimately *because* it pursues human rights, "the end goal of sovereignty." It is bound by liberal-rational global culture, and must accept socialization. The principle that sovereignty takes precedence over human rights applies only if the sovereign state is actively seeking to enhance the human rights of the people living under its jurisdiction. The sovereign state thus emerges as an "agent" implementing human rights on behalf of the hermeneutical "principal" that is liberal-rational global culture. In this respect, Li sounds very similar to the world-polity theorists.

Upon closer inspection, however, Li supports subservience to a transcendent Chinese state. In discussing what fate might befall a state that refuses to implement human rights, Li notes only that the state would face problems in global society because Western countries would criticize it. In Alastair Iain Johnston's terms, this approach suggests a purely "adaptational" response to global society's demands rather than the "learning" that would result from genuine internalization of global cultural values.[85] Moreover, Li apparently reserves the right for the transcendent state to *define* the content of human rights. He lists as key rights the right to existence, right to development, right to expression (*biaodaquan*), and right to participate.[86] But since he does not explain the content of these rights in detail, it is easy to imagine the CCP arguing that all four are already adequately protected in China. Such an approach is suggested by the argument of Xiao Gongqin, the noted neoconservative, in an important article in *Strategy and Management*. Xiao contends, in the course of an otherwise subtle and intelligent discussion of the Kosovo crisis, that "the Chinese people" are more concerned about "collective rights" than they are about "individual rights." Therefore, "the Chinese people" reject US intervention on behalf of human rights when such intervention threatens the strength and dignity of the Chinese nation.[87] Similarly, Xinhua declared in April 2001 that "the right of independence, the right of survival, and the right of development are the human rights of primary importance."[88] Yet the Chinese people are never actually asked their preferences; unaccountable elites employed by the transcendent state speak for them.

Accumulating efforts to "adapt" to global society's demands for human rights protection do hold the potential to evolve into genuine learning—a phenomenon which Risse and Sikkink find to be common globally in socialization to human rights norms.[89] In 1993, the CCP founded the China Human Rights Research Association (CHRRA) as an apparently adaptational organization; taking this cue, provincial and municipal party organizations subsequently established "little brother" human rights associations at educational institutions throughout the country. The CHRRA soon began publishing a yearbook chronicling "the glorious experience and great achievements of the Chinese people in struggling for, safeguarding, and developing human rights." In early 2002, it launched *Human Rights Bimonthly*, a multiple-language magazine endorsed by senior archconservative Li Peng. The CHRRA also set up a Web site in early 2002 with both English and Chinese versions. The State Council began issuing white papers on China's human rights situation in November 1991; and it has issued them annually since 1995.[90]

These efforts suggest that the CCP believes it has no choice but to enter into at least an ersatz dialogue with the West on human rights, which is significant: It cannot simply ignore liberal-rational global culture.[91] Even more potentially significant is the fact that Beijing signed the UN International Covenant on Economic, Social, and Cultural Rights in October 1997 and the UN International Covenant on Political and Civil Rights in October 1998; it ratified the Economic, Social, and Cultural Rights covenant in March 2001.[92] More dramatically still, the Second Session of the 10th National People's Congress (NPC) adopted an amendment to the PRC Constitution in March 2004 which declares starkly that "the State respects and safeguards human rights." CHRRA Vice President and Secretary-General Dong Yunhu proclaimed the amendment to be "a major event in the development of China's democratic constitutionalism and political civilization as well as an important milestone in the development of human rights in China."[93]

Risse and Sikkink argue that authoritarian states can get trapped in their own rhetoric regarding human rights and find themselves on slippery slopes. They present the process as unfolding with the kind of linear logic that suggests (without explicitly predicting) inevitable progress on "the road" to a democratic future.[94] Increasing rights consciousness and certain other developments discussed with "political civilization" in Chapter 5 make clear that important changes are certainly taking place in China, and there is a degree of truth to the popular (among CCP supporters) slogan that "the Chinese human rights situation has never been better." On balance, however, it is important to underscore the fact that the Chinese party-state continues to demonstrate extraordinary adeptness at refusing to get trapped in human rights rhetoric and to avoid the jump from adaptation to uncontrolled learning and unwanted deep socialization. Chinese political and intellectual elites are highly conscious of the need to learn from the West and absorb liberal-rational global culture selectively so that they can avoid what they regard as falling into the hegemonists' trap of deep socialization and "peaceful evolution," which could spell permanent decentering. They continue to stress the primacy of the CCP-defined and -dominated collectivity over the individual, and regard their most important goal as being to amass comprehensive national power for the purpose of defending against hegemonism and consolidating multipolar modernity. As the CHRRA's Dong Yunhu declared in November 2002, "human beings are the most important productive forces. The protection and development of human rights will help to promote the development of productive forces."[95] To this extent, human rights can be regarded as a national priority.

On the other hand, an important corollary of the proviso that rights can be supported as long as they contribute to national strength is that Chinese citizens agitating for improved human rights run the risk of being accused of consorting with hegemonists to "weaken and divide" the nation: one of many epithets heaped upon the Tiananmen demonstrators (and many other dissidents).[96] Suspicion of foreigners runs deep in Chinese political culture, and the CCP took advantage of this fact beginning in the early 1990s to cultivate a prickly new nationalism among younger Chinese.[97] This new nationalism explicitly stresses the primacy of the collectivity over the individual, along with the concomitant notions that "Western" human rights concepts are inapplicable to China and that those who call for their adoption are scheming to halt China's rise. As the CCP Central Committee's "Program for Education in Patriotism" noted in September 1994, "patriotism, in essence, is identical to socialism.... Ideological education in patriotism, collectivism, and socialism constitutes a trinity and is organically integrated in the great practice of building socialism with Chinese characteristics."[98] In the words of a *Renmin Ribao* editorialist writing in June 2000: "The interests of the motherland are overwhelming above anything else. One will devote everything unconditionally without reservation if it is needed by the motherland.... By insisting on making an individual's interest subordinate to collective and state interests, one may fundamentally prevent one's individual interests from being harmed in the long run."[99]

No alternative definition of the Chinese nation—which might emphasize pluralism, the inalienable rights of the individual, or the virtues of multiparty politics—would be acceptable. In Thailand and Taiwan, democracy has become virtually inscribed into the national identity (however imperfectly it may be practiced). Such a transformation in China's national identity and related articulation with liberal-rational global culture is flatly ruled out by the Communist authorities, who proudly proclaim themselves to be "the firmest and most thorough patriots," in fact the "model of patriotism for the Chinese nation."[100] That is, again, why the CCP rounded up and hounded CDP members during the May 1999 Belgrade bombing demonstrations, and why Hu Jintao declared that same month that the May Fourth Movement of 1919 "gave birth to the great spirits of patriotism, democracy, science, and progress, and all the heritage boils down to the Great Patriotism."[101]

Sometimes the CCP justifies crackdowns on dissidents not only by questioning their patriotism, but also by claiming that the government *must* crack down on dissidents to uphold the values of liberal-rational global culture. One example is the Party's repeated justifications for destroying the quasi-Buddhist Falungong network, which came to national and international attention in April 1999 when thousands of its (perhaps millions of) members demonstrated in Beijing against local official harassment. The CCP responded to this plea for tolerance and respect for religious freedom by outlawing the Falungong in July 1999 and declaring it to be an "evil cult." Mass arrests and persecution followed, and the Falungong—whose leader, Li Hongzhi, had already migrated to the United States—claimed that hundreds of its members were killed. The CCP regularly pilloried the organization by accusing it of being "anti-science, anti-mankind, anti-society, and anti-government."[102] Repeatedly, the Party stressed the antiscience aspect of Falungong doctrine, accusing Li Hongzhi of "fabricating preposterous, bizarre, and astounding crooked theories and heretical doctrines . . . in order to create a panic mentality and terrible atmosphere."[103]

This strategy appeared designed to justify the crackdown among Chinese intellectuals and government officials and Western critics—who normally constitute the CCP's most attentive publics—by arguing, in effect, that the Falungong is on the "wrong side of history" and that only the CCP is working hard to bring Enlightenment culture to China. In fact, the Party probably worried less about the superstitious aspects of Falungong doctrine than the network's formidable mobilizational power and its attractiveness to Chinese citizens across regions and socioeconomic strata. With its mystical cult of the nation and chiliastic predictions of China's inevitable global success, the CCP is not averse to appealing to superstitious tendencies in Chinese culture. Edward Friedman has argued that the CCP is jealous of the Falungong because they are, in fact, ideological "soul brothers."[104] Disparaging the Falungong as antiscience and antimankind while branding it a cult rather than a religion helps to legitimate CCP repression among those who are less sympathetic when the Party cracks down on liberal intellectuals.[105]

Suppressing Splittism: Democracy Versus Empire

In 2001, the Singapore-based Chinese scholar Zheng Yongnian wrote an article for *Strategy and Management* stressing the primacy of "state building" (*guojia jianshe*) over democratization. In the course of making this Huntingtonian argument, Zheng lamented recent changes in Indonesian politics, contending that democratization had begun a process of Indonesia's "national disintegration." East Timor had already secured independence and "quite a few other provinces" were demanding it, Zheng asserted gloomily. He also reminded his readers about the collapse of the Soviet Union and asked: "Can we [in China] at a minimum avoid a multi-national country's disintegration while achieving comparatively ideal democratic state construction?" Zheng proceeded to answer the question in the negative by explaining how the CCP must first state-build before indulging in any discussion of democratization. He concluded by arguing that "democratization can easily lead to a multi-national country's disintegration." Zheng was both making what he considered to be a rational argument and subtly appealing to his intellectual readers' pride in empire, signaling that those who call for democratization in fact call for China's unraveling.[106]

Some 64.2 percent of PRC territory consists of officially designated minority "autonomous" regions. About 162 million varied and diverse peoples live in these territories, ranging from the Islamic Uighurs and Kazakhs of Xinjiang to the Buddhist Tibetans of the Tibetan Autonomous Region (TAR) and nearby provinces in the southwest. There are also Buddhist Mongols in Inner Mongolia and numerous other groups in south and southwest China. Many of the regions outside of Xinjiang and Tibet have become Sinified following decades of assimilationist education policies, transmigration, and intermarriage. Within a few years, even Xinjiang and Tibet—extensively colonized by Han settlers since 1949—may be in danger of losing their cultural distinctiveness.[107] For this reason, Uighurs and others in Xinjiang, and Tibetans in the TAR, have waged a low-grade resistance struggle against the Han Chinese for many years, and Beijing's response has been uncompromising repression coupled with incentives to collaborate. Tibetans have, in recent decades, generally eschewed violence in their struggle, but some Uighurs did opt for violence beginning in about 1990. The East Turkistan Independence Movement (ETIM), which the US State Department listed as a terrorist organization in August 2002, may well have been one such group using violence.

The CCP's efforts to cling to empire in Xinjiang and Tibet are integrally related to its commitment to resist democratization—most obviously because if Uighurs, Kazakhs, and Tibetans were allowed to vote on the matter (prior to successful Sinification), they might reject continued Chinese rule. International security is also an important part of this mix, because Tibet and Xinjiang border strategically vital regions populated by resource-rich and sometimes hostile countries and groups. Attempts to pressure Beijing into relaxing its grip on Tibet, in particular, have long met with an outraged response from Chinese leaders and establishment intellectuals, who assert that there is no possibility the United States is genuinely concerned about Tibetans' human rights. By virtue of its status as a hegemonist, the United States can only be committed to weakening China. Thus, Zhang Wenmu of the Institute of Contemporary International Relations wrote in 1999 (at the height of the Kosovo crisis) that "Tibet is the front line for China to enter Central Asia, the Middle East, and Indian Ocean, so Western powers are trying to prevent China from expanding."[108] Zhang worried about a Western alliance with India to separate Tibet from China—a dangerous situation geopolitically because then adversaries would control the headwaters of the Yellow and Yangzi rivers. Similarly, Wang Yizhou of the World Political Economy Research Institute argued that the primary lesson of Kosovo was that the CCP should become even tougher on ethnic minorities. "If we can learn anything from Russia, it is the simple lesson that we cannot be soft-hearted to or tolerant towards any separatist groups, including those in Tibet, Taiwan, and Xinjiang."[109]

In a way analogous to its justification for uprooting the Falungong, the CCP proclaims that it *champions* improved human rights conditions in Xinjiang and Tibet. Indeed, China has taken up the burden of implementing the modern global project in these allegedly backward places. "The old Tibet was a society practicing a feudal serfdom system combining political and religious power, which was darker than the European Middle Ages," the CHRRA declared in 1999. "Serfs were forced to flee from famines and become beggars, and countless numbers died of starvation and disease." But fortunately for the Tibetans, all of that changed when Chinese troops quelled the historic Tibetan uprising of Spring 1959, during which the Dalai Lama fled to India. Afterward, Tibet finally began to make progress—in areas ranging from public sanitation to industrialization to compulsory education. As the CHRRA report concluded:

The tremendous historical changes in Tibet since the launching of Democratic Reform in 1959 indicate that the abolition of the feudal serfdom system and the implementation of regional autonomy for ethnic minorities are the basic reasons for the social development and earth-shaking improvement in human rights there.... Human rights conditions will be constantly perfected along with social and economic development as long as Tibet adheres to the road of socialism with Chinese characteristics.[110]

The CCP apparently believes that it has awakened the Tibetan people and brought them enlightenment and development. On this basis it claims to act, in effect, as an agent for liberal-rational global culture in implementing modernity in Tibet, which would otherwise collapse into medieval barbarism.

The Tibetan economy has indeed grown by about 12 percent annually since the 1980s but many Tibetans are less than appreciative of the CCP's efforts. The exiled Dalai Lama dismisses the notion that he would reinstate feudalism in a genuinely autonomous new Tibet, which would of course mean that Chinese rule is no longer necessary to keep the Tibetans moving forward on the path of modernization. Beijing rejects the Dalai Lama's entreaties: "Narrow nationalists never see their own shortcomings and never think of other nationalities, thus inciting mistrust and strengthening splittist ideas," the official *Tibet Daily* pronounced in 1996. "The Dalai clique has sought to distort history and disrupt unity by spreading reactionary propaganda."[111]

Buddhism forbids the telling of lies and points out that all mortal beings should regard honesty and sincerity as basic virtues; they should not engage in "wild talk and lies." However, the Dalai Lama—who poses as the "religious leader" of Tibetan Buddhism—has taken no heed of these interdictions or the minimum morals that a human being should have; he has made malicious and entirely groundless accusations against the policy of the Chinese Government towards Tibet, and wantonly spread such rumors as "the human rights situation in Tibet is deteriorating," "the Tibetan culture has become extinct," or "there is no religious freedom in Tibet"—thus turning himself into a master of wild lies.[112]

The Dalai Lama's most frequent and outrageous crime is to appear in the centers of world society and argue publicly that Chinese rule violates Tibetans' human rights and their right to self-determination. Given his facility with English, his courteous manners, and his gentle personality, the Dalai Lama has attracted a worldwide network of supporters—a network sufficiently influential that he is routinely invited to meet with Western and other governmental leaders (including the US president) and speak before the European Parliament.[113] Because the Dalai Lama is also a Nobel Peace Prize laureate (1989), Western dignitaries would in any case find it difficult to turn down his requests for visits. Nevertheless, the CCP concludes that the Dalai Lama's presence at major global events is evidence of a Western plot to destroy China by "splitting Tibet from the motherland."[114]

Tibetans tend to resist PRC rule sullenly and silently;[115] in Xinjiang, the situation is far more violent.[116] Deputies to the Sixth Xinjiang Uighur Autonomous Region Party Congress reported in October 2001 that "the last five years were ones in which the destructive acts committed by ethnic separatists were the most rampant since the founding of the PRC."[117] Random bombing incidents and assassinations of low-level functionaries were becoming more frequent, and increasingly the separatists were "joining forces in launching attacks, replacing scattered operations with regional operations—and even with transregional, transnational, multilevel, and joint operations." This was the August 2001 assessment of Pan Zhisheng, Director of the Central Asia Research Institute at the Xinjiang Academy of Social Sciences. Pan argued that the primary reason the situation had deteriorated so rapidly was because Xinjiang separatists had joined forces with Osama bin Laden's network in Afghanistan. Yet Pan also insisted paradoxically that another reason for the upsurge in violence was that "hostile forces in the Western countries" were conspiring with East Turkistan independence groups based overseas.[118] Partly for this reason, the solution to the Xinjiang imbroglio was not democratization, which would undermine China's drive to become a powerful and distinctive pole in IR. The solution was instead to intensify the brutal crackdown already underway, which Pan justified bluntly as "conforming with China's ultimate national interests."[119] UN Human Rights Commissioner Mary Robinson warned Chinese leaders in November 2001 not to use the US-led "war on terror" as an excuse for repressing domestic dissent.[120] But especially after the State Department listed ETIM as a terrorist group in August 2002, the CCP had reason to hope that Washington, at least, would be less likely to lecture it about human rights violations in Xinjiang and Tibet. The CCP could start portraying its struggle to maintain imperial control as a part of the war on terror.

Conclusion

The shock of the 1989 political crisis and alarm generated by the Soviet Union's collapse convinced Chinese leaders and many establishment intellectuals that American hegemony and the democracy it championed posed serious threats to China's national identity. Foreign academic predictions that the "third wave of democratization" might soon sweep the PRC only intensified their concerns. Partly in response, political and intellectual elites developed a new view of IR in which China stood for the forces of resistance to US world domination. They began portraying democratization as a tool by which the United States would weaken and decenter China. Some of their concern was sincere, while some was simply an effort to legitimate the crushing of domestic dissent so that authoritarian power could be stabilized. In either case, too many people embraced the new view, and too many people developed complex elaborations of it, for the concerns to be dismissed as simply cynical propaganda. Most of China's leaders and many of its establishment intellectuals seemed convinced that democratization would weaken China and turn it into a cultural appendage of the United States. To resist one was to resist the other; and indeed, to resist hegemony's imposition *required* resisting democratization.

But will such concerns continue to be effective in stifling demands for political liberalization? There seems little doubt that the economic development and social changes resulting from reform and opening have produced sufficient material conditions for Chinese democracy. Greater wealth, private property, household agriculture, the rise of a middle class, access to wider sources of information, openness to the outside world, and impatience with corruption and other social ills will surely motivate Chinese people to press for democratization in the future.[121] International human rights NGOs, journalists, and some foreign governments will also apply pressure from the outside.

Since most cases of successful democratization require an alliance of moderates in government with moderates in an opposition, CCP leaders would have first to allow moderates in the Party to emerge and let them enunciate a position on democracy and IR that does not equate liberal-rational global culture to American hegemony. They would also have to allow an opposition of some organizational capacity to form within civil society and permit it to cultivate and propagate "new thinking" on Chinese politics and the PRC's global role. To date, however—as explained in Chapter 5—positive developments in these directions have all been stymied by a party-state which, under Hu Jintao, insists upon an undemocratic "political civilization" as China's future, resisting hegemony to uphold the righteous iron law of multipolar modernity. Economic development and social-structural change are obviously insufficient to bring about China's democratization. National identity as currently constructed precludes it.

CHINESE CROSS-CURRENTS COUNTERED BY "POLITICAL CIVILIZATION"

Important nuances to the works of Chinese international relations (IR) specialists (and even some statements of PRC leaders) suggest the possibility that aversion to decentering could fade in China as globalization deepens. Afterward, new formulas could be found for reconciling national identity with democratization. Thai intellectuals were able to finesse the obstacles Siamese Buddhism posed to democracy, and as explained in Chapter 6, Taiwanese intellectuals eventually found formulas for remaking their island society's collective identity. Similar intellectual developments in China could accompany the massive structural changes the country has experienced in recent years, which have increased the functional appropriateness of democratic politics. The rise of a market economy, huge volumes of foreign direct investment and trade, travel and study abroad, and diffusion of the Internet have all transformed the terrain in which the Chinese Communist Party (CCP) and establishment intellectuals strive to maintain and legitimate authoritarian rule.

This chapter first reviews some of the important intellectual cross-currents at play, evaluating the likelihood they can break the bedrock aversion to decentering. Intellectual developments do provide a small cultural opening for democratization activists to use in pursuing political change, but—as explained in the second half of the chapter—the party-state is fully aware of the "danger" and has responded with a number of measures designed to seal the crack: ranging from technical and legal constraints on Internet use to the elaboration of "political civilization with Chinese characteristics" as an answer to democracy. The Party also continues to view democratization as likely to dissolve China in a West-centered cosmopolitan global order, "overwriting" Chinese national identity. In this context, it asserts the *increasing* relevance, rightness, and (therefore) inevitability of multipolarization and "inter*national* democratization."

Intellectual Cross-Currents

Not all of the articles appearing in Chinese IR journals in recent years express a high degree of aversion to decentering, or a high degree of hostility toward democracy. Some, in fact, break new intellectual ground in ways that suggest serious brain power is being applied in some quarters to rethinking China's world position creatively. In 2000 and 2001, *Strategy and Management* published a small series of articles designed to rebut the well-known extremist Wang Xiaodong's popular nationalism.[1] The editors apparently believed that centrist-conservatives should ally with liberals to counter Wang's discourse, which had helped structure the mentalities of those taking part in the anti-American demonstrations of May 1999. Wang, whose popularity in print and on the Internet makes him in some ways analogous to an American radio talk-show host (only even more influential), borrows ideas haphazardly from any number of different sources, especially nineteenth century Social Darwinism, and then lashes them together unsystematically. He hates the West for despising China and declares that American democracy is rooted in the control of a dominant race over slaves. He criticizes Chinese intellectuals as a class for being too "close to America" (*qin Mei*) and mocks liberals who call for democratization as obsequiously worshipping the West.[2] Such a discourse is clearly on the nativist end of the "Chinese political spectrum,"[3] and countering it requires (or so *Strategy and Management* editors seemed to believe) an alliance between eclectic modernizers and those leaning toward the "total Westernization" end of the spectrum.

The most liberal article was written by He Jiadong, a former newspaper editor and head (as of 2000) of the Beijing Social and Economic Research Institute.[4] He argues that world history since the French Revolution—the era of liberal-rational global culture—proves that if a society puts Wang Xiaodong-style nationalism at the center of its discourse, democracy will be cast aside and the society will become authoritarian. In worst-case scenarios, authoritarianism will lead to war—and He points to Japan (a focus of official CCP hatred) and Germany as the two clearest examples. He's piece more broadly discusses the cardinal importance to China of cultivating public morality (*gongde*), citizens' rights and responsibilities, a spirit of universal goodwill (*boai*), and the internationalization of thought, which in this context means the acceptance of liberal-rational global culture. He criticizes Wang's idea of global reordering and China's concomitant recentering as an impossible goal for the PRC to realize unless it can first develop "soft" or ideational power, which He defines as having an ideology with globe-wide appeal. He argues that far from increasing soft power, Wang's insistence on the need for China to expand its "living space" to solve social and economic problems is so offensive that it would, if pursued, actually *reduce* China's soft power. He also argues that Wang's generally racist and Social Darwinistic worldview would make achieving any renaissance of Chinese culture impossible. He contends finally that the democracy and liberalism which the West promotes may be flawed but can still be used to develop the better side of humanity, whereas the nationalistic authoritarianism Wang champions cultivates the worst side of humanity.

Somewhat similarly, Chen Dabai—a well-educated person who worked (as of 2000) in the field of international commerce—argued in the *Strategy and Management* series that there are two traditions in Chinese nationalism, one associated with the late-Qing reformer and intellectual giant Liang Qichao, and the other with the vainglorious and obtuse Chiang Kai-shek. Chen contends that Liang Qichao's nationalism was supportive of democracy because it linked national freedom in international society (a concern for all Chinese) with individual freedom and human rights. Chiang Kai-shek's nationalism, in contrast, suppressed individual freedom and as a direct result weakened China and embroiled it in dangerous international disputes. Wang Xiaodong clearly represents the Chiang Kai-shek school of Chinese nationalism, Chen asserts, and he castigates this nationalism as being like an addictive drug: Chinese with a Boxer or nativist mentality will only want more and more of it until the result is warfare with foreign countries, warfare which will be entirely China's fault.

On the question of multipolarity, Chen writes in a way perhaps reflecting his interests in global commerce that US hegemony is significantly more benign and constructive than many other possible types of hegemony, and that China can derive great benefits from free-riding on it. Wang had argued that all forms of hegemony limit the autonomy of nation-states and constrain their development, but Chen counters that American hegemony can be *enabling* for China, making possible the attainment of a level and kind of development that would otherwise be out of reach. Chen also notes that whereas hegemons certainly do derive unequal benefits from their dominant positions, they also have to pay unequal costs.[5]

At the same time as the liberals were voicing their concerns, noted neoconservative Xiao Gongqin, a historian at Shanghai Normal University, also criticized Wang Xiaodong-type nationalists. Xiao in fact mocked nationalists and nativists generally for proposing "stupid, backward, and blind" policies in a misguided attempt to counter "peaceful evolution."[6]

Since Xiao was already on record as having argued the superiority of collective rights to individual rights,[7] and was generally known to be unsympathetic to democratization, He and Chen might have directed some of their firepower at him and the mainstream Party line for which he stood. This was in fact a central bias in *Strategy and Management*'s series. It gave an outlet to liberals to vent their anger at Wang Xiaodong but in some ways diverted attention from the most serious obstacle to democratization in China: the party-state, and the establishment intellectuals who support it. To be sure, the liberals understood that Wang and his nationalism—however offensive—are not the primary danger. He Jiadong in particular used the opportunity afforded by *Strategy and Management* to suggest obliquely that the CCP, which winks at Wang's excesses, is the main force blocking China's democratization. At several points in his article, He hinted that the popularity of Wang-style nationalism would only encourage the current government more fully to manifest its worst tendencies.[8] But in joining forces with a neoconservative like Xiao Gongqin, He may have inadvertently helped legitimate the party-state and establishment intellectual mainstream.

Another scholar who submitted a cross-current critique is Wang Sirui of (in 2001) the Beijing Contemporary Chinese Language Research Institute, an organization which—despite its name—focuses a great deal of attention on political and social matters. Wang Sirui took issue with those Chinese who argue the PRC should avoid democratization because democratization caused the collapse of Russian comprehensive national power. This popular conservative argument reflects Chinese aversion to decentering because any recentering would be impossible in the event China's comprehensive national power collapsed.

Wang Sirui wants China actively to pursue democratization precisely because he believes that without it, political corruption will lead to collapse. He develops his argument by critically discussing four popular propositions on the relationship between economic development and democratization. First, he dismisses the belief held by some—including many of the CCP's Western apologists—that economic growth will eventually lead automatically to democratization. Wang contends that democratic change will have to be pursued self-consciously and against entrenched resistance.

Second, he dismisses the argument that as long as China democratizes, its strong economic growth will be certain to continue. Here, Wang is signaling that he is no blind believer in democratization as a cure-all for the problems of developing countries. This helps establish his *bona fides* as an objective analyst.

Third, Wang accepts as accurate the notion that economic collapse or crisis can lead to massive political change. But this is a warning for the Party, because he next asserts, in his fourth major point, that an intensification and deepening of political corruption will eventually cause economic growth to slow or stop.

In sum, Wang argues that the Party must pursue political reform (which he defines straightforwardly as democratization) to end political corruption, and through that avenue maintain economic growth—which, in turn, is essential for the Party to survive and for political change to be kept moderate and orderly.[9] The only alternative is a series of developments likely to make it impossible for China to achieve a sustained increase in comprehensive national power. Those Chinese who smirk at Russia's difficulties had better take note of China's actually parlous situation, Wang contends, because "anyone who seriously studies the matter will realize that mocking and laughing at others' strenuous efforts and mindlessly acting smug and self-satisfied is extremely idiotic."[10]

The works of He Jiadong, Chen Dabai, and Wang Sirui are quite atypical for Chinese IR journals, or for that matter any Chinese journals.[11] (He's articles obviously became even less typical after the CCP banned their publication in July 2000.) Much more common (though not as common as frank propaganda) are promising articles that start off sounding like they will differ from the mainstream discourse in a significant way but then soon degenerate into something closer to the Party-sanctioned orthodoxy. Such is the case with Yu Xilai's unusual and stimulating "International Justice and International Democracy," which appeared in *Strategy and Management* in 2003.[12] Yu begins by arguing that instead of trying to replace hegemonism with multipolarism, China should adopt a strategy of working *with* the United States to construct a system of just and fair "global governance" (*quanqiu zhili*), essential to ameliorating the difficulties produced by globalization. Yu makes several important points in the course of this article, which hint at precisely the sort of intellectual breakthrough that would allow Chinese elites to legitimate democratization and finesse decentering.

First, he states that the pursuit of international justice must be made subservient to the larger pursuit of general justice (*yiban zhengyi*), which he identifies with institutional arrangements that stress "the value of people." Such a concept is consistent with both the humanism of liberal-rational global culture and the humanism of Confucianism, but *not* with the CCP obsession to amass comprehensive national power to achieve global recentering. The CCP evidently views human beings as disposable resources. Yu is surely criticizing it implicitly, just as he is when he writes that the traditionally recognized cardinal components of international justice—national self-determination, sovereign equality, and noninterference in foreign countries' domestic affairs—are for good reason under challenge. Yet Yu pulls back from the brink of a split with CCP-sanctioned orthodoxy by concluding this section with an argument that the goals of international justice should be summarized as the pursuit of peace and development (*heping yu fazhan*, a Deng Xiaoping slogan), inter*national* freedom (*guoji ziyou*), and inter*national* democracy (*guoji minzhu*).

Apparently, then, Yu regards states as still the rightfully central actors in international affairs. Yet in his second important point he argues that international justice requires a new "global" (*quanqiu*) rather than "international" democracy and an order in which individual "world citizens" (*shijie gongmin*) rather than national governments would constitute the basic units. This is obviously a striking departure from multipolar modernity and is a vision similar in important respects (at least on the surface) to that of the world-polity theorists.[13] Yu continues in this vein by praising Kant and asserting the validity of democratic peace theory. He writes that to achieve international peace, at the very least all the world's major countries (if not the smaller ones) will have to become liberal democracies. Yu's fourth major point is to argue against Beijing's discourse on hegemonism that prior to the Iraq War, the United States had been earnestly, if sometimes misguidedly, pursuing international justice and frequently standing up for China (such as with the "Open Door" policy after 1898 and during World War II). Even the folly of the Iraq War is not a sufficient reason to denounce the United States angrily, Yu contends. It would be enough to chastise the United States for going astray despite having good intentions. Ultimately China must work with the United States to establish a new regime of international justice because it will not be able to amass the comprehensive national power necessary to replace it.[14]

Yu would appear to be edging close to the position that he wants China to seek recentering *through* democratization, by sharing centrality with the West, Japan, and other democratic countries. This would be an extremely important intellectual breakthrough. But subsequently, Yu makes statements that suggest he is actually committed to adaptation rather than to learning.[15] Most generally, he never faces squarely the full ramifications of the fact that China is nowhere near democratic and yet is becoming substantially more powerful. Given Yu's assumptions, how can international justice be achieved if one of the world's major state actors is authoritarian? In one sense, Yu might be leaving the question hanging to nudge his readers in coming to their own conclusion that international justice cannot be achieved as long as China remains authoritarian. But other factors suggest that he simply has not thought the matter through, or perhaps even thinks that China is on the right track and will automatically become democratic as it develops economically.[16]

Second, Yu interrupts his narrative at one point to make a moderately impassioned plea for the sanctity of national sovereignty, when he criticizes the NATO action in Kosovo.[17] This is clearly inconsistent with his earlier assertions that concepts such as sovereignty are being challenged for good reason, and at the very least demands a critical discussion in an article concerned with the problem of international justice. Yu either honestly shares some of the orthodox CCP view of the sovereignty question or added this section to please the Party.

Third, Yu caters to CCP and mainstream academic views when he asserts that the world can be divided into "mature" (*chengshou*) and "childish" (*youzhi*) countries, and that the mature countries (which obviously includes 5,000-year-old China) must discipline and tutor the childish ones. Any complete international democracy in which all sovereign states enjoy equal rights would become "as raucous as children in a kindergarten voting for group chiefs and lunch menus."[18] Such a discourse seems clearly related to the evident Chinese belief that Tibetans, Uighurs, Mongols, and other non-Han ethnic groups under PRC control are like children who must be led into development by the wise and experienced Chinese.[19] This is a well-documented elite Chinese cultural arrogance with deep roots in history;[20] Yu simply transposes it to the contemporary global scene, under the assumption that China can join the West in claiming a right to be one of the primary Subjects moving world history forward, while childish peoples (including, presumably, the Taiwanese) are denied Subjecthood. Yu also writes that the world can further be divided into responsible and rogue countries, with China once again among the responsible ones. International democracy would come to have the flavor of "criminals electing the police" if rogue countries' participation is not restricted and carefully guided by the responsible countries.[21]

What Yu has in mind is something similar to the nineteenth century Concert of Europe, in which conservative great powers keep the peace and prevent uppity new nationalities from staking a claim to statehood. Yu argues that the state-based (and China-privileging) United Nations should take the lead in establishing international justice. The United Nations is a good organization for the task, Yu contends, because its foundational principles make it less likely that the new international order to emerge would violate the cardinal principle that "international interventions and sanctions must be restricted to publicly-recognized 'international public realms' (*guoji gonggong lingyu*)" and that "there cannot be willful intervention or interference with the freedom of sovereign states in 'international private realms' (*guoji siyu*)."²² This would of course give the Chinese state freedom to pursue any policies it deems desirable within its sovereign territory, despite the implications for democracy and human rights. Yu had earlier asserted "the value of people" as central to the larger justice that the world's states should pursue, but here he fails to address the question of what should be done when one of the major states begins violating this key principle domestically.

Yu also contends that the United Nations should be made "more democratic" by weighting votes in the General Assembly on the basis of member states' population and financial contributions. He argues that such a reform would help bring about "the transformation of the General Assembly from an international discussion forum to a [serious] organization with budgetary and law-making functions." He declares that "since China is the world's most populous country, and its contributions to the UN will inevitably increase as its comprehensive national power increases, China should actively promote and support the UN General Assembly's transformation and reform."²³ A world order more centered on an authoritarian China would thus be legitimate.

The Internet

Even radically creative new intellectual formulas can do little to change national identity if an authoritarian state blocks their propagation. The CCP banned *Strategy and Management* in August 2004, but *Strategy and Management* was in any case read mostly by elites.²⁴ The Internet, in contrast, holds the potential to reach a massive audience (about 110 million at the end of 2005), and the CCP is in no position to ban it. Indeed, Party leaders view Internet development as central to increasing Chinese material power.

The problem is that the Party also controls the Internet far too tightly to allow it to evolve into a reliable platform for circulating new ideas that might reshape national identity. Most Internet users are intellectuals, government officials, and business executives and their children, people who by and large benefit from authoritarian rule. Excluded are laid-off state-owned enterprise (SOE) employees, migrant workers, and most peasants—precisely the people who do not benefit as much from the system (or who suffer from it) and who therefore might be expected to use the Internet to agitate for change. Of course, even elite intellectuals who benefit from the system can become critical, and China has produced a fair number of "cyber dissidents" in recent years, courageous people who challenge CCP propaganda with penetrating posts on discussion boards. The most notably effective or outspoken of these dissidents are, however, very soon subject to harassment or arrest, which serves to reduce the autonomy and effectiveness of the Internet as an electronic public sphere. Other cyber dissidents who manage to post their comments anonymously despite the intrusive tracing techniques employed by the party-state's rumored 30,000 Internet police usually find their posts censored or deleted; thus, Reporters Without Borders calculated that some 70 percent of all "controversial" messages on the main Chinese discussion boards are censored.[25]

The CCP tries to prevent public opinion expressed through the Internet from becoming anything more than inchoate or carefully shaped and steered (as with nationalism).[26] It completely blocks public opinion from informing *organized* opposition—or even, if the Falungong is an accurate indicator, simply networked dissent.[27] Yet organized oppositional public opinion is necessary, in the strong sense of the term, for democratization—or at least for democratization with reasonable prospects of becoming consolidated. Until the Internet radically escapes CCP control, it cannot serve as a strong enough social force to bring democracy to China.

The cardinal question then becomes: Why does the CCP insist on controlling the Internet? Why does it expend enormous governmental resources on hiring tens of thousands of bureaucrats to monitor Internet exchanges and message boards, and on installing advanced eavesdropping and control technologies purchased from such Western telecommunications giants as Cisco? The answer, it would appear, is more than simply that the Party wishes to prevent individual Chinese citizens from exchanging ideas autonomously. Although that is certainly a key factor, a deeper concern is to prevent Chinese citizens from exchanging ideas autonomously with *foreigners*, as well as with overseas Chinese and "compatriots in Hong Kong, Macao, and Taiwan."

Recall the point made in Chapter 4 about culture being associated with countries, not free-floating. The culture floating through the Internet is no exception. Within the ecology of multipolar modernity, all culture must serve the interest of some state; and any *global* culture "out there" must logically be serving the interest of a state driving for hegemony. One pair of authors even goes so far as to *define* cultural identification (*wenhua rentong*) as "a relationship between individuals and national cultures."[28] This formulation assumes a priori that the only cultural units of significance are nation-states; moreover, nation-states are effectively essential and eternal, because these authors explain how national cultures construct individuals but have nothing to say about how individuals construct national cultures. As *Renmin Ribao* editorialized on National Day, 1996:

Without a powerful national soul that collectively embodies the national spirit, a country cannot possibly stand tall independently among the nations of the world, perform exploits that shine eternally, or contribute even more to mankind's progress. Embodying the national interests and representing the national will, this national soul complies with the historical trends [e.g., multipolarization], and its powerful appeal and shaking power can give fuller scope to the nation's potential, rally the strength of the nation most effectively, and turn it into an invincible force that can accomplish great, earthshaking undertakings.[29]

Theorists of global civil society sometimes write about how the information revolution is challenging the states-system. But to Chinese writers, the information revolution is only challenging some *states*. The states-system itself is primary and reflects the world's distribution of cultures. Noting that "information is the carrier (*zaiti*) of spiritual and cultural products," Chen Xiaowei and Yin Fang of the Military Science Academy (as of 2000) argue that "for this reason, the US spares no effort in developing the 'information superhighway' and 'digital globe'; in promoting science and technology and social progress, it enthusiastically pursues 'cultural hegemonism'.... Its goal is to carry out peaceful evolution in non-Western countries, for the purpose of constructing a single, united Western world."[30] This formulation is significant because the victims of peaceful evolution are asserted to be non-Western cultures, not socialist systems. Since peaceful evolution in other contexts is routinely equated with democratization, here it becomes clear that to some authors, at least, democratization is a cultural threat. Similarly, Yang Yang of Fudan University (in 2002) argues that "culture has already become an important aspect of the struggle between strong countries and weak countries," and that Americans are using the new "dissemination opportunities" presented by the Internet and other media "to encourage 'freedom, democracy, and human rights' throughout the world; a primary goal of their diplomatic strategy is to promote Western values and in that way to become a kind of 'cultural power' (*wenhua qiangquan*)."[31]

Sometimes Chinese authors discuss the numerous challenges and problems posed by the Internet in ways that suggest they might be willing to accept the notion that the Internet serves "chaos" more than cultural hegemony. In the end, though, they almost always find order within the chaos. Thus, Zhang Li and Bai Jie of the China Science and Technology University (in 2000) explain how the Internet unsettles world order by facilitating new kinds of crime (such as the circulation of computer viruses) and providing a platform for NGOs and other actors to disseminate what they charge to be lies and distortions. But they conclude that all of the problems the Internet causes ultimately assist in the consolidation of US hegemony. Chaos cannot exist within global society; some national force must be guiding all global developments, especially those of a cultural nature. "The Internet strengthens Western-centric consciousness and causes the globalization of culture in fact to become Westernization.... [The West] carries out purposeful, planned cultural penetration, from early on called 'smokeless war.' "[32]

As Liu Yongtao of Fudan University (in 2001) similarly contends, "American foreign policy has two basic goals: (1) protect the US geopolitical and political identity realm (*rentong fanwei*), and (2) influence and subvert the identities of 'others' so that they do not come to constitute a threat to American identity."[33] Under the circumstances, the CCP obviously has no choice but to control the Internet tightly.[34] It is impossible to these Chinese writers that the Internet actually undermines *all* national cultures, including American national culture, because its content is beyond the capacity of *any* state to control. Every apparently chaotic force in global politics must have a state acting intentionally behind it, and when that force threatens the CCP's vision for China—as shared by intellectual elites—the state is overwhelmingly likely to be the United States.[35]

The purposeful nature of the US strategy is important to stress because it justifies Internet control. "After the Cold War concluded, the reason the US set aside the 'Star Wars' plan and changed to carrying out 'information superhighway' and 'digital globe' research was precisely for the purpose of using domination over future world information circulation to seek advantages in information resources, expand hard and soft power, and assert hegemony over the globe."[36] Such a statement suggests that the United States is a unified actor, "setting aside" research in one area to then turn, in unison, to conducting research in other areas, all for the purpose of implementing a grand design.[37] The assertion is similar to Wang Jisi's claim noted in Chapter 4 that *all* Americans, regardless of political persuasion, seek hegemony—because it suggests an inability or at least strong disinclination to perceive genuine pluralism in American life. It is also similar to Wang's likely mirror-imaging, because if China seeks comprehensive national strength, every other state must be seeking it, too; moreover, China actually is capable of redirecting national research and development strategies in a way that would be difficult for Washington to match in peacetime.[38]

Political Civilization

Through Internet management and other repressive policies, Chinese leaders and establishment intellectuals insist that China will take a different road to the future, but that the road will still be consistent in important ways with core global cultural values. In 2002, the Party

proclaimed that it would establish a nondemocratic "political civilization," to be built alongside "material civilization" and "spiritual civilization." Chinese political development would thus eventuate in a state of
affairs better than democracy and unique to Chinese civilization. It would
wisely eschew what Li Zhongjie of the Central Party School dismissed as
"democratic romanticism":

A foreign scholar once drew this vivid analogy: Jesus Christ is worshipped as
lord only by Christians, Allah only in the Muslim world, and Sakyamuni only by
Buddhists. But there is only one "god" that is worshipped by virtually everybody in
the world and this "god" is none other than democracy. . . . This not only indicates
that democratic values have found their way deep into the hearts of the people,
but also that they entertain a certain unrealistic, romantic fantasy associated with
democracy. . . . In fact, democracy is not a Promised Land in the dreams of poets,
nor is it a children's paradise in one's imagination. It is a very complicated social
phenomenon and historical process.[39]

The roots of the political civilization concept can be traced to the 1980s'
discourse on "socialist democracy with Chinese characteristics"(SDCC).
In justifying crackdowns on democracy movements, Deng Xiaoping had
explained that "when we propagate democracy, we must make a strict
distinction between socialist democracy and bourgeois, individualistic
democracy. We must integrate democracy toward the people and dictatorship toward the enemy; and integrate democracy with centralism,
with law, with discipline, and with leadership by the Party."[40] Accepting
"bourgeois, individualistic" democracy would lead to all sorts of negative
social phenomena, because Western or Japanese pseudo-pluralism is "no
more than an attempt to reconcile the conflicts within the ruling class
by taking turns in power and to create all kinds of false impressions of
democracy by attacking and accusing each other in order to deceive the
laboring people."[41] *Renmin Ribao* commentator Zheng Hangsheng argued in 1996 that it was impossible for such negative phenomena ever to
appear in China:

1. Socialist democracy is based on public ownership of the means of production, which "makes it possible for formal equality gradually to
   change into actual equality" and which causes the "elimination of social injustice."
2. Socialist democracy is under the leadership of the Communist Party,
   which is the vanguard of the working class.
3. Socialist democracy is based on the collectivist spirit, which differs
   fundamentally from Western individualism.[42]

In the years following publication of Zheng's assessment, the Party began implementing sustained SOE reform, laying off millions of workers and managers. This weakened public ownership of the means of production. The SOE system had in any case not created society-wide equality; one of its hallmarks had been the sheltering of an elite class of urban managers and workers. Starting in the late 1990s, tens of millions of even these people were put out of work; some took new jobs in the private sector. Inequality increased sharply throughout China from the early 1990s, and was expected by some observers to increase even more with implementation of the 2001 World Trade Organization (WTO) accords.[43] Jiang Zemin's "three represents" formula—which, among other things, allows private entrepreneurs to enter the CCP—means abolition of even the pretext of the Party acting as the "vanguard of the working class." It now claims to act as the vanguard of society's most "advanced" sectors.

As economic development and structural change in the 1990s transformed China into an enormously complex society, political elites and some establishment intellectuals insisted on the continued validity of communist authoritarianism. One of the most conservative formulations was that of Xing Benxi, a noted theoretician, who in 2000 published a long discourse on the subject of "unity" in the *People's Daily*. Xing argued that the more plural China becomes socioeconomically, the more singular it must become ideologically: "Our plural culture must be plural culture under the guidance of Marxism, and the guiding position of Marxism is the backbone of such plural culture. With this backbone, we can guarantee the socialist character of the culture in our country and guarantee that the culture in our country will always advance in a progressive orientation."[44]

Other intellectuals (and propagandists) continued working vigorously to try to delegitimize "Western" democracy as the global standard. The theorist Xie Hong argued in *People's Daily* in December 2000 that "Western" democracy is essentially flawed and immoral because it inherits the legacy of ancient Greece's slave-system democracy. Socialist democracy, in contrast, "is democracy of the majority and represents the highest form of democracy in human history," the next phase in the march of modern progress.[45] Perhaps sensing the contradiction between arguing that socialist democracy is the democracy of the majority and yet that China must be ruled by a vanguard party, Xie contended in a way consistent with the "three represents" (still several months from formal unveiling) that "the 'majority' must be a majority which is advanced, cohesive, and capable of ruling" so that "the representatives elected by this 'majority'—that is, leading cadres at all levels—always represent the requirements of development of advanced productive forces, the direction of progress of advanced culture, and the fundamental interests of the overwhelming majority of the people."[46]

Yang Jianping of the Central Party School elaborated on this issue in a 2001 article for *Strategy and Management*.[47] Yang first asserted that democratization was the CCP's ultimate goal, but then castigated "Western-style" democracy for (1) producing tyrannies of the majority, such as when Caucasian-Americans rule over African-Americans; (2) producing tyrannies of the minority, such as when George W. Bush climbed to the US presidency in 2000 despite receiving fewer popular votes than Al Gore; (3) allowing political parties to manipulate the system and "become the sources of disaster" (here, Yang does not provide examples); and (4) allowing parties to refuse to cooperate when they are out of power. Developing countries cannot afford such disruptions, Yang argues, because efficiency and discipline are crucial to modernization.

Xiao Gongqin also appears uncomfortable with the word "democracy," but understands that massive changes in Chinese society under reform and opening (and beyond) are going to put pressures on leaders to change the political system. He wrote in a 2000 *Strategy and Management* article that as economic development and social differentiation continue, sometime toward the middle of the twenty-first century "a pluralistic political model with Chinese characteristics" will emerge. What this means exactly is unclear; Xiao writes only that the model "will not necessarily manifest as a Western multi-party model; the concrete details await further research."[48] The preconditions for the new model's emergence have already been established: the rise of a civil society with Chinese characteristics, specialization of economic and social interests, expansion of middle-class culture and influence, development of a "rule of law" culture, flowering of intellectual thought and plural contention, and incipient "democratization" from below based on village elections and related developments (see below). Xiao does use the word "democratization" in this section and his list of preconditions sounds consistent with what might be read in the mainstream Western democratization literature. But he also insists that China is taking its own path toward development and that implementing a Western-style democratic system would (at this point, at least) be a big mistake.[49]

Other writers agree that social, economic, and cultural changes require corresponding adjustments in the political system, but not necessarily democratization. Beijing University political scientist Xu Xianglin expressed his concerns in the pages of *Strategy and Management* that social inequality and other negative side effects of reform and opening are planting the seeds of social unrest. Political reform is certainly necessary to reduce these pressures, Xu writes, but not infrastructural political transformation. Deep transformation would probably make things worse.[50] Proceeding from similar presuppositions, Zheng Yongnian (the PRC expatriate at Singapore National University) argued a few months later in *Strategy and Management* that the social and cultural turmoil produced by reform and, particularly, globalization require a strong state to manage—and that democratic states are weak. State-building must therefore precede democratization.

To justify this position, Zheng contends that there are three (and he implies *only* three) theories of democratization current in the Western scholarly world, which hold as follows:

1. The democratic system can only exist in countries with market economies or capitalist economies.
2. The democratic system can only arise, develop, and flourish in industrialized, wealthy countries.
3. The likelihood of a democratic system flourishing depends heavily on whether the country's traditional political culture stressed the virtues of compromise and balances of power among social forces.[51]

Zheng appears to be trying to convince his readers that even foreign experts believe democracy is unsuitable for China, since China cannot meet the stringent criteria. He continues by arguing that democratization is a subspecies of state-building, or—since he is inconsistent—that state-building precedes democratization in a unilinear process. China has still not completed the state-building stage, despite its "5,000-year" history.

"There can be many roads to democratization," Zheng writes, but only cautious, careful reflection will allow China to choose the best course. This formulation suggests not rejection but actually revision of the road metaphor; to Zheng, there are multiple "roads" (plural) to the future, but all roads lead to the same destination. Even this conclusion is uncertain, however, since to Zheng "democratic politics is only one form of the modern state." Toward the end he writes that "China is in the process of taking its own road" but that "democratization is a great global trend which no country can escape."[52] The confusion inherent in Zheng's piece reflects the broader ambivalence many Chinese intellectuals feel toward the concept of "Western" democracy.

Yang Jianping of the Central Party Office agrees with Zheng that state-building should precede democratization, because he does not accept liberal global culture's dictum that democratization is the best form of governance. "The reason the state exists is to pursue the people's prosperity," Yang writes, "and the form [of government] must serve this goal. Logically

speaking, then, the form of government should match the national conditions; and we should adopt that form of government which can guarantee
the people a fine life."[53] Democratization should only be pursued to the
extent that it supports the larger goal of enhancing the people's prosperity.

Such a utilitarian approach reflects incomplete socialization to liberal-
rational global culture and a commitment to stand out of and apart from
the world and make use of it instrumentally. Yang is suspicious of calls for
China to democratize because he believes that at home Western countries
pursue both liberty and the rule of law, while for developing countries they
promote liberty and human rights but *not* the rule of law. At most they
stress that the ruling party should be subject to the rule of law, and the goal
is to make the developing country unstable and stop it from advancing.[54]
Yang promotes instead "rule-of-law democracy" (*fazhi minzhu*), by which
he means something similar to Zheng Yongnian's call for state-building
well before democratization. The essence of democracy to Yang is a government that both determines and represents "the people's basic interests"
(*genben liyi*), not whatever interests they might articulate for themselves.
The most basic interest is acquisition of comprehensive national power.
No other goal, no matter how ardently promoted by agents of global
socialization, could possibly supplant comprehensive national power in
importance. It is essential to thriving in the ecology of multipolar modernity.

Other writers stress the need to find a political system suited to
China's unique value-system, which—depending on how "China" is
essentialized—might be specified in any number of ways. Li Luqu of
Shanxi University published an article in *International Studies* arguing
at first that democracy would be quite suitable for China because of
its consistency with Confucianism. "The Confucian stress on benevo-
lent governance, elite responsibility-consciousness, and the people's right
to demand political change correspond closely to the civility, fairness,
public transparency, and such demanded by democratization."[55] But Li
continued that Confucianism can serve to counterbalance the "individualist extremism" of Western democracy and what he asserts to be its lack
of community-mindedness. This may seem odd given the value attached
to the civic culture within Western democracies, but Li is convinced that
the West is entirely a place where the strong prevail over the weak and
social norms break down in a way that would be completely unacceptable
to Chinese people. China requires a system less individualist and in fact
less democratic than Western democracy: an authority- and community-
oriented system rooted in distinctive Chinese values.[56]

One of the most vituperative denunciations of democracy to be articulated by a Chinese intellectual in recent years is Fang Ning's 2002 attack.

Fang, then Deputy Director of the Chinese Academy of Social Sciences' Institute of Political Science, gave an interview published on the first-year anniversary of the September 11th terrorist attacks. He denounced US democracy and insisted that China should completely abandon even the terminology associated with democratization. "How can we make ourselves clear when China's reality is described by the linguistic system of other people?" Fang queried, noting that the word "democracy" originated in ancient Greece. China should stop using the term "democratization" and should start actively promoting the new term "political civilization" to describe the status it seeks, alongside material civilization and spiritual civilization.

"Political civilization" was coined as a slogan by CCP General Secretary Jiang Zemin at the 2001 National Propaganda Conference and first promoted publicly in May 2002, as Party conservatives sought to preempt discussion of meaningful political reform in the run-up to the Sixteenth Party Congress (held in November 2002).[57] Experts explained political civilization in numerous articles published on the eve of the Congress. Li Liangdong of the Central Party School's Department of Political Science and Law proclaimed in September 2002 that the concept constituted "a leap forward in the theory of political development," because it reflected the fact that "democracy is a *component* of the modern political civilization of mankind, but not the totality of political civilization."

Political civilization includes not only the construction of democracy but also the construction of the legal system; not only the construction of systems, but also the construction of political culture and legal culture. Political civilization is a concept of a larger category and a wider scope. This shows that since entering the new century, the Party has ascended to a much higher ground in its theoretical understanding of the development of socialist politics than in the past.[58]

Despite political civilization including "the construction of democracy," its precondition is "adhering to the Four Cardinal Principles," which means upholding the CCP's dictatorship. It allows for borrowing concepts and practices from other political civilizations and putting them to use in a utilitarian spirit; useful concepts and practices imported so far include national sovereignty, the minority submitting to the majority (i.e., the Leninist party vanguard), "consultation on the basis of freedom and equality" (considering alternative views that are consistent with the Four Cardinal Principles), and the notion that political processes must be "proceduralized, institutionalized, and standardized." But such specifications obviously make the concept completely consistent with the CCP's traditional authoritarianism.[59]

Jiang Zemin would thus pay lip service to the rhetoric of democracy, such as when he spoke of "adhering to the path of building socialist democracy with Chinese characteristics." Fang Ning rejected even adaptation. He argued that China should abandon liberal-rational global culture's discourse on democracy completely, because global culture is West-centric:

The advancement of this new term—political civilization—is virtually an attempt to remove such an obstacle in the linguistic system of the Chinese language.... In my view, there are no universal standards for political development.... China is in need of political development and political system reforms, but both the starting point and the destination should be China's national interests and the well-being of the Chinese people.... There is no such thing as modernity, no such thing as whether or not [political development] goes in line with the trend of [global] society. In my view, all of these things are dogmatism, foreign dogmatism.[60]

Fang understood that if China continued to develop economically at a rapid pace, the CCP's determination to build a nationalistic and authoritarian political system flouting the constitutive norms of global society would probably cause tensions with other states. Yet he was prepared to accept the consequences for an opportunity to cast China into a world-historical heroic role. "China is a challenger to the irrational, outdated, and ugly order of the world," Fang claimed, while characterizing global society as "inequitable, disgraceful, and unethical." China is well positioned to put an end to the world's "backward, uncivilized, and dark order" as it reestablishes its centrality. If the Chinese people can forge a united will, they will be in a position collectively to "collide" with the dark global order and force it to change. "Since the makers of this order are not willing to put an end to it, what can only be done is to let other people put an end to it." This requires social discipline, nationalistic consciousness, and a spirit of resistance to those aspects of liberal-rational global culture threatening to corrode Chinese identity and delude the Chinese people into thinking that they are not essentially distinct and unique. China should borrow from abroad, but only when "it is good for us because this is conducive to our challenge to the irrational order."[61]

Obviously Fang rejects the notion that the world is marching inexorably toward a future in which all states become liberal-democratic. But by refusing to accept even the language of democracy, he goes much farther than China's leaders and other establishment intellectuals. Yet most Chinese who express opinions on the matter in national newspapers and IR journals seem to share Fang's views on the desirability of finding a distinctive and authoritarian Chinese road. Mainstream discourse pictures China as a society fundamentally distinct and the world as divided ontologically into poles of comprehensive national power. Yielding to democratization under such circumstances would mean accepting the United States and broader West as China's cultural masters and philosophical overlords. Very few Chinese intellectuals or leaders would be comfortable with such a status. The fear of permanent decentering drives them to resist democratization and assert political civilization as a superior substitute.

The Early Stages of Political Civilization in Practice

Chinese commentators sought to elucidate the political civilization concept in greater detail during the months following the Sixteenth Party Congress. Liu Chun of the Central Party School explained that "an advanced political civilization includes a standard and perfect system of democratic politics and a corresponding political operation mechanism and supervision mechanism, as well as a standard procedure for guaranteeing the rational operation of this system and mechanism."[62] Writing in slightly less arcane terms, a Xinhua reporter explained that "to build a socialist political civilization, it is necessary . . . to organically combine adherence to Party leadership and exercise of the people's rights as masters of the country with rule of law in running the country, continuously develop socialist democracy, and build a socialist state under the rule of law." The goal would be "to provide a political and legal guarantee for reform, opening up, and stability" so as to "develop a vivid, lively, stable, and harmonious political situation marked by democracy and unity."[63] At the same time, the purpose of the sister concept of socialist *spiritual* civilization would be (among other things) to consolidate comprehensive national power:

Developing a socialist advanced culture and building a socialist spiritual civilization are related to the prosperity and development of the Party and state and the great rejuvenation of the Chinese nation. . . . In the world of today, the success or failure, plain-sailing or rough-going of all countries in the competition of overall national strength are increasingly determined by their innovation capabilities in terms of knowledge, science and technology, and culture, and by the ideological and ethical standards, as well as the scientific and cultural qualities, of their citizens. In building a well-off society in an all-round way, we should have not only a prosperous economy and civilized politics but also a prosperous culture.[64]

Political civilization would also contribute to increasing comprehensive national strength: necessary, given the dangers and opportunities presented by multipolar modernity. But political development would have to be guided carefully to maximize its effectiveness. Blind submission to the socialization pressures of liberal-rational global culture would spell disaster.

While promoting political civilization as the end goal of political development, CCP commentators continued to trumpet "socialist democracy with Chinese characteristics" as the highest expression of political civilization to date, reflecting the conviction that political (and spiritual) civilization must be built on the material foundations of an advanced economy. Achieving political civilization would require a gradual perfection of SDCC, whose most important institutions at the present time include (1) villages holding elections to choose village committees, known abroad as Chinese "village democracy," (2) "People's Congresses" at every level of the governing hierarchy participating more meaningfully in the drafting of legislation, and (3) the public using the Internet and other new media to monitor government performance and provide feedback. Although these developments have certainly changed the way China is governed, they do not add up to democracy. The Party's explicit intention is to use them not to pave the way for democracy but instead to strengthen the state, increasing national power while deflecting domestic and foreign criticism.

Village elections. After the "Organic Law on Villagers' Committees" was mooted in 1988 (it was officially promulgated in 1998), some 906,000 village committees were constituted through four or more rounds of elections by mid-2002.[65] Although it would go beyond the scope of this chapter to address the significance of village elections in detail, it is important to stress that the Party does not intend for them to supplant the "people's dictatorship" or otherwise lead to changes beyond CCP control.[66] Party leaders seem instead to hope that the elections will enhance the bureaucracy's efficiency and effectiveness and pressure local cadres into becoming less corrupt and more responsive to the central government's concerns. These goals can be achieved partly by recruiting new talent to leadership positions through the election process. The Party does not intend for village elections to become a means by which voters actually take control over leadership-selection, budgeting, taxation, and other important matters. All of the published reports on village elections in such media as the *People's Daily* insist upon this point repeatedly. For example, Yue Yan and Zhen Hai wrote in 1997 that "practice has proved that the system of self-rule by villagers does not contradict the need to strengthen the Party's leadership over rural work," and that "self-rule by villagers has become a solid foundation for the Party to consolidate its leading status."[67] The Party intends to dominate the agenda-setting process, making certain that its key initiatives, such as the one-child policy, are all faithfully implemented.

CCP leaders and intellectuals know that foreigners have seized on village elections as a ray of hope that China might be on the road to "Western-style" democratization. Party outlets publish numerous articles extolling the elections and describing in colorful detail the many ways in which they have transformed the local political scene.[68] But village democracy does not, at root, seem significantly different in terms of the *theory of the political system* (if not the specific practice) from Mao Zedong's "mass line" formulation, which argued that the Party should immerse itself in the life of the masses and open up the channels of communication so that it never becomes overly bureaucratic and divorced from people's real needs. In fact, Wang Zhenyao of the Civil Affairs Ministry found that village elections represent "an institutionalized mass line" and that the concept had to be sold in this way to leftist cadres in 1989 who worried that it was bourgeois-liberal.[69] As a result, village elections are best conceived as an important initiative in the overall pursuit of political civilization rather than as a milestone in democratization.[70]

People's Congresses. In August 2002, the National People's Congress (NPC) Standing Committee received in draft form a proposed Law on Supervision by the NPC and the Local People's Congresses at Various Levels. The purpose of this law would be to "strengthen and standardize...the NPC's supervision over the government, the Supreme People's Court, and the Supreme People's Procuratorate," as well as to help "develop socialist democracy and promote the process of administering the country according to law."[71] Delegates to people's congresses at various levels had already begun cultivating the habit of expressing their dissatisfaction with various matters and contributing to the policymaking process as far back as the 1980s. The purpose of the new draft law would be to systematize these scattered developments, meaning (among other things) to rein them in; that is, prevent them from getting out of hand and coming to constitute a threat to the system. The point in any case would be to "develop *socialist* democracy and build *socialist* political civilization," which means developing under the CCP's authoritarian tutelage and control.[72]

Supervision through the media. As it drafted China's 10th Five-Year Plan, the State Planning Commission reported receiving 10,000 policy suggestions "from ordinary people through special websites;" it claimed to have adopted over 300 of the suggestions.[73] Large numbers of Chinese "netizens" access Xinhua News Agency sites reporting on institutionalized political events such as NPC meetings.[74] They also vigorously debate such events in online chat room sites—though without, of course, having the benefit of access to foreign or overseas Chinese news reports that might evaluate the NPC meetings critically and assess them in a comparative context.[75] As suggested above in the Internet section, none of these developments seems likely to lead (on their own, at least) to China's democratization. At best they serve a steam-valve function while allowing the Party to claim fidelity to key constitutive norms in liberal-rational global culture.

"International Democratization" and Multipolarization

In the immediate aftermath of the September 11th terrorist attacks, Chinese analysts expressed optimism that the decline of the United States had begun in earnest. On October 1, 2001, Tang Tianri explained in the general affairs magazine *Liaowang* ("Outlook") why the inevitable success of multipolarity might now come sooner than expected during the dark days of Kosovo. Tang acknowledged that the United States remained mired in the illusion that it could control the international system during the next fifteen to twenty years and impose its political vision on the world. Four trends, however, would frustrate the Americans. First, "nothing can stop Russia from restoring its status as a great power." Second, "nothing can stop China from rising up and increasing its strength." Third, "the trend towards independence and self-reliance of the EU is beyond control." And fourth, "it is hard to control Japan and prevent it from becoming a big military power."[76]

The departure from the Kosovo discourse is significant. Chinese analysts had always insisted that multipolarity was inevitable; after all, the CCP's vision of a distinctively Chinese political civilization *required* it to be inevitable. During the Kosovo crisis, Chinese elites worried that Europe was becoming a plaything of the United States through NATO and that Japan would join the unholy alliance, which was already directing its pincers toward the Eurasian heartland. But now, in the aftermath of September 11th, an *Outlook* commentator could declare that the United States was no longer capable of controlling Europe and Japan. In the weeks following the attacks, other Chinese writers expressed similar confidence that the end of the unipolar moment had begun.

But the assessment changed abruptly after the successful American counterattack on Al-Qaeda bases in Afghanistan beginning in October 2001. A contributor to the *Jiefangjun Bao* ("Liberation Army Daily") conceded in February 2002 that the picture had become murkier in recent months. The world scene was now "characterized by rapid changes, interwoven contradictions of different categories, and continual adjustments," probably "the most profound changes since the end of the Cold War." At present, things seemed to be favoring the hegemonists again, but the commentator still concluded that, on the whole, multipolarization remained firmly on track and that it was only a matter of time before the United States was dethroned. Multipolarity's victory would certainly come sometime "early in the 21st century," the commentator promised, though achieved in a complex and tortuous struggle.[77]

Victory would at last make possible the attainment of what some Chinese writers called "inter*national* democracy": a system in which every state-level unit acts as an equal, autonomous, rights-bearing member of international society, and in which no actor (state or otherwise) can interfere in sovereign states' internal affairs. International democracy—a "pluralist" vision of IR, in English School terms[78]—is identical to multipolarity insofar as "multipolarization must take international democratization as its basis and goal."[79] As explained by Ni Shixiong and Wang Yiwei of Fudan University (in 2002), both concepts together represent the natural and correct "way" of international affairs:

> Human society and the natural world are alike in being full of plurality and difference; this is objectively a universal phenomenon. . . . If someone were to take one kind of social system, development model, value system, or type of civilization and absolutize, mythologize, and forcibly foist it upon others—while viewing others as perverted (*yiduan*) and therefore rejecting association with them (*jiayi paichi*)—this would completely violate the objective law of the plurality of things.[80]

The only legitimate "road" of political development in global society is consolidation of "world plurality" (*shijie de duoyangxing*). Arguing that democratization is the single road, implicitly privileging the United States and broader West as the global Center, would be evil, heterodox, wrong, and unscientific. Yet promoting world plurality is not a call for nation-states to isolate themselves from each other. They should certainly trade and invest across borders. In fact, Ni and Wang contend that the very basis of international political democratization is international economic democratization, defined as "healthy globalization" and the guarantee of "collective development." In other words, contrary to the predictions of world-polity theory, or even those of neo-Gramscian William Robinson,[81] Ni and Wang believe that economic globalization will lead to *less* likeness among units, or at least to a consolidation of the differences that already exist. The logic might simply be that since the international economic order is currently benefiting the CCP, it should be praised. But since the international political order holds the potential to harm the CCP, it should be criticized.

In a similar move, Wang Yi of the Ministry of Foreign Affairs identifies globalization as the key reason the coming multipolarity will be normatively desirable, whereas the pre-1945 multipolar balance of power (BOP) system had been deeply flawed. Economic interdependence combined with cross-border flows will stabilize the coming multipolar system to render BOP logic superfluous, Wang argues. He finds that globalization is good because it "especially helps reduce opposition to new-rising powers" (read: China).[82] This sanctifies globalization not only as normatively desirable but also as inexorable; Wang in fact argues that multipolarization and international democratization together constitute a joint "inevitable trend and irreversible historical process" precisely *because* economic globalization is inevitable.[83] Since most Western IR specialists believe that globalization weakens states—or at the very least challenges them mightily—Wang's conclusions are surprising, until one remembers that (1) the CCP benefits from multipolarity and (2) the CCP also benefits from economic globalization. Therefore, both of these phenomena *must* covary positively.[84]

Multipolarity of course implies the decline of US hegemony, and that, too, is inevitable. In the words of Wang Jisi, the dean of China's America specialists, "only the timing, process, and nature of [the US] decline are difficult to predict";[85] the decline itself will certainly occur. An obvious question is why—why, that is, it must occur, as opposed to being desirable that it occur. The simplest answer is that it must occur because nothing else would be consistent with CCP desires. Shi Yinhong, Director of the US Research Center at the People's University, draws on the work of William McNeill and other historians in arguing that US hegemony must decline as a natural result of the dispersal of power that always occurs as hegemons disseminate advanced technologies (hardware and software) to late-developers.[86] This provides some theoretical and empirical justification for Chinese optimism.

More radically, Zhang Wenmu, a national security specialist at the Contemporary International Relations Research Institute, contends that multipolarization emerges as a natural result of "southern" countries exercising their "right to development." Zhang dates this concept to the eighteenth century European Enlightenment but it sounds significantly more like nineteenth century European Romantic nationalism. He believes that for a variety of (also) Marxist reasons, northern countries invest in southern countries, with the result that, as Shi Yinhong had also noted, advanced technology flows to the disadvantaged. Next borrowing from A.F.K. Organski (without citing his work),[87] Zhang argues that some new southern power will rise to challenge the hegemon, a process he *defines* as multipolarization—suggesting that multipolarization might simply be a code word for China's rise. The hegemon will in the first phase seek to contain or "strangle" (*ezhi*) the rising power, producing a crisis. There are only two possible outcomes, Zhang asserts, neither of which Organski and colleagues found to be common historically. In the first, the hegemon compromises with the rising power and accepts a new multipolar world political and economic order; in the second, the hegemon yields its place peacefully to the rising power as Britain yielded to the United States between the 1920s and the 1950s.[88]

Zhang does not even mention the outcome that Organski and colleagues found to be most common: The rising power challenges the hegemon before its comprehensive national strength is sufficient, resulting in catastrophic defeat in a global war. Nothing so pessimistic or suggestive of possible CCP miscalculation is acceptable in Chinese public discourse. The only possible outcomes to the struggle between rising power and hegemon are outcomes in which China is victoriously recentered, either by (1) joining the hegemon in a new condominium, *without* having been forced to accept democratization or (2) replacing the hegemon without a serious struggle.

Zhang explores the rise of the United States in the nineteenth and twentieth centuries and discusses as "still having special relevance for contemporary China" geopolitical theorist Alfred Thayer Mann's (1840–1914) musings on the "theory of naval power" (*haiquan lilun*). Zhang is suggesting that China has a right to pursue the same type of development as the United States did by developing a navy that can defend China's expanding global economic interests. Zhang further contends that naval development is essential to China's democratization. He argues that 19th and 20th century Latin American countries only remained dictatorships because of the political interference of Britain and the United States. If Latin American countries had been able to deploy strong navies, they could have defended themselves from Anglo-American predations and would have flowered into democracies with their own national characteristics. Therefore, China needs a strong navy (and strong military forces generally) to prevent US hegemonists from intervening in Chinese politics and stopping China's democratization. "To China—and even to all southern countries—not to oppose hegemonism means not being able to seek development; seeking development requires opposing hegemonism."[89] China's democratization is thus impossible in a hegemonic world, but also is impossible in a multipolar world, except insofar as "political civilization" and "socialist democracy with Chinese characteristics" count as democratic.

Other writers offer additional explanations for why US decline and the success of multipolar modernity are inevitable. Zhang Shenjun of Beijing Normal University argues that the democratic ideology the United States promotes to legitimate hegemony will eventually backfire as world leaders first accept it but then begin demanding that Washington respect international democracy. Zhang predicts a "structural crisis" in the aftermath of the Iraq War, because (1) the United States will try to force

Iraq and the rest of the Middle East to accept domestic democracy, which will backfire, and (2) US unilateralism—bypassing the United Nations and overthrowing other countries' governments—violates international law and is therefore inherently unsustainable.[90] Perhaps because states largely create it, international law is pictured in this way as possessing a kind of primal force, a force rooted in the timeless validity of sovereignty as ontologically presuppositional, and Westphalia as Genesis and Revelation. The United States not only may not, it *cannot* continue to act in ways that violate institutions built on the principle of sovereignty. Therefore, the bid for hegemony is inherently unsustainable. In this picture the United States will decline simply as a result of quasi-natural elemental forces recovering their potency and direction.[91]

As examples of incipient international democratization in action, Li Zhongjie of the Central Party School cites three cases: (1) the complicated maneuvering that resulted in Taiwan's semiforced withdrawal from the United Nations in 1971, (2) Washington's annual inability to have China criticized formally by the UN Human Rights Commission, and (3) the vote to evict the United States from the Commission in May 2001. The vote to reinstate the United States in May 2002 would also have to be considered international democracy in action, Li grudgingly conceded, but it was important to note that the United States "did a great deal of [suspect] work behind the scenes and barred other countries from entering the race" to get itself readmitted. It would therefore be wrong to conclude that international democracy "is the most perfect system," Li acknowledged, but certainly it has its place at the international level as an antidote to hegemonism.[92] In the perfect system, presumably, everything would always go the CCP's way.

Recentering China

Singapore's Zheng Yongnian writes that "a lot of people predict the Chinese economy will quickly surpass America, becoming number one in the world."[93] Similarly, Yu Xilai expects that by mid-century, China will have the world's largest macroeconomy, second largest population, and third largest territorial expanse. At that point, China will become the second most comprehensively powerful country in the world, right after the United States. By 2075, it may even surpass the United States. Chinese material advantages will easily be fungible into ideational or soft power, Yu believes, leading to a situation in which "China's international goals *and values* will, to a great extent, influence the direction of the 21st century world."[94] What kind of direction might the world then take? How would China change the world after recentering?

Chinese writers seem unanimously to agree that, regardless of the specific answer, China should always be a part of the international community. It should remain fundamentally distinctive, and never dissolve into a West-centered global cosmopolitanism, but should always take active part in global affairs. The best kind of world to these Chinese writers is not a world in which individual countries isolate themselves, as Mao isolated China in the 1960s. Countries should not only trade and invest with each other but should also pursue "dialogue across cultures," meaning across civilizations or nation-states. Shen Qurong of the Institute of Contemporary International Relations argues that crude cultural relativism must be rejected because it can easily lead to situations in which "some people defend certain kinds of barbaric, stupid, or un-human thinking and behavior."[95] To Shen, the world must be led—but not by the United States, at least not by the United States alone. Others contend that the world's naturally plural state must be preserved; thus, Yu predicts that the "chief contradiction" in twenty-first century IR will be between those countries (he does not mention nonstate actors) trying to make the world "become a single unit" (*yitihua*, a kind of global cosmopolitanism) and those trying to defend plurality.

Yu identifies four requirements for twenty-first century Chinese diplomacy. First, China should join and participate enthusiastically in existing international regimes and rules of the game. It should not try to "set up a separate stovepipe" (*ling qi lu zao*) of China's own regimes and rules, an alternative Center. The reasons are simply because (1) China will not have the power to set up an alternative Center before at least 2075, and (2) it can benefit extensively by using the current regimes and rules of the game.[96]

Second, China should take the lead in pursuing East Asian regional unification *à la* the European Union. The ultimate goal of regional unification would be to use East Asia as a base from which China could challenge US global hegemony. Yu notes that in recent years, the use of Chinese characters and the Chinese language generally has increased in East Asia, which he defines to include not only Korea, Japan, and Taiwan, but also Vietnam and apparently other parts of Southeast Asia (but not South Asia).[97] China—the pole, the actor, the Subject—"should seize this advantageous opportunity and put efforts into using literature, the humanities and social sciences, and computers and networks to achieve new successes and pursue the goal of making Chinese and English together the chief tools of communication in East Asian culture."[98] Obviously, therefore, Yu sees ideational power as central to achieving regional unification and speculates that an Asian Commonwealth can be established by 2050. Such a Commonwealth would "greatly strengthen the position and functions of China and an integrated East Asia in the process of the globe becoming a single unit."[99]

Third, Yu affirms that China should play an active role in the dialogue across cultures, by which he means civilizations rather than nation-states. Civilizations may, in the twenty-first century, become the new natural basis of power-poles, superseding nation-states. Yu first cites Huntington approvingly because Huntington takes East Asian civilization to be Confucian, ignoring the weight of Buddhism as the popular religion. Yu reiterates the importance of the widespread use of Chinese characters and then declares that "Japanese civilization, Korean civilization, Vietnamese civilization, etc., are all subsidiary civilizations (*zi wenming*) and secondary civilizations (*ya wenming*) in traditional East Asia; therefore, China's own relations with countries to the southwest, northwest, and north implicate civilization-level dialogue with other civilizations."[100] Following regional unification, China will lead and represent East Asia in the dialogue across cultures, because Confucianism belongs to China.[101]

Yu writes that as Asians unite, they face a choice. They can unselectively accept and digest the "modern civilization" bequeathed to them by European imperialists, or they can establish *within* modern civilization an alternative "Asian home" (*Yazhou de jia*). "This kind of collectively-created 'Asian civilization'. . . must on the one hand link and mutually merge with (*jiegui xiangqia*) contemporary Euro-American civilization" and, on the other hand, must "play a special role in global society's shift from an emphasis on utilitarianism to ecological balance and the shift to focus on networks instead of physical entities in the global social architecture." China has the decisive, central role to play in determining whether Asia succeeds in making these shifts.[102] This may seem surprising, given the environmental damage caused by China's utilitarian approach to economic development,[103] and the CCP's state-centered rather than network-centered approach to IR. Perhaps Yu intends for China to abandon developmental Realism on the way to becoming more powerful. But his fascination with China's increasing international stature suggests otherwise. He may be deploying terminology current in the NGO and international governmental organization (IGO) communities to increase Chinese soft power.

Fourth, Yu argues that after the Asian Commonwealth is established, Asia (minus India)—under Chinese leadership—should pursue the creation of a "global federation," whose governance would be rooted in the UN system. China already enjoys enormous power in the United Nations by virtue of its permanent seat on the Security Council. Yu wants to increase that power by weighting General Assembly votes on the basis of national population and financial contributions (see the discussion of Yu's work in the "Intellectual Cross-Currents" section). The result would be a "democratic" global federation in which "Chinese" (meaning the CCP-controlled state) votes would count up to five times as much as US votes, to say nothing of Japan's votes and those of China's other enemies and competitors. In summary, Yu posits a world in which China consolidates some measure of hegemony over East and parts of Southeast Asia and then is weightiest in a UN-based "global federation."

These goals should be attainable by 2050. Afterward, China is recentered—though it may not surpass the United States in comprehensive national power until 2075. "If one day China becomes the world's Number One, and becomes the economic hegemon, everyone will greatly respect us. All the nations and societies of the world will esteem Chinese culture, will research and study Confucian thought, will imitate the interpersonal relations exemplified in the Chinese family, and afterwards will study how Chinese cultivate the person, organize the family, rule the country, and then bring peace to the world."[104] To the extent that Yu's goals are widely shared, Chinese ambitions are to *supplant* the United States to become the new Center and dominant Subject in world history. China would establish precisely the sort of unipolar world that the CCP claims is impossible and immoral and which it accuses the "hegemonistic" United States of trying to establish.

The new world would be Chinese in culture, not liberal-democratic. But would this make it Confucian? Yu implicitly essentializes contemporary China as Confucian, overlooking the intellectual revolutions of the twentieth century that deeply discredited Confucianism.[105] He also avoids analyzing the widely remarked Chinese "spiritual vacuum" and crisis of public morality, which imply that the PRC would face enormous difficulties in offering the world attractive cultural models. Yu concedes that China must first undergo a "civilizational renovation" (*wenming zaizao*) before it can serve as a global model, but he thinks this can rather easily be achieved in the second half of the twenty-first century.[106] In this respect, he supports the CCP's stance on building a socialist spiritual civilization (though he may disagree on specifics), and is confident that the party-state can succeed once the material conditions are propitious.

In like manner, Wang Xiaodong believes that most of the world's great thinkers in the twenty-first century will come from China, because Chinese live on the world's periphery and as a result experience a disproportionate share of the world's poverty, bitterness, and degradation—all essential to producing great thoughts. As Chinese move from the periphery to the

Center, they will replace Westerners as the main source of the world's great scientific and cultural achievements.[107]

Fudan University's Yang Yang asserts similarly that Chinese culture can remake the dominant global culture. He contends that Chinese have always used Confucian persuasion, dialogue, and patience to conduct international affairs, in support of the noble purpose of encouraging the world to achieve a "great unity" (*datong*) or great peace.[108] Yang argues that the Chinese state should make use of this historical "fact" to increase ideational power.[109] Such utilitarianism would violate the Confucian practices and beliefs, but this may be acceptable because achieving a global "great unity" is predicated on China increasing its comprehensive national power.

Yang claims that other Chinese values will also be useful in this endeavor, including the Chinese belief in universalism rather than selfish nationalism, their love of peace, and esteem for friendship. He contends that China can offer the world human-heartedness (*ren*), righteousness (*yi*), ethical conduct (*li*), intelligence (*zhi*), and trustworthiness (*xin*), and that these can be used "to build the cultural basis for a reasonable, just, and stable international order."[110] He assumes that the values Confucianists argued *should* characterize Chinese society actually *did*, and even still *do*. This is akin to arguing that Christian rulers in Italy, France, and Germany always "turn the other cheek" in international affairs because that is what Jesus preached.[111] The hyperrealism that informs the CCP's comprehension of US and Japanese foreign policy motives thus gives way to a pure and unrealistic idealism of Chinese motives.

Conclusion

The primary obstacle to China's democratization is the ruling CCP, and it is a formidable obstacle indeed: supported by the vast majority of China's establishment intellectuals (since joining or remaining in the establishment requires displaying support) and by multinational corporations and foreign governments eager to sell to or invest in China. The CCP and its domestic supporters construct an image of the Party leading China to amass awesome wealth and strength ("comprehensive national power"), after which it will lead most of Asia and—without democratizing—join in a condominium with the United States at the global Center as a primary Subject in world history. It might eventually replace the United States in the leading position. The Party and its intellectual supporters set as an official goal the establishment of a distinctively Chinese Communist "political civilization" as an alternative to despised "Western democracy." They know that the socioeconomic changes associated with reform and opening have transformed China structurally and culturally, especially by making it more plural. They understand the role of the Internet and other advanced communications technologies in facilitating these changes. As a result, they try to channel and direct the changes down the path of political civilization, while promoting nationalism-priming endeavors such as a costly space program and hosting the Olympics and world trade events.

Given the power of this nationalistic vision to mobilize popular support on behalf of a CCP-led Chinese return to greatness, China will not easily transit to democracy. The commitment to recentering Chinese civilization will not likely fade. Such a political culture, carefully constructed and managed by the vanguard party elite, rests on a real economic and military rise of extraordinary proportions. The CCP seems capable of using this culture to neutralize forces of liberalization unleashed by globalization's impact (including liberal-rational global culture) and of defeating those seeking an opening for democracy.

TAIWAN: DEMOCRATIZATION AS DE-SINIFICATION

Taiwan's democratization might at first glance seem to be self-explanatory, needing little reference to liberal-rational global culture. After its economy joined the ranks of the middle-income countries in the 1970s, democratization was in some ways the next logical step for Taiwan. Wealth was distributed fairly evenly on the island, creating a strong and increasingly self-confident middle class.[1] Most Western countries and Japan had democratized after becoming comparably wealthy, and their experiences suggested democracy was functionally the most suitable system for industrialized, capitalist, high-consumption economies.

But as explained in the Thailand and China chapters, democratization does not flow automatically from economic development. China seems to be substantially more distant from democratization today than when it was far less developed economically in 1989. The question then becomes why people in Taiwan began demanding democratization in the 1970s, and why the ruling Chinese Kuomintang (*Zhonghua Kuomintang*; hereafter, KMT) eventually acquiesced. From where did the idea of democracy come to the Taiwanese, and why did they see it as a normatively desirable type of political system? After all, they might have demanded something closer to the efficient, technologically advanced authoritarianism of ethically Chinese Singapore. Where did they get the idea that Taiwan is a "democratize-able" distinct nation-state? The KMT had never promoted this notion; indeed, it brutally punished anyone who publicly suggested it. To the KMT, the Republic of China (ROC) was a nation-state, but not Taiwan. The Chinese Communist Party (CCP) had always refused to accept either Taiwan or the ROC (on Taiwan) as a nation-state, viewing Taiwan instead as a "renegade province" or future People's Republic of China (PRC) "special administrative region" (SAR), akin to Hong Kong.

Why did the Taiwanese insist upon Taiwan being a democratize-able nation-state?

Senior historian Chang Yen-hsien, Curator (since 2000) of the ROC National Museum of History, argues that Taiwan's democratization was causally intertwined with the country's (and he certainly regards Taiwan as a country) emergence as a "Subject in History," not in the sense of playing the kind of dominant world role desired by China, but of a society charting its developmental course autonomously and with dignity as a national collective unit.[2] Chang finds that in the past, Taiwanese were taught that Taiwan could only be some other polity's peripheral territory or insignificant appendage, an object of some other state's subjectivity—whether that of the Manchu Qing, whose Beijing-centered empire annexed Taiwan in 1683 and governed it loosely until 1895; Imperial Japan, which wrested Taiwan from the Qing in 1895 and developed but exploited it until 1945; or the Nationalist Chinese, who occupied Taiwan under American auspices in October 1945 and then relocated to the island completely after losing the Chinese civil war. The Manchus, Japanese, and Chinese Mainlanders successively imposed peripherality on the Taiwanese, most (but not all) of whose ancestors had migrated from the East Asian mainland (Fujian and Guangdong provinces in the contemporary PRC) long before modern nationalism transformed the Qing territories into the contemporary construction "China." Taiwan's eventual emergence as a Subject in History therefore includes both its democratization and "deperipheralization," or emergence as a "new and independent country" (*xin er duli de guojia*)—a common slogan of Taiwanese nationalists.

Consistent with Chang, Juan J. Linz and Alfred Stepan argue that *sovereignty* is an essential precondition for democracy. The CCP promises Taiwan that it may keep its democracy under "one country, two systems": Taiwan's inevitable future status, according to CCP prognosticators. Some foreigners encourage Taiwan to accept this deal. But Linz and Stepan contend that "without a sovereign state, there can be no secure democracy":

Can a democratic political sub-system exist within the overall framework of a totalitarian or post-totalitarian state? Politically, probably not—because of the example that it would provide for the citizens of the larger unit to see one region enjoying freedoms to which they would not have access. This dissonance would generate a persistent temptation for the sovereign state to subvert those democratic institutions.

But there is a more serious and principled constitutional difficulty. The state would still have the right to modify the political status of any component subunit. . . . [I]n any democratic federal state, the citizens of a subunit obviously have their share in the decision-making process in the center through democratic participation in the federal representative bodies. But in a system that is nondemocratic at the center, they would have no share, and the nondemocratic system would make the most important decisions.[3]

Chang and other Taiwanese nationalists agree that defending Taiwanese sovereignty is the basic precondition to consolidating Taiwanese democracy. Without sovereignty and the national project, Taiwan would become like authoritarian Hong Kong or Macau. As explained in Chapter 7, this leads some Taiwanese nationalists to the extreme position of rejecting Chinese culture entirely. But for most, it requires at a minimum the whole-hearted embrace of liberal-rational global culture and identification with the modern world mainstream.

Activists in Taiwan believe that cultivating a new national identity also served in the 1970s and 1980s as a tactical tool for mobilizing sufficient strength to force the KMT to liberalize.[4] Later, democratization facilitated consolidation of an autonomous civil society, which allowed the further cultivation of Taiwanese national identity. An important illustration is the Wu San-lien Taiwan Historical Research Materials Foundation, which in 1993 opened a Taiwan Historical Research Center for public use, allowing motivated citizens more easily to escape KMT ideological hegemony and begin imagining Taiwan as a distinct nation-state.[5] From Chang's synoptic perspective, all such developments can be subsumed under the larger historical trend of Taiwan emerging as a (democratic) Subject in History, which is "not only the aspiration and objective of Taiwan's people over the past century, but also the ongoing driving force behind its historical evolution."[6] As a historical "driving force," Taiwanese subjectivity clashes with the CCP's conviction that Taiwan will become a peripheral part of the alternative political civilization it will inevitably succeed in establishing under multipolar modernity. The implications of this clash are discussed in Chapter 7. The present chapter explains Taiwan's democratization as resulting from a fusion of the Taiwanese subjectivity movement with the values of liberal-rational global culture. Taiwanese nationalists and their liberal Mainlander allies accepted democratization as not threatening the essence or *ti* of the new Taiwan taking shape in the 1970s and 1980s. They believed that absorbing liberal-rational global culture would only enhance Taiwan's identity.

Rooting Taiwanese Subjecthood in History

Chang Yen-hsien is the dean of a new wave of younger Taiwanese historians who have only been allowed to publish their works openly since the early 1990s. Before then, KMT censorship placed sharp restrictions on how Taiwan could be characterized in history. The island was generally cast as an outpost of Chinese civilization since the Ming Dynasty (1363–1644) or even earlier, lost for fifty years to Japanese imperialism, but even under Hirohito's boot heel resisting heroically and bringing glory to the Chinese people.

Obviously in this orthodox history, Taiwan was a peripheral part of China. Since both the ROC and the PRC were at the time undemocratic, Taiwan itself had no indigenous basis on which to build a democracy; it could only follow trends in "Greater China." To promote democratization, Chang and simpatico historians felt impelled to write a new Taiwanese history, one that would transcend KMT ideological hegemony and portray Taiwan as distinct from China and destined to become an independent democratic nation.[7] These new historians conceived Taiwan's democratization to be the latest phase in a long-term struggle for liberation from a series of oppressors, including the Dutch, the Manchu Qing, the Japanese, and the Nationalist Chinese.[8] They insist that there is nothing essential about "China," a concept of convenience first used by Westerners to denote the empires ruling the East Asian mainland and their cultural legacy. Only later was the China concept internalized, essentialized, and abused for nationalistic political purposes by mainland state-builders in both the KMT and the CCP. Taiwanese people became merely one of many unwilling objects of subsequent Chinese state-building and imperial expansion; other victims included the Tibetans, Uighurs, and Mongols. Today, all of these people continue to resist the imposition of a Chinese identity, but only the Taiwanese have found themselves in a position to resist it effectively.

Most of Taiwan's new historians acknowledge that the genetic code and much of the culture of the Taiwanese people originated on the East Asian mainland, making them "related" in important ways to the people of China. But some nationalists insist that the Taiwanese genetic code is distinct as a result of centuries of intermarriage with plains-dwelling Malayo-Polynesian island aboriginals.[9] They also stress that Taiwan borrowed heavily from Japan during the colonial period and later from the United States; thus, Taiwan is both biologically and culturally unique. Nationalist historians compare Taiwan's relationship to China with the American relationship to Western civilization, arguing that countries can share in a civilizational heritage and yet still cultivate national autonomy. There is no obvious reason, they contend, why all peoples influenced by Chinese culture should be governed by a single authoritarian center in Beijing.[10]

The historians frontally challenge claims that Taiwan is inherently and essentially Chinese because it has "always" been a part of China.[11]

They argue that Taiwan has never been integrated tightly into *any* mainland-based political system, and was not even loosely integrated before the (non-Chinese) Manchu Qing seized the island in 1683. When the Dutch occupied Taiwan in 1624, it had never been administered by a mainland-based government. The Han Chinese population was only some 24,000—in contrast to 120,000 aboriginals (classified by KMT and CCP nationalists as "Chinese" despite their ethnic distinctiveness). During the thirty-seven years of Dutch rule, immigration of peasants and laborers from Ming territories increased dramatically as Taiwan came to resemble Batavia, Manila, or Malacca, with European administration, Chinese labor, and a disenfranchised *bumiputra* too disorganized to resist. The key difference was that Taiwan was much closer to China geographically than was the Dutch East Indies, the Philippines, or Malaya.

As a result, when Zheng Chenggong ("Koxinga" to Europeans)— a half-Japanese, half-Fujianese Ming loyalist and enemy of the Qing— occupied Taiwan in 1661, the Manchu authorities came quickly to perceive controlling the island to be essential to imperial security. That was the reason they took Taiwan at gunpoint from the Zheng family in 1683 and turned it into a prefecture of Fujian province. That Taiwan's population had become predominantly Han Chinese made little difference to the Manchus, who were, after all, themselves ethnically distinct. The Manchu concern was that Taiwan should not be used as a springboard to attack Qing territories.[12]

Taiwanese historians explain in detail how Taiwan did not become well integrated into the Qing Empire, politically or culturally. Qing officials (including Han Chinese) dispatched to the island typically spent their three-year tenures making money off a lucrative monsoonal trade so they could retire in luxury on the mainland. They did little governing, sitting back while clans and gangs administered Taiwan rudely. Only in the 1880s, after a brief French military incursion, did the Manchus dispatch a reform-minded and energetic governor, Liu Mingchuan, to assert more effective control over Taiwan and preside over its reincorporation into the Empire as a province.[13] But even this late in history, the reason for the redoubled Qing effort was imperial security, not national sentiment or profound cultural bonding.

There was, to be sure, a degree of Sinification taking place on the island. Only twenty-three Confucian academies were established between 1683 and 1860, but then fourteen more were established between 1860 and 1893. Between 1862 and 1894, Taiwan produced 343 degree-holders, over a third of the island's total output in the two centuries after 1688.[14] When the Qing signed the Treaty of Shimonoseki in 1895, ceding Taiwan to Japan, their chief negotiator, Li Hongzhang, expected that a large number of Taiwanese would want to migrate to the Chinese mainland. He demanded from the Japanese a provision allowing Taiwan residents two years—from May 1, 1895, to May 8, 1897—to decide whether to move. After May 8, 1897, remaining Taiwanese would automatically become (second-class) citizens of Japan. The Japanese agreed because they hoped Taiwan would be evacuated so they could colonize it for "living space." In the event, only 4,456 Taiwanese took up the offer to move, surprising everyone. Those who chose to go were mostly degree-holders, indicating a high social status and *possibly* identification with Chinese culture.[15] The vast majority—the population may have been two million at the time—decided to stay. The very thin umbilical cord linking Taiwan with China was then severed, never to be restored culturally—though the economic relationship has, since the 1990s, become unprecedentedly close.[16]

Politically active Taiwanese are aware of this history and use it self-consciously to articulate a distinctively democratic identity. A Democratic Progressive Party (DPP) municipal official in Kaohsiung explained that

Taiwan is a part of the southeastern Chinese coastal zone, but we've always been very different from people living in inner China and up in Beijing. We are traders, and we've always had a lot of contact with Europeans and Americans. You might date our democracy to 400 years ago, because even in the Dutch period we absorbed some ideas about the modern state. We also have a pioneering spirit, because Taiwan is mostly an immigrant society. This is the kind of spirit that's not conservative and not content with the status quo. We always want change, just like European civilization wanted change. Later, even most Mainlander migrants were from the coast.[17]

From 1683 to 1860, Taiwan was actually a backwater in the global economy and society, not rejoining the global mainstream until Britain forced the Qing to open treaty ports to trade. After 1860, Taiwan became a significant exporter of tea, camphor, and sugar.[18] But following incorporation into the Japanese Empire in 1895, most of Taiwan's trade was redirected to Japan, and the island exited world society again. In this respect, the history of democratic Taiwan is profoundly different from the history of democratic Thailand, as outlined in Chapter 2. But Taiwanese nationalists still identify with an *image* of their country as having always been open to the outside world, patched into the flows of global commerce and culture, and in this way distinct from and superior to China. Believing that they have always been a part of the global mainstream—and never the seat of an alternative Center—makes it easier for Taiwanese nationalists to accept democratization, and even to expect and demand democracy as the only type of political system suitable for a people such as themselves.

Taiwanese historians argue that there was no sense of Taiwan being a distinctive political unit before annexation to Imperial Japan. Modernization of Taiwan under Japanese rule established the basis for a "real feeling of being a national unit" (*guojia danwei zhenshigan*).[19] Before 1895, Han migrants thought of Taiwan as either a place of political refuge or a frontier zone in which to eke out a rough existence. Migrants were divided by place of origin on the mainland, clan, and other factors. Aboriginals were divided by tribe. Genuine Taiwan consciousness only began to emerge in the 1910s and 1920s as a secondary and unintended consequence of Japanese development policies.[20]

The Taiwanese have thus long been accustomed to powerful outsiders transforming them culturally. Lacking a sense of Taiwan-centrality, they were, within the past century, transformed first by Imperial Japan and later by the KMT. Some resisted; and as explained below, this resistance is claimed by some writers to be the essence of the Taiwanese national spirit. But by the 1970s, a basic predisposition to accept transformation at the hand of significant "Others" made it much easier for the Taiwanese to accept socialization to liberal-rational global culture than the Chinese.

Chang Yen-hsien writes of Japanese colonialism that Tokyo first established a basic cultural distinction between Japan as "inner" and Taiwan as peripheral. The long-term goal was "inner-extension" (*neidi yanchang*): Japan the Subject would transform Taiwan the Object into a Japanese clone. This policy was enforced through myriad daily encounters between colonizer and colonized, in all significant institutions of public life. If Taiwanese refused to accept their "object of transformation" status in, for example, schools, government offices, and health clinics, they would be made to suffer material and psychological consequences, and in extreme cases would be subjected to physical punishments.[21] Such an intensive socialization process over two generations primed Taiwanese to regard their society as essentially peripheral and even as requiring transformation by powerful outsiders.

The Japanese also established a legal-institutional foundation for Taiwan's eventual emergence as a country distinct from China. Legal historian Wang T'ai-sheng explains that the Japanese introduced a Western/Continental legal system immediately upon taking control of Taiwan and ruled through law (albeit dictatorially) during the entire fifty-year colonial period.[22] This accustomed Taiwanese to using law to resolve civil and political disputes. It was one reason they, along with liberal Mainlanders, were able to curb, with minimal bloodshed, the wilder and more militaristic tendencies inherent in Chiang K'ai-shek's authoritarian system. After the KMT's legitimacy collapsed in the wake of a series of international crises in the 1970s (discussed below), Taiwanese and liberal

Mainlanders looking for solutions did not generally embrace extralegal methods and goals. Lawyers played a prominent role in Taiwan's largely peaceful transformation. Contemporary leaders continue to regard constitutionalism as the only legitimate path to establishing an internationally recognized independent state. Wang argues that the contrast with China is significant. Chinese people have *never* experienced either rule *of* law or rule *by* law, whether in the PRC or in earlier times. This makes Taiwan and China essentially different.[23]

By implementing a Continental legal system, Japan conveyed key elements of liberal-rational global culture into Taiwan. As Japan itself entered a period of cautious movement toward democratic governance in the 1910s and 1920s, young Taiwanese studying in Tokyo also became exposed to new concepts of nationality, citizenship, and political participation. They returned to Taiwan to found a social movement committed to carving out a more respectable and autonomous place for Taiwan within the Japanese Empire.[24]

In January 1921, Dr. Chiang Wei-shui conceived the idea of establishing an umbrella organization to coordinate the various activities of returned intellectuals, and thus was born the Taiwan Cultural Association (*Taiwan Wenhua Xiehui*), whose activities included not only agitating for a local assembly, but also disseminating modern knowledge. Returned intellectuals—especially doctors, engineers, and teachers—established newspaper-reading centers and gave lectures on Taiwanese history, Western history, the new Continental legal system, public health and sanitation, economics, basic science, and other academic topics. They also established publishing houses to import and sell books on the social sciences and politics from both Japan and China. A common slogan from this period was "Taiwan belongs to the Taiwanese" (*Taiwan shi Taiwanren de Taiwan*), indicating that the Taiwanese deserved a say in how Taiwan was governed, and deserved to be educated and enlightened. Chang Yen-hsien contends that here can be found the roots of "Taiwanese subjectivity" (*Taiwan zhutiguan*).[25]

Although the Taiwanese movement's leaders were partly inspired by Chinese political developments after the May 4th Movement of 1919, the Taiwanese generally considered their struggle to be distinct. Historian Lee Hsiao-feng classifies the Taiwanese groups into four "factions," according to whether they (1) identified primarily with China or Taiwan, and (2) made revolutionary or reformist demands.[26] The revolutionary pro-China groups were in the minority, and most of their members eventually fled to the mainland to escape Japanese repression and join the Communist insurgency. Reformist pro-China groups made up the institutional mainstream, but were not necessarily the numerical majority.

Lee calls these groups the "wait for an opportunity faction" (*daijipai*), because they wanted to "wait and see" whether an opportunity would arise for unification with China and, if so, to seize it. The special characteristic of this group was that its members were wealthy and usually had investments in China—not unlike their successors among contemporary Taiwanese businesspeople.[27] The opportunity faction's control of the institutional mainstream was ensured by its ownership of Taiwanese newspapers. The faction also benefited from the fact that Tokyo pursued a policy of moderation toward China before 1927, encouraging cross-Strait trade and investment.

The opportunity faction did not necessarily identify with China culturally, even though its members did use China economically and as symbolic capital to defend Taiwanese dignity. They deployed the symbols of China's "5,000-year" history as a shield to deflect Japanese insults. What could backward Taiwan be in relation to this powerful Other—modern Japan—if not glorious ancient China? Taiwanese had yet to discover a distinctively indigenous tradition that could serve as a similar source of pride. Asserting a Chinese heritage at such junctures was psychologically gratifying and politically useful. Many Taiwanese deploying the China symbol in this way possessed an idealized image of China. Businessmen who traveled to the mainland had a clearer idea, but they restricted their movements to China's urban areas to benefit from special privileges under Japanese protection. Very few people in Taiwan identified with, or even particularly knew much about, the *real* China of the time. As explained below, once they confronted this China face to face in 1945, they were shocked to discover that all along they had been distinctively Taiwanese.[28]

The remaining two factions of the 1920s and 1930s movements were the revolutionary pro-Taiwan and reformist pro-Taiwan groups. They differed in the scope and scale of their political activities. The revolutionary groups organized peasant and other lower-class social movements, while the reformist groups concentrated on such endeavors as encouraging the development of Taiwanese themes in literature. The pro-Taiwan groups were in some ways antecedents of today's antiunification Taiwan Solidarity Union (TSU) and the more moderate DPP. During the imperial era, the pro-Taiwan groups lacked the wealth and social stature to contest Japanese rule, since higher-status Taiwanese supported it. Contemporaries in the TSU and DPP face a similar, if less severe, conundrum, with the United States replacing Japan in the position of (a much milder) imperial-like authority demanding moderation in the assertion of identity. But US influence over Taiwan is far less extensive and intensive than was Japanese imperial control. US democracy also allows Americans who might sympathize with Taiwanese aspirations to influence policy. For these reasons and others, Taiwanese subjectivity—repressed in the 1920s and 1930s, and later under the KMT—finally flowered in the 1980s and 1990s. Today it takes deep root.[29]

Forced Sinification Under KMT Dictatorship

If the KMT had taken over Taiwan in 1925 or 1930, it might have been able to use the pro-China sentiment present in some quarters to help legitimate its rule. But the KMT did not begin administering Taiwan until 1945, and in the interim—during the 1937–45 period—Japanese authorities implemented a thoroughgoing and successful "Japanization" (*huangminhua*, literally "citizen-of-the-emperor-ization") movement on Taiwan, producing a deep gulf between Taiwanese and Chinese.

At the same time Chinese nationalism was crystallizing in the face of Japan's brutal invasion and occupation, Taiwanese were taking Japanese surnames and competing with each other to master the Japanese language. Only 51 percent of Taiwanese "understood" Japanese in 1940, but by 1943, 80 percent "understood" the language. In 1942, 425,921 Taiwanese males volunteered for Japanese military service, about 14 percent of the eligible male population. By the end of the war, 207,183 Taiwanese had served in the military in some capacity, and 30,304 lost their lives—fully 0.5 percent of the population.[30] Much of this participation was coerced, but not all of it; and even forced participation had the effect of socializing Taiwanese into a significantly different historical experience from that of Chinese people. Taiwanese entered the postwar period with a profoundly underdeveloped Chinese national consciousness, quite in striking contrast to China itself, where the war's ferocity had mobilized and united people to a degree they had never experienced before.

The new Taiwanese historians are in agreement that despite these diametrically diverging experiences, Taiwanese generally welcomed the KMT soldiers and officials who arrived to take Japan's surrender in October 1945. Weary of war and weary of deprivation, most Taiwanese appeared willing to make the effort to redefine themselves as Chinese, in line with KMT demands. The KMT and the China for which it stood certainly seemed to be special entities. They claimed credit for defeating powerful Japan, Taiwan's overlord and most significant Other for the previous fifty years. How could the Taiwanese fail to admire and respect the KMT and China, especially given the turbulence of the times and the lack of a viable alternative?

But the honeymoon period ended almost immediately as KMT corruption, arrogance, and incompetence alienated the Taiwanese.[31] Chiang K'ai-shek had been forced to send his least educated and most undisciplined troops to Taiwan so that superior forces could be kept on the mainland to fight Mao's Communists. Cultural conflicts developed. As related by Peng Ming-min, the dean of Taiwan's democracy and independence activists:

> In the dog-eat-dog confusion of Chinese life during the war years, these men [Chiang's soldiers and officials] had survived and reached their present positions largely through trickery, cheating, and double-talk, often the only means of survival in the Chinese cities from which they came. To them we were country bumpkins and fair game. . . . The continental Chinese have traditionally looked upon the island of Formosa [Taiwan] as a barbarous dependency. Addressing a large gathering of students soon after he arrived, the new Commissioner of Education said so, with blunt discourtesy, and this provoked an angry protest. On the other hand, Formosans laughed openly and jeered at newcomers who showed so often that they were unfamiliar with modern equipment and modern organization.[32]

Up to one million Republican Chinese migrated to Taiwan between 1945 and 1952. According to Chang Yen-hsien, they propagated with a single voice the notion that Taiwan's six million people had been mentally "enslaved" (*nuhua*) by the Japanese, convinced to deny the "fact" that that were essentially Chinese. Mainlanders also charged that Taiwanese behaved obsequiously in the face of colonialism, especially during the Japanization movement.[33] They became incensed when Taiwanese shopkeepers would shout Japanese-language words of welcome at people entering stores and restaurants, bowing in Japanese-style clothes. They hated to hear the clicks of women's *geta* shoes on the streets.[34]

The KMT soon embarked upon a full-scale Sinification program by implementing in schools and other public places—anywhere Taiwanese were likely to encounter symbols—"education" in Sun Yat-sen's Three People's Principles, the spirit of the great Chinese nation (as forged, to an important degree, during the War of Resistance against Japan), and the Mandarin language, which the vast majority of Taiwanese could not speak. Names of roads, parks, and other public spaces were changed to such important KMT symbols and slogans as "Zhongshan," "Jianguo," "Minsheng," and "Xinhai."[35] Japanese-language newspapers were banned in October 1946 with the effect of rendering educated Taiwanese publicly mute. "The result was to make Taiwanese people feel the presence of Chinese culture and the KMT at all times and places." It was nothing less than a comprehensive remaking of the symbolic environment for the purpose of realizing *Da Zhongguo Minzuzhuyi*, the "great China nationalism" that cast Taiwanese into an insignificant, subordinate role.[36]

Some suggest that Chinese contempt toward Taiwanese was motivated by jealousy. Taiwan had prospered under Japanese rule, and even though its economy had been devastated by World War II, it was still significantly wealthier, more orderly, and more efficiently administered than almost anyplace in China. As early as 1911, Liang Qichao acknowledged on a visit to Taiwan that the Japanese were doing a remarkably good job developing the island. In February 1947, the Shanghai *Ta Kung Pao* praised Taiwan for its nascent modernization.[37]

But most Chinese found it exceedingly difficult to credit Japan or the Taiwanese for Taiwan's relative prosperity. In later years, they would foster the myth that the KMT was responsible for Taiwan's postwar "economic miracle." Contemporary Taiwanese nationalists see this myth as clear evidence of Chinese efforts to deny Taiwanese subjectivity and agency in their own development. They find it particularly ironic and galling in light of the fact that the Chinese who arrived in the first few waves of migration between 1945 and 1947 were actually (to the Taiwanese) extremely unimpressive bureaucrats and poor and unkempt soldiers who spit and blew nasal mucous on the street, broke line, ran red lights, stole bicycles, and even invaded homes—none of which, contemporary Taiwanese insisted, had ever been a problem under the Japanese.[38] Not only were the Mainlanders arriving in the first few waves unpleasant people, but they were also going to *rule* us, Taiwanese realized. This appalling situation prompted some to resort to gallows humor to attempt to take control of the situation psychologically. "The dogs have left us but the pigs have arrived," they joked among themselves, the dogs being the Japanese and the pigs the Chinese. Later Taiwanese nationalists would consider the expression of such resistance to KMT ideological hegemony (and to earlier Japanese hegemony) important events in the development of Taiwanese subjectivity, though it did the Taiwanese little tangible good at the time.[39]

Sinification also entailed attacking Taiwanese culture on the literature and arts front. Historian Lin Jui-ming finds that a distinctive Taiwanese literature had emerged as early as the 1920s and 1930s as part of the general formation of a Taiwanese collective consciousness.[40] Following retrocession, the Nationalist Chinese (not only KMT propagandists, but even liberal intellectuals) redefined Taiwanese literature mockingly as at best "Chinese literature in Taiwan" (*zai Taiwan de Zhongguo wenxue*), or at worst "frontier literature" reflecting the slavish and backward mentality of a people who had succumbed to Japanese imperialism and intermarried with island aboriginals. Given such backwardness, it was essential for Taiwanese writers to transform themselves so that they could become like the universally awakened and enlightened Mainlanders. At a minimum, they should immediately stop writing in the Japanese language. More proactively, they should start addressing themes and topics exploring "the problems of China as a whole," as developed by Mainland literati after the May 4th Movement of 1919. Beginning in the 1950s, with the descent into White Terror, this policy line meant that Taiwanese writers should heroically support anti-Communism and resist "Russian influence on the mainland."

By the 1960s, a new generation of Taiwanese writers rediscovered the original 1920s–1930s literature and developed the concept that Taiwanese literature had always been in essence "tragic" (*beiqing*) in tone. Chinese critics argued that this tragic mindset reflected Taiwanese society's slavishness to the Japanese and passivity in the face of oppression. But Ch'en Wan-i of Ch'ing-hua University found that the generation of the 1960s refashioned "tragic" as a subtle form of resistance—akin to gallows humor.[41] Over the next two decades, and especially after the "nativist literature" (*xiangtu wenxue*) movement of the 1970s began, Taiwanese writers developed the tragic theme and established the notion that Taiwanese literature is essentially a literature of resistance: resistance to both imperialism (Japan) and feudalism (China). In associating feudalism with China, they were implicitly identifying much of what they denigrated culturally to be coterminous with the KMT and Mainlanders. As early as the 1920s, the Japanese had explicitly taught Taiwanese to despise in themselves a list of negative traits that the Japanese called *Shina* (Chinese: *Zhina*), a derogatory term used to connote Chinese backwardness and disorder. The Taiwanese replaced "feudal" for *Shina* and deployed the term strategically to turn the tables on Mainlander intellectuals who had defined *them* as "backward."

This move undermined the possibility of later imagining anything good about a political association with the PRC, or a fusion of Taiwanese and Chinese identities. Some historians believe that any possibility of such a fusion was lost forever as a result of the tense encounters between Mainlanders and Taiwanese in the years immediately following retrocession. Most significant was the brutal slaughter and repression of the 1947 February 28th incident and aftermath, which Taiwanese historians discuss extensively.[42] But tensions flared in every type of encounter, including in literature and the arts—caused usually, the historians assert, by Mainlander arrogance and dismissal of Taiwanese subjectivity.

Ch'iu K'un-liang, ex-director of the Institute for Theatrical Arts, writes about the tensions that developed in theater, an especially important medium in the initial postwar period because Taiwan did not yet have television and films were still scarce.[43] An indigenous Taiwanese theater "with a profound popular basis" had emerged in the 1920s. After retrocession, some Taiwanese playwrights hoped to cooperate with refugee Mainlander playwrights in projects that would contribute to the creation of a fused new identity. The problem was that Mainlander playwrights denied the Taiwanese even a semblance of equality on the stage. Soon, in fact, Mainlanders drove the Taiwanese almost entirely out of the life of the theater, not only on stage but even as critics and commentators. Their chief tool: enforced use of Mandarin. Use of Japanese on stage was outlawed with its use in other public places in October 1946. Soon afterward, Mainlanders sought to ban the use of Taiwanese.[44] One KMT cultural commissar asserted in the September 21, 1946, *New Taiwan Life* newspaper (*Taiwan xinsheng bao*) that "if we were really to use local dialects in staging plays, that would suggest a complete misunderstanding of the meaning of plays. . . . Anyone who understands theater will recognize the truth of this statement."[45] The Taiwanese language was only a local dialect, reflecting Taiwan's peripheral status and lack of subjectivity. Since the function of plays was to glorify the Chinese nation, plays staged in Taiwanese would be absurd.

In subsequent years, under the influence of more liberal Mainlanders—such as those associated with the *Free China Fortnightly* (*Ziyou Zhongguo*)—the KMT reformed cultural policy to reduce Taiwanese alienation. Chang Yen-hsien explains how the change was reflected in history-writing, which continued to deny the Taiwanese subjectivity or autonomous agency in the world of nation-states, but did stop depicting them as slaves. In *An Outline of Taiwan's History* (*Taiwan shishi gaishuo*), Academia Sinica historian Kuo T'ing-i portrayed the Taiwanese as exemplifying the spirit of resistance of the great Chinese people, from Ming loyalist Zheng Chenggong through the War of Resistance Against Japan.[46]

But Sinocentrism continued to be the dominant theme and reached its zenith in November 1966, with the KMT's launching of a Chinese Culture Renaissance Movement (*Zhonghua wenhua fuxing yundong*), Chiang Kai-shek's answer to Mao's Great Proletarian Cultural Revolution. The Renaissance Movement depicted Sun Yat-sen and Chiang as the latest incarnations of a brilliant Chinese spirit going back to the semimythical sage kings Yao, Shun, and Yu. Chinese culture was humankind's greatest accomplishment, while Taiwanese "provincial" culture was vulgar and low. Because of the propaganda blitz that accompanied the Renaissance Movement—including revision of school textbooks—"the Taiwanese people did not have confidence in their own culture" at the time.[47] They were not yet in a position to cultivate Taiwanese subjectivity or to pursue democratization.

The KMT's Explanation of Taiwan's Democratization

The KMT showed no intention of democratizing until the 1980s. It repressed the Mainlander-based "Free China" liberalization movement of 1957–60 and imprisoned its leader, Lei Chen, for eleven years.[48] Nevertheless, interviews of KMT officials in 1999 and 2002 revealed a strong disinclination to accept the Chang Yen-hsien thesis that Taiwan's democratization resulted from the assertion of Taiwanese subjectivity.[49] The officials argued that eventual democratization was inherent in the ROC's political development path as laid down by Sun Yat-sen in the 1920s and faithfully implemented by Chiang K'ai-shek and his son Chiang Ching-kuo (r. 1975–88) in later decades. They contended that unless one adopts the cynical view that Sun's *Three People's Principles* and Chiang K'ai-shek's various works and utterances were designed to hoodwink a populace and disguise a dictatorship, they should be taken seriously. Whereas CCP leaders have consistently vowed that they will *never* allow the PRC polity to evolve (peacefully or otherwise) into a "Western-style" democracy, neither Sun, Chiang K'ai-shek, nor Chiang Ching-kuo, ever said such things. In fact, they said quite the opposite, and in the process, the KMT officials insisted, planted seeds deep into the collective identity of the ROC on Taiwan that eventually flowered into democracy.

In a typical passage from the *Three People's Principles*, Sun Yat-sen wrote (in 1924) that

after China secures a powerful government, we must not be afraid, as Western peoples are, that the government will become too strong and out of control, because our plan for the reconstructed state includes the division of political power of the whole state into two parts. The political power will be given into the hands of the people, who will have a full degree of sovereignty and will be able to control directly the affairs of state; this political power is popular sovereignty. The other power is government, and we will put that entirely in the government's organs, which will be powerful and will manage all the nation's business. . . . If the people have a full measure of popular sovereignty and the methods for exercising popular control over the government are worked out, we need not fear that the government will become too powerful and uncontrollable.[50]

Eventually, as a KMT official explained, the Sun system was expected to evolve into a democracy:

There were three phases to implementing the Three People's Principles: the phase of military dictatorship, the phase of tutelary democracy, and then the democratic period. Sun never thought that in his lifetime China could pass beyond the military dictatorship phase. It's hard to know what Chiang K'ai-shek might have thought in 1925 [the year Sun died], but the circumstances never allowed him to try to implement democracy, even assuming he wanted to, because the government was always being threatened by Communists and the Japanese. In fact, we never even had total control over the country. After the move to Taiwan, the reason Chiang maintained a dictatorship was because the ROC was always in danger. . . . Maybe he didn't really believe in Sun's theories, but even so, the government's legitimacy was closely connected to them so he could never renounce them.[51]

Chiang declared in a commentary on Sun's works that "in our endeavor to build up China as an independent, free, and democratic country in the current anti-Communist, anti-Russian struggle, we must have plans and proceed step by step in order to reconstruct a free and secure Chinese society to serve as the foundation for the independent democratic country that will emerge in the course of change."[52] Chiang seemed never to pass up a public opportunity to contrast "Free China" with "Communist China." These terms saturated his annual New Year's and other holiday speeches. They filled the newspapers and relevant school textbooks. There was in fact limited "freedom" in Chiang's Taiwan in the form of tightly controlled local assembly elections and elections in schools and universities. These probably did create a mild expectation that Taiwan would some day democratize.

But KMT officials reserved most of the credit for Taiwan's democratization not for Sun or for Chiang K'ai-shek, but for Chiang Ching-kuo, who in many ways is a hero for liberal Mainlanders. In the estimation of one KMT historian, Chiang Ching-kuo probably did believe in Sun's Three People's Principles and thought he was implementing them in the 1970s and 1980s with his decisions to relax media controls and eventually allow the legal establishment of opposition parties and lift martial law. Chiang Ching-kuo probably thought that Taiwan was ready to enter the tutelary stage in 1975 and then advance to full democracy after 1987. At a minimum, liberalizing in the name of Sun's ideology legitimized reforms in the eyes of KMT conservatives. A reform-minded political entrepreneur such as Chiang Ching-kuo could manipulate Sun-ism to neutralize conservative opposition.[53]

Taiwanese nationalists agree that KMT ideology and rhetoric played a role in the democratization movement by providing them with symbolic resources to use in "hoisting the KMT on its own petard."[54] But they reject the notion that it took Chinese leadership to democratize Taiwan. Democratization resulted from the assertion of Taiwanese subjectivity in the face of unremitting KMT and broader Mainlander repression. "We had nothing against Sun," a former activist reported. "The problem was that they refused to implement him."[55] "We always used the Three People's Principles as a tool to attack the KMT," said another, "because it was embarrassing for them and effective for us."[56] A third activist contended that Chiang Ching-kuo "was produced by the democratization movement, not the other way around. He was forced by domestic developments and global trends finally to allow the DPP to form legally and to lift martial law. He did not have a decisive personality; he was enacted, not an actor. But at least he was smart enough to recognize reality and not block it like a stubborn old dictator."[57]

Chiang K'ai-shek effectively ruled out democratization of a Chinese ROC with his crushing of the "Free China" reform movement in 1960, in which liberal Mainlanders critical of the KMT in the *Free China Fortnightly* tried to ally with native Taiwanese leaders at the subprovincial level.[58] But most of the leaders of the *dangwai* ("outside the [KMT] party") resistance movement in the late 1970s and early 1980s did first encounter the symbols of democracy at school in KMT textbooks. They later began developing their political awareness by reading such liberal Mainlander magazines as *Free China Fortnightly* and then *Daxue Zazhi* and *Wenxing*.[59] Liberal Mainlanders who arrived after 1945 changed Taiwan in a myriad subtle ways, making numerous contributions to democratization. Many Mainlander migrants were scientists, engineers, artists, and writers. They helped to structure the mindsets of Taiwanese nationalists, giving their thought a liberal cast. Although Taiwanese thus played the primary role in democratization, the role liberal Mainlanders played was also crucial. Most of them had abandoned the extremes of Sinocentrism by the 1970s at the latest.

International Shocks and the Intrusion of Global Society

Although the ROC on Taiwan held China's seat as a permanent member of the UN Security Council through 1971, by 1960, very few on Taiwan harbored the illusion that the KMT would ever restore its rule on the mainland. American diplomatic support combined with massive CCP policy mistakes and expressions of hostility toward the outside world to give Taiwan and the KMT a measure of security and prestige at this time. The KMT benefited from the support of most overseas Chinese, from Asia to North America—since there was little that these people found attractive in Mao's PRC. With Mao assaulting the Chinese heritage, the KMT came to represent a legitimate offshoot of the main development of Chinese history.

This quickly unraveled after Richard Nixon and Henry Kissinger took office in January 1969.[60] US–China rapprochement signaled that maintaining the fiction the KMT represented China was no longer tenable. In 1971, the PRC entered the United Nations. Chiang K'ai-shek then decided to withdraw the ROC's membership, asserting that there could be only one China in international society and that he was its president.[61] KMT policy thus presented an outdated Sinocentrism when international changes were rapidly transforming Taiwan into a peripheral actor in world affairs. Japan recognized the PRC in 1972. Other countries quickly followed suit. By the time the United States recognized the PRC in 1979, the KMT was isolated internationally and its domestic legitimacy was in tatters. The resulting cultural and political crisis on Taiwan eventually found resolution in democratization and de-Sinification. Surviving as an autonomous entity required that the ROC become a "model country" by the standards of liberal-rational global culture. Large historical forces were at work.[62]

Chiang's decision atavistically to assert an authoritarian Sinocentric pride at the United Nations in 1971 alienated liberal Mainlanders, who were at the forefront of those arguing that unprecedented creativity was required to keep Taiwan from being absorbed by the PRC. Upon his release from eleven years in prison in July 1971, *Free China Fortnightly* editor Lei Chen called for a "two countries, two governments" (*liang guo liang fu*) solution to the looming UN contest. This would also allow hope for Taiwan's eventual democratization. After the KMT dismissed Lei's proposal and withdrew its membership, Lei suggested that Taiwan's name be changed from the Republic of China (*Zhonghua Minguo*) to the "Chinese Taiwan Democratic Republic" (*Zhonghua Taiwan Minzhuguo*).[63] This, Lei believed, would make it more difficult for the PRC to put forward a case justifying annexation. Lei opposed a "Taiwan Republic" (*Taiwan Gongheguo*) because he did not want Taiwan to be independent of cultural China.

The independence movement was at this time active abroad but ineffective inside Taiwan. The only partial exception was the Presbyterian Church (*Zhanglao Jiaohui*), which had been conveying not only Christianity but also modern liberal humanism into Taiwan since 1865. The Presbyterians supported *bentu* (native Taiwanese) causes, leading nonviolent resistance efforts against both the Japanese and the KMT. They encapsulated the fusion of liberal-rational global culture with Taiwanese identity that animates democratization and de-Sinification.

On December 17, 1971, risking Chiang K'ai-shek's wrath, the Presbyterians issued a statement demanding that the KMT not sell Taiwan out to China and that Taiwan more broadly pursue political reform to win back the respect of international society. The statement linked the ROC's international isolation directly to the KMT's failure to democratize. On August 16, 1977, echoing the rhetoric of US President Jimmy Carter, the Presbyterians issued a Human Rights Declaration (*renquan xuanyan*) asserting that Taiwan's future should be decided by the Taiwan people and that the end goal should be Taiwan's emergence as a "new and independent country."[64] The willingness of the Presbyterians to take risks such as these underscored the rapid decline of the KMT's prestige and reflected a new confidence on the part of *bentu* forces to give voice to their grievances. The Presbyterians joined the *dangwai* leaders in finding that action was necessary to avert the United States, China, and the KMT all conniving to turn Taiwanese into PRC citizens.

Outside of Taiwan, the independence movement was even more active. In 1964, Peng Ming-min, Hsieh C'ong-min, and Wei T'ing-ch'ao issued a Taiwan Self-Reliance Declaration (*Taiwan zijiu xuanyan*) asserting the existence of "one China, one Taiwan." Peng emerged as the most visible of the TIM (Taiwan independence movement) leaders. Historian Shih Ming, author of *The Taiwan People's 400-Year History* (*Taiwanren sibainian shi*), which first appeared in 1962, presided over formation of the Taiwan Independence Union (*Taiwan duli lianhehui*) in 1967. By the early 1970s, this group had dissolved and then re-formed with others into the World United Formosans for Independence, WUFI (*Taiwan duli jianguo lianmeng*).[65] Two years after Shih Ming produced his pathbreaking history, Wang Yu-te published in 1964 *Taiwan: A History of Struggle* (*Taiwan: kumen de lishi*).

Chang Yen-hsien finds that as the first works of history written from a Taiwanese perspective, these books were milestones in the development of Taiwanese subjectivity. They would not circulate openly inside Taiwan until the 1990s, and the overseas independence activists would not be allowed to return to the island until about the same time: the KMT blacklisted them. But "Taiwan people had only to go abroad to hear surreptitiously about the independence movement" and to read the histories. Overseas Taiwanese developed "an unconscious feeling of the movement's existence," especially in the United States, Canada, and Japan.[66] One activist who studied in the United States said that "there were only dozens of us involved at first, but within a decade or so we were hundreds. We were only loosely organized, though, and always had to be on the lookout for KMT spies."[67] The activists could not easily communicate with people in Taiwan because KMT censors read suspect people's letters and international long-distance telephone calls were expensive. As a result, independence activities inside Taiwan were limited.[68]

After 1965, as the KMT began concentrating on economic development, the number of overseas Taiwanese students and intellectuals increased.[69] Only a trickle of students went abroad in the 1950s and early 1960s, but after the decision to focus on export-oriented development, tens of thousands went.[70] Overseas students of the 1960s and 1970s were mostly engineers and natural scientists, professionals whose talents were needed for economic development. Social scientists and students of the humanities did not go abroad in large numbers until the 1980s. KMT leaders did not see such fields as contributing much of value to economic development. They were also worried that nonscientists would be more likely to become politically dangerous.

Yet engineers and natural scientists easily absorbed democratic values while abroad and reflected critically on Taiwan's predicament. Some made direct contact with independence activists. Others, including Mainlanders, developed an intense hostility to KMT authoritarianism, identifying with the freedoms of American, Canadian, and Japanese society. Many remained abroad after graduating, but some started returning to Taiwan in the mid- and late-1970s as international diplomatic shocks undermined the KMT's prestige.[71] Chiang K'ai-shek's death in March 1975 created an opportunity for moderate reform. Even more students then returned, bringing back alternative images of what a good polity might be like, reflecting new values absorbed in the centers of world society. Taiwan was in no position to try to establish an alternative global Center at this time, as the PRC tries to do today. Taiwan had become a diplomatic outcaste, and consequently much less secure. To Taiwanese intellectuals, as well as to liberal Mainlanders, the burning question became simply how to restore political legitimacy and a modicum of international security. The answer to most seemed obvious: democratization.[72]

Some overseas Taiwanese students became avid admirers of the Western and Japanese social movements of the 1960s and 1970s, an important source of the global *oppositional* culture. These movements convinced the Taiwanese students of the value of confronting traditional authority. Several informants who eventually became democracy activists and then politicians reported that they and their friends particularly admired the youth and hippie movements, despite themselves being too conservative and fearful of KMT spies to take part. Some Mainlanders saw in this activism echoes of China's own sociopolitical movements of the 1910s–1930s, in which their parents or grandparents might have participated. To all of these students, it was refreshing and inspiring to witness firsthand young Americans demanding *and winning* freedom from traditional restrictions and constraints.[73]

One individual who later became a leading activist and then a politician went to the United States not as a student but as a special guest of the US State Department for forty-five days in 1969. He first visited San Francisco and Berkeley to witness the hippie and antiwar movements and then transited through several cities in the South, meeting with activists in the civil rights movement. He was most impressed when, during a swing through Chicago, he stumbled across a church and civil rights rally led by a young Jesse Jackson. While in the Bay Area and then in Washington, the activist met with China specialists in academia and government to discuss what might happen should the United States derecognize Taiwan. He spent a brief period at the Library of Congress reading about international relations and, more importantly to him, the history of US social movements. The visit lasted only forty-five days, but the activist reported that "it completely opened my eyes to the ways we could change Taiwan."[74]

Even in the absence of direct contact with independence activists, some overseas Taiwanese began for the first time while abroad to reconceive their island as a nation-state—an occupied nation-state. As explained by a longtime activist and eventual DPP legislator:

We graduate students [in the US] were all reading about the decolonization of Asia and Africa in our comparative politics classes while the Vietnam War protests raged outside. It didn't take long for some of us to put two and two together and see that Taiwan had gone from being a Japanese colony to a Chinese colony. In many ways, Taiwan was a classic imperial outpost. For example, ethnicity determined how high up you could go in the government and the military and exactly what positions you could hold. We were being forced to speak a foreign language in public places [Mandarin instead of Taiwanese], especially at school. We were constantly indoctrinated with the notion that we were citizens of 'China,' and we weren't allowed to study Taiwan's history objectively.[75]

Ethnic Taiwanese could take active part in Taiwan's economic development, but could not at first share in the wealth of the giant state- and KMT-owned enterprises, since these were largely controlled by Mainlanders. Nor could they take up important political and cultural positions, influencing Taiwan's future development through normal channels.[76] They had been stymied by what one activist called an "informal apartheid system."[77] But their experiences abroad in the centers of world society were now helping them to imagine viable alternatives. Of course there were already complaints about the system inside Taiwan. As deputy premier, Chiang Ching-kuo began cautiously co-opting ethnic Taiwanese into the KMT power structure in the late 1960s. But there were still colonial-style *nomenklatura* lists in place (however hidden), limiting certain key positions to Mainlanders, well into the 1990s. The KMT was not going to end this system voluntarily.[78]

Despite their support for social movements, most of the overseas Taiwanese and Mainlander students staunchly opposed the anti-Vietnam War movement. They found little attractive about Communism during the height and then the aftermath of Mao's Cultural Revolution. They feared that an American military withdrawal from Southeast Asia would hold ominous implications for Taiwan. Taiwanese and liberal Mainlanders thus *selectively* absorbed from the oppositional global culture. They were not passively socialized. They did not simply "enact," as some of the world-polity theorists might have predicted;[79] instead they acted, *choosing* to pursue democratization and establishment of an independent country over more radical alternatives. Undoubtedly, the reality of Taiwan's successful market economy and export-led model of growth trumped Leninist-inspired theories that demonized the world market and promoted autarky, delinkage, and statization of the economy.

In 1960, a young Taiwanese Presbyterian went to study in Canada and in September of that year came across a copy of the Japanese-language magazine *Taiwan Youth* (*Taiwan qingnian*), a journal promoting Taiwanese political consciousness.[80] The Presbyterian—who before was a *Chinese* nationalist—was intrigued, and innocently sent to Japan for a subscription. Soon KMT spies on his Canadian campus intercepted a copy of the magazine, after which the Presbyterian was put on the blacklist and forbidden to return to Taiwan until 1995. Angry and perplexed, he became progressively more involved in independence activities. Sometime in the early 1970s, he became acquainted with Liberation Theology, itself an important stream of the global oppositional culture steeped in both Catholic Christianity and modern humanism. In a way that Thailand's Sulak Sivaraksa and other socially engaged Buddhists would recognize, the Presbyterian became convinced that the solution to Taiwan's transformation lay in convincing overseas students to return to Taiwan and work quietly at the community level to begin rebuilding society from the ground up. Eventually, this process would effect national and international-level political change.

After the Formosa Incident of December 1979 (see below), the Presbyterian became convinced, as did many others, that conditions were ripe for pushing full-steam for Taiwan's democratization. In the early 1980s, he systematized his work by running annual training programs abroad for young Taiwanese activists, rotating the sites among Toronto, San Francisco, and Tokyo. Each program included two weeks of intensive training sessions followed by two or more months of reflective study, discussion, and travel. The curriculum included social structural analysis (to impart a "sociological imagination"), analysis of specific sociopolitical problems, and training in street tactics: how to organize and conduct demonstrations, protests, and sit-ins. KMT spies knew about the programs and harassed anyone who attended and then returned; consequently, only about sixty people "graduated" the training camps before 1988. In the decade after 1988, as KMT conservatism crumbled, another 1,000 people received training, and they became critical to efforts to build and consolidate democracy.

A later DPP legislator, who attended a Toronto program in 1988, first became active in politics after the Formosa Incident.[81] Initially, this activist was a moderate, working under the tutelage of the more senior activist who had visited the United States for forty-five days in 1969. But the younger activist became a relative radical after the vicious murder of *dangwai* leader Lin I-hsiung's mother and two twin daughters (seven-years old) on February 28, 1980, while Lin was in prison for his role in the Formosa Incident. The young activist himself had daughters about the same age as Lin's. He felt a profound mixture of sadness, sympathy, anger, and fear at the brutality, especially the cruel mockery of those who would kill a Taiwanese leader's family on the anniversary of the February 28th incident. The young activist's anger increased as the KMT began saturating the media with a bogus explanation implicating variously "a thief" and/or "a bearded foreigner" for the killings, which occurred despite the secret police having Lin's house (where his mother and daughters were staying) under surveillance. The young activist then decided to join a study group of *dangwai* members committed to learning Taiwanese history. He experienced an identity-transformation, coming to identify himself as an independence activist. To his surprise and later embarrassment, he soon found himself generalizing that *all* Chinese people must be killers; and he became convinced that the only way to fight Chinese violence would be to use violence himself, with like-minded others.

The Presbyterian training camp pulled this activist back from the brink of what could have become a tragic career by teaching him, as he later explained, to think less in terms of destroying a hated enemy than in terms of constructing a better society, step by step, for weaker groups deserving support. The curriculum that summer (1988) consisted of only three courses: one on Mahatma Gandhi, one on Martin Luther King, and one on the 1960s US antiwar movement. The reading load was not particularly heavy but the discussion and case analysis were intense, teaching the activist to channel his anger down more effective pathways. Before the training course, he was leaning toward lashing out at Taiwan's authoritarian enemies with violence. Afterward, he understood that although elections were frequently shams in the KMT's Taiwan, nonelectoral forms of participation (which were therefore completely necessary) did not need violence. Demonstrations, civil disobedience, media campaigns, and other tactics would be much more effective.

Taiwan's democratization clearly owes a great deal to the influence of both the mainstream and oppositional global cultures. Thousands of Taiwanese and liberal Mainlander students who went abroad in the 1960s, 1970s, and beyond found themselves in the centers of world society at a time when the authoritarian KMT's very *definition* of the ROC had been mortally wounded by the leading powers' decision to switch recognition to the PRC. With Taiwan's identity uncertain, and its international security threatened, many students concluded that Taiwan must be remade as a new and independent country along the general lines of such impressive, powerful, and seemingly secure host countries as the United States, Canada, and Japan. These countries were not paragons of virtue, the students understood, as their social and political problems were often intractable and appalling. But people in these countries generally resolved their problems not by lying about them or denying they existed; rather, they discussed them openly and, through legal channels—including nonelectoral political participation—sought their remedy. For many Taiwanese students, seeing Americans bring Nixon down was particularly inspiring, because it demonstrated that even when things start going terribly wrong in a democracy, when liberal institutions are challenged to the core, the system can be restored in such a way that institutional legitimacy is preserved and in some ways even enhanced.[82]

Disseminating the New Vision: *Dangwai* Magazines

Calls for the ROC's democratization and Taiwanization dominated the pages of the *dangwai* magazines and journals that flourished in the years following Chiang K'ai-shek's death in March 1975. Readers numbered in the tens of thousands.[83] Their ranks grew even larger as thousands of overseas students began returning in significant numbers during the 1980s and then fanned out across the island to take up positions in colleges and high schools, the media, social service organizations, law firms, and businesses. Returned students became in many locales and workplaces "social opinion leaders" who disseminated both the values of liberal-rational global culture which they had absorbed abroad and images of a new and democratic Taiwanese nation.[84] For *dangwai* leaders in particular, the magazines created a community feeling and a sense of involvement in a shared and dangerous enterprise. "That's why we published them," said an editor of *Taiwan Zhenglun* (*Taiwan Political Review*), which first appeared in August 1975. "We had to stay united and focused on our cause, and we had to attract more people to support us." The task was not easy because vendors had to hide the magazines to keep them from being confiscated. People lucky or well connected enough to purchase them would share the magazines with others, since few Taiwanese had access to photocopiers or fax machines until well into the 1980s.[85]

Earlier magazines of a somewhat dissenting nature—including *Free China Fortnightly* (which eventually became extremely dissenting), *Wenxing*, and *Daxue Zazhi*—had all been published with explicit KMT approval, and had all been edited by Mainlanders. *Taiwan Political Review* was the first exclusively Taiwanese-edited magazine of political discussion and commentary, a point which Chang Yen-hsien argues is significant in the development of Taiwanese subjectivity. It demonstrated that Taiwanese intellectuals were finally emerging from the trauma of the February 28th Incident ready to play a leadership role.[86] In Chang's assessment, *Taiwan Political Review* challenged the KMT by (1) discussing Taiwan's future critically, in the light of deleterious international developments; (2) criticizing "great China consciousness" and taunting those who controlled only Taiwan but boasted they represented all of China; (3) calling for multiparty politics; (4) demanding freedom of the press; (5) arguing that candidates for election should be allowed to criticize "fundamental national policy," not just minutiae; and (6) demanding that martial law be lifted. Although it called for democratization, *Taiwan Political Review* did not demand Taiwan's independence from China. That would have led to prison sentences or worse.[87]

A *Taiwan Political Review* editor later explained that in selecting content, he and his associates would keep three goals in mind. First, they wanted to unite all elements of the scattered opposition, including disaffected Mainlanders. This was yet another reason the *Review*'s articles avoided the Taiwan independence issue. Second, they sought to attract young professionals (such as the budding attorney Chen Shui-bian) to their cause. They realized that most members of the general public accepted the KMT smears that painted *dangwai* members as rabble-rousers who flirted with Communism. The *Review* editors wanted to convince the new middle class that the opposition was moderate and could be trusted with political power. The more professionals they could attract, the more convincing they would become to broader members of the middle class. Their third goal was to undermine the KMT's legitimacy by simply reporting its shortcomings, to which could now be added (in the wake of Chiang K'ai-shek's death) the problem of disorganization and lack of focus. The KMT was split after mid-1975, disagreeing over the problems of leadership, localization, and international legitimacy.[88]

Taiwan Political Review was banned in December 1975, after only five issues. Successor magazines soon appeared, usually with some of the same personnel involved, always disappearing after only a few issues. The second genuinely landmark *dangwai* magazine was *Meilidao (Formosa)*, a more radical journal published monthly from August through December 1979.[89] As word leaked in December 1978 that the United States would switch recognition from the ROC to the PRC on January 1, the KMT—in panic, and probably looking for a good excuse anyway—suspended Legislative and National Assembly elections and imposed a state of emergency. The *dangwai* leaders had been coordinating their activities more effectively in the months leading up to the elections and had been expected to do well. The sudden cancellation infuriated the opposition camp, whose members vowed as a consequence to press the KMT even more tenaciously for reform. This required organization, but the *dangwai* were disallowed by law from forming a political party. They decided instead to begin publishing *Formosa* while at the same time establishing a string of "Formosa Magazine Service Centers" in a dozen or so cities and counties throughout Taiwan and in the United States, Canada, and Japan. The idea was to create an island-wide network of antihegemonic opinion and activism linked to centers of support for the Taiwanese cause (and liberal-rational global culture) abroad.[90] This was something very new for Taiwan, as disaggregated *dangwai* activists were joining together in a *movement* devoted to democratization—and to the assertion of a Taiwanese national identity.[91]

Few contributors to *Formosa* justified democratization in terms of the Chinese experience or Chinese history. To them, the Chinese experience was evidently irrelevant, except for a few formulaic asides. *Formosa* contributors justified reform by the experiences of Western countries, and they used Western civilization as a legitimate yardstick against which to measure contemporary Taiwan. For example, attorney You Ch'ing, who had studied law in West Germany and who would later become a DPP legislator, contributed an article to the second *Formosa* on the right of a people to resist illegitimate government.[92] Editors prefaced the main body of the article with a reference to Mencius on the justifiability of overthrowing tyranny (*nuezheng*), but You devoted his efforts entirely to explicating how the concept of the right to resist—"even using violence"—emerged in the European Middle Ages through the cross-fertilization of the Roman legal tradition, Christianity, and contemporary praxis. He then stressed how the right to resist had evolved, by the end of the eighteenth century, into a right to stage revolutions, and he noted with approval that the right to revolt was written into the revolutionary 1793 French Constitution as "sacred" and "the highest responsibility." You further explained how the experiences of Fascism and Communism confirmed for all the relevance of the right to rebel even under modern conditions. You did not argue explicitly that the Taiwanese people should rebel against the KMT. But he certainly implied that such a rebellion would be justified by the standards of liberal-rational global culture.

In the third *Formosa* issue, editors published under the name of the publishing house an article on the subject of political legitimacy, which drew entirely on Western political philosophy and legal history to discredit the KMT.[93] After declaring that the historical experience of all of humankind demonstrates that democracy is the sole path to freedom and prosperity, the article castigates the KMT for asserting that order, or rule by law, necessitates denial of democratic liberties. The article particularly criticizes the KMT (and its supportive intellectuals) for trumpeting conservative American political science theories which argued that countries in the process of economic development must be ruled by autocratic institutions or else they will dissolve into chaos. The article ridicules the KMT's unique corollary to this theory, which contended that the only form of democracy suitable for East Asia is one-party democracy, as alleged to be practiced in Japan (a democracy where opposition parties were actually voted into many offices).[94] The article continued that *there was nothing distinctive about Taiwanese people that required them to be ruled in ways any different from Westerners*, since democracy had been confirmed as the most reasonable, just, and effective political system in the *human* experience.

The *dangwai* leaders who wrote this article did not consider Taiwan to be essentially different from the West, and did not believe that they had to justify democratization on the basis of the Chinese experience or any distinctive Taiwanese experience. In fact, Taiwan did not yet have a clearly identifiable "essence" or *ti* whose core values might conflict with democracy. Still in the process of emerging from Chinese KMT (and, earlier, Japanese) dominance as a distinctive Subject in History, Taiwan was not yet associated with a set of practices and beliefs requiring reconciliation with liberal-rational global culture. The notion of Taiwan as Chinese had not taken sufficiently deep root in the 1950s and 1960s for it to survive the international shocks of the 1970s intact. *Formosa* contributors argued that the KMT had lost its right to rule Taiwan not because it violated the Chinese essence, but because it violated the constitutive norms of liberal-rational global culture.

Dissident Mainlanders agreed that there was no way to relegitimate the ROC government by reference to Chinese history. It could only be relegitimated by reference to liberal-rational global culture, whose socialization agents were, by the late 1970s and early 1980s, actively encouraging governance in accord with human rights. In a broad-ranging analytical discussion in *The China Tribune* (*Zhongguo Luntan*), an erudite Mainlander bimonthly which, like the *dangwai* magazines, also appeared after Chiang K'ai-shek's death, Wang Er-min acknowledged that "we must Westernize. Whether from a historical perspective or the realistic requirements of the nation, it can affirmatively be said that we must learn from the Western powers and must accept Westernization. Everything in the world today takes the West as the mainstream; in other words, the Western powers are the world's leaders."[95] Had the KMT continued to rule all of China, it might have been every bit as unlikely as the CCP to accept democratization. But the KMT on Taiwan suffered a massive collapse of legitimacy during the 1970s, followed by a dizzying increase in international insecurity, both of which necessitated yielding to *dangwai* demands to democratize. Even KMT intellectuals concluded that the ROC's only choice was to accept socialization to liberal-rational global culture.

But dissident Mainlanders did *not* believe Taiwan should establish a "new and independent country" (as the Presbyterians and the *dangwai* were insisting), separate from China. Even as generous and thoughtful a publication as *The China Tribune* editorialized against the Taiwan independence movement, branding it in March 1976 a tool of the "Mao Coms" (*Mao gong*) and a "stupid course" inviting "suicide."[96] Even liberal Mainlanders continued to insist that Taiwan's history was a part of China's history, and that Taiwan's role was subsidiary. In April 1976, *The China Tribune* published a "special report" by Ch'en Te-sheng on the "national spirit" of the Taiwanese people during the Japanese colonial period, claiming that "not a day passed when the Taiwanese people did not consider themselves to be Han [Chinese] and were keeping the motherland fondly in heart."[97] Yet many Taiwanese joined enthusiastically in the Japanization movement of the 1930s and served the Japanese Army that occupied China. The article also insisted that Chiang Wei-shui, the founder of the Taiwan Cultural Association in 1921, "was a completely loyal disciple" of Sun Yat-sen.[98] (He was probably influenced by him, but was not a "disciple.") Taiwanese wishing to give voice to their "local" identity could thus follow the good and loyal Chiang Wei-shui or could take the "stupid" and "suicidal" independence route.

Formosa magazine approached Taiwan's history differently. In the third issue, Liu Feng-sung declared that when people "assert vaguely that Taiwanese are Chinese, either they lack self-confidence [in their Taiwaneseness] or they speak with a chauvinistic sense of superiority or affliction (*youyuegan huo bingtai*)."[99] Liu wrote that when the Mainlanders arrived in 1945, they got along with the Taiwanese terribly, "leading to the February 28th Incident, whose scars are still fresh for those who experienced it personally—even 30 years later."[100] This was an extraordinary statement to appear in a Taiwanese magazine of the 1970s, when no other media outlet dared to mention the February 28th Incident, let alone use it explicitly to stimulate ethnic consciousness and opposition to Mainlander dominance. Liu was careful not to stir up too much ethnic hatred, however. He noted that "Mainlander friends" have now become "new Taiwanese" (*xin Taiwanren*, a slogan appropriated by Lee Teng-hui in the 1990s), and have a positive role to play in Taiwanese history.[101] That is, Mainlanders can play a role in *Taiwanese* history (shifting the locus of subjectivity). They could no longer impose "central plain consciousness." Liu added that "Taiwan's identification with China is a cultural identification, not a political identification." Taiwan must have a distinctive nation-state, based on its distinctive history and other unique characteristics.[102]

As *Formosa* magazine became increasingly critical and effective, right-wing vigilante groups began attacking its Service Centers. By late fall 1979, the environment had became dangerous for the *dangwai*. Nevertheless determined to maintain their pressure on the KMT, *Formosa* activists planned to hold a commemoration in the southern city of Kaohsiung on World Human Rights Day, December 10, 1979. This event would legitimate the *dangwai* movement through association with liberal-rational global culture. The KMT refused to grant a permit to demonstrate. Formosa activists and supporters nevertheless assembled in Kaohsiung's Rotary Park about 6:30 p.m. and began giving speeches. Soon police surrounded the gathering. After a tense couple of hours, they began spraying tear gas, precipitating a melee that lasted into the early morning hours. Up to 200 people (including police officers) were injured.

Three days later, the KMT used the "Formosa Incident" (sometimes "Kaohsiung Incident") as a pretext to order almost all the *dangwai* opposition leaders arrested; it also banned *Formosa* magazine.[103] The voice of the liberal Mainlander intellectual establishment, *The China Tribune*, approved of these arrests, arguing that although the *dangwai* had shown positive potential to become an effective opposition force, it went astray when it began publishing *Formosa*, which used distorted arguments to arouse people to violence. Those instigators of the Formosa Incident (referring to the *dangwai*, not the police) scheming to destabilize the government (*you panluan yitu*) must be dealt with sternly and according to law, the *Tribune* argued, while minor-role Incident participants should be treated more gently. The KMT should resume liberalization.[104]

Democratization and Taiwanese Subjectivity

The KMT portrayed the Formosa Incident activists as low-life thugs seeking Taiwan independence, with left-wing maniacs precipitating a riot and beating innocent police officers. But the KMT's media could not counter the impact of subsequent events. The first was the murder of Formosa Incident prisoner Lin Yi-hsiung's mother and daughters. The second was the spring 1980 Formosa Incident military trial, convicting the eight most important *dangwai* leaders (the "Kaohsiung Eight") of subversion and sentencing them to terms ranging from twelve years to life in prison. In April and May 1980, an additional thirty-three people who had taken part in the demonstrations were convicted in civil court and sentenced to prison terms ranging from two to four years. A third group of ten Presbyterians was convicted of helping to hide *dangwai* leader Shih Ming-teh (who feared execution); among members of this group, the general-secretary of the Presbyterian Church, Kao Chun-ming, was sentenced to seven years in prison, while the others received lighter terms.[105]

In the assessment of a later DPP legislator who, at the time of the Incident, lived safely in the United States, the Formosa Incident and its aftermath changed Taiwan politics fundamentally. The younger *dangwai* members who remained free to contest local elections secured the sympathy of voters who felt for those imprisoned. The KMT appeared repressive and quasi-alien (i.e., Chinese). Because of the new global movement, the KMT would have a hard time silencing these younger *dangwai* members or canceling local elections. With the US Congress and Jimmy Carter promoting human rights, "big brother was watching."[106] Politically conscious Americans were appalled by the KMT's conduct. They knew the United States, which now treated China almost as an ally against Brezhnev's Soviet Union, could threaten the KMT with a withdrawal of military and diplomatic support if it rejected political reform.

US pressure further gutted the KMT's legitimacy and prestige, especially in the eyes of the native Taiwanese population. The *dangwai* now "played the ethnicity card" in the struggle to end the KMT's dictatorship. Historian Huang Hsuan-fan counts more than 1,500 incidents of popular resistance in Taiwan between 1983 and 1987, many related to ethnicity and language issues.[107] In 1983, the united *dangwai* adopted as a slogan for the restored legislative elections "democracy and self-determination (*zijue*) to save Taiwan." In 1987, the new DPP (established in December 1986) adopted a platform whose first line read that "the future of Taiwan should be decided together by all Taiwan residents on the basis of equality and universality."[108] Also in 1987, DPP members established an Organization for Promoting the Consolation of the February 28th Incident, which sponsored seventeen commemorative activities throughout the island. These commemorations "openly introduced the Incident to the broader public, strengthening support for the political opposition by historicizing current ethnic tensions and antigovernment sentiment. The DPP used the issue to drive open the public sphere, and linked demands specific to the memory of the Incident . . . to the DPP's broader program for liberal democratization and Taiwanese independence."[109] Underground radio and cable television stations amplified the message and intensified pressure on the KMT. By the early 1990s, the underground stations could, in alliance with taxicab drivers, paralyze the city of Taipei in protest on a couple of hours' notice.[110]

KMT leader (and president) Chiang Ching-kuo finally legalized opposition political parties in December 1986 and lifted martial law in July

1987. He died in January 1988. His successor as president—the ethnically Taiwanese agricultural economist Lee Teng-hui—committed Taiwan to a course of full democratization. Lee sped Chiang's policy of KMT "Taiwanization" so that the party might survive in power in a democratic ecology. The DPP's Chen Shui-bian, who had helped defend the Kaohsiung Eight, was elected mayor of Taipei in 1994. In March 2000, the ethnically Taiwanese Chen was elected president of the ROC on Taiwan. This transfer of power to Taiwanese nationalist forces through a democratic process aroused the wrath of Mainlanders and the hostility of the CCP. In some ways, Taiwan's democratization seemed to contain the seeds of its own destruction.

THREATS TO THE CONSOLIDATION
OF TAIWANESE DEMOCRACY

On May 1st, 2002, the Chinese Communist Party's (CCP's) *China Daily* criticized Taiwanese president Chen Shui-bian:

Chen's audacity in ignoring both history and reality is outrageous. He has taken over from [former president] Lee Teng-hui as cheerleader of the de-Sinification movement in Taiwan. He masterminded "localized education," cultivation of a "sense of national identity," and desertion of the island's long self-claimed identity as the "Republic of China." He is behind attempts to change the names of the local currency units as well as the island's representative offices overseas, as well as attempts to bestow on a local dialect the status of a "national language" and moves to delete the word "China" from everywhere possible and to reduce coverage of China in school textbooks.... But his crusade is destined to fail. Taiwan and the mainland have grown too close to be separated.[1]

The CCP seeks to block the realization of Taiwanese subjectivity and in this way it threatens democracy. Expanding cross-Strait ties have not, contrary to expectations, reduced Chinese hostility, nor diluted Taiwanese identity. To the extent economic integration facilitates the rise of a class of interests in Taiwan who argue for appeasing the CCP, it endangers the subjectivity project. Already, Taiwanese nationalists *perceive* businesspeople with investments in China to be acting as vanguards of Taiwan's "Hongkongization," or transformation into a PRC Special Administrative Region (SAR).[2] For those who equate democratization with the achievement of Taiwanese subjectivity, the prospect of "reperipheralization" as a Chinese SAR is unacceptable.

But resistance is also dangerous, because the CCP threatens Taiwan with violence. Wang Zaixi of China's State Council warned in March 2002 that "advocating 'Taiwan independence' and separatism is absolutely a dead-end road" that will "lead to a war which will cause misery to Taiwan compatriots."[3] Senior leader Jiang Zemin reportedly set a deadline of 2020 for Taiwan to relinquish its nation-building ambitions and accept a fate as a SAR, or else face military assault.[4] Defense Minister Cao Gangchuan warned on August 1, 2004 (Army Day) that "if Taiwan independence forces continue to act willfully, the People's Liberation Army has the determination and capability to resolutely smash any 'Taiwan independence' splittist conspiracy.... China's sovereignty and territorial integrity is the supreme objective, and the will of 1.3 billion Chinese cannot be violated."[5]

To date, the constant stream of threats has had the effect not of deterring the Taiwanese nationalists but of hardening them in the conviction that any political association with China must be rejected. However, the threats do combine with domestic political developments to cause the nationalists to worry—and *increasingly* to resent the ignominy to which Taiwanese were subjected after Mainlanders took control of their island in the late 1940s. The nationalists thus express a determination to remake the ROC in ways that will exalt Taiwanese culture, even at the expense of alienating or frightening Mainlanders and antagonizing the CCP. In response, many Mainlanders charge that Taiwan is becoming less democratic as the DPP and its "Green" (Taiwanese nationalist) allies refuse to recognize their traditional privileges and take dangerous risks with China. Most Mainlanders do not want Taiwan to become a SAR, but do want it to remain "ROC Chinese."

After Chen Shui-bian's reelection as president in March 2004, Taiwan's "ethnic" conflict threatened increasingly to corrode the quality and legitimacy of its democracy.[6] One indicator was that KMT presidential candidate Lien Chan (born in China but of Taiwanese descent) and his running mate, People's First Party (PFP) chairman James Soong (a Mainlander), refused to acknowledge Chen's victory. PFP members openly accused Chen of staging his own assassination attempt the day before the election to elicit sympathy votes. Radio and television stations catering to "Blue" (KMT, PFP, and prounification New Party) audiences succeeded through repetition in constructing the assassination attempt as inherently suspicious and Chen's presidency as inherently illegitimate. One demoralizing result was a growing conviction that Taiwan's democratic institutions are flawed. Another was an increasing realization that the gulf between Mainlanders and Taiwanese might have become too wide to bridge.[7] Within the context of intensifying cross-Strait integration and the PRC's military threats, Taiwan faced multiple crises of democratic consolidation probably even more serious in the long term than Thaksin's challenges to Thai democracy.

Managing Cross-Strait Flows

Despite CCP bellicosity, cross-Strait economic and other forms of integration continue to deepen, presenting Taiwan's government with the problem of managing lucrative transborder exchanges with an avowed enemy while still upholding democratic principles. Greens, who worried about Taiwan's eventual absorption into China under "one country, two systems" (the formula used for Hong Kong), openly expressed doubts about the loyalty of Taiwanese doing business with China. They pointed to historical precedent: In the 1920s and 1930s, Taiwanese capitalists and landlords benefiting from Japanese rule had used their control of newspapers to restructure *bentu* (native Taiwanese) public discourse, making it both more supportive of the imperial system and of "peace and order in East Asia," which was a code phrase for close economic relations with China.[8]

By 1937, some 100,000 Taiwanese businesspeople and their families lived under Japanese protection in China and Hong Kong. These *sekimin* initially supported the Japanese war effort, but following the Cairo Declaration of 1943, "more Taiwanese became directly involved in Kuomintang politics" and "urged that Taiwan again be made a separate province of China."[9] Some contemporary Taiwanese nationalists point to *sekimin* as opportunists and worry that today's businesspeople will follow in their footsteps, selling Taiwan out. These Greens call for slowing down, stopping, or even reversing the cross-Strait integration process. Democracy, liberalism, and sheer economic necessity currently make this impossible, but some insist that beyond a certain point, economic benefit and the niceties of democratic praxis must be sacrificed. They insist that Taiwan's core interest lies in defending sovereignty and realizing subjecthood.

But abandoning democracy would violate the constitutive norms of liberal-rational global culture and thereby undermine Taiwan's security. It would destroy the multiethnic "new Taiwanese" identity laboriously forged by Taiwanese and liberal Mainlanders from the 1970s to the 1990s. Few people on Taiwan would support sacrificing the economy to establish a formally independent nation-state. Therefore, the Taiwanese nationalists face a huge dilemma.

Trade and Investment

Cross-Strait trade and investment ties first "took off" in the mid-1990s, even as a June 1995 Cornell University speech by President Lee Teng-hui led to deteriorating cross-Strait political relations. From 1995 to 2001,

Taiwan–China trade exceeded $163 billion, with Taiwan amassing a surplus of $109 billion. After both sides entered the World Trade Organization (WTO) at the end of 2001, annual trade volume ballooned, increasing from $32.3 billion in 2001 to $61.6 billion in 2004—during which time China surpassed the United States to become Taiwan's largest trading partner.[10] Each year, Taiwan racked up surpluses amounting to about 40 percent of total trade, with the result that, by 2003, the China trade accounted for 10 percent of Taiwan's total GDP.[11] At the same time, Taiwan's unemployment rate increased from 3.6 percent in the first quarter of 2001 to 5.1 percent in the first quarter of 2002.[12] By March 2005, it had slowly descended back to about 4.1 percent.[13] Far too many Taiwanese jobs were now dependent on the China trade for any democratic government seriously to consider trying to halt the integration process.

Trade with China increased Taiwanese jobs, but investment by Taiwanese firms in China increased domestic unemployment. From 1995 to 2001, Taiwan companies contracted to invest $31.2 billion in China in nearly 24,000 projects, utilizing $21.1 billion. Precisely as unemployment was soaring during 2001, Taiwanese capital was relocating to China, with $6.9 billion contracted and $3.1 billion utilized in 4,000 projects. These projects were becoming increasingly large-scale and capital-intensive, as elements of the information technology industry moved across the Strait.[14] The geographic targets for Taiwanese investment also expanded beyond traditional Fujian and Guangdong provinces to the Yangzi River valley and to such northern cities as Beijing, Tianjin, and Shenyang.[15]

Of the 1,910 Taiwanese companies that had invested abroad by the end of 2001, 74.7 percent had operations in the PRC, and an additional 9.1 percent had operations in Hong Kong that were often backward-linked to businesses in China.[16] Cross-Strait investment continued to increase rapidly, despite political tensions. Even during the first half of 2004, in the midst of the contentious presidential election campaign and aftermath, Taiwanese firms poured $3.39 billion into China, a 68.2 percent increase over the comparable period in 2003.[17]

These China-invested firms coalesced into a powerful interest group demanding removal of obstacles to even deeper cross-Strait integration, such as the "three direct links" of trade, transportation, and communication. They won an important victory in the summer of 2001, when the DPP agreed to end former president Lee's "go slow, be patient" policy—in place since September 1996—and replace it with a new "active opening, effective management" policy. The new policy removed a $50 million ceiling on any single investment and increased from $3 million to more than $20 million the size of projects that would be permitted without special government approval. A new body would screen projects valued at $20 million and more.[18] A securities analyst explained that "Taiwanese enterprises have no choice but to move to the mainland for survival."[19]

After Taiwan and China joined the WTO, Taipei announced (in January 2002) that it would increase the number of products legally importable from China from about 6,000 to 8,000. By 2006, all but 100 strategically sensitive items would be importable. The government would also consider allowing investments by Chinese individuals and institutions in Taiwan, including in such sensitive sectors as real estate.[20] The CCP pushed for more, with a leading figure in Taiwan policymaking reminding Taiwanese of the costs to be incurred if they delayed implementation of the WTO accords. Delays would only "affect the rational allocation of resources on both sides of the Strait, affect Taiwan enterprises' competitiveness in the world market, and affect the interests of Taiwan consumers who hope to benefit from the import of good and cheap mainland products."[21]

The CCP hoped to convince businesspeople to pressure the DPP into accepting Hongkongization. This frightened Taiwanese nationalists and increased tensions in domestic politics. An official with the Taiwan Solidarity Union (TSU) charged in 2002 that 10 percent of Taiwanese businesspeople invested in China already were acting as "mouthpieces" (*chuanshengtong*) for Beijing. He gave the example of Wang Yung-ch'ing, the Formosa Plastics mogul, who argued publicly that "we are all Chinese" and "there is only one China." The TSU official claimed that "most of the Taiwan companies are small- and medium-sized, and they support Taiwan quietly."[22] A few, though, were traitorous.

In May 2004, reacting to Chen Shui-bian's reelection, the PRC State Council's Taiwan Affairs Office suddenly announced that Taiwanese businesspeople supporting the independence movement would no longer be welcomed to invest in China. The office singled out Hsu Wen-lung, whose Chi Mei Group owned large-scale factories in South China producing ABS, a material used in consumer electronics and household appliances. *People's Daily* charged that "even though he benefited a lot from the vast market and low cost in the Chinese mainland, Hsu said that 'the Chinese Mainland is in a way like Taiwan's economic colony. Investment in the Chinese Mainland has nothing to do with love for Taiwan. It is just a way for enterprises to survive.'" The paper also complained that "in his daily life, Hsu does not speak Mandarin; instead he likes to talk with others in Taiwan local twang or Japanese."[23]

Beijing's hard-line approach angered the Taiwanese nationalists. "China has never changed its goals," a senior Chen adviser charged. "It alters tactics sometimes but never changes goals. Beijing can use businesspeople and even a few Taiwan politicians to try to divide and conquer, for example by cultivating people who will oppose the government just for the sake of opposing it. In fact, this is already happening, which is one reason the DPP government is facing so many difficulties."[24] The adviser asserted that "there are certainly a lot of Taiwanese businessmen out there in financial difficulty who would be very thankful for a loan from China and the chance to become Tung Chee-hwa the Second" (a reference to the Hong Kong SAR's unpopular first Chief Executive, thought beholden to Beijing for a loan in the 1980s).

Semiconductors

A debate between those taking an economistic view of cross-Strait integration and others worried about the implications for Taiwanese subjectivity heated up in the winter of 2002 over Taiwanese semiconductor manufacturers establishing foundries in China. The global recession of 2000–2001 gutted the information industry, leaving Taiwan's manufacturers operating at only about 70 percent of capacity. The Chinese market—expected to increase in size from $25 billion in 2002 to $41 billion in 2005—beckoned, as did the mainland's inexhaustible supply of inexpensive labor.[25] Taiwanese chip manufacturers lobbied the government to allow investment in eight-inch wafer production on the mainland. In March 2002, the Taipei Computer Association issued a position paper arguing that the question "should not be politicized; rather, it should be a pure matter of economics."[26] This and related economistic arguments stimulated the TSU—guided by Lee Teng-hui—to mobilize a demonstration. "What are they thinking about?" an incredulous Lee asked. He said that semiconductors were central to Taiwan's security and to its identity as an advanced, high-technology country.[27]

Following the election of thirteen of its leading members to the Legislative Yuan in December 2001, the TSU had become Taiwan's chief voice arguing for the complete realization of sovereignty even at the risk of damaging the economy. Integration was not purely an economic issue, TSU leaders insisted. It was a political issue threatening Taiwan's Hongkongization, which would extinguish both democracy and autonomy. All "normal" countries protect strategic industries. Lee Teng-hui observed that "both the US and Japan forbid their semiconductor companies to shift their manufacturing bases to China. It would be odd for Taiwan to be so generous."[28]

The DPP found itself walking a politically charged tightrope over the eight-inch wafer issue. On the one hand, its leaders were committed to preserving Taiwan's de facto independence and to deepening cultivation of a distinctive Taiwanese identity. On the other hand, they had no choice but to respect the demands of the large section of Taiwanese business (especially in the IT industry) benefiting from cross-Strait economic relations. For the DPP to turn its back on this powerful constituency would be political suicide. It would also be ideologically difficult to justify because the government was committed to free markets, open trade, and foreign investment.

The Ministry of Economic Affairs (MOEA) favored allowing the transfer of eight-inch wafer plants, while the Mainland Affairs Council (MAC) opposed it.[29] President Chen remained publicly noncommittal. But Vice President Annette Lu asserted that she opposed allowing the plants to move because they served as a "lifeline of Taiwan's industry."[30] Premier Yu Shyi-kun said the decision should be made taking *both* economic efficiency and national security in mind.[31] In the end, the MOEA won and announced in late April 2002 that transfer of eight-inch technology would be allowed on the condition that chipmakers replaced their eight-inch plants in Taiwan with plants producing the more advanced twelve-inch chips.[32] Perhaps pointedly to assert "effective management" alongside the seemingly inexorable trend of "active opening," the government also announced at this time that it would withdraw development fund investments from the Semiconductor Manufacturing International Corporation, run largely by Taiwanese computer specialists but based in Shanghai.[33] The DPP did not want to appear to be encouraging integration.

Meanwhile, groups favoring expanded cross-Strait ties maintained relentless pressure on the government. In the spring and summer of 2002, opposition legislators played up an April survey of 363 Taiwan-based firms that found the business community dissatisfied with the DPP's China policy. Only 9.4 percent of businesspeople accepted President Chen's assertion that agreeing to the 1992 consensus on "one China" would be tantamount to caving in to "one country, two systems." Two-thirds of the businesspeople said that "active opening, effective management" was simply "old wine in a new bottle."[34] The American Chamber of Commerce on Taiwan warned that the ROC would face "economic irrelevance" if it continued to "drag its feet on embracing economic integration." The DPP should "accept economic reality" and open the doors to "unrestricted investment and trade and the free movement of goods, services, and people" across the Strait.[35]

After the wafer decision, groups pushing for deepened integration shifted their focus to ending the ban on the "three direct links." Direct transportation between the port of Kaohsiung in southern Taiwan and the Chinese ports of Fuzhou and Xiamen had been inaugurated experimentally in April 1997. On the experiment's fifth anniversary, the ROC

Ministry of Transportation and Communications pronounced it a success, but said the volume of goods shipped was reaching the saturation point.[36] A simultaneous report issued on the "mini three links" between Kinmen and Fuzhou and Xiamen—opened in January 2001—indicated similar success: more than 15,000 passengers crossed in fifteen months.[37]

Now businesses with a mainland interest began increasing pressure to open up the "maxi" three links. Having to go through Hong Kong and other transshipment centers increased costs at a time when the global recession had made profit margins razor-thin. Opposition politicians reported that polls showed 80 percent of businesses wanted direct links.[38] The KMT and PFP jointly drafted legislation to create a framework for direct links. The legislation quickly cleared committee.[39] A KMT leader argued that "if Taiwan wants to become a world planning and logistics center, there will have to be harmony between the two sides of the Strait and Taiwan must face squarely the issue of direct transportation." He said that the government should address the issue "pragmatically"—that is, from an economistic point of view—by not insisting on negotiating with the PRC state to state.[40] In response, the *Taipei Times* warned that "national security" (including the security of democracy) should take precedence:

Between Taiwan and China, a fierce competitive relationship exists, both economically and militarily. It is futile and naïve to hope for a "win-win" cross-Strait situation. Undeniably, so far, Taiwan has suffered tremendous economic losses in this race. Once the "three direct links" are open, the scales will tip even more in China's favor. In other words, so long as China remains Taiwan's biggest threat, if the two sides open direct links, Taiwan's survival will become more precarious. No leader of this country should remove this safety net and cave in to pressure from special business interests.[41]

At a May 2002 conference in Kaohsiung, the MAC chairwoman agreed. She said that businesses "should not forget that Beijing works to annex Taiwan." People in the private sector are certainly free to take risks with China "but the government cannot risk our national security and the well-being of our people by trying to woo Beijing's friendship."[42] Earlier in the spring, an ROC National Security Council adviser had told an audience in Washington that Taiwan cannot have normal economic relations with China as long as the PRC seeks to "denationalize" the ROC.[43] But within a few weeks, Taipei started to yield. It accepted the face-saving solution of allowing NGOs (with close government links) to open negotiations on the three direct links.[44]

Talent

The flow of highly trained scientific and technical personnel across the Strait became another heated issue pitting Taiwanese of an economistic mindset against those trying to forestall Hongkongization. In January 2002, the BBC cited a report by the Taiwan Institute of Economic Research that up to 500,000 ROC citizens had relocated to China to work for the 50,000 or more Taiwanese firms there. In October 2003, an *Asia Times* article estimated that as many as 750,000 to 1 million Taiwanese might be living in China.[45] With the nature of investment changing from low-end manufacturing to advanced computer-component fabrication and assembly, the DPP worried Taiwan would suffer a brain drain. It mooted laws in April 2002 that would restrict the movement of specially trained personnel across the Strait. Such personnel "are part of the country's assets," Premier Yu proclaimed, and they should be "protected from being hired by mainland firms." Yu justified restrictions on freedom of movement, arguing that they were consistent with the norms of international society because advanced countries like the United States and Japan use similar restrictions.[46]

Accepting the need to legitimate government policy by reference to global norms, Academia Sinica president Lee Yuan-tseh—who held an honored position in global society as cowinner of the 1986 Nobel Prize in Chemistry—testified before a legislative committee that imposing controls on the movement of trained personnel would tarnish Taiwan's image as a liberal and democratic country.[47] A PFP legislator echoed these claims, contending that the policy would smear Taiwan's reputation internationally.[48] These rejoinders were significant because they went beyond economistic logic. Taiwan had benefited from an open, liberal economic system, and could not prosper from a closed system. If it failed to uphold the principles of openness, the United States and Japan, Taiwan's major allies, would react negatively. Taiwan must remain a good global citizen to stay secure.

"Being democratic" currently appears firmly central to the Taiwanese collective identity, but the stresses of integration could cause that to change. The DPP also floated a trial balloon in April 2002, testing responses to a policy that would register science and technology personnel so that they could be monitored and their movements possibly restricted. Officials of the National Science Council discussed this proposal at a meeting in the Hsinchu Science and Industrial Park on April 15th. Even while acknowledging the desirability of restricting some talented people's movements, the scientists and others present vehemently opposed registration and forced the government to back down.[49] The CCP joined this debate with a Xinhua editorial on April 25th:

Taiwan authorities and Taiwan independence elements cannot accept the fact that people across Taiwan have been increasingly enthusiastic about mainland China in recent years. Instead, they fiercely scold the people for "betraying" Taiwan....

They should be aware: Given the current economic globalization, the flow of professionals cannot be stopped. That Taiwan high-technology industries choose to shift to mainland China is an unavoidable choice under the current environment for international competition.... If Taiwan authorities really care for the people's well-being, they should immediately reverse from the path of hostility and unwiseness.[50]

The CCP appealed directly to the Taiwanese public to ignore the political and cultural implications of deepened integration. Their real interest—indeed, their only future—was to let integration run its course. "Listen to the PFP and KMT," the Xinhua commentary effectively exhorted. "The DPP and TSU will lead you to economic distress."

In the end, the DPP relented. The government had hoped to restrict the movement of people with expertise in semiconductor wafer research, design, and fabrication, as well as military aviation, shipbuilding, and anesthetics. But by the end of April it had decided to restrict the movement only of people with expertise in semiconductor wafer fabrication plant photolithography.[51] Even this limited restriction was unlikely to prove effective. A source in the semiconductor industry disclosed that "we can play around with the words used in professionals' profiles to avoid mentioning their familiarity with lithography."[52] Meanwhile, the MAC decided to start facilitating entry into Taiwan of PRC citizens with specialized expertise. This was apparently in response to the demands of multinationals whose operations span the Strait.[53] The integration inherent in globalization seemed a juggernaut.

Students

"People flows," by mid-2001, included some 3,300 Taiwan students matriculating in Chinese universities. By 2003, up to 15,000 younger students attended Chinese elementary, middle, and high schools.[54] The DPP responded by moving toward recognizing PRC schools' academic accreditation; by establishing a Taiwan-oriented school in Dongguan, Guangdong to teach overseas Taiwanese children, using an ROC curriculum; and by making use of the "mini three links" between Kinmen and Fujian to allow Taiwanese businessmen in China to send their children to school in a nearby place under ROC jurisdiction. It had taken seven years of lobbying by the 2,000-member Dongguan Taiwan Businesspersons Association before the Dongguan school finally secured permission from Guangdong's provincial government to begin offering instruction in September 2000. This school employed teachers and teaching materials from Taiwan. In Kinmen, an ROC Education Ministry official said that Taiwanese businesspeople working in Fujian would be able to send their children there to receive an education—"in their own motherland."[55] They would also be able to take the ferry to see the children on weekends. Integration increased the difficulties of raising Taiwanese children as Taiwanese.

Spouses

Cross-Strait marriages reached 210,000 by mid-2004. Almost 20 percent of all marriages registered in Taiwan included PRC females. Many joined old bachelors with young women. Some Taiwanese questioned the women's motives, even suggesting that some were spies.[56] Taiwanese consciousness, identity, and subjectivity seemed under siege.

Workers

Each day in 2001, the ROC government arrested on average a dozen PRC citizens working in Taiwan illegally, most in the sex trade. In 2004, a high-ranking police official estimated that there were 10,000 PRC citizens working illegally in Taiwan.[57] Typically, these migrants were smuggled across the Strait by Chinese criminal gangs, who also shipped drugs and weapons.[58] Sometimes Chinese criminals cooperated with Taiwanese criminals. Lawless parts of Fujian and Guangdong proved to be helpful hinterlands to which Taiwanese criminals could flee when their situation became precarious at home. From 1991 to 2001, ROC law enforcement authorities requested that their PRC counterparts assist in the apprehension of 335 suspects who had escaped to the mainland. But only eighty-seven had been caught as of December 2001.[59] The Taiwan police official interviewed in 2004 complained that Fujian and Guangdong police are both incompetent and often unwilling to cooperate because of political reasons.

Retired Officials

Integration sometimes threatened Taiwan's security more directly. The Control Yuan reported in late 2001 that as many as 200 of Taiwan's 414 recently retired military and intelligence officials violated restrictions on their travel to China.[60] The most infamous was Liu Kuan-chun, a former National Security Bureau cashier who allegedly embezzled $5.48 million and then fled to the mainland in September 2001. Liu's flight set in motion a chain of events that culminated in *Next* magazine's publication in March 2002 of revelations that former president Lee Teng-hui had maintained a secret fund of over $100 million to use for influencing foreign governments. The TSU charged that PFP Chairman James Soong had conspired with Liu to release this information to the public.[61] In any case, the *Next* saga pitted those favoring a more forceful assertion of Taiwanese national identity against those like Soong who argued that Taiwan is ultimately a part of China. The *Taipei Times* president stated the case for the Taiwanese nationalists:

The TSU believes that the PFP is a co-conspirator and is therefore also criminally liable. If this is so, then the PFP's hope was nothing less than to destroy former president Lee Teng-hui by exposing the secret accounts. Conduct of this nature would demonstrate that the PFP is not loyal to the ROC, its president, or its people. It is more like a propaganda machine for China in Taiwan.[62]

He warned that many senior military officers do not identify with Taiwan or respect President Chen. The military had been Mainlander dominated until 2000 and was still suffused with the ethos of the old KMT. How the military would respond to a Chinese attack was always a question. Now, Taiwanese nationalists worried about retired military officers taking secrets to China or exposing them in the media.

On March 20, 2002, police and investigators raided *Next* magazine's Taipei offices and confiscated thousands of copies of the offending issue. Investigators also searched the home of the journalist who wrote the explosive article. The Public Prosecutor's Office charged that *Next* was "endangering state security" as well as "the rights and security of foreign friends."[63] In response, *Next*, opposition politicians, and some foreign media outlets criticized the DPP for attacking press freedom. The DPP soon backed down, and President Chen reiterated Taiwan's commitment to freedom of speech. But some DPP legislators—one step ahead of the TSU—filed a complaint of "high treason" against PFP Chairman Soong. Calling itself the "anti-betrayal alliance," they asked the Public Prosecutor's Office to investigate whether Soong had violated Article 109 of the Criminal Code, which mandates a prison term of from one to seven years for anyone who "discloses or delivers a document, or any other form of secret information concerning national defense" to enemies of the ROC.[64] President Chen told a gathering of National Security Bureau officials on April 10, 2002 that "the achievement of democratization should not become a factor that decreases our loyalty to the country and . . . an excuse to neglect the government's intelligence system."[65] As everywhere, war and the threat of war created a hostile environment for protecting democratic liberties.

Water

A severe drought struck Taiwan during the winter and spring of 2002, increasing the general sense of vulnerability by raising the specter of having to import water from China. Some feared Taiwan becoming completely dependent on China for natural resources in a way similar to Hong Kong. Rainfall in the greater Taiwan region from November 2001 to April 2002 was only one-third the normal amount, drying up reservoirs first on rocky Kinmen and Matsu. Kinmen authorities contacted their counterparts in Fujian to inquire about importing water. A spokesman for Taiwan's prounification New Party called for the construction of a permanent water pipeline linking Kinmen to Fujian. The MAC hesitated to give its approval even for emergency imports. The chairwoman explained that "we must make sure there is a mechanism to ensure that Taiwan will not be held hostage on the water supply front."[66] *People's Daily* responded:

Although Fujian is also short of water, yet how can it pay no heed to the requests of the blood relations? Therefore, it has made appropriate preparations to deliver fresh water in its vicinity to quench the burning thirst of the Taiwan compatriots, whereas the Taiwan authorities are flaunting the banner of "human rights" to mislead the public and wangle votes, refusing to rescue the dying people at the moment of emergency, disregarding the Taiwan compatriots' rudimentary right to subsistence, ... and prating about the so-called security and guarantee. They are simply deceiving themselves as well as others.[67]

The water issue intersected with worries about economic dependence to increase the sense of vulnerability. Semiconductors require huge amounts of water to manufacture: up to 3,000 gallons prior to filtering to clean a single eight-inch wafer, and even more to clean twelve-inch wafers. Even with recycling, a single semiconductor factory consumes two to three million gallons of water per day. Industry insiders in Hsinchu warned that they would have faced a "critical problem" if the drought had continued beyond June 2002. They would have been unable to produce to capacity at precisely the point when the global recession was easing and orders were beginning to increase.[68] Fortunately for them the summer rains came and the government lifted restrictions on water use. But the industry insiders warned that in any future drought, they might well have to rely on China.

CCP "Sticks"

Beyond economic enticements, the CCP also uses sticks to discipline Taiwan when it disapproves of Taiwanese behavior. After the DPP's election as the largest party in the legislature in December 2001, Chinese officials intensified their ongoing harassment of mainland-based Taiwanese businesspeople. Taiwan's Straits Exchange Foundation (SEF) revealed in April 2002 that some seventy Taiwanese had been detained in Dongguan in recent years for "unclear reasons." After the elections, PRC authorities added to this harassment by rejecting, without explanation, 2,025 notarized documents that Taiwanese businesspeople presented in the course of conducting their normal affairs between December 2001 and April 2002. Taiwanese in sixteen provinces and cities were inconvenienced.[69] The message was that fair treatment of Taiwanese would be contingent on supporting parties and policies Beijing approved.

Businesspeople suspected of ardently supporting Taiwan's independence were specially harassed. The Deputy Director of the PRC's Taiwan Affairs Office warned straightforwardly in 2000 that Beijing would not allow Taiwanese businesspeople "to make money in mainland China while supporting Taiwan independence at home." During 2001, several Taiwanese corporations thought by the CCP to support independence reported being hounded in various ways, such as by being subjected to surprise account audits and fire safety inspections from which other firms were exempt.[70] In the run-up to the March 2004 presidential elections, Beijing arrested twenty-six Taiwanese "spies" (twenty-four in December 2003 and two more in February 2004), accusing them of helping to pinpoint the locations of Chinese missiles aimed at Taiwan. Some "spies" were paraded on television.[71]

The problem for China was that such attacks tended to backfire. After 2001, Taiwanese businesspeople began taking extra precautions, such as maintaining funds offshore in case PRC authorities decided to seize their assets. They also found it less easy to identify with the Chinese nation when, while living in China, they had to worry about being harassed. Some reported that the more exposure they had to China, the more deeply they identified with Taiwan.[72]

Rumors swirled in December 2001 that Beijing was pressuring Taiwanese businesspeople into joining the CCP. A DPP legislator charged in a parliamentary session that the CCP was "aggressively absorbing" Taiwanese businesspeople in an attempt to "sharpen united front work." The Minister of Economic Affairs acknowledged in response that a CCP branch had probably been set up in a Shenzhen company affiliated with Taiwan's Hon Hai Precision Industry Corporation. "That is not a good thing," he conceded, and he reminded the legislator that Taiwan's government "does not encourage" Taiwanese businesspeople to join the CCP. But so far only four Chinese employees of Hon Hai appeared to have joined; therefore, it was too early to draw dramatic conclusions from the reports and legislators should not exaggerate the threat.[73] Meanwhile, a CCP spokesman said that "it is ridiculous for some Taiwanese to make a fuss about this issue" and that "they are ignorant of the truth or are being malicious."[74]

De-Sinification as the Antidote to Creeping Hongkongization

Most of the outside world seems sanguine about Taiwan's economic integration with the PRC, regarding it as a blessing that could lead to permanent peace. Once the two sides' economies become firmly intertwined, neither will want to go to war, and they might even enter willingly into political integration. To most outsiders, Taiwanese are essentially Chinese. But to those Taiwanese nationalists concerned about realizing subjectivity, integration is a nightmare scenario. They fear that their project is too young and fragile to withstand the pressure. They call for steps to be taken to stiffen the Taiwanese people's resolve and dissuade them from identifying with China. Otherwise, they see little hope of realizing a Taiwanese future.

Economist Ch'en Po-chih, former chairman of the Economic Planning and Development Council, attempts to develop a convincing academic case for slowing or reversing integration in a contribution to Chang Yen-hsien's edited volume, *March to the 21st century*.[75] Ch'en argues that it would be naïve to view the China–Taiwan relationship purely from the standpoint of economics, because Chinese leaders "said a long time ago" that they wanted to solve the Taiwan problem by "using businesspeople to surround the government" (*yi shang wei zheng*) and "using citizens to pressure officials" (*yi min bi guan*). The only way to avoid the trap, Ch'en contends, is to slow the investment rush. He claims this would be perfectly feasible because firms can secure adequate profits elsewhere, especially in South and Southeast Asia. But even if costs there were higher, and a mainland presence necessary to secure access to the China market, helping Taiwanese businesses to make profits should not be the ROC government's primary goal. "It is not correct to argue that internal and external investment should be decided on the basis of individual firms' profits." Investment decisions have larger consequences. The government must take into account all the social costs and benefits of investment decisions to Taiwanese workers, upstream and downstream suppliers and consumers, and to the government itself, which depends heavily on large Taiwanese firms for tax revenue. The government must also take national security into account. "For the government to liberalize blindly is not an appropriate policy."[76]

In this way, Ch'en—as a respected economist—counters the economism that undergirds optimists' contention that integration will lead inexorably to a just peace. Yet business people continue to agitate for opening the three direct links, for loosening restrictions on manufacturing advanced computer components in China, and for loosening restrictions on talented Taiwanese engineers who want to go to work for Chinese firms.

President Chen aligned himself rhetorically with Lee Teng-hui's preferred "Go South" policy, which would divert China-bound investment to Southeast Asia; but in practice, the DPP continues to loosen restrictions on Taiwanese businesses in China and would allow NGOs to negotiate the three direct links.

Given deepened integration's seeming inevitability, Taiwanese nationalists began in 2002 to intensify efforts to cultivate the Taiwanese collective identity. They took their struggle to the media and to the streets. Lee Teng-hui was the most visible actor. Lee gave a highly publicized interview to *Open* magazine in July 2002, arguing that the primary problem facing Taiwan was not economic integration with China but the underdeveloped sense of "Taiwanese subjectivity" (*Taiwan zhuti de wenti*).[77] "Right now the most important thing is identity," Lee said, a "national consciousness." Developing subjectivity requires that people "identify with Taiwan's history, geography, and values." The task was too pressing to wait for glacially paced intellectual efforts. Lee was concerned that Taiwanese might lose their will to resist Chinese blandishments and pressures. "In 2008, Chinese nationalism will reach its pinnacle. The Three Gorges Dam will be completed, the highway connecting Nanjing to Chongqing will be finished, and Beijing will host the Olympic Games."[78] Awed by such glories, Taiwanese might find themselves attracted not only by the economic benefits that would come with subordination to China, but also by pride in associating with a new superpower. Such a development would end any hope of establishing Taiwanese subjectivity and sound the death knell for Taiwanese democracy. Therefore, before 2008, Taiwanese should be made acutely conscious of Chinese hostility and Taiwanese distinctiveness. Their self-confidence and morale should be raised.

To these ends, the TSU proposed "de-Sinification" of Taiwanese society. Beginning in January 2002, when the party's thirteen legislators assumed their seats, the TSU—in alliance with independence activists in civil society and more nationalist elements of the DPP—took a number of steps to communicate to China and to the world that Taiwan is not a part of China.

Promoting Public Use of the Word "Taiwan"

On May 11, 2002, an estimated 10,000 Taiwanese took to the streets of Taipei to advocate changing the name of the country to the "Republic of Taiwan." The march was organized by the Alliance to Campaign for Rectifying the Name of Taiwan, an umbrella group of more than seventy civil society organizations aligned with the TSU. An Alliance convener declared that the march's purpose was to "encourage the people of Taiwan to take pride in being Taiwanese and to identify Taiwan as their sole motherland."[79] Another convener said authorities should promote use of the word "Taiwan" first in government agencies and embassies abroad and later in the private sector.[80] The TSU chairman, who read a supportive statement by Lee Teng-hui (said to be ill), explained that the name change was necessary to promote a sense of Taiwan's national distinctiveness.[81] The march was to become an annual Mother's Day event, signifying that Taiwan is mother to the Taiwanese people. The May 2003 march had to be cancelled because of the SARS outbreak, but was rescheduled for September 2003 and attracted some 50,000 participants. An even larger event with a similar purpose was the February 28, 2004 "Hold Hands to Protect Taiwan" demonstration, in which an estimated 1.2 million people formed a human chain along the entire length of Taiwan's west coast. Their purpose was to express unity and resolve in the face of 500 or more Chinese missiles aimed at the island. Most of this event's organizers were the same as those who organized the "Rectify Taiwan's Name" demonstrations.[82]

De-Sinifying the Education Curriculum

From 1995 to 1997, a committee chaired by Nobel laureate and Academia Sinica president Lee Yuan-tseh approved a new high school history and social studies curriculum called "Knowing Taiwan" (*Renshi Taiwan*). The committee rejected the KMT's traditional "Great China chauvinism" and developed a new Taiwan-focused curriculum that, among other things, discussed the Japanese colonial period objectively and gave Aboriginals a larger role in Taiwan's history. The goal was to teach young Taiwanese to "establish themselves on Taiwan, have concern for the mainland, and open their eyes to the world" (*lizu Taiwan, xionghuai dalu, fangyan shijie*). The new textbooks described Taiwan's "ethnic pluralism" as producing a distinctive "Taiwanese consciousness," and noted how Taiwanese people repeatedly resisted authoritarian rule from abroad.[83]

The new textbooks were products of political compromises between Lee Teng-hui and the Mainlanders who still dominated ROC education in the 1990s. After Chen Shui-bian's election in 2000, Taiwanese nationalists decided that such compromises were no longer necessary. They began agitating for deeper change. During the first half of 2002, the TSU chairman repeatedly called on the DPP government to revise the new textbooks to eliminate passages suggesting that Taiwan might still be a part of China.[84] Before the December 2001 legislative elections, the DPP employed independent-minded psychology professor Ovid Tseng as Minister of Education. During his tenure, Tseng antagonized Lee Teng-hui and other Taiwanese nationalists by his reluctance to press de-Sinification in the classroom. Tseng also promoted the Hanyu Pinyin Mandarin translit- eration system instead of Taiwan's own Tongyong Pinyin system. Because Hanyu Pinyin is the system used in China, Lee and other Greens opposed its use in Taiwan, since that might imply Taiwan's subjugation. Imme- diately after the December 2001 legislative elections made the DPP the largest party, Tseng's opponents demanded his ouster. This prompted the CCP to issue criticism in *Ta Kung Pao*:

Pro-independence organizations are anxious to...thoroughly instill the Taiwan independence concept into school textbooks. They entertain the wishful thinking of breaking the umbilical cord relationship between Taiwan and the motherland and creating public opinion in preparation for the founding of "Taiwan's state- hood." ... The Chen Shui-bian administration is propagating the tricks of "de- Sinification," engaging in maneuvers promoting Taiwan's cultural independence, and inculcating the younger generation with the Taiwan independence concept. Its intentions are sinister indeed![85]

Chen relieved Tseng of his duties as Education Minister in January 2002, replacing him with another former psychology professor (and social activist), Huang Jung-tsun. Huang announced in July that Taiwan would adopt the Tongyong Pinyin system and that classroom curricula would be reviewed for possible future revisions.[86]

Proposing That Only Taiwan-Born Citizens Be Eligible for Election as President

Although this initiative seemed to be aimed at evicting powerful oppo- sition figures such as James Soong, Lien Chan, and Ma Ying-jeou from presidential politics, TSU officials claimed in an interview that actually they were thinking ahead to when younger Mainlanders might migrate to Taiwan, swamping the island demographically and then electing only their own kind as leaders.[87] Taiwanese subjectivity would clearly be compro- mised in such a scenario. But the TSU proposal violated the Constitution. The Chen administration distanced itself from the proposal on precisely these grounds and for trampling on the rights of a class of citizens.[88]

Although the TSU held only thirteen of 225 seats in parliament (and lost two in 2004), Chinese policymakers regularly vilified the party and its spiritual leader, Lee Teng-hui. In one April 2002 blast, the official Xinhua News Agency declared:

On the one hand, on the pretext of localization, the TSU has stepped up its cam- paign aimed at gradual Taiwan independence, with unreserved efforts in this re- gard, coming up with a new move on almost a daily basis—with an eye to sowing

discord among different groups of people and on sustaining and escalating political wranglings and conflicts. On the other hand, with a blind eye to the Taiwan
people's demand for revitalizing the economy and improving their livelihood, the
TSU has also been seeking to block economic and trade exchanges between the
two shores.

Indeed, the TSU's frenzied clamors for Taiwan independence—coupled with its
relentless pursuit of turbulence and intranquility in Taiwan society in the name of
"love for Taiwan"—are smothering Taiwan's future, including the Taiwan people's
wishes. In fact, what they are doing is aimed at murdering Taiwan. As things are
set to turn out contrary to its wishes, the TSU is bound to be cast aside by the
entire Chinese people, including Taiwan compatriots.[89]

Such commentary suggested that the CCP was worried the TSU voiced
sentiments that most people in Taiwan shared but were too cautious to
articulate. The TSU's interpenetration with an increasingly rich and vibrant civil society suggested a dynamization of Taiwanese subjectivity.
The *Taipei Times* contended in its coverage of the first "Rectify the Name
of Taiwan" march that the large turnout reflected increasingly wide acceptance of the TSU's agenda. Prior to May 2002, the largest demonstrations
in Taipei during the Chen presidency had numbered only 5,000. Issues
such as environmental protection and unemployment failed to muster
more than half of the 10,000 who turned out for the "Rectify the Name
of Taiwan" march, which itself was a minor fraction of the 1.2 million
who assembled in February 2004 for the "Hold Hands to Protect Taiwan"
event. A senior advisor to the National Security Council argued that the
large turnouts indicated mainstream Taiwanese society increasingly considered Taiwan and China to be two separate entities and that "Taiwan
does not accept 'one country, two systems.' "[90] The search for subjectivity
had become widespread and deeply rooted.

Radical De-Sinification

To some Taiwanese nationalists, mass demonstrations and parliamentary
maneuvers are insufficient for achieving subjectivity. A literature professor, Ch'iu Kwei-fen, argues that the "first and most important task" is
nothing less than "to recast (*chongsu*) the culture."[91] This is a subject
that particularly animates Lee Chiao, president (in 2002) of the Taiwan
Pen Association (*Taiwan bihui*). Lee promotes complete cultural renovation in an essay entitled "Taiwanese Culture and a New Nation State."[92]

Lee contends that the Taiwanese people's primary problem is that they
unconsciously and uncritically accept the Sinocentric myths propagated
by the KMT and the CCP, which are reinforced through encounters with

Westerners. These myths presume that "Chinese culture is superior within the world" and that "the Chinese people are the world's most outstanding." Hence, "the best thing that China has to attack Taiwan with is its culture."[93] Wrongly believing that "blood is thicker than water," many Taiwanese see their culture as a subsidiary of Chinese culture. But Lee believes that "Taiwanese culture and Chinese culture are as different from each other as Taiwanese culture is from American culture." Taiwanese and Chinese people do share basic human biology, but then again, Taiwanese and Americans share basic human biology. What Taiwanese must do in this situation is to "get rid of the virus" (*jiedu*) that Sinocentrism constitutes by "exposing its vacuousness" (*xushi*), puncturing and deflating the myths of Chinese culture so that a new Taiwanese culture can rise in its place.

Lee argues that accepting Chinese culture by definition peripheralizes and dwarfs (*aihua*) Taiwan. Chinese culture asserts China's centrality and superiority within the world. It "takes that which is Chinese as the beginning and ending of all thought; takes those things that are uniquely China's as the standard for all countries and places; takes China's survival as a microcosm of the world's survival; and takes Chinese values as the center, using them to judge all values everywhere."[94] Premodern Sinocentrism survived essentially intact through the revolutions of the twentieth century and into the twenty-first. Those aspects of modernity that Sinocentrism did absorb made it worse. Leninism in particular—which helped shape both KMT and CCP worldviews—taught Chinese people to stand outside their culture and use it as a tool cynically to pursue material self-interests. Especially in the PRC during the Cultural Revolution (1966–76), "the great Chinese culture" was "instrumentalized" (*gongjuhua*) so that it could be used domestically for selfish political aims and internationally to increase Chinese comprehensive national power.

To Lee, Chinese culture stands for nothing of any higher value. Its imposition on Taiwan after 1945 caused an innocent people to become unable to judge right from wrong, distinguish things of genuine value from dross, or filter incoming foreign culture. It reduced the standards of intellectual and political elites' public behavior and destroyed the island society's wholesome values. Chinese culture peripheralized Taiwan and denied it subjecthood. It created a huge array of specific social and political problems that continue to fester—and for whose solution some people wrong-headedly assert the need to rely even *more* on Chinese culture, especially Confucianism.

Lee therefore suggests that Taiwanese jettison Chinese culture entirely and replace it with a newly constructed Taiwanese culture. This new culture would draw from the ethnically Han people who emigrated from

the East Asian mainland virtues such as persistence, diligence, and prag-
matism, but would also draw from Japan an appreciation of discipline,
social norms, and the rule of law, and from the West an appreciation of
the spirit of scientific inquiry and democracy. The new culture would fuse
these varied elements together while remaining distinctively Taiwanese,
and would reject from Han culture tolerance for public disorder and pol-
lution, from Japanese culture a tendency toward political corruption and
paralysis, and from Western culture a disposition toward "extremist" and
"corrosive" doctrines such as deconstructionism and postmodernism.

Lee writes that as Taiwanese people begin imagining a new national
identity, they should focus on four major tasks whose successful comple-
tion would result in profoundly positive change. First, they should discuss
critically the cynical (*xianshi*) and materialistic lifestyles corrupting the
society, lifestyles which Lee believes are ultimately imported from China.
Taiwanese should strive to replace the corrupting lifestyles with new ones
based on worldviews rooted in "new concepts of humanity, love, and the
Earth." Reconstructing the mass media is crucial in this regard because
far more people are exposed to popular media products than to historical
debates. Lee contends that with only a few exceptions, Taiwanese television and radio stations, newspapers, and book publishers act unwittingly
as tools of Chinese cultural imperialism, by using news broadcasts, glitzy
entertainment shows, and historical dramas constantly to inculcate the
notion that Taiwan is a part of China. If Taiwan is to achieve subjectivity,
political and cultural elites must de-Sinify media content and reorient it
toward Taiwanese themes.[95]

Second, Taiwanese must work harder to understand the lives of fellow
citizens in other social strata and in earlier historical times. One cardinal
problem Lee perceives is that "Taiwanese traitors" (*Taijian*), concerned
only with their own material interests, are willing to sell the country
out by disinvesting in Taiwan and investing in China. This phenomenon
contributes to an increasingly dread-filled atmosphere in Taiwan and a
fatalistic sense that the island's days of prosperous autonomy are numbered. "Taiwanese traitors" must be pressured to recognize the implications of their actions for fellow citizens and must start putting the collective good ahead of their private interests. If the "traitors" refuse to
change, Lee predicts that more people in Taiwan will start trying to anticipate everything China wants (economically and politically) and will
provide it subserviently, at the cost of Taiwan's national dignity and independence. What matters should be the fate of all Taiwanese people, not
just rich businesspeople—and certainly not the *Chinese* people in whose
name some of the businesspeople grandiosely legitimate their selfishness
by claiming that they "are helping the motherland to develop." Such

tactics only play into the hands of the CCP and its supporters and abuse the Taiwanese people's lingering mesmerization by the illusions of "Great China nationalism."

Third, Lee recommends that the government transform the spatial and temporal landscapes in which Taiwanese people lead their daily lives. It should change the public holidays to eliminate all vestiges of the old KMT ROC, replacing Chinese holidays with new, ecologically aware commemorations linked to important events in the history of Taiwanese subjectivity. For example, May 20th—the date of an important farmer's demonstration in the 1980s, and the date Chen Shui-bian was first inaugurated as president in 2000—should be commemorated as Farmers' Day.[96] The government should also recast space, rectifying such serious social problems as: general chaos in the cities, dangerously speeding vehicles, haphazardly built architectural eyesores, iron-barred windows communicating social hostility, foul-smelling garbage piled high in parks and streets, animal carcasses and other "road kill" befouling streets and sidewalks, lascivious advertisements and television programs promoting appearance-obsessed vanity, polluted and unkempt natural scenic spots, and bronze statues of great personages in Chinese history "littering" schoolyards and other public spaces. Lee wants Taiwan to be remade clean, orderly, wholesome, and non-Chinese. Only in this way can the Taiwanese achieve the cultural renovation necessary to replace their psychological peripherality and "tragic" self-perception with a dignified and authentic new Taiwanese subjectivity.

The last cultural change that Lee believes essential is spiritual reformation. The Taiwanese government, in alliance with social activists, should actively cultivate religious sentiment among the people, specifically to counter what Lee contends is a destructive Chinese tendency to put humans at the center of the universe. The government should uproot the human-centered arrogance of the Chinese worldview and replace it with a healthier and more modest ethos. Taiwanese should cultivate a sense of humility in the face of nature and awe at the fragility of life. They should end their abuse of the environment.[97] They should become more resistant to the blandishments of advertising and illicit sex and drugs. Religion would make the Taiwanese more cooperative and compassionate, concerned about social problems and motivated to work to try to remedy them.

Despite the apparently radical nature of Lee's proposals, he argues that his vision is simply for Taiwan to become a "modern country," a "nation-state" (*guomin guojia*) formed contractually by free citizens, with a government constituted by elections. He envisions Taiwan remaining a multiethnic nation-state, with all ethnic groups—including Mainlanders—enjoying equality under the law and in daily experience. His vision is consistent with political scientist and activist Shih Cheng-feng's formulation, which holds that "the 'Taiwanese nation' (*Taiwan minzu*) refers to all people who love Taiwan, identify with Taiwan, and are willing to struggle for Taiwan, regardless of race, ethnicity, or provincial background. The stress is on loving Taiwan, not on the blood and cultural ties of the 'Chinese nation' (*Han minzu*)." Even North Americans of European ancestry would be welcomed as members of the Taiwanese nation as long as they meet these requirements.[98]

But there is a catch. Lee Chiao demands radical de-Sinification of culture. Shih Cheng-feng cannot accept as members of the Taiwanese nation people who say "yes, I identify with Taiwan, but I identify more closely with China." They are belittling their Taiwanese identity, reinforcing historical peripherality.[99] Ch'iu Kwei-fen finds that part of what *defines* "Taiwanese" is resisting Chinese culture, since Chinese culture is the culture of an imperialist oppressor.[100] But if China serves as a negative "Other" for a new Taiwanese nation, the status of Taiwan's Mainlanders becomes uncertain. For some of them, de-Sinification is sufficiently threatening that it reduces their commitment to democratic rules of the game. They charge that Taiwanese nationalists devalue democracy, since implementing radical de-Sinification schemes would require a powerfully invasive state. Each side suspects the other, prompting both sides to take actions (such as, in the case of some Mainlanders, refusing to recognize President Chen's reelection) that undermine the quality of Taiwan's democracy.

The DPP and Radical De-Sinification

Though President Chen evidently sympathized with the Taiwanese nationalist agenda, his government—at least until 2006—charted a middle course between the TSU's demands and those of unificationists in the PFP and KMT. Chen the candidate suggested his acceptance of the nationalists' agenda during the 2004 presidential campaign. But after his reelection, Chen as president resumed a centrist course, promising in his May 2004 inauguration speech that in revising (rather than replacing) the ROC Constitution, he would not change the name or flag of the country or in other ways use constitutional revisions to formalize Taiwan's de facto independence. Chen's promises came as other DPP leaders articulated a "new cultural discourse" designed to appeal to Mainlanders and the PRC. Yet the DPP ultimately accepted the goal of realizing Taiwanese subjectivity. It would not bow to CCP demands to surrender sovereignty and accept the "one China principle," but neither would it risk Taiwan's security by unnecessarily provoking China.

Over the years, the DPP was forced to deflect a number of the TSU's more radical initiatives. After the TSU proposed making Taiwanese the

ROC's second official language (after Mandarin), President Chen countered that English should be made the second official language instead. This move suggested Chen's determination to uphold openness to liberal-rational global culture and not retreat into antidemocratic ethnic chauvinism. But a subtext was that Taiwanese should learn the international language simply to reduce the likelihood of becoming completely dependent on China economically. Under the DPP, the Education Ministry was already expanding English teaching in elementary schools and would soon encourage college and university professors to start using English as a primary medium of instruction.[101]

Chen also celebrated Taiwan's ethnic diversity. He proclaimed in an April 2002 speech to the National Culture Association that he was committed to "forging an environment favorable for various ethnic groups to preserve and resurrect their cultural legacies." The speech was designed partly to counter TSU calls for nativization centered on the Taiwanese majority, and was targeted not only at Mainlanders but also at Hakka and Aboriginal groups. Chen said that "the openness and exuberance of Taiwan's democratization have contributed to the development of grassroots folk culture." Anyone wishing to protect this culture would not seek to close Taiwan off and foster hostility among its ethnic groups, but would instead open up to the outside world while celebrating ethnic diversity.[102]

Chen's relationship with the TSU—and with Lee Teng-hui personally—was delicate. Chen sympathized with many of the TSU's initiatives, but as president of a complex society, and with numerous constituencies, his only option was to take a centrist course, which also reduced the chances of antagonizing the CCP excessively or alienating the United States. Lee at several points questioned Chen's centrist approach, such as when he called in 2002 for a realignment of the ROC party system into two groups, "one devoted to Taiwan and the other not so devoted to Taiwan." But Lee also demanded that opposition parties give Chen "a free hand" in running the country, even in the face of (mostly cynical) criticism that a "free hand" might lead to the restoration of dictatorship.[103]

By August 2004, even the TSU was moderating its rhetoric. The Alliance to Campaign for Rectifying Taiwan's Name announced that it would play down the name-change issue during the next mass demonstration, scheduled for November 2004. The protest would still be devoted to "the promotion of a Taiwan-centered consciousness," but in a "less aggressive" way, consistent with the pursuit of "national harmony."[104] The change in tone was in response to President Chen's May 2004 inaugural address and perhaps also in recognition of the need to reduce ethnic tensions in the wake of the polarizing March 2004 election.

Prospects

In 2006, three threats clouded prospects for the consolidation of Taiwanese democracy and the improvement of its quality. First, and most seriously, China continued to insist that Taiwan be incorporated into the PRC under "one country, two systems." Second, the Taiwanese nationalists' de-Sinification project threatened Mainlander rights and culture. Third, the Mainlanders' resulting political alienation reduced the commitment of some of them to democratic rules of the political game.

Some Mainlanders worked *for* the DPP government, and this was a source of hope for those who wanted the "new and independent" Taiwan to remain democratic and multiethnic. In the early 1990s, Mainlander T'ien Hsin formed an association of Mainlanders pledging to work for the early realization of Taiwanese independence. T'ien became sufficiently visible in his activities and trusted among Taiwanese subjectivity activists that the DPP selected him in 2000 for special cultivation. Educated in the United States, and fluent in English, T'ien was appointed to a post liaising with foreigners, while awaiting an opportunity to run in a legislative race.

One of the reasons T'ien was attractive was because he wrote an article for Chang Yen-hsien on the political views of liberal Mainlanders associated with *Free China Fortnightly* in the 1950s. T'ien presented the liberal Mainlanders as models for contemporary Mainlanders.[105] He detailed how the liberals—Chinese nationalists and anticommunists, but also critics of the KMT—were forced over the course of the 1950s to the 1970s to come to terms with the fact that the KMT would never again rule the Chinese mainland. What, then, should become of the ROC on Taiwan? T'ien traced the evolution of the political views of Lei Chen (founder of *Free China Fortnightly*), Yin Hai-kwang, and Fu Cheng. T'ien argued that over two decades, all three respected intellectuals became progressively more committed to the notion of an independent Taiwan—independent from the PRC, though not from cultural China. (Yin eventually allowed for the possibility of independence even from cultural China.) T'ien contended that the liberal Mainlanders' views "should be reflected upon and referenced" by all Mainlanders today.

But the problem in presenting them as contemporary models is twofold. First, the PRC is no longer "Communist" in any meaningful sense, and yet the reason Lei, Yin, and Fu came to identify with Taiwan was precisely because they loathed Communism. The PRC's current system of corrupt authoritarianism is ironically similar in key respects to the system the KMT brought to Taiwan in the 1940s.

Second, Taiwan is no longer in an uncontested way "Chinese."

As a result of both of these considerations, the PRC is substantially less alien today for Taiwan's Mainlanders than it had been in the 1960s and 1970s, while Taiwan has become significantly *more* alien. To be sure, most of Taiwan's Mainlanders find little attractive about the CCP's Leninist politics. But they hold out hope for the PRC's early democratization, and they perceive the DPP and TSU to be destroying Taiwan's democracy and undermining their traditional privileges.

Asian democratization succeeds when the polity is open to liberal-rational global culture and accepts socialization to its constitutive norms as exalting national identity. This was precisely the condition that characterized Taiwan in the 1970s and 1980s, when the collapse of KMT legitimacy shattered the thin veneer of modern Chinese identity in Taiwan. In its place, Taiwanese nationalists and liberal Mainlanders together constructed a new national identity that fused elements from Taiwan's complex heritage with cardinal values in liberal-rational global culture. This paved the way for Taiwan's democratization in the 1980s and 1990s.

But the CCP, after crushing the spring 1989 democracy movement, became suspicious of Taiwan's democratization. It linked developments in Taiwan with "peaceful evolution" in China and the collapse of Leninist authoritarianism in the Soviet Union, Mongolia, and Eastern Europe. All were declared to be manifestations of "American hegemonism." Thus when Lee Teng-hui gave his speech at Cornell University in June 1995, CCP elites were already primed to see in the Taiwanese quest for subjectivity US manipulation. They intensified military pressure by staging exercises and deploying missiles. They launched fusillades of harsh rhetoric. The resulting tensions led some Taiwanese nationalists to abandon their commitment to democratic rules of the game, and some Mainlanders also reduced theirs. Moderates in the DPP sought to keep Taiwan open to liberal-rational global culture, firmly on a democratic path. They held the upper hand as of 2006, but with the CCP unyielding in its pressure, Taiwanese society showed signs of cracking. The future of its democracy was highly problematic.

THE FUTURE OF DEMOCRACY AND LIBERAL-RATIONAL GLOBAL CULTURE IN ASIA

Understanding democratization requires acknowledging the world-polity theorists' important insight that modern states acquire their identities *partly* through socialization to the constitutive norms of a liberal-rational global culture. But world-polity theory should be revised to account for the fact that not all global cultures are liberal-rational, and that among those stressing democratic values, some are more radical than others. Among the liberal-rational variants, there is, at any given time, at least a mainstream and an oppositional global culture. Even finer distinctions are possible.

More importantly, world-polity theory should be revised to note that states vary in their propensity to *accept* socialization. China's aversion to decentering within world society and history impedes socialization to the contemporary norm of democratic governance. The CCP accepts much of mainstream liberal-rational global culture, particularly those elements useful for increasing comprehensive national power. But it rejects elements, especially in the global oppositional culture, valuing democracy. CCP leaders and intellectuals believe that cultures serve states; hence, any "global" culture must actually be serving an international power pole, most likely the United States. China can borrow from other states' (including "global") culture selectively, but the CCP rejects reconstitution from abroad at the level of identity. It perceives democratization as likely to lead to this result by weakening the state and turning China into a cultural "stooge" (*fuyong*) of the United States. Resistance—and, ultimately, amassing sufficient comprehensive national power to recenter China—requires upholding "the people's democratic dictatorship."

In contrast, a lack of concern about decentering in Thailand and Taiwan combines with the perception that liberal-rational global culture is universally valid to facilitate state socialization and, since the 1970s, democratization. Siamese of the nineteenth century became convinced that the global culture's rationalism was consistent with pure Siamese Buddhism. Their felicitous resolution of the *tiyong* dilemma established the precondition for later Thai elites not only to accept reconstitution by liberal-rational global culture, but even to seek it proactively.

The distinctively Taiwanese identity only started taking shape in the 1920s, well after liberal-rational global culture had already begun disseminating widely. Taiwan thus never faced a *tiyong* crisis, and has always been predisposed to accept identity reconstitution at the direction of external forces. When Chinese hegemony began crumbling on the island in the 1970s, Taiwanese nationalism blossomed. Its historical "lateness" helped ensure that resistance to liberal-rational global culture would be minimal, as did the need to refashion Taiwan into a "model country" so that it could survive as an autonomous entity.

Thai, Taiwanese, and Chinese identities could change. In particular, as people in China continue to expand their cultural and intellectual horizons, they might pressure the CCP into redefining the democratization *problematique* in ways that finesse decentering. Increasingly in future years, the CCP's highest ranks will likely fill with people educated in the West. They might soften their resistance to decentering or accept "sharing Subjecthood" with the West as the architects of modern world history. After all, there is no denying China's stunning contributions to contemporary human civilization.[1]

At present, however, the trend seems the opposite. The CCP under Hu Jintao has strengthened authoritarian control and proclaimed its commitment to building an alternative new nondemocratic political civilization. Party leaders and intellectuals assert the validity of "world plurality" over (in English School terminology) the liberal "solidarism" of world-polity and democratic-peace theory. The CCP demands the annexation of democratic Taiwan and seeks to extend its influence throughout Asia, the South Pacific, and Africa. If it succeeds in establishing an alternative new political civilization, authoritarian but wealthy, people in Taiwan, Thailand, and other Asian countries might begin to question democracy's universal validity. The possibility would appear to be especially strong in the case of Thailand because of Thaksin Shinawatra's popularity from 2001 to 2005 and the tradition of looking abroad to the great powers for models of governance.

The deeper problem is that, in the *longue duree* of world history, democracy may be *abnormal*. Political scientist S. E. Finer concludes his three-volume masterwork on "The History of Government Since Ancient Times" by noting the paucity of democratic governments in the past:

The Forum [i.e., democratic] polity is comparatively rare in the history of government, where the Palace [authoritarian] polity and its variants are overwhelmingly the most common type. Only in the last two centuries has the Forum polity become widespread. Before then its appearance is, on the whole, limited to the Greek *poleis*, the Roman Republic, and the medieval European city-states. Furthermore, most of them for most of the time exhibited the worst pathological features of this kind of polity. For rhetoric read demagogy, for persuasion read corruption, pressure, intimidation, and falsification of the vote. For meetings and assemblies, read tumult and riot. For mature deliberation through a set of revising institutions, read instead self-division, inconstancy, slowness, and legislative and administrative stultification. And for elections read factional plots and intrigues. These features were the ones characteristically associated with the Forum polity down to very recent times. They were what gave the term "Republic" a bad name, but made "Democracy" an object of sheer horror.[2]

Democratization specialists and world-polity theorists sometimes imply that democracy is normal and that all countries are embarked upon "the road" to a democratic future. But Finer's conclusions suggest the opposite. Viewed from the long span of history, back to ancient times, authoritarian governance is normal to human society. The short modern period esteeming democracy *may* be exceptional, unlikely, and, therefore, transitory.

There are other reasons to question the security of democracy's future in Asia (and elsewhere). New computer- and telecommunications-driven transformations to the ecology of globe-level human interaction threaten to undermine liberal-rational global culture's integrity. Advances in surveillance and control technologies provide authoritarian governments and democracies enticed by their functionality with easy-to-use tools for monitoring populations and constraining their activities. Within this context, democracy can prevail in Asia against those disdaining it as a pointless impediment to power and plenty only if concerned actors exercise agency to nurture and defend it.

Global Culture Versus the Network Society

The basic assumption of world-polity theory is that ideational (soft) power ultimately triumphs over material power. The diffusion of liberal-rational global culture from its West European birthplace to the rest of the world did initially require European military and economic supremacy, a material-power advantage that owed an enormous debt to East and Southeast Asia and the Islamic world. But at some undefined point during (probably) the twentieth century, global culture transcended the countries that created it and achieved a transnational status. Afterward, not even the leading Western states could escape its constitutive power. International NGOs (INGOs) became the most important actors socializing states, and they continue today faithfully to implement global culture's constitutive norms. World-polity theory does not consider the possibility of a rising state accumulating sufficient material power to challenge global culture's hegemony and one day overturn it. But this is the potential challenge posed by authoritarian China's rise.

What is the relationship between ideational and material power? What will be the fate of liberal-rational global culture and democracy in Asia? To try to answer these questions, it is useful briefly to review two seminal contributions to contemporary sociological theory: Michael Mann's *The Sources of Social Power* (1986) and Manuel Castells' *The Rise of the Network Society* (1996).

Michael Mann on Power and Interstices

In *The Sources of Social Power*, Mann presents world society as constituted neither by a hegemonic global culture nor the CCP's asserted autonomous power poles.[3] Instead, Mann sees the world as constituted by "multiple overlapping and intersecting networks of power," which may or may not covary positively in any particular time-space juncture. Human needs and desires can be satisfied collectively using four kinds of power resource: ideology, economy, violence (military force), and politics. Using each resource generates an organized power network, such as religion for ideology, the market for economic production and exchange, military and police forces for violence, and the state for politics.

Power can be further subdivided along two dimensions: whether it is *authoritative* or *diffused*, and whether it is *intensive* or *extensive* (see Table 2). Authoritative power is consciously willed by groups and institutions and is characterized by explicit commands and conscious obedience. Diffused power is exerted through relatively spontaneous, unconscious, decentered processes exemplifying power relations not explicitly commanded. Within the second dimension, intensive power is concentrated, coercive, and highly mobilized, thoroughly penetrating the lives of those under its influence. Extensive power affects large numbers of people over a vast geographical expanse but cannot easily mobilize positive commitments or significantly penetrate the lives of those affected.

The development of what Mann terms "enabling facilities" has resulted in authoritative and diffused power becoming more extensive over time—while also, in some ways, increasing the efficacy of intensive power

TABLE 2

Mann's Power Categories

	Authoritative	Diffused
Intensive	Army command structure	A general strike
	Organized religion	INGO activism
Extensive	Militaristic empire	Market exchange
		Language
		Social norms
		Global culture

SOURCE: Adapted from Michael Mann, *The Sources of Social Power, Vol. 1: A History of Power from the Beginning to AD 1760* (Cambridge and New York: Cambridge University Press, 1986), pp. 1–33.

applications. In earlier centuries, steady improvements in communication, transportation, weapons, and related technologies made it logistically feasible to create successively larger land- and sea-based empires. The ancient Roman, Chinese, Persian, and other empires were, Mann contends, loosely governed federated structures. Only in the past two centuries have truly extensive applications of authoritative power appeared.

Other kinds of enabling facilities extended the reach of diffused forms of power. Mann cites as examples the spread of literacy in shared languages, coinage, financial institutions, law codes, and national consciousnesses. Here is the category in which liberal-rational global culture would appear (though Mann does not discuss the concept). Originally backed by the authoritative power of European and later US military and economic empires, global culture eventually took the form of a diffused/extensive power, similar to language or social norms.

But Mann would presumably be skeptical that any global culture could maintain its diffused/extensive power to socialize world elites forever. To Mann, history does not end. Constantly restless and creative human beings always think of new and more effective ways to use ideology, production and exchange, violence, and politics to satisfy their needs and wants. Importantly, in those zones not "covered" by current institutions—zones which Mann terms "interstices"—restless and creative humans "tunnel." The result of their efforts is significant change in the institutional expression of one or another source of social power. Subsequently, pressure to bring the other institutions into alignment should spawn additional social changes. The development and diffusion of enabling facilities ensures that these processes reach over increasingly larger geographic expanses.

The CCP's resistance to world decentering suggests liberal-rational global culture is still not completely global in reach, and may never become truly global. The Party accepts socialization to this culture only to the extent it is useful for increasing comprehensive national strength.

When socialization occurs anyway, and people in China show signs of becoming "polluted" by liberalism, the Party punishes them. Dissatisfied with the structure of global politics, the CCP and its intellectual supporters seek to tunnel through the interstices made possible by the liberal-rational global culture's incomplete hegemony (an ideological source of power) and the US military's incomplete hegemony (violence) to change the system, recentering China. The first steps would be to force Japan to acknowledge Chinese preeminence in East and Southeast Asia and to coerce Taiwan into annexation. Securing veto rights over key foreign and domestic policy decisions in Central Asia, Southeast Asia, Australia, and New Zealand might be next. Depending on how ambitious the CCP becomes, recentering could extend to disrupting the recent Asia-Pacific democratization trend and impeding efforts to improve democratic quality in the region.

Manuel Castells on the "Network Society"

Other developments threatening the integrity of liberal-rational global culture might undermine democracy in Asia. Castells' theory assumes three ideal-typical ways of organizing the human race: (1) hierarchically, (2) in sovereign-autonomous units, and (3) in a multinodal network.[4] With the proviso that Castells' models are ideal-types, the ancient Roman and Chinese empires can be considered examples of hierarchical organization, as their autocratic leaders sought to rule most of the entire known civilized world (to the extent feasible). A less obvious example would be the contemporary world—*if* the world-polity theorists are correct. Though materially, the human race might be divided into sovereign-autonomous units, or into networks, world-polity theorists would argue that, culturally, it is unified. People everywhere are "subjects" of global culture, because it informs the identities of all significant actors.

Despite Realism's former dominance in the study of IR, the world has never been organized into truly sovereign-autonomous units (the second ideal type). Transborder trade and communications flows have always compromised state autonomy, and dependence on powerful foreign states combined with an inability to exercise complete domination at home inevitably limited sovereignty. Some states—the powerful, the continental, the insular—were "more sovereign-autonomous" than others; but even these states frequently perceived advantages to pooling sovereignty on some issues and sacrificing it on others. Yet the CCP's determined resistance to the constitutive norm of democratic governance suggests that although economic power may be transnational, ideational power is not necessarily. Sovereign-autonomy or something approximate to it *might* still be valid in the realm of culture and identity, given a sufficiently committed state such as China's armed with advanced enabling facilities.

The third ideal-typical way of organizing humanity is in multinodal networks. Castells develops a "network society" model in which power is neither structured hierarchically nor distributed neatly among independent states. It is, instead, dispersed widely among interconnected and ephemeral "nodes."

[Nodes] are stock exchange markets, and their ancillary advanced service centers, in the network of global financial flows. They are national councils of ministers.... They are street gangs and money-laundering financial institutions in the network of drug traffic.... They are television systems, entertainment studios, computer graphics milieus, news teams, and mobile devices generating, transmitting, and receiving signals in the global network of the new media at the roots of cultural expression and public opinion.[5]

Castells shares with Mann the conviction that sources of social power do not always covary positively, structuring situations rigidly. But Castells goes beyond Mann to argue that power can be radically ephemeral and transient, frustrating the efforts of state leaders and other elites to control events. Most of Castells' examples are taken from the world of international business and finance, but his logic applies equally well to other realms of activity. The United States is incapable of preventing the flow of dangerous drugs across its borders, despite prodigious interdiction and suppression efforts by several government agencies. To Castells, facts such as these add up to serious challenges to the hierarchical and sovereign-autonomous unit models of globe-wide human organization.

Theories positing the domination of a hegemon (the United States or broader West) are far too crude to capture the subtleties of networked reality, since hegemons frequently find it impossible to achieve their goals. Theories positing sovereign-autonomous units exaggerate the power of national governments even inside their own territories. States and state agencies, parliaments, and individual leaders can influence transnational events as components of nodes, but almost never act in an effective way autonomously—except on those rare occasions when they self-consciously commit maximum effort to a coherent course of action. To Castells, state power is normally a background or conditioning variable in decision-making situations but not necessarily the most important one. Almost all states are now densely crosscut by transnational networks; none is genuinely autonomous. The concept of sovereignty is highly problematic.

Castells sees power in the international system as being everywhere and yet nowhere, here today on this issue and in this node, gone tomorrow or shifted to another node. To be sure, key actors find themselves regularly taking part in the activities of several different nodes and tend to institutionalize their participation. Nodes interconnect at "switches," and here significant power can be applied—as when "financial flows take control of media empires that influence politics."[6] But no actor participates in the operations of all or even most nodes, and none is capable of asserting hierarchical control over the giant worldwide network ("the Net") which the nodes comprise. Network logic trumps the efforts of any individual or group to exert "international agential power"[7] over the contours of the system.

If Castells' model of emerging world society is accurate, the fate of liberal-rational global culture becomes problematic. To the world-polity theorists, global culture is effectively "out there": a hermeneutical force structuring the mindsets and actions of everyone "inside." But to Castells, culture itself is *inside the Net* of human exchange and therefore structured by network logic. The liberal-rational global culture can only prevail if the actors who contribute most significantly to cultural construction, through the Net, decide in their dispersed settings to promote this particular kind of culture and value system. There is no "power center" in Castells' model that can ensure a global culture's continued hegemony. There is no master socialization mechanism to ensure that contributors to cultural construction will have internalized liberal-rational values. Images and information flowing through the Net will not necessarily be consistent with liberal, democratic, and rationalistic values. Global culture *might* prevail, because its institutionalization affords excellent advantages over competing hegemonic projects entering the network ecology age. But Castells is impressed by the cultural reactions against globalization manifest in new identity movements. Some of these movements reject liberal-rational values. Like the CCP—but often more radically—they associate global culture with Western power.[8]

World-polity theorists view culture as "closed," but Castells views it as open-ended with possibilities—though not *all* possibilities—since by implication he considers it unlikely that, given network logic, a single culture could establish ideational hegemony worldwide. Castells would reject the assertion that INGOs all function to socialize states into a hegemonic liberal-rational global culture. *Some* INGOs socialize some states in this way, but others have completely different agendas, and contribute radically different values to a global cultural mélange.

One of the INGO activists interviewed in Thailand agreed with Castells. She said: "I don't think global culture is closed at all. There are many parallel universes existing at the moment, and the dominant culture is carried only by a small elite." Moreover, "just because it's hegemonic doesn't mean it's reality. What's actually going on in the world at any given moment—day-to-day, in every place, by all kinds of people—isn't usually what's visible to most of us from what we see in the media, and isn't necessarily affected by that kind of global culture."[9] Network logic might subvert liberal-rational global culture. Through their mobilization efforts, INGOs "can make things visible that were invisible" and, in the process, restructure the culture. What results may not necessarily be consistent with liberal-rational principles.

INGOs of all orientations use the Internet and other new communications technologies to corrode state sovereignty and undermine hierarchy. But technology strengthens states as well as citizens. Potentially it strengthens states more than citizens because states are usually better organized and have access to more resources. New surveillance, monitoring, and control technologies make it increasingly easy and affordable for states to track citizens' movements and preemptively neutralize those who might become "threatening."[10] The US government, while purporting to promote democracy, uses these technologies to monitor citizens' (and foreigners') behavior at home and to wage wars abroad. INGOs could use some of these technologies to pursue democracy. But in a country such as China, they are far too weak to offer a credible defense of civil society should the state commit to crushing it.

In sum, there is no current global trend or tendency that inspires confidence in the inevitability of democracy's triumph worldwide, or in assertions that all countries are embarked upon "the road" to a democratic future. Technology empowers but also undercuts; economic development helps, but not if citizens sacrifice liberties willingly in exchange for material plenty (or excess). Asian democracy, like democracy elsewhere, can only survive and flourish if it is nurtured self-consciously and in clear-eyed awareness of the numerous threats to destroy it. The CCP blocks democratization for one-fifth the human race and might empower putative autocrats elsewhere in Asia. With China rising and the CCP committed to establishing a new authoritarian political civilization, Asian democracy faces a challenging future. Worldwide, democracy is comparatively rare historically, while authoritarianism is normal. For the liberal-rational global culture to prevail in this context, concerned agents must act.

REFERENCE MATTER

NOTES

Chapter 1

1. "APEC Warning," 2003.
2. "APEC Warning," 2003.
3. See Chapter 3.
4. Yuwadee, "Thaksin Urges."
5. The standard study on this period is Morell and Chai-anan 1981. Also see Van Praagh, *Thailand's Struggle for Democracy*, pp. 180–96.
6. Yuwadee, "Thaksin Urges."
7. Interview 328. "Farang" is the Thai word for a Western Caucasian foreigner.
8. For insightful discussions of this complex issue, see Kelly and Reid 1983; Diamond and Plattner 1998; Diamond, Linz, and Lipset 1989; Rodan 1996; Chee 1998; and Wood 2004.
9. See Zhao, "Chinese Nationalism."
10. On this point applied generally, see Hobson, "What's at Stake."
11. Whitehead 1996; also see Carothers, *Aiding Democracy Abroad*.
12. For concise overviews of the democratization literature, see Geddes, "What Do We Know"; and Bunce, "Comparative Democratization."
13. Moore 1966; Almond and Verba 1963.
14. A few of the most important such works include Keane 1988; Weigle and Butterfield 1992; Putnam 1993; Diamond 1994; Foley and Edwards 1996; Jones 1998; Kim 2000; and Alagappa 2004.
15. For methodological discussions of the problems that can result, see Geddes, "How the Cases You Choose Affect the Answers You Get"; King, Keohane, and Verba, *Designing Social Inquiry*, pp. 128–39; and Collier, Mahoney, and Seawright 2004. Collier, Mahoney, and Seawright—who use the term "truncate" on the dependent variable—note rightly that the practice is only problematic in cross-case designs or when the researcher proposes to generalize systematically on the basis of a within-case design.
16. For example, Przeworski et al. 2000.
17. Munck, "The Regime Question," p. 132.

18. Carothers, "The End of the Transition Paradigm." Also see O'Donnell 2002. O'Donnell argues that the transition paradigm Carothers criticizes is supple and does not presuppose—even subtly—that transitions will end in democracy.

19. Huntington, *The Third Wave*, p. 316.

20. Whitehead, *The International Dimensions*, p. 21.

21. Robinson 1996. For a more sanguine interpretation of democracy-promotion, see Carothers, *Aiding Democracy Abroad*, pp. 19–64.

22. Robinson, *Promoting Polyarchy*, pp. 32–33.

23. One implication of Robinson's theory is that China should soon become politically democratic because of the PRC's rapid and deep integration into the global economy and its emergence as "the workshop of the world": the primary destination for global flows of foreign direct investment (FDI). To date, however, transnational capitalists have been content to work with China's labor-repressing authoritarian regime.

24. Cox, *Approaches to World Order*, pp. 88–89.

25. On the other hand, Larry Diamond—perhaps the leading democratization specialist in the field of Comparative Politics—develops a notably subtle and nuanced discussion of democratization's future in *Developing Democracy*, pp. 24–63 and 261–78.

26. Gilley, *China's Democratic Future*, p. xiii.

27. As does Hobson, "What's at Stake."

28. Gilley, *China's Democratic Future*, p. xv.

29. Meyer, "Globalization"; also see Meyer, "The World Polity"; Meyer, Thomas, and Ramirez, "World Society"; and Boli and Thomas, "World Culture."

30. See Meyer, "The Changing Cultural Content."

31. Note that world-polity theorists are using "global culture" in a very specific sense. They do not mean "global culture" generally, as some speak of "global society," "global politics," or "global problems."

32. World-polity theorists do not consider the possible "Eastern origins of Western civilization." They do not concern themselves with Enlightenment culture's extensive debt to Islam, China, and other non-Western influences. They bracket the question of ultimate origins and confine their analysis to the period since the French and Industrial Revolutions. For challenges to Western-centrism, see Frank 1998; Pomeranz 2001; and Hobson 2004.

33. See Boli and Thomas, "INGOs," especially pp. 39–41; and Boli, "Conclusion," pp. 277–79.

34. Three of the most important works in the voluminous English School literature relevant for this discussion are Wight 1992 (his essays from the 1950s); Bull 1977; and Bull and Watson 1984.

35. Buzan, *From International to World Society?* p. 59 and p. 145 (emphasis added).

36. Buzan, *From International to World Society?* pp. 146–47.

37. The term might also be translated as "world diversity."

38. Finnemore, *National Interests in International Society*, p. 25.

39. Finnemore, *National Interests in International Society*, p. 30.

40. See Finnemore's chapter on "Norms and War: The International Red Cross and the Geneva Conventions," in *National Interests in International Society*, pp. 69–88. Also see Barrett and Frank 1999.

41. On the general subject of hermeneutical (culturally deterministic) approaches to social explanation, see Alexander, *Twenty Lectures*, especially pp. 281–301.

42. Boli and Thomas, "INGOs," p. 18.

43. Boli and Thomas, "INGOs," p. 17.

44. Boli and Thomas, "INGOs," p. 47.

45. Risse and Sikkink 1999.

46. Risse and Sikkink, *The Power of Human Rights*, p. 2.

47. Risse and Sikkink, *The Power of Human Rights*, p. 5. Also see Keck and Sikkink 1998.

48. Risse and Sikkink, *The Power of Human Rights*, p. 3.

49. Compared to 1966 or 1976, the human rights situation in China has certainly improved in important respects. But there is no evidence the CCP is embarked upon a course of embracing liberal human rights standards. (See Chapters 4 and 5)

50. Risse and Sikkink, *The Power of Human Rights*, p. 24.

51. Risse and Sikkink, *The Power of Human Rights*, p. 12.

52. Hobson, *The State and International Relations*, especially pp. 145–73 and 217–35.

53. See Levenson 1965; Duara 1995; and Zhao, "Chinese Nationalism."

54. The *tiyong* dilemma was not, of course, the only important factor causing social and political change in Asia. Population pressures, indigenous intellectual debates, dislocations caused by secular economic dynamics, and many other internal factors figured prominently. But the *tiyong* dilemma was central, interacting with these other factors to deepen turbulence.

55. As Bjorn Wittrock notes, "the existence of this common global condition [modernity] does not mean that members of any single cultural community are about to relinquish their ontological and cosmological assumptions, much less their traditional institutions. It means, however, that the continuous interpretation, reinterpretation, and transformation of those commitments and institutional structures cannot but take account of the commonality of the global condition of modernity" (Wittrock, "Modernity: One, None, or Many?" p. 56).

56. See Rice, *Mao's Way*, especially pp. 212–29 and 349–81.

57. Levenson 1965; also see the essays in Unger 1996.

58. See Lynch, *After the Propaganda State*, pp. 219–23.

59. See Hobsbawm, *The Age of Extremes*, pp. 109–77.

60. Eisenstadt, "Multiple Modernities," p. 5.

61. Wittrock, "Modernity: One, None, or Many?" pp. 47–48.

62. Boli and Thomas, "INGOs," p. 40.

63. See Castells, *The Power of Identity*.

64. See Chapter 8.

65. See Geddes, "What Do We Know About Democratization," pp. 117–19; and Bunce, "Comparative Democratization," pp. 706–7.

66. Przeworski et al., *Democracy and Development*, pp. 78–136. Boix and Stokes declare at the end of their 2003 *World Politics* article that "we have shown that economic development both causes democracy and sustains it." But they lack a solid causal explanation; thus "a full answer as to why this is so requires us to understand the hidden mechanisms and consequences of economic development." They believe that, in any case, understanding democratization requires no reference to cultural and identity factors. (Boix and Stokes, "Endogenous Democratization," p. 545.)

67. "Suchinda's Near Impossible Task," 1992.

Chapter 2

1. The Democracy Monument had been built in the 1940s to commemorate the 1932 end of the absolute monarchy. As explained in Chapter 4, the end of the absolute monarchy did bring initial constitutional rule to Thailand and (sometimes) electoral politics, but not democracy in any meaningful sense.

2. See Barme, *Luang Wichit Wathakan and the Creation of a Thai Identity*, pp. 27–31.

3. Frank E. Reynolds, "Legitimation and Rebellion," pp. 140–41.

4. Interviews 304 and 325.

5. See Van Praagh, *Thailand's Struggle for Democracy*, p. 149; and Frank E. Reynolds, "Legitimation and Rebellion," p. 144.

6. Quoted in Morell, "Thailand: Military Checkmate."

7. The most comprehensive English-language assessment of this period is Morell, *Power and Parliament in Thailand*. For a summary of events, see Pasuk and Baker, *Thailand*, pp. 299–304.

8. Pasuk and Baker, *Thailand*, pp. 162 and 301.

9. Wyatt, *Thailand: A Short History*, p. 289.

10. Interview 325.

11. Sulak, *Powers that Be*, p. 48.

12. Interviews 305, 309, and 311.

13. Interview 327.

14. Interviews 305, 309, and 311.

15. See Frank E. Reynolds, "Legitimation and Rebellion," p. 139.

16. Interview 327.

17. Pasuk and Baker, *Thailand*, p. 91.

18. Pasuk and Baker, *Thailand*, p. 404. Also see Amara 2001.

19. See Wyatt, "The 'Subtle Revolution.'"

20. Kirsch, "Modernizing Implications," p. 59.

21. Jackson, "Thai-Buddhist Identity," p. 201.

22. Thongchai, *Siam Mapped*, pp. 39–40; Sulak, "The Crisis of Siamese Identity," p. 42; and Kirsch, "Modernizing Implications," p.61.

23. Thongchai, *Siam Mapped*, p. 38.

24. Thongchai, *Siam Mapped*, p. 41.

25. Europe could not have been the global center to Mongkut—nor could Siam—because as an accomplished astronomer, he knew that the Earth "was nothing but a planet like other stars," a planet whose "surface was full of countries, and Siam was merely one of them." (Thongchai, *Siam Mapped*, p. 44.) Such a perspective was strikingly different from the one then prevailing in China, which held that the Qing Empire was the global center, certainly not "just another country."

26. See Wyatt, "King Chulalongkorn the Great."

27. See Tambiah 1978.

28. Wyatt, "Education and the Modernization of Thai Society," p. 225.

29. Wyatt, "King Chulalongkorn the Great," p. 276; Pasuk and Baker, *Thailand*, p. 242.

30. Pasuk and Baker, *Thailand*, p. 222.

31. Wyatt, "Interpreting the History of the Fifth Reign"; also see Seksan 1989.

32. Quoted in Murashima, "The Origin of Modern Official State Ideology," p. 84.

33. Murashima, "The Origin of Modern Official State Ideology," p. 85.

34. Quoted in Wyatt, *Thailand: A Short History*, p. 211.

35. Quoted in Barme, *Luang Wichit Wathakan and the Creation of a Thai Identity*, pp. 35–36.

36. Quoted in Barme, *Luang Wichit Wathakan and the Creation of a Thai Identity*, p. 21.

37. Space limitations preclude a full discussion, but see Barme 1993; and Murashima 1988.

38. See Thongchai, *Siam Mapped*, pp. 95–112.

39. Thongchai, *Siam Mapped*, pp. 107–12; Pasuk and Baker, *Thailand*, pp. 221–26.

40. Kirsch 1978; Tambiah 1978.

41. Jackson, "Thai-Buddhist Identity," p. 195.

42. Visalo, "Buddhism for the Next Century," p. 237.

43. Sulak, "The Crisis of Siamese Identity," pp. 43–44.

44. Not all NGOs are influenced by socially engaged Buddhism. Those that are fall into Naruemon's Type 3 NGO, the kind that emphasizes political empowerment in the belief that "social and political change depends more on strong self-reliant groups than on policy reform by the government." Type 1 NGOs "emphasize a policy of cooperation" and work closely with government agencies to increase the effectiveness of state development and social welfare policies. Type 2 NGOs are more critical of government policies and try to "highlight economic and social problems . . . as political issues, and not the products of economic conditions alone." (Naruemon 2002.)

45. Interview 304. The "new model of society" has yet to be spelled out in convincing detail, making the socially engaged Buddhists vulnerable to the charge of utopian idealism. Nevertheless, the vision motivates their activism.

46. Besides McCargo, *Chamlong Srimuang*, two very useful studies of the May 1992 upheaval taking substantially different perspectives are Khien 1997; and William Callahan 1998.

47. McCargo, *Chamlong Srimuang*, p. 102.

48. Data in McCargo, *Chamlong Srimuang*, p. 115; also see pp. 226–29.

49. See Suthichai, "92: Beyond Soul-Searching"; and "The Social Cost of Development," 1992.

50. McCargo, *Chamlong Srimuang*, pp. 135–36.

51. "Suchinda on Religious Belief," p. 49.

52. "Suchinda Addresses Closing," p. 36. Suchinda also hinted darkly that General Chavalit Yongchaiyudh—another rival—was a closet Communist.

53. "Pro-Democracy MPs Continue Protest," 1992. After leading the coup that overthrew the elected government of Chatichai Choonhavan in February 1991, Suchinda promised he would preside over passage of a new constitution and then step down, vowing explicitly in November 1991 and on several subsequent occasions that he would not use the stacked deck he had created to seek the premiership. But Suchinda was not known for keeping his word. On May 8, 1992, he also solemnly declared in a nationwide television address that "I promise that I will never order the armed forces or police authorities to use violent means against the people." ("Prime Minister Addresses Nation," p. 45; see, also, "An Unforgivable Betrayal," p. 64; and "National Letdown in the Making," p. 63.)

54. William Callahan, *Imagining Democracy*, p. 119.

55. "Anti-Suchinda Rally Held," 1992. For a variety of reasons, Chamlong quickly aborted the fast. See McCargo, *Chamlong Srimuang*, pp. 247–54.

56. The academic-activists in interviews 309 and 319 separately made this observation.

57. McCargo, *Chamlong Srimuang*, p. 274.

58. Sukhothai continued to flourish autonomously for a few decades until Ayutthaya reduced it to vassalage in the 1420s. See Taylor, "The Early Kingdoms," pp. 168–73.

59. Quoted in Jackson, "Thai-Buddhist Identity," p. 211.

60. Quoted in Wyatt, "Contextual Arguments."

61. Quoted in Jackson, "Thai-Buddhist Identity," p. 211.

62. Quoted in Jackson, "Thai-Buddhist Identity," p. 215.

63. Quoted in Jackson, "Thai-Buddhist Identity," p. 211.

64. The informant in Interview 318, a scholar of Thai Buddhism, stressed this "counter-hegemonic thrust" of socially engaged Buddhism. On government efforts to cultivate a more conservative collective identity—especially through operations of the Office of the Prime Minister's National Identity Board, established in 1980—see Craig J. Reynolds, "Introduction: National Identity and Its Defenders"; and Michael Kelly Connors, *Democracy and National Identity in Thailand*, pp. 136–43.

65. For excellent overviews, see Sulak, ed., *Socially Engaged Buddhism for the New Millennium*; Chappell 2003; Doneys 2002; and Naruemon 2002.

66. Jackson, *Buddhadasa*, p. 2. Theravada Buddhism is the Buddhism of Thailand, Cambodia, Laos, Burma, and Sri Lanka; Mahayana Buddhism is the Buddhism of Tibet, China, Taiwan, Japan, Korea, and Vietnam. For a concise overview of the doctrinal differences and their origins, see Harvey, *An Introduction to Buddhism*, pp. 73–169. For a discussion of Theravada Buddhism's arrival in mainland Southeast Asia, see de Casparis and Mabbett, "Religion and Popular Beliefs of Southeast Asia," pp. 286–304.

67. Sulak, *Powers that Be*, p. 10; and see Chapter 3.

68. Jackson, *Buddhadasa*, p. 282.

69. McCargo, *Chamlong Srimuang*, p. 74.

70. Jackson, *Buddhadasa*, p. 289.

71. Quoted in Jackson, *Buddhadasa*, p. 80.

72. Quoted in Jackson, *Buddhadasa*, p. 151.

73. Jackson, *Buddhadasa*, p. 151.

74. Interview 318.

75. Jackson, *Buddhadasa*, pp. 177–81; Interview 318.

76. Jackson, *Buddhadasa*, p. 177.

77. Jackson, *Buddhadasa*, p. 203.

78. Quoted in Jackson, *Buddhadasa*, p. 181. See, also, Pasuk and Baker, *Thailand*, pp. 376–80.

79. Buddhadasa, *Keys to Natural Truth*, p. 141.

80. Visalo, "Buddhism for the Next Century," pp. 243–44.

81. See Jackson, *Buddhadasa*, pp. 33–36 and pp. 215–24.

82. Jackson, *Buddhadasa*, p. 223.

83. Visalo, "Buddhism for the Next Century," p. 249.

84. Jackson, *Buddhadasa*, pp. 239–51, quotation on p. 244. In the context of the 1970s, Buddhadasa's position was moderate. See Keyes 1978.

85. See Vasana 2003.

86. Quoted in Pasuk and Baker, *Thailand*, p. 299.

87. Mulder, *Inside Thai Society*, p. 129.

88. Quotation from "S.J.'s" introduction to Sulak, *Powers That Be*, pp. 10–11. Also see Ito 2003.

89. See Sulak, *Loyalty Demands Dissent*.

90. Interview 327.

91. See Chapter 1. Given the networked nature of Thailand's NGO movement, most of the larger Thai NGOs are internationally linked, directly or indirectly. Not all receive funds from foreign NGOs, but most are hooked into the broader NGO network (in some cases tenuously, however). (Interviews 305, 308, 312, and 319.)

92. Risse and Sikkink 1999.

93. Amara and Nitaya 1997; and Naruemon 2002.

94. The situation is changing in China, but very slowly and within sharply drawn parameters. (See Chapter 5.)

95. Interview 327.

96. See Green 2003.

97. Interview 327. "We even teach our students not to hate Prime Minister Thaksin," Sulak says. "It's no good to hate Thaksin. It's very difficult to *love* him, but it's no good to hate him." (See Chapter 3.)

98. Interview 324.

99. Surin Maisrikrod 1999.

100. Even the relatively conservative National Identity Board decided in 1983 to embrace "democracy with the King as head of state" as the official goal of Thai political development. See Craig J. Reynolds, "Introduction: National Identity and Its Defenders," pp. 13–29; and Connors, *Democracy and National Identity*, pp. 136–43.

101. Sulak, "Buddhism and Human Rights in Siam," p. 195. On the other hand, Sulak believes that the very *need* for formal human rights standards indicates that something is wrong with global society. (Interview 327.)

102. Interview 324.

103. "Ajarn" is an honorific title meaning "teacher."

104. Quoted in Connors, *Democracy and National Identity*, p. 232.

105. Cited in Connors, *Democracy and National Identity*, p. 232.

106. In some ways, therefore, Forum-Asia appears to be a Type 1 NGO in Naruemon's scheme, but in other ways it appears more like a Type 2 or Type 3 NGO. See Note 44.

107. See Chapter 3.

108. Interview 324.

109. The NGO activists in interviews 322, 323, and 326 said they also frequently receive calls for help on stories from the media, and view it as a general practice for the better-known NGOs.

110. Interview 324.

111. Interview 320.

112. See Chapter 3; and see Lynch, "International 'Decentering' and Democratization."

113. See Chapter 3.

114. Khun X said that "military officers are usually very good people" and that she first developed a good professional relationship with the military when it needed help preparing for a postindependence peacekeeping mission in East Timor. (Interview 324.)

115. Interviews 324 and 330.

116. By the end of 2003, there were over 10,000 NGOs in Thailand, with a huge variety of platforms and concerns. Most were unregistered. (Interviews 325 and 329.)

117. Interview 320. Also see Naruemon, "NGOs and Grassroots Participation," pp. 187–88; and "PM Vows to Resolve Pak Mool Crisis His Way," 2002.

118. Interview 326.

119. See Chapter 1.

120. Information in the paragraphs to follow on Focus on the Global South comes primarily from interviews 322 and 323.

121. Short for *muubaan*.

122. See Pasuk and Baker, *Thailand*, pp. 48–88 and pp. 395–415. In the mid-1980s, socially engaged Buddhist Prawase Wasi argued that the state should cease administering the villages and that they should be left to govern themselves. "Prawase did not simply contrast 'village' against 'state,' but contrasted the village as the site of true Buddhist values against the state as the weapon of capitalism. To defend the Thai nation [therefore] meant opposing the state, either by withdrawing into self-reliance, or by endeavoring to change the state's character." (Pasuk and Baker, *Thailand*, p. 388.)

123. Pasuk and Baker, *Thailand*, p. 294.

124. Interview 330. Many of these students, if not most, were influenced by the Marxist critiques of development flourishing in Western social science departments in the 1970s—linking Thai youth to the global oppositional culture.

125. Interviews 302, 305, 308, 311, 319, 326, and 330.

126. Interview 301 and 302.

127. Interview 322; on the Assembly of the Poor, see Chapter 3.

128. Interview 312 spelled out the logic in detail.

129. Interview 323.

Chapter 3

1. At the time, the King was concerned that Thailand might soon go the way of neighboring Cambodia, Laos, and Vietnam, whose governments had recently fallen to communist insurgencies.

2. "Constitution of the Kingdom of Thailand," 1991.

3. Hewison, "The Monarchy," p. 63.

4. On the King's political perspicacity, see "Former Premier [Anand Panyarachun] Examines Role of King," 1995.

5. See Connors, *Democracy and National Identity*, pp. 132–87.

6. See "Former Premier [Anand Panyarachun] Examines Role of King," 1995. Note that no comparable "essence-embodying figure" exists in China, which is yet another reason why democratization in that country will be so difficult. Any Chinese leader who suddenly came out in favor of democratization—no matter how apparently strong his position—would soon be likely to find himself the target of devastating attacks for promoting "total Westernization." Taiwan, too, lacks an essence-embodying figure, but since Taiwan never faced a *tiyong* crisis and is so thoroughly open to liberal-rational global culture, it does not presently need such a figure to legitimate democracy (see Chapter 6).

7. Officially forty-four people were killed, but several hundred went missing and never returned. Hundreds more were injured. See Khien 1997; and William Callahan 1998.

8. "King Meets Suchinda, Chamlong," 1992.

9. In fact, the King boldly and somewhat surprisingly chose Anand to replace Suchinda despite the fact that Anand would also be an unelected prime minister. Yet it was understood that the highly regarded Anand—a cultured diplomat

and international businessman—would serve only for a few months, and that his primary task would be to prepare Thailand for a new general election in September. See McCullough 1992; and "Anand Panyarachun Interviewed," 1992.

10. "Liberal royalism" is a concept developed by Michael Kelly Connors on pp. 185–86 of *Democracy and National Identity*.

11. Oksenberg and Goldstein 1974.

12. See Meisner 1999; Link 1992; and Goldman 1995.

13. See Chapters 4 and 5 for a fuller discussion.

14. The activist-intellectuals of interviews 302 and 322 actually date Thailand's democratization from October 1997, not May 1992. For overviews of the constitution-drafting process, see the essays in McCargo, ed., *Reforming Thai Politics*.

15. S. J., "Introduction," p. 14. On the 1932 revolution, see Batson 1984.

16. Pridi, *Pridi by Pridi*, pp. 70–72.

17. It was during Phibun's rule that, in 1939, the government changed the name of the country from the multiethnic and cosmopolitan "Siam" to the narrower and more chauvinistic "Thailand."

18. Pridi, *Pridi by Pridi*, p. xvii (from Baker and Pasuk's "Introduction").

19. Sulak, *Powers That Be*.

20. See Suthichai, "Chuan Urged to Set Vision"; "Pak Mun Debacle Due to Communications Gap," 1993; and Phaisan 1993.

21. Pasuk and Baker, "Power in Transition."

22. "Chamlong: Protesters Did Not Die in Vain," 1992.

23. On the significance of this point for Thailand, see Connors, "Framing the 'People's Constitution.'"

24. Even "the process" itself was plural. McCargo writes that in addition to political reform, Thai people were discussing educational reform, media reform, medical reform, reform of academic research, and several other kinds of reform in the 1990s. Thailand had become a society abuzz with change. (McCargo, "Introduction: Understanding Political Reform in Thailand." See, in addition, Chang Noi, "Cultural Revolution in Thailand.")

25. "Student Body Hands Out Manual on Possible Coup," 1992.

26. "Anand Urges Peaceful Resistance to Coup Attempts," 1992.

27. "Time to Focus on How to Deal with the Military," 1992.

28. "Professional Leadership Needed for State Firms," 1992.

29. "PollWatch Submits Suggestions for Fair Elections," 1992.

30. Nophakhun, "Comment."

31. See "Anand Urges Peaceful Resistance to Coup Attempts," p. 48.

32. Interviews 322 and 328.

33. "Decentralization a Priority of 1993," 1993.

34. Interview 330. This activist argued that one of Prime Minister Thaksin's techniques for securing support was to "buy" poor people through his low-interest, state-backed loan programs (see below).

35. Thirayuth, "Good Governance." Also see Prudhisan 1998.

36. Frank E. Reynolds, "Legitimation and Rebellion," p. 137.

37. See Chapter 2.

38. See "Overhauling Thai Politics towards Reforms," 1994.

39. "Thousands Rally to Demand New Constitution," 1994. See, also, "Senior Academic on Political Development," 1994.

40. "Now, There Is No-Win Situation in the Country," 1994.

41. "A Day of Madness and Treachery," 1994. See, also, "The Principle of the Obsolete Politicians," 1994.

42. Prawase, "An Overview of Political Reform," pp. 26–27.

43. McCargo, *Chamlong Srimuang*, p. 207.

44. Connors, "Framing the 'People's Constitution,'" pp. 41–42.

45. Prawase, "An Overview of Political Reform," p. 23.

46. See "Political Reform Only Real Way to Achieve Maturity," 1995.

47. "Appalling Backtrack on Political Reform," 1995; and "Opposition on Government's Political Reform Drive," 1995.

48. See "Democracy Group Sets Political Reform Deadline" 1995; and "Growing Frustration over Political Reform," 1995.

49. "Political Reform: A Serious Question of Sincerity," 1995.

50. Prudhisan, "Thailand," p. 271.

51. Former President of Parliament Uthai Pimjaichon chaired the umbrella CDA.

52. Interview 312.

53. For a detailed overview, see Doneys 2002.

54. Interview 316. On independent commissions, see below.

55. Doneys, "Political Reform," p. 176.

56. Interview 330.

57. See Chapter 2.

58. Interviews 312, 316, and 330. For a detailed overview of the drafting process, see Prudhisan 1998.

59. Chang Noi, "Challenging the Powerful."

60. Interview 330; and Prudhisan 1998. As explained below, the emphasis on community rights is considered by some participants in the drafting process to be the most important distinctively Thai element in the Constitution.

61. For a broad and thoughtful assessment of the crisis and its context, see Laird 2000.

62. Chang Noi, "Challenging the Powerful."

63. Somchai and Supawadee 1997. Snoh was surely making a play on the Maoist strategy of surrounding the cities from the countryside.

64. Supawadee and Ampa 1997.

65. Interview 300.

66. "'Yes' Vote Paves Way for New Era," 1997; and Sirikul and Yuwadee 1997. See, also, Prudhisan, "Thailand," especially pp. 280–83.

67. "Constitution of the Kingdom of Thailand," October 11, 1997.

68. Interview 331.

69. Chang Noi, "Challenging the Powerful."

70. Interviews 328 and 331 are the primary sources of information about the NHRC. See, also, "Interview with Former Thai Prime Minister Anand Panyarachun," 2002.

71. Quotations taken from background materials provided for Interview 328.

72. See below.

73. See Voice of the Asia-Pacific Human Rights Network.

74. The informant in Interview 306—a historian—very helpfully discussed Thai popular perceptions of Burma in historical context. See, also, Sunait and Than, *On Both Sides*, especially pp. 10–31.

75. The problem was so severe that half of Thailand's two million prison inmates in 2000 were serving drug-related sentences. About 3 percent of the population may have been addicted to *yaa baa*, while hundreds of thousands of other people were experimenting with the drug. See Greenfield 2001. For a detailed medical overview, see Davidson et al. 2001.

76. Interview 310.

77. Interview 313.

78. Interview 320.

79. This argument was made with particular eloquence by the informant in Interview 325, a former activist and in 2003 a senior history professor.

80. Interview 302; and Kiatchai 1994. See, also, Rotberg 1998; and Mary P. Callahan 2000.

81. Quoted in Nutsara 1997. Also see Acharya, *Constructing a Security Community*, pp. 108–14.

82. Yindee 1997.

83. "Shameful for ASEAN to Embrace Burma," 1997.

84. Veera 1997. SLORC is the acronym for "State Law and Order Restoration Council," then the euphemistic name for the Burmese junta.

85. "House Panel Opposed to ASEAN Entry for Burma," 1997.

86. Nutsara 1997.

87. "Thailand Supports ASEAN Commission on Human Rights," 1998.

88. Quoted in Marisa, "Minister."

89. "Surin Sees Benefits in Intervention Policy," 1998.

90. Kavi, "Good Ideas Need Discreet Lobbying."

91. Achara 1998; and Kavi, "Towards an Enhanced Interaction."

92. Quoted in Phanrawi and Nutsara 1998.

93. "Abridged Version of Address," 1998. See, also, Surin Pitsuwan 1998.

94. "Abridged Version of Address," 1998.

95. Information for the following paragraphs was provided by the informant in Interview 329.

96. Quotations taken from background materials provided for Interview 329.

97. Quotations taken from "PM's Declaration: Democracy Is Not My Goal," 2003. In the event, the TRT won 377 seats (with 60.1 percent of the popular vote), against ninety-six for the second-largest party, the Democrats (who took 18.3 percent of the popular vote). Thaksin was buoyed by an impressive performance in managing the tsunami disaster that struck Thailand on December 26, 2004,

giving him an opportunity to display his effective administrative skills. (See "PM's Rating Soars after Tsunami Hit," 2005.)

98. Wichit and Watcharapong (2004) summarize the logic.

99. See Chapter 2.

100. See Voice of the Asia-Pacific Human Rights Network.

101. Informants in interviews 324, 325, 327–29, and 331 all stated that Thaksin reminded them of Sarit.

102. Sarit's fortune eventually amounted to $140 million, which of course was a lot of money in the 1960s. See Thak, *Thailand*, pp. 336–37.

103. Note that eighty-one was also a lot of mistresses in the 1960s. "Practically no one was immune from his [Sarit's] overtures: beauty queens, movie stars, night-club hostesses, university and secondary school students. . . . His elaborate network of procurers was the envy of many" (Thak, *Thailand*, p. 339).

104. Thak, *Thailand*, p. 339.

105. Thak, *Thailand*, pp. 160–61. Also see Barme 1993.

106. Thak, *Thailand*, pp. 148–50.

107. See Shari 2003; and Perrin 2003. Thaksin's Shin Corporation also became 50 percent owner of Thai Air Asia, established in November 2003 as a no-frills carrier offering low-priced domestic and international flights: a boon for Thai people of modest income.

108. Quoted in Yuwadee, "Essay Competition for the Poor."

109. Quoted in Thak, *Thailand*, pp. 193–94.

110. Thak, *Thailand*, p. 195. The possibility of pyromania cannot be discounted.

111. Quoted in Thak, *Thailand*, p. 166.

112. Thak, *Thailand*, p. 164.

113. Thak, *Thailand*, p. 190.

114. Dabhoiwala 2003; and Kazmin 2003.

115. Dabhoiwala 2003.

116. Dabhoiwala 2003.

117. See "Thaksin's 'War on Dark Influences,'" 2003.

118. Quoted in Dabhoiwala 2003. One of the major criticisms of the drug campaign was that in fact only "small fry" were killed. The big, well-connected dealers were said to have been left alive and comfortable. See Adams, "Thailand's Crackdown."

119. Quoted in Yuwadee, "Essay Competition for the Poor." In fact, Thaksin did not always or even usually demonstrate significant concern for the downtrodden. Much like Sarit, he sometimes found that they got in the way of a smoothly operating Thailand, Inc. This was the key reason he ordered the Bangkok streets cleared of prostitutes, beggars, stray dogs, and NGO activists in the weeks leading up to the October 2003 APEC conference. He even ordered the Air Force to transport Cambodian beggars back to Phnom Penh. See Adams, "Thaksin's Potemkin Welcome for APEC"; Dimmock, "Hiding the Human Evidence"; and Aphaluck 2003.

120. Cited in "Thaksin's 'War on Dark Influences,'" 2003.

121. See Shari 2003.

122. Quoted in Pasuk and Baker, *Thailand*, p. 309.

123. Quoted in Pasuk and Baker, *Thailand*, p. 310.

124. Interviews 322, 324, 327.

125. Cited in "Thaksin's 'War on Dark Influences,'" 2003.

126. Barnes 2002.

127. "King Wants Drug Toll Explained," 2003.

128. Interview 326.

129. Interviews 319, 322, and 328; and Supara Janchitfah, "Enemies of the State?" *Bangkok Post*, 5 January 2003 <http://www.bangkokpost.com>.

130. On the promises and perils of "Thaksinomics," see Daniel Lian, "Thaksin's Model," *Asiaweek*, 17 August 2001 <http://www.asiaweek.com>; Chang Noi, "Understanding Thaksin's Pluto-Populism," *The Nation*, 18 February 2002 <http://www.nationmultimedia.com>; Shari 2003; and Perrin 2003.

131. Interviews 322 and 330; Supara 2003; and Yuwadee, "PM Denies Trying to Cut NGO Funding."

132. See Supara 2003.

133. Quoted in Chang Noi, "NGOs, Violence, and Money."

134. "PM Slams 'Anarchists,'" 2002.

135. Quoted in Marisa, "UN Envoy."

136. "PM Slams UN Envoy as Biased," 2003.

137. Quoted in Voice of the Asia-Pacific Human Rights Network.

138. See "Former Premier [Anand Panyarachun]," 1995.

139. "King Calls for End to Intolerance," 2001.

140. Quoted in "Thaksin Taught the Value of Criticism," 2003.

141. Fullbrook 2006.

142. On Thaksin's ideological influences—most from the business world—see Nophakhun, "Watchdog."

Chapter 4

1. Sometimes PRC state leaders and supportive intellectuals assert that democracy is an eventual goal, but "eventually" always means several decades into a hazy future. As detailed in Chapter 5, the official goal of political reform since mid-2002 has been establishment of a new "political civilization" that would transcend democracy and be superior to it.

2. Almost all Chinese intellectuals are directly or indirectly employed by the party-state. This fact sharply constrains the range of opinions intellectuals express publicly and channels their views down paths not usually supportive of democratization. A lifetime of socialization into the Party-dominated environment ensures that successful intellectuals will have internalized "correct" views starting from an early age. Of course, there are also dissidents—numerous in absolute terms—but they rarely get the chance to publish their views. Sometimes mavericks flourish

briefly but they are always subject to arrest, exile, or imprisonment. The CCP seems significantly more tolerant of mavericks who err on the side of nationalistic extremism; for example, it winked at the authors of mid-1990s chauvinistic tracts such as *China Can Say "No"* (1996). Mavericks erring on the side of liberalism frequently get themselves into serious trouble, while those who err on the side of quasi-atavistic antimodernism (such as the Falungong Buddhists) are subject to ruthless repression.

3. On this point, see Friedman, *National Identity and Democratic Prospects*, noting especially his argument that a counterhegemonic southern-oriented national identity could serve as the cultural basis for future democratization efforts (pp. 87–114).

4. Even leaders and establishment intellectuals disagree among themselves, though not, apparently, about the core assumptions explained in this chapter and Chapter 5. What they think privately might also differ from what they articulate in print.

5. For an excellent discussion of the roles these IR journals play in PRC policymaking, see Shambaugh 2002.

6. The literature on obstacles to, and prospects for, China's democratization is voluminous and rich, and cannot be reviewed satisfactorily in this limited space. Notably important works include (but are not limited to) Nathan 1985; Friedman, *National Identity and Democratic Prospects*; Goldman 1995; and Zhao, *China and Democracy*. Also see the special January 2004 issue of the *Journal of Democracy*, which focuses exclusively on China. Most of the writers cited here explicitly analyze the cultural obstacles to China's democratization, but conclude with varying degrees of optimism that since culture is evolving and can be reconstructed consciously, democracy is possible in China. But to evaluate democracy's prospects fully, the specific cultural variable of elite aversion to decentering must be analyzed within the context of Chinese articulation with liberal-rational global culture.

7. O'Donnell and Schmitter 1986.

8. See Gallagher 2004.

9. "Hegemonic" in English-language political science and IR generally means "dominant," but the word "hegemonistic" in Chinese (*badao*) has the much stronger connotation of dominating unreasonably and by force, ruling by might instead of right, acting high-handedly and bullying the weak. Ancient Chinese kings and eventually emperors might be civilized and persuaded to abandon such rude hegemonistic behavior by the precepts of Confucianism; they would then exemplify "the way of kings" (*wangdao*). Since the 1960s, the CCP has used "hegemonistic" to describe and denounce its primary geostrategic opponent, first the Soviet Union and, since the 1989 democracy movement, the United States. The term is intentionally deployed not only to suggest hostility and disapproval, but also the notion that China's enemies are playing outside the rules of the game of even Realist international relations—for example, by "interfering in other sovereign countries' internal affairs."

10. See Minxin Pei 2000.

11. On the economic and regulatory dimensions of China's opening to the outside world, see Zweig's meticulously researched *Internationalizing China*.

12. For the effects on Taiwan, see Chapter 7.

13. They do not envision a "postmodern" world except insofar as the West is decentered. At least judging from published works, Chinese understanding of postmodernism is distorted by nationalism and Sinocentrism; hence, most Chinese intellectuals fail to appreciate the possibility of China becoming decentered vis-à-vis Tibet, Xinjiang, Mongolia, and Taiwan.

14. Of course it is challenged in Taiwan, but Beijing's leaders and intellectuals dismiss the Taiwanese challenge as merely despicable splittism (see Chapter 7).

15. Western scholars of international relations have traditionally dated the origins of the modern states-system to the 1648 Treaty of Westphalia, in which European states acknowledged each other's sovereignty over religious and other matters inside the territories they sought to govern. In recent years, critical and historically minded IR scholars have uncovered evidence that Westphalia was actually not such an important treaty at the time. Nineteenth century state-builders exaggerated its importance to enhance efforts to legitimate the states-system. See Krasner 1999; Osiander 2001; and Teschke 2003.

16. On the concept of enabling facilities, see Mann, *The Sources of Social Power*, especially pp. 1–33.

17. If the world begins before Westphalia, Chinese writers must explain why Qin succeeded in establishing hegemony over all the known world (*tianxia*) in 221 BCE, and why this condition has been sanctified ever since. The multipolar modernity concept requires that an essential China arrived on the stage of international relations as a fully coherent power pole after 1648.

18. Ni and Wang, "Shilun guoji guanxi minzhuhua," p. 24.

19. Ni and Wang, "Shilun guoji guanxi minzhuhua," p. 24.

20. On this point, also see Wang Yi 2000.

21. Zhang Wenmu, "Zhongguo guojia anquan zhexue," p. 24.

22. Zhang Yan, "Xinxi shidai de diyuan zhengzhi yu 'kejiquan,'" p. 20. On information space, see Chapter 5.

23. Zhang Yan, "Xinxi shidai de diyuan zhengzhi yu 'kejiquan,'" p. 18.

24. Wang Zhijun, "'Hou lingtu shidai' yu diyuan zhanlue de shanbian," p. 33.

25. Huntington, *The Clash of Civilizations*.

26. See Li Luqu 2002. Judging from the tone of some of their articles, another factor motivating Chinese specialists to accept Huntington's categories is that they are flattered the famous Harvard professor would assign China a central role in pan-Asian history and assert that premodern Chinese Confucianism undergirds wider East Asian civilization.

27. See Chapter 1.

28. Thus, Yan Xuetong writes that the chief contemporary international "contradiction" is the US drive for hegemony and the other great powers' efforts to stop it. (Yan, "Lishi de jixu," pp. 9–10).

29. Zhang Yan, "Xinxi shidai de diyuan zhengzhi yu 'kejiquan,'" p. 18.

30. Song Yimin, "2010 nian qian wo guo zai shijie shang mianlin de jiyu yu tiaozhan," p. 3.

31. Note that although many people in other countries find American arrogance and unilateralism offensive, they do not usually regard with jealousy the possibility that the United States is the Center. Thai and Taiwanese intellectual and political elites who sometimes find themselves aghast at US foreign policy do not argue that, as a result, their countries should reject democratization.

32. Song Yimin, "2010 nian qian wo guo zai shijie shang mianlin de jiyu yu tiaozhan," p. 3.

33. Zhang Minqian 2000.

34. On the inevitability of US failure and ultimate triumph of multipolarism, see the concluding sections of Chapter 5.

35. Wang Jisi, "Meiguo baquan de luoji," p. 12. Wang appears partly to be taking President George W. Bush's January 2002 "axis of evil" speech and extrapolating from it to all of America, past and present. Indeed, another author argued essentially that Bush is one of the most American presidents in history, by first establishing that self-righteousness is the essence of Americanness, and then arguing that Bush is one of the most self-righteous presidents in US history. (Shi Aiguo, "'Minzhu heping lun' pouxi," p. 1.)

36. Ultimately, even the opinions and judgments of American IR specialists are "basically the same" (*datongxiaoyi*); and their influence on the general public results in a unity of American views (*yanlun yilu*). (Wang Jisi, "Meiguo Baquan," pp. 20–27.)

37. Here it would appear that Wang is partly "mirror-imaging" from his own society, where divergent views exist, but on key issues can be extremely dangerous to articulate. The result is an impression of uniformity, which the party-state encourages with frequent statements such as "The Chinese people are united in their determination to prevent Taiwan from becoming independent."

38. Chomsky's official Web site is <http://www.chomsky.info>.

39. Wang Jisi, "Meiguo Baquan," pp. 20–25. Liu Jianfei of the Research Center for International Strategy in the Central Party School (as of 2002) also argues that Americans agree on the goal of hegemony, and that there is no genuine pluralism in US society. (Liu Jianfei, "Leng zhan hou Meiguo," pp. 16–17.)

40. See Keane 2003.

41. The CCP allows environmental NGOs to work in China, but not human rights NGOs such as Forum-Asia and Focus on the Global South. See Economy, *The River Runs Black*, pp. 129–75.

42. See Chapter 1.

43. Wang argues that hegemonism will only end if people in developing countries stop lining up at US consulates the world over trying to emigrate to the United States. This is because Americans boast that "yes, the world hates us, but everyone keeps trying to come to the United States." If people in developing countries would stop making the Americans feel so proud of themselves, their self-confidence would weaken and eventually their "hegemonistic mindset" (*baquan*

xintai) would shatter. After that, the new "multipolar epoch" (*duojihua shidai*) would begin—an event which, as explained in Chapter 5, is in any case inevitable. (Wang Jisi, "Meiguo Baquan," p. 29.)

44. Lu, Zhang, and Wang, "Mei yu zai ti renquan fan Hua yi'an de tedian he beijing," pp. 8–10; quotations on p. 9.

45. Shan Min 2001. On Kosovo, see below.

46. Lu, Zhang, and Wang, "Mei yu zai ti renquan fan Hua yi'an de tedian he beijing," p. 10.

47. Shi Aiguo, "'Minzhu heping lun' pouxi," pp. 2–3.

48. Shi Aiguo, "'Minzhu heping lun' pouxi," pp. 4–5.

49. Zheng Hangsheng 1996.

50. "Peaceful evolution" refers to China's slow transformation into an American-style capitalist democracy. After the Tiananmen massacre of June 4th, 1989 and the subsequent collapse of East European and Russian Communism, Chinese propagandists and many intellectuals began arguing that Secretary of State John Foster Dulles predicted in the 1950s that the West would be able to destroy international communism in a "smokeless war" entailing subversion through cultural and social penetration. "Peaceful evolution" therefore connotes dangerous American cultural and social influence that will, if not resisted, lead to China's democratization and ultimate transmogrification through decentering.

51. Jiang and Li 1999.

52. For a related argument, see Huang Zhaoyu 2000.

53. Wang Xiaode, "Guanyu 'Meiguohua' yu quan qiu duoyuan wenhua fazhan de sikao," especially pp. 87–91.

54. See Chapter 5.

55. Jiang visited the United States in October 1997 and Clinton visited China in June 1998.

56. Huang Qing 1997. Also see Huang Yi 2001.

57. Wright 2002.

58. See Xiao Gongqin, "Shixi Zhong Mei zhengzhi wenhua zhangli," pp. 42–43.

59. Wang Tianxi 1999.

60. See Wang Zhijun, "'Hou lingtu shidai' yu diyuan zhanlue de shanbian," especially pp. 33–4; and Fan Guoxiang 2000.

61. Ma Ling 1999.

62. See Zhang Tiegang 2001.

63. Shih Chun-yu 1999.

64. Zhang Zhengdong 1999.

65. He Chong, "NATO Has Changed Its Role."

66. See Yang Yonghong 1999; Yan, "Lishi de jixu," p. 10; and Gu, "Xifang rendao zhuyi ganyu lilun pipan yu xuanze," pp. 33–34.

67. Quoted in Ma Ling 1999.

68. Yao quoted in Ma Ling 1999. Following a twenty-day inspection visit to ninety-one Yugoslav cities, towns, and villages, Human Rights Watch calculated

that about 500 civilians died in the bombing. <http://www.hrw.org>. See, also, Zhang and Yuan 1999.

69. "*Renmin Ribao* Commentator on Embassy Bombing," 1999. Three Chinese "journalists" (who actually might have been intelligence officers) were killed and 20 people were injured in the bombing.

70. "Aggression and Atrocities Make One Boil with Anger," 1999.

71. Quoted in Li and Wang 1999.

72. Quoted in Li and Wang 1999.

73. "Embassy Attack Exposes 'Rights Champion,'" 1999.

74. "Chinese Human Rights Specialists Denounce NATO Bombing," 1999.

75. "Chinese in Belgrade, Beijing Protest Embassy Bombing" 1999; "More on US Ambassador to PRC," 1999.

76. Quoted in Mudie 1999.

77. Pollack 1999.

78. "Democracy Party Warned to Stay Clear of NATO Protest," 1999.

79. "*Renmin Ribao* Condemns 'Pro-Democracy' Elements," 1999.

80. Tang Runhua 1999.

81. Huang and Ji 1999.

82. For an overview, see Wang Xingfang 2000.

83. See Fan Guoxiang, "Renquan, zhuquan, baquan," pp. 10–11; and Liu Wenzong 2000.

84. Li Zhimin, "Zhishi jingji shidai guojia zhuquan zai renshi," p. 25.

85. See Johnston, "Learning Versus Adaptation"; and Johnston, "International Structures and Chinese Foreign Policy."

86. Li Zhimin, "Zhishi jingji shidai guojia zhuquan zai renshi," p. 27.

87. Xiao Gongqin, "Shixi Zhong Mei zhengzhi wenhua zhangli," especially p. 41.

88. "China's Efforts to Establish Socialist Human Rights," 2001.

89. Risse and Sikkink 1999; also see Foot, *Rights Beyond Borders*, pp. 113–250.

90. "China's Efforts," 2001; "China Launches First Magazine on Human Rights," 2002; and Wu Jing, "China's Largest Human Rights Website Opens."

91. But it can certainly reject US State Department criticism of China's human rights situation. For one of many examples, see "US Criticism of China's Human Rights Record Reveals Cold War Mentality," 2004.

92. He Chong, "Great Significance of China's Ratification."

93. Dong Yunhu 2004.

94. See the discussion of Risse and Sikkink's work in Chapter 1.

95. Quoted in "Chinese Experts Discuss Human Rights Protection," 2002.

96. Note the striking contrast with Thailand, where student democracy protestors in 1973 "succeeded in creating a firmly-entrenched public image of themselves as the true defenders of the most sacred values of the Thai civic order, and in thoroughly discrediting the continuing efforts of the government to tar their protest with the brush of either youthful irresponsibility or communist subversion." (Frank E. Reynolds, "Legitimation and Rebellion," p. 41.)

97. For a penetrating analytical overview, see Zhao, "Chinese Nationalism."

98. "A Program for Education in Patriotism," 1995.

99. Ren Zhongping 2000.

100. Ren Zhongping 2000.

101. "Hu Jintao," 1999.

102. For example, see "On Li Hongzhi and the Political Nature and Serious Harm of his 'Falun Dafa,'" 1999; and Xin Wen, "Methods Used by 'Falungong' to Trample on Human Nature."

103. Wang Leiming 2000.

104. Friedman, "The Most Popular Social Movement in China During the 1990s."

105. Although the CCP accused the Falungong of violating liberal-rational global culture norms, it also argued that the organization was working closely with external hostile forces seeking to Westernize and split China, primarily in the United States. ("It Is Necessary to Maintain Vigilance," 2001.)

106. Zheng Yongnian 2001; quotations on pp. 2, 6, and 10.

107. See Bovingdon 2002; and Baranovitch 2001.

108. Quoted in Becker 1999.

109. Quoted in Becker 1999.

110. China Society for Human Rights Studies 1999.

111. Quoted in "Beijing Warns Against 'Narrow Nationalism,'" 1996.

112. "Why Dalai Tells Wild Lies," 2000.

113. Thailand's Sulak Sivaraksa considers the Dalai Lama "a friend and a hero" (Interview 327).

114. See, for example, "Article Blasts US for Backing Dalai's Separatist Activities," 2001.

115. For one example of many, see "Tibetan Monks Suffer China Patriotism Campaign," 1997.

116. For an unusually candid and detailed elaboration of the (at the time, at least) deteriorating situation in Xinjiang, see Wang Xinhong 2001.

117. Chen Feng 2001.

118. Quoted in Bao 2001.

119. According to Amnesty International, by the late 1990s Xinjiang had become the region of China with the most executions per capita—in a country that already executed more people than all other countries combined. See "PRC's Xinjiang Anti-Crime Campaign Targets Muslim Separatists," 2001.

120. "Abdurixit on Stepped-Up Ideological Battle," 2002. See, also, "Xinjiang Mobilizes the Whole People to Launch Anti-Separatism Struggle," 2002.

121. Also see Johnston, "Chinese Middle Class Attitudes Towards International Affairs."

Chapter 5

1. *Strategy and Management* was by far the most provocative and intellectually stimulating of the Chinese IR journals before the Party banned it in August

2004. The journal's offense, apparently, was to publish an article criticizing North Korean dictator Kim Jong-il, a CCP ally. See Tkacik 2004.

2. Wang Xiaodong 2000.

3. See Chapter 3.

4. He Jiadong 2000. He's article went to press at almost exactly the same time as the CCP was ordering a ban on all his publications and those of other liberal scholars such as Li Shenzhi and Liu Junning. See "Veteran Diplomat Writes Article," 2000.

5. Chen Dabai 2000. Chen's liberalism is somewhat compromised by his insistence that Mao Zedong exemplified Liang Qichao-style nationalism. However, this may have been a tactical move on Chen's part, since Mao can be used as a symbol to legitimate all sorts of political discourses.

6. Xiao Gongqin, "Shixi Zhong Mei zhengzhi wenhua zhangli," p. 45.

7. See Chapter 4.

8. He Jiadong, "Zhongguo wenti yujing xia de zhuyi zhi zheng," especially pp. 107–11.

9. Wang Sirui, "Zhongguo jingji zengzhang yu zhengzhi gaige," especially pp. 71–73. In addition to corruption, Wang writes that worsening inequality, environmental destruction, low investment in education, and other factors are all preparing the ground for serious economic difficulties in China, and perhaps a collapse.

10. Wang Sirui, "Zhongguo jingji zengzhang yu zhengzhi gaige," p. 77.

11. But "closet liberalism" may be more widespread. See Fang Jue 1998; Mao Yushi 1998; and Liu Junning 2000.

12. Yu, "Guoji zhengyi." Yu formerly worked at the Beijing Contemporary Chinese Language Research Institute, but by 2003 had moved to the Zhong-Mei Wenhua Feituo Gongcheng Lianhe Zuweihui, an organization whose mission is uncertain but which evidently works in the field of cultural exchanges with the United States. This would seem to reflect Yu's *relatively* broad-minded position on democratization and decentering.

13. See the discussion in Chapter 1 of the work of John Boli and George Thomas, in particular.

14. Yu, "Guoji zhengyi," pp. 54–60. Also see Yu, "21 shiji Zhongguo xiandaihua yicheng (shang)."

15. See Chapter 4.

16. This is suggested by another of Yu's articles, discussed below.

17. Yu, "Guoji zhengyi," p. 52.

18. Yu, "Guoji zhengyi," p. 53.

19. Note that Yu contended in an earlier article on "Chinese Culture within World Civilization" that Tibetan culture, Zhuang culture, and other minority cultures were all subsumed under Chinese culture and therefore not allowed a direct interface with world civilization. (Yu, "Shijie wenming zhong de Zhongguo wenhua.")

20. See Bovingdon 2002; and Baranovitch 2001.

21. Yu, "Guoji zhengyi," p. 53.

22. Yu, "Guoji zhengyi," p. 60.

23. Yu, "Guoji zhengyi," p. 61.

24. See note 1, this chapter.

25. See "Living Dangerously on the Net," 2003. Also see Chase and Mulvenon 2002.

26. For a detailed explanation of the rationale, see Ding 2001.

27. Sometimes the CCP's intolerance for organized dissent becomes tragically ridiculous. For example, see Philip P. Pan 2004.

28. Zhang Ji and Li Hui, "Leng zhan hou guoji zhengzhi zhong de wenhua chongtu," p. 46 (emphasis added).

29. "*Renmin Ribao* Editorial," 1996. Also see Li Zhimin 2001; and Liu Jianfei, "Lun yishi xingtai."

30. Chen Xiaowei and Yin Fang, "Xin shiji Meiguo de 'shuzi diqiu' jihua," p. 30.

31. Yang Yang, "Qian xi wenhua zai guoji guanxi zhong de zuoyong," p. 40. Also see Yang Cheng 2002.

32. Zhang Li and Bai Jie, "Hulianwang de fazhan dui guoji guanxi de yingxiang," quotations on pp. 13 and 15.

33. Liu Yongtao, "Lengzhan hou Meiguo dui wai wenhua zhanlue touxi," p. 14.

34. In August 2000, President Jiang Zemin called in a speech before the 16th World Computers Conference in Beijing for the establishment of an international (state-based) convention on Internet content and security. The Chinese bureaucracy does not appear to have followed up the proposal with significant diplomatic attention. ("It Is High Time to Formulate an International Convention on the Internet," 2000.)

35. Also see Hu Lianhe, "Lun lengzhan jieshu hou de guojia wenhua anquan," especially pp. 33–34; and Zhang Ji and Li Hui, "Leng zhan hou guoji zhengzhi zhong de wenhua chongtu," especially pp. 44–45.

36. Chen Xiaowei and Yin Fang, "Xin shiji Meiguo de 'shuzi diqiu' jihua," p. 30.

37. Also see Zhang Yan 2001. Zhang argues that the US National Information Infrastructure and Global Information Infrastructure plans are schemes designed "to destroy international restrictions and control cross-border information flows" (Zhang Yan, "Xinxi shidai de diyuan zhengzhi yu 'kejiquan,'" p. 21). Similarly, Zhan Jiafeng and Zhang Jinrong argue that the US "is scheming to use information networks to achieve its goal of controlling the world" (Zhan Jiafeng and Zhang Jinrong, "Keji geming yu diyuan zhengzhi lilun de yanbian," p. 34).

38. For the classic Chinese case, see Lewis and Xue 1991.

39. Li Zhongjie 2002.

40. Quoted in Zhou 1995.

41. Zhou 1995.

42. Zheng Hangsheng 1996.

43. See Wang Shaoguang 2000.

44. Xing Benxi 2000.

45. Xie Hong 2000.

46. See, also, Xiao Ping 2001.

47. Yang Jianping 2001.

48. Xiao Gongqin, "Hou quanneng tizhi," p. 1.

49. Xiao Gongqin, "Hou quanneng tizhi," pp. 2–3.

50. Xu Xianglin, "Yi zhengzhi wending wei jichu de Zhongguo jianjin zhengzhi gaige," especially pp. 21–24.

51. Zheng Yongnian, "Zhengzhi gaige yu Zhongguo guojia jianshe," p. 4.

52. Zheng Yongnian, "Zhengzhi gaige yu Zhongguo guojia jianshe," quotations on pp. 3 and 6.

53. Yang Jianping, "Fazhi minzhu: houfa guojia de zhengzhi xuanze," p. 87.

54. Yang Jianping, "Fazhi minzhu: houfa guojia de zhengzhi xuanze," p. 86.

55. Li Luqu, "Dongya wenhua yu minzhu de goujian," p. 36.

56. Note that Li's formulation cannot solve the *tiyong* problem because the *ti* of China today is no longer Confucianism but is instead "socialism with Chinese characteristics." Confucianism can fairly easily be squared with democratization, as Li's article suggests. Squaring "socialism with Chinese characteristics" with democracy is, on the other hand, an apparently insurmountable challenge.

57. See "To Grasp In-Depth Important Thinking of 'Three Represents,'" 2003.

58. Sun Chih 2002 (emphasis added).

59. Arch-conservative Li Peng offered precisely this interpretation during an inspection trip to Fujian in December 2002. See Zhang Sutang and Wu Yilong 2002.

60. "No Foreign or Indigenous Dogmatism," 2002.

61. Quoted in "No Foreign or Indigenous Dogmatism," 2002.

62. Quoted in Li Shufeng, Wu Huanqing, and Tian Yu 2002.

63. "To Grasp In-Depth Important Thinking," 2003. Also see Wang Xialin 2003.

64. "To Grasp In-Depth Important Thinking," 2003.

65. The numbers are difficult to specify precisely, because practice seems to vary widely on the basis of idiosyncratic factors. See Li Du 1998; and "Unswervingly Promote Democracy at Rural Grassroots Levels" 2002.

66. The political transformation of the villages in the past decade is a topic of great depth and complexity that cannot even begin to be addressed adequately here. For excellent overviews and analyses, see Wang Zhenyao 2000; O'Brien 2001; and the voluminous resources available online at the joint Carter Center-Beijing University "China Elections and Governance" Web site.

67. Yue Yan and Zhen Hai 1997.

68. These articles also seem to be directed at domestic audiences. See, for example, Luobuciren and Gamaduji 1997; "Beijing Villagers Said Practicing 'Village Democracy,'" 2001; and Wang Jinfu and Chen Binhua 2002.

69. At a key central meeting in 1989, elder Peng Zhen stood up and argued that village self-rule meant no more or less than institutionalization of the mass

line. Peng declared: "If the Communist Party doesn't want the mass line, then it isn't even the Communist Party." (Quoted in Wang Zhenyao, "Zhongguo de cunmin zizhi yu minzhuhua fazhan daolu," p. 101.)

70. The elections are sometimes legitimated as superior to Western elections. Thus, one Chinese reporter declared that the "special feature" of Chinese village democracy is that "many candidates are nominated" for individual positions, and that this practice "is an innovation in the election history of the world." (Li Weiwei 2002.)

71. Wang Jinfu and Chen Binhua 2002.

72. See Xu Xianglin 2000.

73. "Xinhua Reports on Internet Bringing Major Changes to China," 2002.

74. "PRC Officials View New Role Played by Internet," 2001.

75. See, for example, "Common People Attending On-line NPC Session," 2002. Also see Zittrain and Edelman <http://cyber.law.harvard.edu/filtering/china/>.

76. Tang Tianri 2001.

77. Lu Baosheng 2002.

78. See Chapter 1.

79. Ni and Wang, "Shilun guoji guanxi minzhuhua," quotation on p. 23.

80. Ni and Wang, "Shilun guoji guanxi minzhuhua," p. 23.

81. See Chapter 1.

82. Wang Yi, "Quanqiuhua beijing xia de duojihua jincheng," quotation on p. 2. Praising globalization in this way should put China at odds with international NGOs in the global oppositional culture, but some Chinese intellectuals have sought to argue that the CCP and global civil society are united in opposing US hegemony. For example, see Cai and Liu 2002.

83. Wang Yi, "Quanqiuhua beijing xia de duojihua jincheng," p. 3. Wang does not explain what causes economic globalization to be inevitable.

84. Also see Li Zong, "Dangjin shidai tedian manyi," especially p. 4. Li argues that world historical development is governed by "laws" (*guilu*); he cites by way of example the collapse of the Soviet Union, which—though very few people predicted it, including Chinese Communists—"had a law-like and inevitable nature."

85. Wang Jisi, "Lue lun dangqian shijie de zhengzhi tezheng," p. 6.

86. Shi Yinhong, "Geju, chaoliu, shidai tezheng," especially p. 9. Shi does not cite McNeill, however.

87. See Kugler and Organski 1989.

88. Zhang Wenmu 2000.

89. Zhang Wenmu, "Zhongguo guojia anquan zhexue," p. 31.

90. Zhang Shenjun, "Quan qiu jiegou chongtu yu Meiguo baquan de hefaxing weiji," especially pp. 37–41. Also see Song Yimin, "2010 nian qian wo guo zai shijie shang mianlin de jiyu yu tiaozhan," pp. 6–8; and Hu Lianhe, "Lun lengzhan jieshu hou de guojia wenhua anquan," especially p. 34.

91. Also see Pan Zhongqi 2003; and Wang Xiaode 2003.

92. Li Zhongjie 2002.

93. Zheng Yongnian, "Zhengzhi gaige yu Zhongguo guojia jianshe," p. 8.

94. Yu Xilai, "21 shiji Zhongguo xiandaihua yicheng (xia)," quotation on p. 1 (emphasis added).

95. Shen, "Wenming duihua de guoji guanxi yihan," quotation on p. 25.

96. Yu Xilai, "21 shiji Zhongguo xiandaihua yicheng (xia)," p. 3. Xiao Gongqin agrees that China should not at present lead a world-scale struggle against hegemonism but should instead follow Deng Xiaoping's dictum "to not stick out" (*bu yao dang tou*). It should only contest hegemonism when CCP-defined "core Chinese interests" are threatened, such as in Taiwan. (Xiao Gongqin, "Shixi Zhong Mei zhengzhi wenhua zhangli," p. 44.)

97. Yu grants India a separate sphere, both because of its obvious civilizational differences and because, he says, Samuel Huntington predicted that India will have awesome comprehensive power by the mid-twenty-first century. This is a fact worthy of some respect, and Yu chides his fellow Chinese for frequently denigrating India, just as (he says) the West denigrates China. (Yu Xilai, "21 shiji Zhongguo xiandaihua yicheng [xia]," p. 5.)

98. Yu Xilai, "21 shiji Zhongguo xiandaihua yicheng (xia)," p. 4. Also see "Is Korea a Forward Base for the Globalization of Chinese?" 2005.

99. Yu Xilai, "21 shiji Zhongguo xiandaihua yicheng (xia)," p. 5.

100. Yu Xilai, "21 shiji Zhongguo xiandaihua yicheng (xia)," p. 5.

101. Shen Qurong gives as an example of dialogue across cultures the Shanghai Cooperative Organization, the group formed by China with Russia, Kazakhstan, Uzbekistan, Kyrgyzstan, and Tajikistan as a club of authoritarian states trying to suppress separatists and Muslim extremists. (Shen, "Wenming duihua de guoji guanxi yihan," p. 28.)

102. Yu Xilai, "21 shiji Zhongguo xiandaihua yicheng (xia)," p. 6.

103. See Economy 2004.

104. Yu Xilai, "21 shiji Zhongguo xiandaihua yicheng (xia)," p. 8.

105. For the classic explanation, see Levenson 1965.

106. Yu Xilai, "21 shiji Zhongguo xiandaihua yicheng (xia)," pp. 8–11.

107. Wang Xiaodong, "Qian tan renquan baozhang," p. 73.

108. Alastair Iain Johnston devastates this image in Johnston, *Cultural Realism*; and in Johnston, "China's Militarized Interstate Dispute Behavior 1949–1992."

109. Yang Yang, "Qian xi wenhua zai guoji guanxi zhong de zuoyong," p. 42.

110. Yang Yang, "Qian xi wenhua zai guoji guanxi zhong de zuoyong," p. 42.

111. Lu Yaohuai of Zhongnan University argues that the Internet, currently "choking with Western values," can be reformed for the better by remodeling on the basis of Chinese ethics. He gives as an example the Confucian/Mencian virtue that a person should monitor himself and act as a gentleman even when alone (*shendu*). If only the world's Internet users would adopt this Chinese virtue, flame-wars and other Internet rowdiness would cease. (Lu Yaohuai 2002.)

Chapter 6

1. On Taiwan's general social and economic development through the mid-1980s, see Gold 1986; Winckler and Greenhalgh 1988; and Rubinstein, "Political Taiwanization and Pragmatic Diplomacy," especially pp. 436–40.

2. Chang Yen-hsien, "Taiwan shi yanjiu yu taiwan zhutixing."

3. Linz and Stepan, *Problems of Democratic Transition and Consolidation*, p. 19.

4. The informant in Interview 223 made this case most cogently. But also see Wachman 1994, who argues that democratization was more a tool which the Taiwanese used as an ethnic group to achieve socioeconomic gains vis-à-vis Mainlanders.

5. This was necessary because, as Ch'en Fang-ming wrote in 1995, "even though [the KMT's] colonial system and martial law system have already broken up, the colonial mentality and martial law mentality have not evaporated" (Ch'en Fang-ming, "Taiwan zuoyi yundong shi yu zhengzhi bianqian" p. 465). Much of the research for the Taiwan chapters of this book was conducted at the Taiwan Historical Research Materials Center, which is located on Nanjing East Road in Taipei. Under Chang Yen-hsien's leadership, the Center has become a busy place, with scholars and students from many different institutions making use of its small but growing collection. At the same time, by the end of the 1990s—and especially after the DPP took power in 2000—Taiwan experienced an explosion of social interest in "Taiwan Studies" as most major bookstores established "Taiwan Studies" sections. This popularized the intellectual interest in Taiwanese identity. Such developments would have been impossible in the absence of democratization.

6. Chang Yen-hsien, "Towards a New 21st Century Taiwan." Also see Lin Miao-jung, "Historians Alter Their Perspective."

7. The generalizations to follow concerning the main themes of this new Taiwan history are based primarily on a reading of the following works: Ch'en Hao-yang, *Taiwan sibainian shuminshi*; Huang Hung-hsiung, *Taiwan kangri shihua*; Shih Ming, *Taiwan bu shi Zhongguo de yibufen*; Chang Te-shui, *Jidong! Taiwan de lishi*; Huang Chao-t'ang *Taiwan lunxian lunwenji*; Chang Yen-hsien et al., eds., *Taiwan jinbainianshi*; Chang Yen-hsien, Lee Hsiao-feng, and Tai Pao-cun, eds., *Taiwan shi lunwen jingxuan*; and Chang Yen-hsien, Tseng Chiu-mei, and Chen Chao-hai, eds., *"Maixiang 21 shiji de taiwan."*

8. Most accept that liberal Mainlanders can become "new Taiwanese" if they embrace democracy and reject Sinocentrism.

9. See Stainton 1999.

10. See Lee Chiao, "Taiwan wenhua yu xin guojia," pp. 350–51.

11. See the CCP's "A History of Taiwan."

12. For an authoritative English-language account consistent with the Taiwanese interpretation, see Wills 1999.

13. See Chang Sheng-yen et al., eds., *Taiwan kaifa shi*, especially pp. 189–96.

14. Gardella, "From Treaty Ports to Provincial Status, 1860–1894," pp. 180–81.

15. See Hsu Hsueh-ji, especially pp. 77–87. Hsu notes that many of Taiwan's degree holders actually bought their titles, suggesting the possibility that holding a degree did not always imply identification with Chinese culture.

16. See Chapter 7.

17. Interview 223.

18. Gardella, "From Treaty Ports to Provincial Status, 1860–1894," , p. 173.

19. Ch'en I-shen, "Lun Taiwan er er ba shijian de yuanyin," p. 323.

20. Sun Ta-ch'uan 1996; also see below. The physical presence of Japanese on Taiwan would become quite large, reaching 270,000 (about 5 percent of the population) by 1935. Japanese governors tightly centralized administration to maintain order and implement development policies. They organized Taiwan into a hierarchy of household groups (*ho* and *ko*) and mobilized the groups for public health campaigns, construction of public works such as roads and harbors, and eventually the wholesale importation of Japanese culture. (See Lamley, "Taiwan Under Japanese Rule, 1895–1945," especially pp. 213–23.)

21. Chang Yen-hsien, "Taiwan shi yanjiu yu taiwan zhutixing," p. 433. Also see Leo T. S. Ching, *Becoming Japanese*, especially pp. 51–132.

22. Wang T'ai-sheng, "Bainian lai taiwan falu de xifanghua"; and Wang T'ai-sheng, "Zhonghua minguo fatizhi de taiwanhua."

23. The lawyer-activists (two eventually became politicians) in interviews 216, 219, and 228 also stressed the importance of Taiwan's distinctive legal history in its eventual democratization.

24. Lamley writes that "students from Taiwan [in Japan] began to increase appreciably after 1915. By 1922, at least 2,400 Taiwanese students were reportedly enrolled in educational institutions in metropolitan Japan. . . . Around 1945, the total number of Taiwanese living there may have grown to between twenty and thirty thousand." (Lamley, "Taiwan Under Japanese Rule, 1895–1945," pp. 230–31.)

25. Chang Yen-hsien, "Taiwan wenhua xiehui de chengli yu fenlie." The movement later splintered as a radical wing sought to mobilize peasants to contest Japanese *zaibatsu* economic exploitation. Later Taiwanese nationalists appropriated Chiang Wei-shui as a symbol of subjectivity and democracy. See Huang Hung-hsiung, "Dajia lai jinian Jiang Weishui xiansheng."

26. Lee Hsiao-feng 1996a.

27. Lin Ch'i-yang 1996; and see Chapter 7.

28. Lee Hsiao-feng 1996a.

29. Chang Yen-hsien, "Taiwan shi yanjiu yu taiwan zhutixing"; Chang Kuo-hsing 1996; and Hsiau, *Contemporary Taiwanese Cultural Nationalism*, pp. 29–49.

30. Data taken from Chou, "Cong bijiao de guandian kan Taiwan," pp. 171–73 and 186–87.

31. See Lee Hsiao-feng 1996b; and Ch'iu K'un-liang 1996.

32. Peng, *A Taste of Freedom*, p. 62.

33. Chang Yen-hsien, "Taiwan shi yanjiu yu taiwan zhutixing," especially pp. 433–35.

34. See Lee Hsiao-feng, "Zhanhou chuqi Taiwan shehui de wenhua chongtu," pp. 284–89.

35. "Zhongshan" was Sun Yat-sen's formal personal name; "Jianguo" means "build the country"; "Minsheng" means "people's livelihood"; and "Xinhai" is the Chinese name for the year of the Republican Revolution (1911).

36. Chang Yen-hsien, "Taiwan shi yanjiu yu taiwan zhutixing," p. 434; also see Phillips 1999.

37. See Lee Hsiao-feng, "Zhanhou chuqi Taiwan shehui de wenhua chongtu," pp. 278–89.

38. Lee Hsiao-feng, "Zhanhou chuqi Taiwan shehui de wenhua chongtu," p. 296.

39. See Lee Hsiao-feng 1996b, "Zhanhou chuqi Taiwan shehui de wenhua chongtu," p. 299; also see Hsiao Ch'iung-jui 1996. Even today, some nationalist Taiwanese politicians curse Mainlanders as *waisheng zhu* ("Mainland pigs"), which the Mainlanders consider to be offensive.

40. Lin Jui-ming 1996.

41. Ch'en Wan-i 1996. Also see Ch'iu K'un-liang 1996.

42. See Ch'en I-shen 1996; Lee Hsiao-feng 1996b; and Phillips 1999. The Incident itself began as an altercation between KMT police and a street merchant selling cigarettes outside the state monopoly, but soon exploded into a larger conflict between Taiwanese social elites and the provincial Mainlander authorities. On the Taiwanese side, a Management Committee (*chuli weiyuanhui*), selected to negotiate with KMT provincial authorities, demanded in effect democratization and a relatively autonomous position within the ROC. The Management Committee's demands escalated slightly a few days after the Incident began, finally prompting Provincial Governor Ch'en Yi to call secretly for backup forces from the Mainland. These forces invaded Taiwan with shocking brutality in the early weeks of March 1947, shooting their way ashore from the island's northern ports. The troops quickly fanned out across the island, killing or "disappearing" thousands of Taiwanese elites in subsequent weeks. The most cautious estimate given for the number killed immediately is 10,000. Historian Lee Hsiao-feng calculates that, subsequently—from the early 1950s to 1987—the KMT executed an additional 3,000–4,000 ROC citizens (including dissident Mainlanders), imprisoned about 29,000 for political reasons, and otherwise tormented an additional 100,000. Also see Wu Nai-te and Ch'en Ming-tung 1996.

43. Ch'iu K'un-liang 1996.

44. The motivation was both cultural and economic. When the KMT took over Taiwan's governmental administration, it fired 30,000 Taiwanese civil servants and replaced them with Mainlanders. The law requiring public use of Mandarin proved to be a useful tool for less-qualified Mainlanders seeking to drive Taiwanese out of coveted jobs. (Ch'iu K'un-liang, "Zhanhou Taiwan juchang de xingshuai qiluo," p. 162.)

45. Quoted in Ch'iu K'un-liang, "Zhanhou Taiwan juchang de xingshuai qiluo," p. 164.

46. Chang Yen-hsien, "Taiwan shi yanjiu yu taiwan zhutixing," pp. 444–46.

47. Chang Yen-hsien, "Taiwan shi yanjiu yu taiwan zhutixing," p. 435.

48. See Ma Chih-su 2002.

49. This section is based primarily on interviews 201, 202, 207, 209, 211, and 218.

50. Sun Yat-sen, *San Min Chu I*, pp. 140–41.

51. Interview 211.

52. Chiang in Sun Yat-sen, *San Min Chu I*, p. 215.

53. Interview 208; also see, on this period and Chiang Ching-kuo's role, Cheng 1989; and Hong-Mao Tien 1989. For an overview from the perspective of the democratic opposition, see Rigger 2001.

54. For a good illustration, see "Minzhu wansui" ("Long Live Democracy"), the lead editorial in the first *Meilidao* (*Formosa*).

55. Interview 217.

56. Interview 222.

57. Interview 224.

58. See T'ien Hsin 1996. For a contemporary KMT attack on *Free China Fortnightly*, see "Ying bu rongxu tiaobo suowei 'Taiwanren yu Daluren' de ganqing," 1960. The tone of these articles is similar to present-day CCP attacks on its "enemies," underscoring the commonality of CCP and KMT worldviews before the KMT was forced to start de-Sinifying in the 1970s.

59. Almost all of the Taiwanese nationalists interviewed conceded these points.

60. For the feel from inside the KMT at this time, see Huang Chu-kwei 1972.

61. See Ch'iu Hung-ta 1971.

62. See, from the *dangwai* perspective, "Mei you gaige jiu mei you qiantu," 1979; and, from the liberal Mainlander perspective, "Zai Meiguo chengren Zhonggong de zhenhan zhong kaizhan xinju," 1978.

63. T'ien Hsin 1996; Interview 230.

64. The Presbyterian declarations are reprinted in Tung Fang-yuan 1996.

65. For an overview of these developments, see Lee Hsiao-feng 1996a. Also see the World United Formosans for Independence Web site.

66. Chang Yen-hsien, "Meilidao shijian yu taiwan minzhu yundong de zhuanzhe," quotation on p. 193. Also see Shih Cheng-feng 2002.

67. It was rational to be fearful because KMT intimidation abroad was brutal and intense. See Kaplan 2001.

68. Interview 232. As late as the 1980s, some 75 percent of US-based WUFI members held either an MA or a Ph.D. degree (Shu, "Who Joined the Clandestine Political Organization?" p. 61).

69. See Fan Kwang-ling 1965.

70. Interviews 203 and 220; Lee Chen-ching 1998. According to Lee's data, there were only an aggregate 6,780 ROC students in the United States in 1965, but by 1970 the number had almost doubled, to 12,029. By 1980, the number had risen further still, to 17,560, and by 1990 it had reached 30,960. (Lee Chen-ching, "Sweeping Educational Reform in Taiwan," p. 16.)

71. Executive Yuan figures indicate that a total of 57,592 ROC students returned from the United States between 1971 and 1998 (Interview 220).

72. Most—but not all—of Taiwan's best-known *dangwai* leaders of the 1970s and 1980s spent at least some time abroad; Chen Shui-bian is an important exception. Among intellectuals, most of the historians working with Chang Yen-hsien studied or lived abroad during the 1970s and 1980s.

73. Interviews 203–5, 209, 226, and 232. Taiwanese did not necessarily have to go abroad to encounter the global oppositional culture. As the activist in Interview 229 noted,

during the 1960s, you could hear all kinds of Western popular music here in Taiwan: Bob Dylan, Joan Baez, the Beatles, the Rolling Stones. The KMT limited the importation of Japanese popular culture but not usually Western popular culture. After all, we had thousands of US soldiers here....We could also read about the US anti-war movement in magazines and see it in movies. The KMT would censor sex and Mao, but not the counter-culture movement.

In this respect, Taiwan was similar to Thailand (See Chapter 2).

74. Interview 215. Another leading activist and politician reported that her most important formative political experience was encountering the women's movement in the United States, which she said thoroughly transformed her understanding of Taiwan society (Interview 228).

75. Interview 205.

76. On this point, see Phillips 1999; Shih Cheng-feng 2002; and Dickson, *Democratization in China and Taiwan*, pp. 122–29.

77. The informant in Interview 204 used the term "informal apartheid system"—in English. Informants in interviews 210, 215–17, 222–24, 227, and 228 agreed that it was apt.

78. About half of the KMT's Central Committee members were Mainlanders as late as 1995, even though Mainlanders represented only about 15 percent of the general population. (Cited in Chu 1998.)

79. See Chapter 1.

80. This section is based on Interview 226.

81. This section is based upon Interview 217.

82. See Lin Hai 1975. In contrast, so restricted were the media in Taiwan at the time that newspapers were not even allowed to report the October 1973 overthrow of Thailand's Thanom–Praphat dictatorship—because the dictators had fled to sanctuary in Taipei. (See Chuang Po-shi 1975).

83. Chang Yen-hsien, "Meilidao shijian yu Taiwan minzhu yundong de zhuanzhe."

84. The informant in Interview 210 stressed the importance of returned students as social opinion leaders. Note the similar function played by the *Social Science Review* and underground journals in Thailand prior to October 1973.

85. Interview 215.

86. Chang Yen-hsien, "Meilidao shijian yu Taiwan minzhu yundong de zhuanzhe," p. 194.
87. Chang Yen-hsien, "Meilidao shijian yu Taiwan minzhu yundong de zhuanzhe," pp. 195–97.
88. Interview 215.
89. See the lead *Formosa* article, "Minzhu wansui!" This article is a *tour d'horizon* linking together all of the themes of Taiwan politics of the 1970s, including international derecognition, collapsed domestic legitimacy, and ethnic politics. It argues that democratization is the tide of history and that KMT resistance is futile.
90. See Chang Yen-hsien, "Meilidao shijian yu Taiwan minzhu yundong de zhuanzhe," p. 200.
91. *Formosa* editors hinted at Taiwan's independence in subtle ways throughout all five issues. For example, they published a poem by Ch'en Hsiu-hsi entitled "Meilidao" ("Formosa") on p. 48 of the first issue. This poem declares Taiwan to be, among other things, a cradle, a mother's warm embrace, a land of brave pioneers, and a free land nourished by the Pacific Ocean (not the East Asian mainland). These are all symbols associated with the independence movement. The poem makes no identifiable reference to China.
92. You Ch'ing 1979.
93. "Minzhu, fazhi, yu hefaxing weiji" 1979; also see "Mei you gaige jiu mei you qiantu," 1979.
94. Both the theory and its corollary are still popular in the PRC today. (See Chapter 4.)
95. Wang Er-min, "Xihua wenti de huisi," p. 42.
96. "'Taidu yundong' de mishi yu yumei," 1976.
97. Ch'en Te-sheng, "Ridi shidai Taiwan de minzu jingshen," quotation on p. 42.
98. Ch'en Te-sheng, "Ridi shidai Taiwan de minzu jingshen," p. 45.
99. Liu Feng-sung 1979. Also see Huang Hung-hsiung, "Dajia lai jinian Jiang Weishui xiansheng"; and Wang Shih-liang 2000.
100. Liu Feng-sung, "Yi qian ba bai wan ren de Taiwan shi," p. 71.
101. Liu Feng-sung, "Yi qian ba bai wan ren de Taiwan shi," p. 71.
102. Liu Feng-sung, "Yi qian ba bai wan ren de Taiwan shi," p. 72. Liu could claim this statement is not quite a call for Taiwan independence, since the Taiwan he envisioned would still identify with cultural China. As explained in Chapter 7, some Taiwanese nationalists now reject *any* kind of identification with China.
103. For a riveting account of these events from the activists' perspective, see Chang Yen-hsien, "Meilidao shijian yu Taiwan minzhu yundong de zhuanzhe," especially pp. 204–8.
104. "Women dui 'Meilidao shijian' de yixie ganxiang," p. 2.
105. "The Kaohsiung Incident of 1979," 2000. All of those convicted—in all three groups—were released from prison later in the 1980s.
106. Interview 205. Also see Bush, *At Cross Purposes: US-Taiwan Relations Since 1942,* pp. 179–218.

107. Huang Hsuan-fan, "Jin wushinian Taiwan yuyan zhengce de bianqian," pp. 34–36; also see Rubinstein, "Political Taiwanization and Pragmatic Diplomacy,'" p. 443.

108. "Taiwan qiantu ying you Taiwan quanti zhumin, yi pubian qie pingdeng fangshi gongtong jueding," cited in Lee Hsiao-feng, "Yibainian lai Taiwan zhengzhi yundong zhong de guojia rentong," p. 292.

109. Edmondson, "The February 28 Incident and National Identity," p. 35.

110. Interview 215.

Chapter 7

1. "Trouble Continues under Chen Shui-bian," 2002.

2. For what might be the effects, see Lam 2004.

3. Quoted in Liao Yi, "Forum on Cross-Strait Relations."

4. Some predicted that a military attack would come sooner. See "Rhetoric, Military Manoeuvres Reflect Growing Chinese Angst," 2004.

5. Quoted in "China warns army can and will 'smash' Taiwan independence," 2004.

6. Outsiders think of Taiwanese and Chinese as ethnically the same. But on Taiwan, analysts refer to Taiwanese versus Mainlander (or Aboriginal, Hakka, etc.) conflict as ethnic (*zuqun*) conflict.

7. But the popularity among Taiwanese of Taipei Mayor Ma Ying-jeou, a Mainlander elected Chairman of the KMT (replacing Lien Chan) in July 2005, was a sign that the situation could improve.

8. Lin Ch'i-yang 1996.

9. Lamley, "Taiwan Under Japanese Rule, 1895–1945," p. 245.

10. Sun Zhaozhen 2002; "Taiwan-China Trade Up 33.1% in 2004," 2005.

11. See Keliher and Meer 2003. Taiwan was China's third largest trading partner.

12. "Taiwanese Workers March Against Rising Unemployment," 2002.

13. "Taiwan's Unemployment Rate Hits 4.09 Percent," 2005.

14. Sun Zhaozhen 2002.

15. "Taiwan Businesses Invest More on Chinese Mainland," 2002.

16. Maubo Chang, "Mainland Is Most Popular Destination."

17. "Taiwan's first half investment in China up 68 percent," 2004.

18. "Taiwan Eases Controls on PRC-Bound Investment," 2001.

19. "Analyst Says Lifting of Ban to Fuel Taiwan's China-Bound Investment,"2001.

20. Deborah Kuo, "Taiwan Opens to Direct Import of 2,126 Mainland Products"; "Taiwan's Cabinet Decides to Ease Half-Century Ban on Chinese Investments," 2002.

21. Zhu Huaying 2002.

22. Interview 234. The informant in Interview 231—also a nationalist—made similar accusations.

23. "'Green' Taiwan businessmen not welcomed," 2004. Caving in to the pressure, Hsu finally issued a statement on March 26, 2005 saying that "Taiwan independence will lead to war and drag the Taiwanese people to disaster." ("Taiwan Warned of Courting Disaster," 2005.)

24. Interview 232.

25. Frank Ching 2002.

26. Lillian Lin, "IC Industry Hopes."

27. Quoted in Frank Ching 2002.

28. Quoted in Frank Ching 2002.

29. Lillian Lin, "MAC Says 8-Inch Wafer Foundries Transfer Is Thorny Issue." The Ministry of Finance also hesitated to support the transfer for fear of losing a revenue source.

30. Victor Lai, "Taiwan's VP Opposes Transfer of 8-Inch Wafer Plants to Mainland." Also see Maubo Chang, "Vice President Urges Businessmen to Keep Roots in Taiwan."

31. Fang Wen-hung, "Cabinet Ponders Wafer Issue with National Security in Mind."

32. There were other restrictions. See Victor Lai, "MOEA Gives Conditional Approval for Eight-Inch Wafer Transfer."

33. "Taiwan Cabinet Fund to Withdraw Investment in PRC-Based Semiconductor Firm," 2002.

34. Lilian Wu, "Businesses Dissatisfied with Government's Mainland Policy."

35. "US Business Group Says Taiwan Risks Making Itself Irrelevant," 2002.

36. David Hsu, "Anniversary of Cross-Strait Transshipping Operations."

37. Maubo Chang, "More than 15,000 Passengers Take Advantage of Mini Three Links."

38. Lilian Wu, "Businesses Dissatisfied with Government's Mainland Policy."

39. Bradsher 2002.

40. Lilian Wu, "Legislative VP Says Direct Cross-Strait Transport Crucial for Taiwan."

41. "Beware of Business Interests," 2002.

42. Maubo Chang, "MAC Chief: Too Early to Purchase Water from Mainland China."

43. James Kuo and Maubo Chang 2002.

44. See "Vice-premier Qian Qichen on Cross-strait Negotiations," 2003. Negotiations stalled in the summer as the CCP became dissatisfied with domestic Taiwanese political developments.

45. Leavey 2002; Keliher and Meer 2003. The migrants were concentrated in the Shanghai and Pearl River Delta regions.

46. Maubo Chang, "Premier: Taiwan Not Alone in Limiting Technology Exports."

47. Sofia Wu, "Talent Control Would Tarnish Democratic Taiwan."

48. Chiu Yu-tzu 2002.

49. Lilian Wu, "NSC Will Not Register High-Tech Personnel in Taiwan."

50. Liao Yi, "Hostility and Unwiseness."

51. Fang Wen-hung, "High-Tech Personnel Control Narrowed Down."

52. Chiu Yu-tzu 2002.

53. Maubo Chang, "Taiwan Cuts Red Tape for More Mainland Chinese Experts."

54. Sofia Wu, "More than 10,000 Taiwan Students Studying in Mainland China"; and Fanchiang 2003.

55. Lillian Lin, "School for Taiwan Children on Mainland"; Lilian Wu, "Kinmen Schools to Accept Children of Taiwan Businesspeople."

56. Sofia Wu, "MAC to Review Legal Issues Regarding Cross-Strait Marriages"; and Gluck 2004.

57. Private communication, Taipei, July 2004.

58. Deborah Kuo, "Cross-Strait Crimes." Other PRC citizens in Taiwan illegally are thought to be current or former soldiers in the People's Liberation Army or agents of the People's Armed Police. See Deborah Kuo, "Mainlanders Find New Way to Sneak into Taiwan."

59. Deborah Kuo, "Cross-Strait Crimes."

60. "Plan to Restrict Movement of High-Tech Workers Seen as Exercise in Futility" 2002.

61. The suspicion remains unconfirmed as of this writing, and Soong denies it. The allegations may have hurt the Lien-Soong ticket slightly in the March 2004 election. See Lee Chang-kuei 2002; and Maubo Chang, "DPP Lawmakers File Complaint of High Treason against PFP Chairman."

62. Lee Chang-kuei 2002.

63. "Further on Taiwan Police Raid on HK Magazine Office," 2002.

64. Maubo Chang, "DPP Lawmakers File Complaint"; Lin Mei-chun, "'Anti-Betrayal Alliance' Accuses PFP Chair of Leaking NSB Secrets."

65. Lin Chieh-yu, "Taiwan's President Reminds Intelligence Community." Also see "Official's Move to China Sparks Security Concerns," 2002.

66. Yeh 2002.

67. Wang Zhi 2002.

68. Hesseldahl 2002.

69. Lin Miao-jung, "Taiwan MAC Says Cross-Strait Ties Stable."

70. "Taiwan Businesses in PRC Discover Political Risks," 2001. Also see Lilian Wu, "Government to Improve Help for Taiwan Businessmen in Mainland."

71. "China claims two more Taiwan 'spies' in custody," 2004.

72. Personal communications 2002, 2004.

73. Deborah Kuo, "Economics Ministry Doesn't Support CCP-Taiwan Business Links." Also see Lilian Wu, "No Taiwan Businessmen on Mainland Have Joined CCP."

74. "PRC Says Party Groups Not to Affect Taiwan Companies," 2001.

75. Ch'en Po-chih 2002.

76. Ch'en Po-chih, "Liang'an jingji guanxi zai taiwan guoji jingji guanxi zhong de dingwei," p. 93.

77. "Lee Teng-hui chuanshou A-bian si da zhizheng mijue," 2002. The terminology is the same as historian Chang Yen-hsien's.

78. Quoted in Lee Mei-chun, "Lee Cautions 2008 Carries China Threat."

79. Sofia Wu, "Pro-Taiwan Activists to Promote use of 'Taiwan' in Group Names."

80. Lin Mei-chun, "'Taiwan' Takes to the Taipei Streets."

81. Sofia Wu, "Pro-Taiwan Activists to Promote use of 'Taiwan' in Group Names." The ROC government added the name "Taiwan" to passports in January 2002. For an angry Chinese reaction, see Mao Zhongwei 2002.

82. "Human Chain Protest Spans Taiwan," 2004.

83. See Stephane Corcuff, "The Symbolic Dimension of Democratization."

84. Lilian Wu, "TSU Promoting Taiwan as National Title."

85. Wu Yuan 2002.

86. The central government was unable to enforce the use of Tongyong Pinyin in Taipei City, where Mainlander Ma Ying-jeou's KMT administration insisted on using Hanyu Pinyin.

87. Interview 234.

88. Edward Chen 2002. Also see David Hsu, "MOI Opposes 'Born-in-Taiwan' Requirement for Taiwan Presidential Candidates."

89. Chen Jianxing 2002.

90. Lin Chieh-yu, "March Shows Civil Groups' Role." Also see Xi Xin 2002.

91. Ch'iu Kwei-fen, "Zai tan taiwan wenxue shiguan," quotation on p. 307.

92. Lee Chiao 2002.

93. Lee Chiao, "Taiwan wenhua yu xin guojia," p. 348.

94. Lee Chiao, "Taiwan wenhua yu xin guojia," p. 349.

95. The new head of the aptly-named Chinese Television System (CTS), a major network, vowed to do precisely this upon her appointment by President Chen in June 2004. See Yiu 2004.

96. Ch'iu Kwei-fen similarly argues that the government and civil society should create new "cultural products" (*wenhua chanpin*) to induce identification with Taiwan; for example, national days of commemoration, new maps, new music, and a new history. (Ch'iu Kwei-fen, "Zai tan taiwan wenxue shiguan.")

97. On this point, also see Wang T'u-fa 2002. Wang argues that the authentic Taiwanese identity is inherently environmentally friendly.

98. Shih Cheng-feng, "Taiwan minzuzhuyi de jiexi," p. 325; interview 231.

99. Shih Cheng-feng, "Taiwan minzuzhuyi de jiexi," p. 332.

100. Ch'iu Kwei-fen, "Zai tan taiwan wenxue shiguan."

101. Lillian Lin, "Official Language Should Be Unified: Education Minister." Also see Ko Shu-ling and Lindy Yeh 2002.

102. Sofia Wu, "President Credits Latest Taiwan Cultural Boom to Democratization."

103. Maubo Chang, "Former President Calls for Regrouping of Political Parties."

104. Chang Yun-ping 2004.

105. T'ien Hsin 1996; interview 230.

Chapter 8

1. See Frank 1998; Pomeranz 2001; and Hobson 2004.

2. Finer, *The History of Government I*, pp. 46–47.

3. Mann 1986. Note that Mann himself does not address the global culture concept. The observations to follow derive from an interpretation and adaptation of his theory.

4. As with Mann, Castells does not address the global culture concept directly; this section is adapted from his work. See Castells, *The Rise of the Network Society*.

5. Castells, *The Rise of the Network Society*, p. 470.

6. Castells, *The Rise of the Network Society*, p. 471.

7. Hobson, *The State and International Relations*.

8. See Volume II of Castells' trilogy, *The Power of Identity*.

9. Interview 323.

10. See Electronic Privacy Information Center and Privacy International.

Bibliography*

"Abdurixit on Stepped-Up Ideological Battle in Muslim-Dominated Xinjiang." Agence France-Presse, January 18, 2002. Reprinted in *FBISDCR*, January 22, 2002.

"Abridged Version of Address by Thai Deputy Foreign Minister M.R. Sukhumbhand Paribatra at Singapore's Institute of Southeast Asian Studies on 31 July 1998." *The Nation*, August 4, 1998. Reprinted in *FBISDREA*, August 11, 1998.

Achara Ashayagachat. "Minister: Thailand Entitled to Comment on Burma." *Bangkok Post*, July 12, 1998. Reprinted in *FBISDREA*, July 14, 1998.

Acharya, Amitav. *Constructing a Security Community in Southeast Asia: ASEAN and the Problem of Regional Order*. New York: Routledge, 2001.

Adams, Brad. "Thailand's Crackdown." *International Herald Tribune*, April 24, 2003. <http://www.iht.com>.

———. "Thaksin's Potemkin Welcome for APEC." *Asian Wall Street Journal*, October 17, 2003. <http://www.awsj.com>.

"Aggression and Atrocities Make One Boil with Anger." *Ta Kung Pao*, May 9, 1999, A2. Translated in *FBISDCR*, May 11, 1999.

Alagappa, Muthiah, ed. *Civil Society and Political Change in Asia: Expanding and Contracting Democratic Space*. Stanford, CA: Stanford University Press, 2004.

Alexander, Jeffrey. *Twenty Lectures: Sociological Theory Since World War II*. New York: Columbia University Press, 1987.

Almond, Gabriel A. and Sidney Verba. *The Civic Culture: Political Attitudes and Democracy in Five Nations*. Princeton, NJ: Princeton University Press, 1963.

Amara Pongsapich. "Chinese Settlers and Their Role in Modern Thailand." In Tong Chee Kiong and Chan Kwok Bun, eds., *Alternate Identities: The*

*The following abbreviations are used in the Bibliography: FBISDCR, Foreign Broadcast Information Service Daily China Report; FBISDREA, Foreign Broadcast Information Service Daily Report (East Asia).

Chinese of Contemporary Thailand. Singapore: Times Academic Press, 2001, 85–106.

Amara Pongsapich and Nitaya Kataleeradabhan. *Thailand: Non-Profit Sector and Social Development.* Bangkok: Chulalongkorn University Social Research Institute, 1997.

"Analyst Says Lifting of Ban to Fuel Taiwan's China-Bound Investment." Agence France-Presse, November 9, 2001. Reprinted in *FBISDCR*, November 13, 2001.

"Anand Panyarachun Interviewed on Appointment." *Naeo Na*, June 11, 1992, 14. Translated in *FBISDREA*, June 11, 1992, 43–45.

"Anand Urges Peaceful Resistance to Coup Attempts." *The Nation*, June 25, 1992, A1. Reprinted in *FBISDREA*, June 25, 1992, 47–48.

"Anti-Suchinda Rally Held; Leader Begins Fast." *The Nation*, May 5, 1992, A1–A2. Reprinted in *FBISDREA*, May 5, 1992, 46–47.

"APEC Warning: Protestors to be Denied Aid." *The Nation*, October 2, 2003, 1A.

Aphaluck Bhatiasevi. "PM Urged to Explain Meeting's Benefits." *Bangkok Post*, October 14, 2003. <http://www.bangkokpost.com>.

"Appalling Backtrack on Political Reform." *Bangkok Post*, August 3, 1995, 4. Reprinted in *FBISDREA*, August 3, 1995, 77–78.

"Article Blasts US for Backing Dalai's Separatist Activities." Xinhua News Service, May 25, 2001. Reprinted in *FBISDCR*, May 29, 2001.

Bao Lisheng. "Three Evil Forces Threatening Xinjiang's Stability." *Ta Kung Pao*, August 10, 2001. Translated in *FBISDCR*, August 16, 2001.

Baranovitch, Nimrod. "Between Alterity and Identity: New Voices of Minority People in China." *Modern China* 27(3), July 2001, 359–401.

Barme, Scot. *Luang Wichit Wathakan and the Creation of a Thai Identity.* Singapore: Institute of Southeast Asian Studies, 1993.

Barnes, William. "Thais Debate a Legal Limit to Thaksin's Term in Office." *South China Morning Post*, December 12, 2002. <http://www.scmp.com>.

Barrett, Deborah and David John Frank. "Population Control for National Development: From World Discourse to National Policies." In John Boli and George M. Thomas, eds., *Constructing World Culture: International Non-Governmental Organizations since 1875.* Stanford, CA: Stanford University Press, 1999, 198–221.

Batson, Benjamin A. *The End of the Absolute Monarchy in Siam.* Singapore: Oxford University Press, 1984.

Becker, Jasper. "The Heart of Chinese Sovereignty." *South China Morning Post*, June 12, 1999, 17.

"Beijing Villagers Said Practicing 'Village Democracy,'" Xinhua News Service, March 23, 2001. Reprinted in *FBISDCR*, March 26, 2001.

"Beijing Warns Against 'Narrow Nationalism.'" Agence France-Presse, December 1, 1996. Reprinted in *FBISDCR*, December 3, 1996.

"Beware of Business Interests." *Taipei Times*, April 21, 2002. <http://www.taipetimes.com>.

Boix, Carles and Susan C. Stokes. "Endogenous Democratization." *World Politics* 55, July 2003, 517–49.

Boli, John. "Conclusion: World Authority Structures and Legitimations." In John Boli and George M. Thomas, eds., *Constructing World Culture: International Non-Governmental Organizations since 1875*. Stanford, CA: Stanford University Press, 1999, 267–300.

Boli, John and George M. Thomas. "INGOs and the Organization of World Culture." In John Boli and George M. Thomas, eds., *Constructing World Culture: International Non-Governmental Organizations Since 1875*. Stanford, CA: Stanford University Press, 1999, 13–49.

———. "World Culture in the World Polity." *American Sociological Review* 62(2), 1997, 171–90.

Bovingdon, Gardner. "The Not-So-Silent Majority: Uyghur Resistance to Han Rule in Xinjiang." *Modern China* 28(1), January 2002, 39–78.

Bradsher, Keith. "Taiwan Under Pressure to Allow Freighter Link with Mainland." *New York Times*, May 5, 2002. <http://www.nytimes.com>.

Buddhadasa Bhikkhu. *Keys to Natural Truth* (translated by Santikaro Bhikkhu and Rod Bucknell). Bangkok: The Dhamma Study and Practice Group, 1988.

Bull, Hedley. *The Anarchical Society: A Study of Order in World Politics*. New York: Columbia University Press, 1977.

Bull, Hedley and Adam Watson, eds. *The Expansion of International Society*. Oxford: Oxford University Press, 1984.

Bunce, Valerie. "Comparative Democratization: Big and Bounded Generalizations." *Comparative Political Studies* 33(6/7), August/September 2000, 703–34.

Bush, Richard C. *At Cross Purposes: US-Taiwan Relations Since 1942*. Armonk, NY: M.E. Sharpe, 2004.

Buzan, Barry. *From International to World Society? English School Theory and the Social Structure of Globalisation*. Cambridge, UK: Cambridge University Press, 2004.

Cai Tuo and Liu Zhenye. "Quanqiu shimin shehui yu dangdai guoji guanxi (Shang)" ("Global Civil Society vs. Contemporary International Relations"). *Xiandai Guoji Guanxi* (*Contemporary International Relations*) 2002 (12), 1–7. [蔡拓、刘贞晔。"全球市民社会与当代国际关系(上)"。现代国际关系, 2002 (12), 頁 1–7。]

Callahan, Mary P. "Cracks in the Edifice? Changes in Military-Society Relations in Burma Since 1988." In Morten B. Pedersen, Emily Rudland, and R. J. May, eds., *Burma/Myanmar: Strong Society, Weak State?* London: C. Hurst & Co., 2000, 22–51.

Callahan, William A. *Imagining Democracy: Reading "The Events of May" in Thailand*. Singapore: Institute of Southeast Asian Studies, 1998.

Carothers, Thomas. *Aiding Democracy Abroad: The Learning Curve*. Washington, DC: Carnegie Endowment for International Peace, 1999.

———. "The End of the Transition Paradigm." *Journal of Democracy* 13(1), 2002, 5–21.

Carter Center-Beijing University. "China Elections and Governance" (Web site). <http://www.chinaelections.org>.

Castells, Manuel. *The Information Age: Economy, Society, and Culture, Volume I: The Rise of the Network Society*. Malden, MA: Blackwell Publishers, 1996.

————. *The Information Age: Economy, Society, and Culture, Volume II: The Power of Identity*. Malden, MA: Blackwell Publishers, 1997.

"Chamlong: Protesters Did Not Die in Vain." *Bangkok Post*, June 9, 1992, 6. Reprinted in *FBISDREA*, June 9, 1992, 55–56.

Chang Kuo-hsing. "Riben zhimin tongzhi shidai taiwan shehui de bianhua" ("Changes in Taiwanese Society During the Era of Japanese Colonial Control"). In Chang Yen-hsien, Lee Hsiao-feng, and Tai Pao-cun, eds., *Taiwan shi lunwen jingxuan* (*Selected Essays on Taiwanese History*). Taipei: Yushan She, 1996, 55–76. [張國興。「日本殖民統治時代台灣社會的變化」。張炎憲、李筱峯、戴寶村編。*台灣史論文精選*。(台北：玉山社, 1996), 頁 55–76。]

Chang, Maubo. "DPP Lawmakers File Complaint of High Treason against PFP Chairman." Central News Agency (Taiwan), April 2, 2002. Reprinted in *FBISDCR*, April 3, 2002.

————. "Former President Calls for Regrouping of Political Parties." Central News Agency (Taiwan), February 19, 2002. Reprinted in *FBISDCR*, February 20, 2002.

————. "MAC Chief: Too Early to Purchase Water from Mainland China." Central News Agency (Taiwan), May 4, 2002. Reprinted in *FBISDCR*, May 6, 2002.

————. "Mainland Is Most Popular Destination for Taiwan Investors." Central News Agency (Taiwan), March 11, 2002. Reprinted in *FBISDCR*, March 12, 2002.

————. "More than 15,000 Passengers Take Advantage of Mini Three Links." Central News Agency (Taiwan), April 18, 2002. Reprinted in *FBISDCR*, April 19, 2002.

————. "Premier: Taiwan Not Alone in Limiting Technology Exports." Central News Agency (Taiwan), April 10, 2002. Reprinted in *FBISDCR*, April 11, 2002.

————. "Taiwan Cuts Red Tape for More Mainland Chinese Experts." Central News Agency (Taiwan), April 29, 2002. Reprinted in *FBISDCR*, April 30, 2002.

————. "Vice President Urges Businessmen to Keep Roots in Taiwan," Central News Agency (Taiwan), April 25, 2002. Reprinted in *FBISDCR*, April 26, 2002.

————. "Challenging the Powerful with a Piece of Paper." *The Nation*, July 25, 1997. <http://www.geocities.com/changnoi2/main97.htm>. Retrieved October 17, 2003.

Chang Noi. "Cultural Revolution in Thailand." *The Nation*, August 29, 1996 and September 22, 1996. <http://www.geocities.com/changnoi2/main96.htm>. Retrieved October 17, 2003.

————. "NGOs, Violence, and Money." *The Nation*, January 3, 2003. <http://www.geocities.com/changnoi2/main03.htm>. Retrieved October 17, 2003.

————. "Understanding Thaksin's Pluto-Populism." *The Nation*, February 18, 2002. <http://www.geocities.com/changnoi2/main02.htm>. Retrieved October 17, 2003.

Chang Sheng-yen, ed. *Taiwan kaifa shi (The History of Taiwan's Development)*. Taipei: Guoli Kongzhong Daxue, 1996. [張勝彥編。台灣開發史。台北：國立空中大學，1996。]

Chang Te-shui. *Jidong! Taiwan de lishi: taiwanren de ziguo renshi (It's Time to Pay Attention to Taiwan's History as the Source of Taiwanese National Recognition)*. Taipei: Qianwei Chubanshe, 1992. [張德水。激動！台灣的歷史：台灣人的自國認識。台北：前衛出版社，1992。]

Chang Yen-hsien. "Meilidao shijian yu taiwan minzhu yundong de zhuanzhe." In Chang Yen-hsien, Tseng Chiu-mei, and Chen Chao-hai, eds., *"Maixiang 21 shiji de taiwan minzu yu guojia" lunwenji ("Collected Essays on 'the Taiwanese Nation and State's March to the 21st century'")* (Taipei: Wu Sanlian Jijinhui, 2002), pp. 191–212. [張炎憲。「美麗島事件與台灣民主運動的轉折」。張炎憲、曾秋美、陳朝海編，「邁向21世紀的台灣民族與國家」論文集。(台北：吳三連基金會，2002)，頁191–212。]

————. "Taiwan shi yanjiu yu taiwan zhutixing" ("Taiwan Historical Research and Taiwanese Subjectivity"). In Chang Yen-hsien, Chen Mei-jung, and Lee Chung-kuang, eds., *Taiwan jinbainianshi lunwenji (Collected Essays on Taiwan's Recent 100 Years of History)* (Taipei: Wu Sanlian Jijinhui, 1996), pp. 431–51. [張炎憲。「台灣史研究與台灣主體性」。張炎憲、陳美蓉、黎中光編，台灣近百年史論文集。(台北：吳三連基金會，1996)，頁431–51。]

————. "Taiwan wenhua xiehui de chengli yu fenlie" ("The Establishment and Disintegration of the Taiwanese Culture Association"). In Chang Yen-hsien, Lee Hsiao-feng, and Tai Pao-cun, eds., *Taiwan shi lunwen jingxuan (Selected Essays on Taiwanese History)* (Taipei: Yushan She, 1996), pp. 131–59. [張炎憲。「台灣文化協會的成立與分裂」。張炎憲、李筱峯、戴寶村編。台灣史論文精選。(台北：玉山社，1996)，頁131–59。]

————. "Towards a New 21st Century Taiwan." *Taiwan News*, January 7, 2002. <http://www.etaiwannews.com>.

Chang Yen-hsien, Lee Hsiao-feng, and Tai Pao-cun, eds. *Taiwan shi lunwen jingxuan (Selected Essays on Taiwanese History)*. Taipei: Yushan She, 1996. [張炎憲、李筱峯、戴寶村編。台灣史論文精選。台北：玉山社，1996。]

Chang Yen-hsien, Tseng Chiu-mei, and Chen Chao-hai, eds. *"Maixiang 21 shiji de taiwan minzu yu guojia" lunwenji ("Collected Essays on 'the Taiwanese Nation and State's March to the 21st Century'")*. Taipei: Wu Sanlian Jijinhui, 2002. [張炎憲、曾秋美、陳朝海編。「邁向21世紀的台灣民族與國家」論文集。台北：吳三連基金會，2002。]

Chang Yun-ping. "Name-Change Lobby Group Changes Tack." *Taipei Times*, August 6, 2004, 3. <http://www.taipeitimes.com>.

Chappell, David W., ed. *Socially Engaged Spirituality: Essays in Honor of Sulak Sivaraksa on His 70th Birthday*. Bangkok: Sathirakoses-Nagapradipa Foundation, 2003.

Chase, Michael S. and James C. Mulvenon. *You've Got Dissent! Chinese Dissident Use of the Internet and Beijing's Counter-Strategies*. Santa Monica, CA: RAND, 2002.

Chee, Soon Juan. *To Be Free: Stories from Asia's Struggle Against Oppression*. Melbourne: Monash Asia Institute, 1998.

Chen Dabai. "Minzuzhuyi de Zhongguo daolu: ping Wang Xiaodong dui Zhongguo minzuzhuyi de yanshuo" ("The Road of Nationalism in China: Comment on Mr. Wang Xiaodong's Nationalist Narration"). *Zhanlue yu Guanli (Strategy and Management)* 2000 (3), 98–104. [陈大白。"民族主义的中国道路: 评王小东对中国民族主义的言说"。*战略与管理*, 2000(3), 頁 98–104。]

Chen, Edward. "TSU Tries to Restrict Citizens Not Born in Taiwan from Running for President." Central News Agency (Taiwan), February 6, 2002. Reprinted in *FBISDCR*, February 7, 2002.

Ch'en Fang-ming. "Taiwan zuoyi yundong shi yu zhengzhi bianqian" ("The History of Taiwan's Left-Wing Political Movements and Political Change"). In Chang Yen-hsien, Chen Mei-jung, and Lee Chung-kuang, eds., *Taiwan jinbainianshi lunwenji (Collected Essays on Taiwan's recent 100 Years of History)* (Taipei: Wu Sanlian Jijinhui, 1996), pp. 453–67. [陳芳明。「台灣左翼運動史與政治變遷」。張炎憲、陳美蓉、黎中光編。*台灣近百年史論文集*。(台北：吳三連基金會, 1996), 頁 153–67。]

Chen Feng. "Jointly Create a Stable Overall Order." *Xinjiang Ribao*, October 28, 2001. Translated in *FBISDCR*, December 11, 2001.

Ch'en Hao-yang. *Taiwan sibainian shuminshi (The Taiwan People's 400-Year History)*. Taipei: Zili Wanbao She, 1992. [陳浩洋。*台灣四百年庶民史*。台北：自立晚報社, 1992。]

Ch'en Hsiu-hsi. "Meilidao" ("Formosa"). *Meilidao (Formosa)* 1(1), 1979, 48. [陳秀喜。「美麗島」。*美麗島*, 1(1), 1979, 頁 48。]

Ch'en I-shen. "Lun taiwan er er ba shijian de yuanyin" ("On the Reasons for the February 28th Incident"). In Chang Yen-hsien, Lee Hsiao-feng, and Tai Pao-cun, eds., *Taiwan shi lunwen jingxuan (Selected Essays on Taiwanese History)* (Taipei: Yushan She, 1996), pp. 303–49. [陳儀深。「論台灣二二八事件的原因」。張炎憲、李筱峯、戴寶村編。*台灣史論文精選*。(台北：玉山社, 1996) 頁 303–49。]

Chen Jianxing. "Suicidal Act Harmful to Taiwan." Xinhua, April 22, 2002. Translated in *FBISDCR*, April 23, 2002.

Ch'en Po-chih. "Liang'an jingji guanxi zai taiwan guoji jingji guanxi zhong de dingwei" ("The Position of Cross-Strait Economic Relations in Taiwan's International Economic Relations"). In Chang Yen-hsien, Tseng Chiu-mei, and Chen Chao-hai, eds., *"Maixiang 21 shiji de taiwan minzu yu guojia" lunwenji ("Collected Essays on 'the Taiwanese Nation and State's March to the 21st Century'")* (Taipei: Wu Sanlian Jijinhui, 2002), pp. 91–103. [陳博志。「兩岸經濟關係在台灣國際經濟關係中的定位」。張炎憲、曾秋美、陳朝海編。「*邁向21 世紀的台灣民族與國家*」論文集。(台北：吳三連基金會, 2002), 頁 91–103。]

Ch'en Te-sheng. "Ridi shidai taiwan de minzu jingshen" ("Taiwan's National Spirit During the Period of the Japanese Occupation"). *Zhongguo Luntan (The China Tribune)* 2(2), April 25, 1976, 41–48. [陳德生。「日帝時代台灣的民族精神」。*中國論壇* 2(2), 1976 年 4 月 25 日, 頁 41–48。]

Ch'en Wan-i. "Lun taiwan wenxue de 'beiqing'" ("On Taiwanese Literature's 'Tragic' Tone"). In Chang Yen-hsien, Chen Mei-jung, and Lee Chung-kuang, eds., *Taiwan jinbainianshi lunwenji (Collected Essays on Taiwan's Recent 100 Years of History)*. Taipei: Wu Sanlian Jijinhui, 1996, 95–103. [陳萬益。「論台灣文學的『悲情』」。張炎憲、陳美蓉、黎中光編。*台灣近百年史論文集*。(台北 : 吳三連基金會, 1996), 頁 95–103。]

Chen Xiaowei and Yin Fang. "Xin shiji Meiguo de 'shuzi diqiu' jihua" ("The US Plan for a 'Digital Globe' in the New Century"). *Xiandai Guoji Guanxi (Contemporary International Relations)* 2000 (5), 28–31. [陈效卫、股方。"新世纪美国的'数字地球'计划"。*现代国际关系* 2000(5), 頁 28–31。]

Cheng, Tun-jen. "Democratizing the Quasi-Leninist Regime in Taiwan." *World Politics* 41(4), July 1989, 471–99.

"China Claims Two More Taiwan 'Spies' in Custody." *Taipei Times*, February 10, 2004, 4. <http://www.taipeitimes.com/News/taiwan/archives/2004/02/10/2003098197>. Retrieved June 22, 2004.

"China Launches First Magazine on Human Rights." Xinhua, February 10, 2002. Reprinted in *FBISDCR*, February 11, 2002.

"China's Efforts to Establish Socialist Human Rights with Chinese Characteristics." Xinhua, April 12, 2001. Reprinted in *FBISDCR*, April 24, 2001.

China Society for Human Rights Studies. "Historical Progress in Guaranteeing Human Rights in Tibet." Xinhua News Service, July 16, 1999. Reprinted in *FBISDCR*, July 19, 1999.

"China Warns Army Can and Will 'Smash' Taiwan Independence." Channel News Asia, August 1, 2004. <http://www.channelnewsasia.com/stories/afp_asiapacific/ view/98656/1/.html>. Retrieved August 2, 2004.

"Chinese Experts Discuss Human Rights Protection Under CCP Leadership." Xinhua, November 21, 2002. Reprinted in *FBISDCR*, November 22, 2002.

"Chinese Human Rights Specialists Denounce NATO Bombing." Xinhua News Service, May 9, 1999. Reprinted in *FBISDCR*, May 10, 1999.

"Chinese in Belgrade, Beijing Protest Embassy Bombing." CNN, May 9, 1999 <http://www.cnn/com>.

Ching, Frank. "Mainland China Is Taiwan's Best Friend and Worst Enemy." *China Post*, May 17, 2002. <http://www.chinapost.com.tw>.

Ching, Leo T. S. *Becoming Japanese: Colonial Taiwan and the Politics of Identity Formation*. Berkeley, CA: University of California Press, 2001.

Ch'iu Hung-ta. "Wo guo tuichu lianheguo hou suo mianlin de wenti" ("Problems Our Country Will Face After Withdrawing From the UN"). *Daxue Zazhi* 47, November 1971, 9–16. [丘宏達。「我國退出聯和國後所面臨的問題」。*大學雜誌* 47(1971 年 11 月), 頁 9–16。]

Ch'iu K'un-liang. "Zhanhou taiwan juchang de xingshuai qiluo" ("The Rise and Fall of Theater in Postwar Taiwan"). In Chang Yen-hsien, Chen Mei-jung, and Lee Chung-kuang, eds., *Taiwan jinbainianshi lunwenji* (*Collected Essays on Taiwan's Recent 100 Years of History*). Taipei: Wu Sanlian Jijinhui, 1996, 157–68. [邱坤良。「戰後台灣劇場的與衰起落」。張炎憲、陳美蓉、黎中光編。台灣近百年史論文集。(台北：吳三連基金會, 1996) 頁 157–68。]

Ch'iu Kwei-fen. "Zai tan taiwan wenxue shiguan: xingbie, zuqun shuxing yu Taiwan wenxue shi chonggou" ("Re-Exploring Historical Perspectives on Taiwanese Literature: Gender, Ethnic Belonging, and the Reconstruction of Taiwanese Literature"). In Chang Yen-hsien, Tseng Chiu-mei, and Chen Chao-hai, eds., *"Maixiang 21 shiji de taiwan minzu yu guojia" lunwenji* (*"Collected Essays on 'the Taiwanese Nation and State's March to the 21st Century'"*). Taipei: Wu Sanlian Jijinhui, 2002, 307–21. [邱貴芬。「再探台灣文學視觀──性別、族群屬性 與台灣文學史重構」。張炎憲、曾秋美、陳朝海編。「邁向21世紀的台灣民族與國家」論文重。(台北：吳三連基金會, 2002), 頁 307–21。]

Chiu Yu-tzu. "Regulation of Movement of High-Tech Workers Watered Down." *Taipei Times*, April 30, 2002. <http://www.taipeitimes.com>.

Chou Wan-you. "Cong bijiao de guandian kan taiwan yu hanguo de huang-minhua yundong" ("Examining the Japanization Movement in Taiwan and Korea from a Comparative Perspective"). In Chang Yen-hsien, Lee Hsiao-feng, and Tai Pao-cun, eds., *Taiwan shi lunwen jingxuan* (*Selected Essays on Taiwanese History*). Taipei: Yushan She, 1996, 161–201. [周婉窈。「從比較的觀點看台灣與韓國的皇民化運動」。張炎憲、李筱峯、戴寶村編。台灣史論文精選。(台北：玉山社, 1996), 頁 161–201。]

Chuang Po-shi. "Women de xinwen ziyou" ("Our News Freedom"). *Taiwan Zhenglun* (*Taiwan Political Review*) October 3, 1975, 22–25. [莊柏仕。「我們的新聞自由」。臺灣政論, 1975 年 10 月 3 日, 頁 22–25。]

Chu, Yun-han. "Taiwan's Unique Challenges." In Larry Diamond and Marc F. Plattner, eds., *Democracy in East Asia*. Baltimore, MD: The Johns Hopkins University Press, 1998, 133–46.

Collier, David, James Mahoney, and Jason Seawright. "Claiming Too Much: Warnings About Selection Bias." In Henry E. Brady and David Collier, eds., *Rethinking Social Inquiry: Diverse Tools, Shared Standards*. Lanham, MD: Rowman & Littlefield, 2004, 85–102.

"Common People Attending On-line NPC Session." Xinhua News Agency, March 8, 2002. Reprinted in *FBISDCR*, March 11, 2002.

Connors, Michael Kelly. *Democracy and National Identity in Thailand*. New York: RoutledgeCurzon, 2003.

———. "Framing the 'People's Constitution.'" In Duncan McCargo, ed., *Reforming Thai Politics*. Copenhagen: Nordic Institute of Asian Studies, 2002, 37–55.

"Constitution of the Kingdom of Thailand." *Royal Gazette* 108 (special ed.), December 9, 1991, 1–59. Translated in *FBISDREA*, February 4, 1991, 49–67.

———. October 11, 1997. <http://www.krisdika.go.th/html/fslaw_e.htm>.

Corcuff, Stephane. "The Symbolic Dimension of Democratization and the Transition of National Identity Under Lee Teng-hui." In Stephane Corcuff, ed., *Memories of the Future: National Identity Issues and the Search for a New Taiwan*. Armonk, NY: M.E. Sharpe, 2002, 73–101.

Cox, Robert. "Social Forces, States, and World Orders: Beyond International Relations Theory." In Robert Cox (with Timothy J. Sinclair), *Approaches to World Order*. Cambridge, UK: Cambridge University Press, 1996, 85–123.

Dabhoiwala, Meryam. "A Chronology of Thailand's 'War on Drugs.'" *Article 2* 2(3), June 2003, 10–16.

Davidson, Colin, Andrew J. Gow, Tong H. Lee, and Everett H. Ellinwood. "Methamphetamine Neurotoxicity: Necrotic and Apoptotic Mechanisms and Relevance to Human Abuse and Treatment" *Brain Research Reviews* 36(1), August 2001, 1–22.

"A Day of Madness and Treachery." *Bangkok Post*, June 17, 1994, 4. Reprinted in *FBISDREA*, June 17, 1994, 54–55.

de Casparis, J. G. and I. W. Mabbett. "Religion and Popular Beliefs of Southeast Asia Before c. 1500." In Nicholas Tarling, ed., *The Cambridge History of Southeast Asia, Volume One, Part One: From Early Times to c. 1500*. Cambridge, UK: Cambridge University Press, 1999, 286–304.

"Decentralization a Priority of 1993." *Bangkok Post*, January 5, 1993, 4. Reprinted in *FBISDREA*, January 5, 1993, 64–65.

"Democracy Group Sets Political Reform Deadline." *Bangkok Post*, August 28, 1995, 1. Reprinted in *FBISDREA*, August 28, 1995, 71–72.

"Democracy Party Warned to Stay Clear of NATO Protest." Agence France-Presse, May 9, 1999. Reprinted in *FBISDCR*, May 10, 1999.

Diamond, Larry. *Developing Democracy: Toward Consolidation*. Baltimore, MD: The Johns Hopkins University Press, 1999.

———. "Rethinking Civil Society: Towards Democratic Consolidation." *Journal of Democracy* 5, July 1994, 4–17.

Diamond, Larry, Juan Linz, and Seymour Martin Lipset, eds. *Democracy in Developing Countries, Volume 3: Asia*. Boulder, CO: Lynne Rienner, 1989.

Diamond, Larry and Marc F. Plattner, eds. *Democracy in East Asia*. Baltimore, MD: The Johns Hopkins University Press, 1998.

Dickson, Bruce J. *Democratization in China and Taiwan: The Adaptability of Leninist Parties*. Oxford: Oxford University Press, 1998.

Dimmock, Matthew. "Hiding the Human Evidence." *Green Left Weekly*, October 15, 2003. <http://www.greenleftweekly.com>.

Ding Guan'gen. "With the New Century as the New Starting Point, Make Every Effort to Take Ideological Propaganda Work to a New Level." *Renmin Ribao (People's Daily)*, March 20, 2001, 5. Translated in *FBISDCR*, April 6, 2001.

Doneys, Philippe. "Political Reform Through the Public Sphere: Women's Groups and the Fabric of Governance." In Duncan McCargo, ed., *Reforming Thai Politics*. Copenhagen: Nordic Institute of Asian Studies, 2002, 163–82.

Dong Yunhu. "Inclusion of 'Human Rights' in the Constitution." Xinhua, March 14, 2004. Reprinted in *FBISDCR*, March 14, 2004.

Duara, Prasenjit. *Rescuing History from the Nation: Questioning Narratives of Modern China*. Chicago: The University of Chicago Press, 1995.

Economy, Elizabeth C. *The River Runs Black: The Environmental Challenge to China's Future.* Ithaca, NY: Cornell University Press, 2004.

Edmondson, Robert. "The February 28 Incident and National Identity." In Stephane Corcuff, ed., *Memories of the Future: National Identity Issues and the Search for a New Taiwan.* Armonk, NY: M.E. Sharpe, 2002, 25–46.

Eisenstadt, S. N. "Multiple Modernities." *Daedalus: Journal of the American Academy of Arts and Sciences* 129(1), Winter 2000, 1–29.

Electronic Privacy Information Center and Privacy International. *Privacy and Human Rights 2002.* <http://www.epic.org>.

"Embassy Attack Exposes 'Rights Champion.'" Xinhua News Service, May 10, 1999. Reprinted in *FBISDCR*, May 11, 1999.

Fanchiang, Cecilia. "Debate Surrounds Issue of Degrees from China." ROC Government Information Office, December 5, 2003. <http://publish.gio.gov.tw/FCJ/past/03120521.html>. Retrieved July 30, 2004.

Fan Guoxiang. "Renquan, zhuquan, baquan" ("Human Rights, Sovereignty, and Hegemony"). *Guoji Wenti Yanjiu* (*International Studies*) 2000 (2), 9–14. [范国祥。"人权、主权、霸权"。*国际问题研究* 2000 (2), 頁 9–14。]

Fang Jue. "A Program for Democratic Reform." *Journal of Democracy* 9(4), 1998, 9–19.

Fang Wen-hung. "Cabinet Ponders Wafer Issue with National Security in Mind." Central News Agency (Taiwan), March 15, 2002. Reprinted in *FBISDCR*, March 18, 2002.

———. "High-Tech Personnel Control Narrowed Down to One Category." Central News Agency (Taiwan), April 29, 2002. Reprinted in *FBISDCR*, April 30, 2002.

Fan Kwang-ling. "Zhei yi dai de liuxuesheng" ("This Generation's Students Abroad"). *Wenxing* (*Apollo Magazine*) 96, October 1, 1965, 62–63. [范光陵。「這一代的留學生」。*文星* 96 (1965 年 10 月 1 日), 頁 62–63。]

Finer, S. E. *The History of Government I: Ancient Monarchies and Empires.* Oxford: Oxford University Press, 1997.

Finnemore, Martha. *National Interests in International Society.* Ithaca, NY: Cornell University Press, 1996.

Foley, Michael and Bob Edwards. "The Paradox of Civil Society." *Journal of Democracy* 7, July 1996, 38–52.

Foot, Rosemary. *Rights Beyond Borders: The Global Community and the Struggle over Human Rights in China.* Oxford: Oxford University Press, 2000.

"Former Premier [Anand Panyarachun] Examines Role of King." *The Sunday Post*, March 12, 1995, 17. Reprinted in *FBISDREA*, March 21, 1995, 51–53.

Frank, Andre Gunder. *ReOrient: Global Economy in the Asian Age.* Berkeley, CA: University of California Press, 1998.

Friedman, Edward. "The Most Popular Social Movement in China During the 1990s." Paper for the Duisburg Conference on Discourses on Political Reform and Democratization in East and Southeast Asia, May 2002 (unpublished).

———. *National Identity and Democratic Prospects in Socialist China.* Armonk, NY: M.E. Sharpe, 1995.

Fullbrook, David. "Why the Shin Corp Sale Was Good Business." *Asia Times*, February 18, 2006. <http://www.atimes.coms>. Retrieved February 25, 2006.

"Further on Taiwan Police Raid on HK Magazine Office over Leaking Secrets." Agence France-Presse, March 30, 2002. Reprinted in *FBISDCR*, March 21, 2002.

Gallagher, Mary E. "China: The Limits of Civil Society in a Late Leninist State." In Muthiah Alagappa, ed., *Civil Society and Political Change in Asia: Expanding and Contracting Democratic Space*. Stanford, CA: Stanford University Press, 2004, 419–52.

Gardella, Robert. "From Treaty Ports to Provincial Status, 1860–1894." In Murray A. Rubinstein, ed., *Taiwan: A New History*. Armonk, NY: M.E. Sharpe, 1999, 180–81.

Geddes, Barbara. "How the Cases You Choose Affect the Answers You Get: Selection Bias in Comparative Politics." *Political Analysis* 2, 1990, pp. 131–50.

———. "What Do We Know About Democratization After Twenty Years?" *Annual Review of Political Science* 2, June 1999, 115–44.

Gilley, Bruce. *China's Democratic Future: How It Will Happen and Where It Will Lead*. New York: Columbia University Press, 2004.

Gluck, Caroline. "Chinese Brides Cold-Shouldered in Taiwan." BBC News, July 29, 2004. <http://news.bbc.co.uk/2/hi/asia-pacific/3936169.stm>. Retrieved July 30, 2004.

Goldman, Merle. *Sowing the Seeds of Democracy in China*. Cambridge, MA: Harvard University Press, 1995.

Gold, Thomas B. *State and Society in the Taiwan Miracle*. Armonk, NY: M.E. Sharpe, 1986.

Greenfield, Karl Taro. "Need for Speed." *Time Asia*, March 5, 2001.

Green, Paula. "Sulak as Activist: Balancing the Global and Local." In David W. Chappell, ed., *Socially Engaged Spirituality: Essays in Honor of Sulak Sivaraksa on His 70th Birthday*. Bangkok: Sathirakoses-Nagapradipa Foundation, 2003, 64–69.

"'Green' Taiwan businessmen not welcomed." *People's Daily*, June 3, 2004. <http://english.people.com.cn/200406/01/eng20040601_145031.html>. Retrieved July 31, 2004.

"Growing Frustration over Political Reform." *Bangkok Post*, October 23, 1995, 4. Reprinted in *FBISDREA*, October 23, 1995, 77.

Gu Shengkai. "Xifang rendao zhuyi ganyu lilun pipan yu xuanze" ("Western Concepts of Humanitarian Intervention: Criticism and Choices"). *Xiandai Guoji Guanxi* (*Contemporary International Relations*) 2002 (6), 28–34. [谷盛开。"西方人道主义干预理论批判与选择"。*现代国际关系*, 2002(6), 頁 28–34。]

Harvey, Peter. *An Introduction to Buddhism: Teachings, History, and Practices*. Cambridge, UK: Cambridge University Press, 1990.

He Chong. "Great Significance of China's Ratification of the International Human Rights Covenant." Zhongguo Tongxun She, March 29, 2001. Translated in *FBISDCR*, April 2, 2001.

————. "NATO Has Changed Its Role and Become an International Gendarme." *Zhongguo Tongxun She*, April 24, 1999. Translated in *FBISDCR*, April 27, 1999.

He Jiadong. "Zhongguo wenti yujing xia de zhuyi zhi zheng" ("The Struggle of 'Isms' in the Context of China's Problems"). *Zhanlue yu Guanli (Strategy and Management)* 2000 (6), 101–11. [何家栋。"中国问题语境下的主义之争"。战略与管理 2000(6), 頁 101–11。]

Hesseldahl, Arik. "Taiwan's Dry Chips." *Forbes*, May 13, 2002. <http://www.forbes.com>.

Hewison, Kevin. "The Monarchy and Democratisation." In Kevin Hewison, ed., *Political Change in Thailand: Democracy and Participation* (London: Routledge, 1997), pp. 58–74.

"A History of Taiwan." Xinhua News Agency. <http://news3.xinhuanet.com/english/2003-12/04/content_1213639.htm>. Retrieved July 12, 2004.

Hobsbawm, Eric. *The Age of Extremes: A History of the World, 1914–1989*. New York: Vintage Books, 1996.

Hobson, John M. *The Eastern Origins of Western Civilization*. Cambridge, UK: Cambridge University Press, 2004.

————. *The State and International Relations*. Cambridge, UK: Cambridge University Press, 2000.

————. "What's at Stake in 'Bringing Historical Sociology *Back* into International Relations'? Transcending 'Chronofetishism' and 'Tempocentrism' in International Relations." In Stephen Hobden and John M. Hobson, eds., *Historical Sociology of International Relations* (Cambridge, UK: Cambridge University Press, 2002), pp. 3–41.

"House Panel Opposed to ASEAN Entry for Burma." *The Nation*, June 2, 1997, A6. Reprinted in *FBISDREA*, June 3, 1997.

Hsiao Ch'iung-jui. "'Taiwanren xingxiang' de ziwo xingsu: bainian lai taiwan meishujia yanzhong de taiwanren" ("The self-Creation of the Taiwanese Form: Taiwanese in the Eyes of Artists During the Past 100 Years"). In Chang Yen-hsien, Chen Mei-jung, and Lee Chung-kuang, eds., *Taiwan jinbainianshi lunwenji (Collected Essays on Taiwan's Recent 100 Years of History)* (Taipei: Wu Sanlian Jijinhui, 1996), pp. 105–56. [蕭瓊瑞。「『台灣人形象』的自我形塑—百年來台灣美術家眼中的台灣人」。張炎憲、陳美蓉、黎中光編。台灣近百年史論文集。(台北：吳三連基金會, 1996), 頁 105–56。]

Hsiau, A-Chin. *Contemporary Taiwanese Cultural Nationalism*. London: Routledge, 2000.

Hsu, David. "Anniversary of Cross-Strait Transshipping Operations Marked Friday." Central News Agency (Taiwan), April 18, 2002. Reprinted in *FBISDCR*, April 19, 2002.

————. "MOI Opposes 'Born-in-Taiwan' Requirement for Taiwan Presidential Candidates." Central News Agency (Taiwan), March 8, 2002. Reprinted in *FBISDCR*, March 11, 2002.

Hsu Hsueh-ji. "Rizhi shiqi de Banqiao Lin jia—yige jiazu yu zhengzhi de guanxi" ("The Lin Family of Banqiao in the Period of Japanese Rule—The

Relationship Between a Clan and Politics"). In Chang Yen-hsien, Lee Hsiao-feng, and Tai Pao-cun, eds., *Taiwan shi lunwen jingxuan (Selected Essays on Taiwanese History)*. Taipei: Yushan She, 1996, 77–130. [許雪姬。「日治時期的板橋林家──一個家族與政治的關係」。張炎憲、李筱峯、戴寶村編。 *台灣史論文精選*。(台北：玉山社, 1996), 頁 77–130。]

Huang Chao-t'ang. *Taiwan lunxian lunwenji (Essays on the Fall of Taiwan)*. Taipei: Xiandai Xueshu Yanjiu Jijinhui, 1996. [黃昭堂。*台灣淪陷論文集*。台北：現代學術研究基金會, 1996。]

Huang Chu-kwei. "Ni-Zhou gongbao hou de wo guo jushi" ("Our Country's Situation After the Nixon-Zhou Communiqué"). *Daxue Zazhi* 51–52, April 1972, 14–17. [黃祝貴。「尼周公報後的我國局勢」。*大學雜誌* 51–52 (1972 年 4 月), 頁 14–17。]

Huang Hong and Ji Ming. "United Under the Great Banner of Patriotism." *Renmin Ribao (People's Daily)*, May 27, 1999, 9. Translated in *FBISDCR*, June 7, 1999.

Huang Hsuan-fan. "Jin wushinian taiwan yuyan zhengce de bianqian" ("Changes in Taiwan's Language Policy During the Past Fifty Years"). In Chang Yen-hsien, Chen Mei-jung, and Lee Chung-kuang, eds., *Taiwan jinbainianshi lunwenji (Collected Essays on Taiwan's Recent 100 Years of History)*. Taipei: Wu Sanlian Jijinhui, 1996, 34–36. [黃宣範。「近五十年台灣語言政策的變遷」。張炎憲、陳美蓉、黎中光編, *台灣近百年史論文集*。(台北：吳三連基金會, 1996), 頁 34–36。]

Huang Hung-hsiung. "Dajia lai jinian Jiang Weishui xiansheng" ("Everyone Come and Commemorate Mr. Chiang Wei-shui"). *Meilidao* 1(1), August 1979, 93. [黃煌雄。「大家來紀念蔣渭水先生」。*美麗島* 1(1), 1979 年 8 月, 頁 93。]

———. *Taiwan kangri shihua (The Story of Taiwan's Resistance to Japan)*. Taipei: Qianwei Chubanshe, 1992. [黃煌雄。*台灣抗日史話*。台北：前衛出版社, 1992。]

Huang Qing. "The Clashes of Western Civilization." *Renmin Ribao (People's Daily)*, July 18, 1997. Translated in *FBISDCR*, August 25, 1997.

Huang Yi. "Leng zhan hou Meiguo dui Hua zhengce linian tan yuan" ("Conceptual Sources of Post-Cold War US Policy Towards China"). *Xiandai Guoji Guanxi*, 2001 (4), 1–6. [黃毅。"冷战后美国对华政策理念探源"。*现代国际关系*, 2001(4), 頁 1–6。]

Huang Zhaoyu. "Cong xin zongtong nanchan kan Meiguoshi minzhu de biduan" ("Defects of US-Style Democracy Seen Through the Difficult Birth of a New President"). *Xiandai Guoji Guanxi* 2000(12), 21–25. [黃昭宇。"从新总统难产看美国式民主的弊端"。*现代国际关系*, 2000(12), 頁 21–25。]

"Hu Jintao: May 4th Heritage Boils Down to Patriotism." Xinhua, May 4, 1999. Reprinted in *FBISDCR*, May 5, 1999.

Hu Lianhe. "Lun lengzhan jieshu hou de guojia wenhua anquan" ("On National Cultural Security in the Post Cold War Period"). *Xiandai Guoji Guanxi (Contemporary International Relations)* 2000(8), 31–34. [胡联合。"论冷战结束后的国家文化安全"。*现代国际关系*, 2000(8), 頁 31–34。]

"Human Chain Protest Spans Taiwan." Cable News Network, February 28, 2004. <http://www.cnn.com/2004/WORLD/asiapcf/02/28/taiwan.protest.reut/>. Retrieved February 28, 2004.

Huntington, Samuel P. *The Clash of Civilizations and the Remaking of World Order*. New York: Touchstone, 1996.

———. *The Third Wave: Democratization in the Late Twentieth Century*. Norman, OK: University of Oklahoma Press, 1991.

"Interview with Former Thai Prime Minister Anand Panyarachun." *Bangkok Post*, April 29, 2002. Reprinted in *FBISDREA*, April 30, 2002.

"Is Korea a Forward Base for the Globalization of Chinese?" *Chosun Ilbo*, January 28, 2005. <http://english.chosun.com>.

"It Is High Time to Formulate an International Convention on the Internet." *Wen Wei Po*, August 29, 2000. Translated in *FBISDCR*, September 1, 2000.

"It Is Necessary to Maintain Vigilance Against the Political Attempt of Hostile Elements in the West to Utilize 'Falungong.'" *Renmin Ribao (People's Daily)*, January 8, 2001. Translated in *FBISDCR*, January 9, 2001.

Ito Tomomi. "Sulak and Engaged Buddhists in Contemporary Thai History." In David W. Chappell, ed., *Socially Engaged Spirituality: Essays in Honor of Sulak Sivaraksa on His 70th Birthday*. Bangkok: Sathirakoses-Nagapradipa Foundation, 2003, 241–50.

Jackson, Peter A. *Buddhadasa: Theravada Buddhism and Modernist Reform in Thailand*, 2nd ed. Chiang Mai, Thailand: Silkworm Books, 2003.

———. "Thai-Buddhist Identity: Debates on the *Traiphuum Phra Ruang*." In Craig J. Reynolds, ed., *National Identity and Its Defenders: Thailand, 1939–1989*. Chiang Mai, Thailand: Silkworm Books, 1991, 192–203.

Jiang Zhaoyong and Li Xiaoguang. "The Cultural Roots of the Sino-US Conflict." *Ta Kung Pao*, September 21, 1999, C1. Translated in *FBISDCR*, October 8, 1999.

Johnston, Alastair Iain. "China's Militarized Interstate Dispute Behavior 1949–1992." *The China Quarterly* 153, March 1998, 1–30.

———. "Chinese Middle Class Attitudes Towards International Affairs: Nascent Liberalization?" *The China Quarterly* 179, September 2004, 603–28.

———. *Cultural Realism: Strategic Culture and Grand Strategy in Chinese History*. Princeton, NJ: Princeton University Press, 1998.

———. "International Structures and Chinese Foreign Policy." In Samuel S. Kim, ed., *China and the World: Chinese Foreign Policy Faces the New Millennium*, 4th ed. Boulder, CO: Westview Press, 1998, 55–87.

———. "Learning Versus Adaptation: Explaining Changes in Chinese Arms Control Policy in the 1980s and 1990s." *The China Journal* 35, January 1996, 27–61.

Jones, David Martin. "Democratization, Civil Society, and Illiberal Middle Class Culture in Pacific Asia." *Comparative Politics* 30, January 1998, 147–69.

"The Kaohsiung Incident of 1979: A Turning Point in Taiwan History." *Taiwan Communique* 89, January 2000. <http://www.taiwandc.org/twcom/89-no3.htm>. Retrieved July 15, 2004.

Kaplan, David E. *Fires of the Dragon: Politics, Murder, and the Kuomintang*. New York: Scribner, 2001.

Kavi Chongkittavorn. "Good Ideas Need Discreet Lobbying." *The Nation*, June 29, 1998. Reprinted in *FBISDREA*, June 30, 1998.

———. "Towards an Enhanced Interaction." *The Nation*, July 27, 1998. Reprinted in *FBISDREA*, July 28, 1998.

Kazmin, Amy. "Amnesty Denounces 'Murder Spree' in Thai War on Drugs." *Financial Times*, November 5, 2003. <http://www.ft.com>.

Keane, John, ed. *Civil Society and the State: New European Perspectives*. London: Verso, 1988.

———. *Global Civil Society?* Cambridge, UK: Cambridge University Press, 2003.

Keck, Margaret and Kathryn Sikkink. *Activists Beyond Borders: Advocacy Networks in International Politics*. Ithaca, NY: Cornell University Press, 1998.

Keliher, Macabe and Craig Meer. "Taiwan and China: Too Close for Comfort?" *Asia Times*, October 24, 2003. <http://www.atimes.com/atimes/China/EJ24Ado1.html>. Retrieved July 20, 2004.

Kelly, David and Anthony Reid, eds. *Asian Freedoms: The Idea of Freedom in East and Southeast Asia*. Cambridge, UK: Cambridge University Press, 1998.

Keyes, Charles F. "Political Crisis and Militant Buddhism in Contemporary Thailand." In Bardwell L. Smith, ed., *Religion and Legitimation of Power in Thailand, Laos, and Burma*. Chambersberg, PA: Anima Books, 1978, 147–64.

Khien Theeravit. *Thailand in Crisis: A Study of the Political Turmoil of May 1992*. Bangkok: Thailand Research Fund and Institute of Asian Studies, Chulalongkorn University, 1997.

Kiatchai Phongphanit. "Burma-ASEAN, An Expensive Investment." *Matichon*, March 7, 1994, 4. Translated in *FBISDREA*, March 8, 1994, 51–52.

Kim, Sunhyuk. *The Politics of Democratization in Korea: The Role of Civil Society*. Pittsburgh, PA: University of Pittsburgh Press, 2000.

"King Calls for End to Intolerance." *Bangkok Post*, December 5, 2001. Reprinted in *FBISDREA*, December 6, 2001.

King, Gary, Robert O. Keohane, and Sidney Verba. *Designing Social Inquiry: Scientific Interferecne in Qualitative Research*. Princeton, NJ: Princeton University Press, 1994.

"King Meets Suchinda, Chamlong; Urges Cooperation." Bangkok Radio Thailand Network, May 21, 1992. Translated in *FBISDREA*, May 21, 1992, 34–35.

"King Wants Drug Toll Explained." *The Nation*, December 5, 2003. <http://www.nationmultimedia.com>.

Kirsch, A. Thomas. "Modernizing Implications of Nineteenth Century Reforms in the Thai Sangha." In Bardwell L. Smith, ed., *Religion and Legitimation of Power in Thailand, Laos, and Burma*. Chambersberg, PA: Anima Books, 1978, 52–65.

Ko Shu-ling and Lindy Yeh. "Taiwan Premier Promotes English as Second 'Semi-Official' Language." *Taipei Times*, May 1, 2002. <http://www.taipeitimes.com>.

Krasner, Stephen D. *Sovereignty: Organized Hypocrisy*. Princeton, NJ: Princeton University Press, 1999.

Kugler, Jacek and A. F. K. Organski. "The Power Transition." In Manus Midlarsky, ed., *Handbook of War Studies*. Boston: Unwin Hyman, 1989, 171–94.

Kuo, Deborah. "Cross-Strait Crimes Challenging Taiwan's Law Enforcement." Central News Agency (Taiwan), December 24, 2001. Reprinted in *FBISDCR*, December 26, 2001.

———. "Economics Ministry Doesn't Support CCP-Taiwan Business Links." Central News Agency (Taiwan), December 19, 2001. Reprinted in *FBISDCR*, December 20, 2002.

———. "Mainlanders Find New Way to Sneak into Taiwan." Central News Agency (Taiwan), February 6, 2002. Reprinted in *FBISDCR*, February 7, 2002.

———. "Taiwan Opens to Direct Import of 2,126 Mainland Products." Central News Agency (Taiwan), January 16, 2002. Reprinted in *FBISDCR*, January 17, 2002.

Kuo, James and Maubo Chang. "Taiwan Security Official Says Beijing Is Trying to Denationalize Taiwan." Central News Agency (Taiwan), February 7, 2002. Reprinted in *FBISDCR*, February 8, 2002.

Laird, John. *Money, Politics, Globalisation, and Crisis: The Case of Thailand*. Singapore: Graham Brash, 2000.

Lai, Victor. "MOEA Gives Conditional Approval for Eight-Inch Wafer Transfer." Central News Agency (Taiwan), April 24, 2002. Reprinted in *FBISDCR*, April 25, 2002.

———. "Taiwan's VP Opposes Transfer of 8-Inch Wafer Plants to Mainland." Central News Agency (Taiwan), February 22, 2002. Reprinted in *FBISDCR*, February 25, 2002.

Lamley, Harry J. "Taiwan Under Japanese Rule, 1895–1945: The Vicissitudes of Colonialism." In Murray A. Rubinstein, ed., *Taiwan: A New History*. Armonk, NY: M.E. Sharpe, 1999, 201–60.

Lam, Willy. "Beijing's Hand in Hong Kong Politics." *China Brief* (Jamestown Foundation) 4(12), June 10, 2004.

Leavey, Helen. "Social Cost of Taiwan Exodus to China." BBC News, January 3, 2002. <http://www.bbc.com>.

Lee Chang-kuei. "Country, Not Party, Must Come First." *Taipei Times*, April 23, 2002.

Lee Chen-ching. "Sweeping Educational Reform in Taiwan." Paper presented at the 2nd ASEAN Asian Symposium on Educational Management and Leadership, Darwin, Australia, December 14–16, 1998.

Lee Chiao. "Taiwan wenhua yu xin guojia" ("Taiwan's Culture and New Nation"). In Chang Yen-hsien, Tseng Chiu-mei, and Chen Chao-hai, eds., *"Maixiang 21 shiji de 'Taiwan minzu yu guojia' lunwenji"* ("Collected Essays on 'the Taiwanese Nation and State's March to the 21st Century'"). Taipei: Wu Sanlian Jijinhui, 2002, 345–57. [李喬。「台灣文化與新國家」。張炎憲、曾秋美、

陳朝海編。「*邁向21世紀的台灣民族與國家*」論文集。(台北：吳三連基金會, 2002), 頁 345–57。]

Lee Hsiao-feng. "Yibainian lai Taiwan zhengzhi yundong zhong de guojia rentong." In Chang Yen-hsien, Chen Mei-jung, and Lee Chungkuang, eds., *Taiwan jinbainianshi lunwenji (Collected Essays on Taiwan's recent 100 Years of History)*. Taipei: Wu Sanlian Jijinhui, 1996a, 275–301. [李筱峯。「一百年來台灣政治運動中的國家認同」。張炎憲、陳美蓉、黎中光編。*台灣近百年史論文集*。(台北：吳三連基金會, 1996a), 頁 275–301。]

———. "Zhanhou chuqi Taiwan shehui de wenhua chongtu" ("Cultural Conflicts in Taiwanese Society in the Immediate Postwar Period"). In Chang Yen-hsien, Lee Hsiao-feng, and Tai Pao-cun, eds., *Taiwan shi lunwen jingxuan (Selected Essays on Taiwanese History)*. Taipei: Yushan She, 1996b, 273–302. [李筱峯。「戰後初期台灣社會的文化衝突」。張炎憲、李筱峯、戴寶村編。*台灣史論文精選*。(台北：玉山社, 1996b), 頁 273–302。]

Lee Mei-chun. "Lee Cautions 2008 Carries China Threat." *Taipei Times*, July 25, 2002, 1. <http://www.taipeitimes.com>.

"Lee Teng-hui chuanshou A-bian si da zhizheng mijue" ("Lee Teng-hui Bestows to A-Bian Four Secrets of Governing"). *Open*, July 24–30, 2002, 18–25. [「李登輝傳授阿扁四大執政秘訣」。*開放*, 2002 年 7 月 24–30, 頁 18–25。]

Levenson, Joseph. *Confucian China and Its Modern Fate: A Trilogy*. Berkeley, CA: University of California Press, 1965.

Lewis, John Wilson and Xue Litai. *China Builds the Bomb*. Stanford, CA: Stanford University Press, 1991.

Lian, Daniel. "Thaksin's Model." *Asiaweek*, August 17, 2001. <http://www.asiaweek.com>.

Liao Yi. "Forum on Cross-Strait Relations Concluded in Shenzhen." Xinhua, March 27, 2002. Translated in *FBISDCR*, April 19, 2002.

———. "Hostility and Unwiseness: Commenting on Taiwan's Scientific and Technological Curfew." Xinhua, April 25, 2002. Translated in *FBISDCR*, April 26, 2002.

Li Du. "The Practice of Rural Grassroots Democracy." *Renmin Ribao (People's Daily)*, October 21, 1998, 11. Translated in *FBISDCR*, October 31, 1998.

"On Li Hongzhi and the Political Nature and Serious Harm of his 'Falun Dafa.'" *Qiushi (Seeking Truth)*, August 11, 1999. Translated in *FBISDCR*, August 25, 1999.

Li Luqu. "Dongya wenhua yu minzhu de goujian" ("Construction of Culture and Democracy in East Asia"). *Guoji Wenti Yanjiu (International Studies)* 2002 (5), 33–37. [李路曲。"东亚文化与民主的构建"。*国际问题研究* 2002 (5), 頁 33–37。]

Lin Chieh-yu. "March Shows Civil Groups' Role." *Taipei Times*, May 12, 2002. <http://www.taipeitimes.com>.

———. "Taiwan President Reminds Intelligence Community to Continue Guarding Against Nation's Enemies." *Taipei Times*, April 11, 2002. <http://www.taipeitimes.com>.

Lin Ch'i-yang. "Rizhi shiqi taiwan wenhua lunshu zhi yishi xingtai fenxi" ("Analysis of Ideology in Taiwanese Cultural Discourses During the Period of Japanese Rule"). In Chang Yen-hsien, Chen Mei-jung, and Lee Chung-kuang, eds., *Taiwan jinbainianshi lunwenji* (*Collected Essays on Taiwan's Recent 100 Years of History*"). Taipei: Wu Sanlian Jijinhui, 1996, 41–62. [林淇瀁。「日治時期台灣文化論述之意識形態分析」。張炎憲、陳美蓉、黎中光編。台灣近百年史論文集。(台北：吳三連基金會, 1996), 頁 41–62。]

Lin Hai. "Xinwen ziyou yu yanlun baoguo" ("News Freedom and Making Opinion Serve the Country"). *Taiwan Zhenglun* (*Taiwan Political Review*) 2, September 1975, 39–41. [林海。「新聞自由與言論報國」。(臺灣政論 2, 1975 年), 頁 39–41。]

Lin Jui-ming. "Zhanhou taiwan wenxue de zai biancheng" ("The Postwar Re-Invention of Taiwanese Literature"). In Chang Yen-hsien, Chen Mei-jung, and Lee Chung-kuang, eds., *Taiwan jinbainianshi lunwenji* (*Collected Essays on Taiwan's Recent 100 Years of History*). Taipei: Wu Sanlian Jijinhui, 1996, 81–93. [林瑞明。「戰後台灣文學的再編成」。張炎憲、 陳美蓉、 黎中光編。台灣近百年史論文集。(台北：吳三連基金會, 1996), 頁 81–93。]

Link, Perry. *Evening Chats in Beijing: Probing China's Predicament*. New York: Norton, 1992.

Lin, Lillian. "IC Industry Hopes Eight-Inch Wafer Foundry Remains Economic Issue." Central News Agency (Taiwan), March 4, 2002. Reprinted in *FBISDCR*, March 5, 2002.

———. "MAC Says 8-Inch Wafer Foundries Transfer Is Thorny Issue." Central News Agency (Taiwan), March 5, 2002. Reprinted in *FBISDCR*, March 6, 2002.

———. "Official Language Should Be Unified: Education Minister." Central News Agency (Taiwan), March 25, 2002. Reprinted in *FBISDCR*, March 26, 2002.

———. "School for Taiwan Children on Mainland to Offer 12-Year Education." Central News Agency (Taiwan), December 4, 2001. Reprinted in *FBISDCR*, December 4, 2001.

Lin Mei-chun. "'Anti-Betrayal Alliance' Accuses PFP Chair of Leaking NSB Secrets." *Taipei Times*, April 3, 2002. <http://www.taipeitimes.com>.

———. "'Taiwan' Takes to the Taipei Streets," *Taipei Times*, May 12, 2002. <http://www.taipeitimes.com>.

Lin Miao-jung. "Historians Alter Their Perspective." *Taipei Times*, March 27, 2002. <http://www.taipeitimes.com>.

———. "Taiwan MAC Says Cross-Strait Ties Stable Despite Problems." *Taipei Times*, April 20, 2002. <http://www.taipeitimes.com>.

Linz, Juan J. and Alfred Stepan. *Problems of Democratic Transition and Consolidation: Southern Europe, South America, and Post-Communist Europe*. Baltimore, MD: The Johns Hopkins University Press, 1996.

Li Shufeng and Wang Leiming. "Legal Principles Will Not Stand a Clear-Cut Savage Act." Xinhua News Agency, May 10, 1999. Translated in *FBISDCR*, May 13, 1999.

Li Shufeng, Wu Huanqing, and Tian Yu. "Pushing Forward Building of Socialist Civilization to New Peaks." Xinhua, November 14, 2002. Translated in *FBISDCR*, November 15, 2002.

Liu Feng-sung. "Yi qian ba bai wan ren de taiwan shi" ("History of the 18 Million People of Taiwan"). *Meilidao (Formosa)* 1(3), October 1979, 69. [劉峯松。「一千八百萬人的台灣史」。美麗島 1(3), 1979 年 10 月, 頁 69。]

Liu Jianfei. "Leng zhan hou Meiguo dui Hua zhengce zhong de yishi xingtai yinsu" ("Ideological Factors in US China Policy During the Post-Cold War Years"). *Xiandai Guoji Guanxi (Contemporary International Relations)* 2002 (8), 13–17 ff. [刘建飞。"冷战后美国对华策中的意识形态因素"。现代国际关系, 2002 (8), 页 13–17。]

——. "Lun yishi xingtai yu guojia liyi de guanxi" ("On the Relationship Between Ideology and State Interests"). *Xiandai Guoji Guanxi (Contemporary International Relations)* 2001 (7), 33–37. [刘建飞。"论意识形态与国家利益的关系"。现代国际关系, 2001 (7), 页 33–37。]

Liu Junning. "Classical Liberalism Catches on in China." *Journal of Democracy* 11(3), 2000, 48–57.

Liu Yongtao. "Lengzhan hou Meiguo dui wai wenhua zhanlue touxi" ("Analysis of Post-Cold War U.S. Foreign Cultural Strategy"). *Xiandai Guoji Guanxi (Contemporary International Relations)* 2001 (5), 12–15. [刘永涛。"冷战后美国对外文化战略透析"。现代国际关系 2001(5), 页 12–15。]

Liu Wenzong. "The Principle of Sovereignty is Unshakeable." *Renmin Ribao (People's Daily) (Overseas Edition)*, February 4, 2000. Translated in *FBISDCR*, February 7, 2000.

"Living Dangerously on the Net: Censorship and Surveillance of Internet Forums." Reporters Without Borders, May 12, 2003. <http://www.rsf.org>.

Li Weiwei. "Thirty-One Provinces." Xinhua News Agency, November 24, 2002. Translated in *FBISDCR*, November 26, 2002.

Li Zhimin. "Zhishi jingji shidai guojia zhuquan zai renshi" ("Rediscovery of State Sovereignty in the Era of the Knowledge Economy"). *Xiandai Guoji Guanxi (Contemporary International Relations)* 2001 (7), 24–27. [李志敏。"知识经济时代国家主权再认识"。现代国际关系·, 2001(7), 页 24–27。]

Li Zhongjie. "How to Understand and Push Ahead with Democratization of the International Community." *Liaowang (Outlook)*, June 3, 2002. Translated in *FBISDCR*, August 20, 2002.

Li Zong. "Dangjin shidai tedian manyi" ("Special Characteristics of the Contemporary Period"). *Xiandai Guoji Guanxi (Contemporary International Relations)* 2002 (7) 3–5. [李琮。"当今时代特点漫议"。现代国际关系 2002 (7), 页 3–5。]

Lu Baosheng. "A New Configuration, New Challenges, and New Opportunities." *Jiefangjun Bao (People's Liberation Army Daily)*, February 6, 2002. Translated in *FBISDCR*, February 14, 2002.

Luobuciren and Gamaduji. "Socialist Democracy Practiced in Tibet." Xinhua News Service, November 30, 1997. Translated in *FBISDCR*, December 5, 1997.

Lu Qichang, Zhang Yanyu, and Wang Wenfeng. "Mei yu zai ti renquan fan Hua yi'an de tedian he beijing" ("The Characteristics and Background of Another US Anti-China Human Rights Initiative"). *Xiandai Guoji*

Guanxi (Contemporary International Relations) 2000 (3), 8–10. [吕其昌、张焱宇、王文峰。"美欲再提人权反华议案的特点和背景"。*现代国际关系*, 2000(3), 頁 8–10。]

Lu Yaohuai. "Lun quanqiuhua shidai de xinxi lunli" ("On Information Ethics in the Global Era"). *Xiandai Guoji Guanxi (Contemporary International Relations)* 2002 (12), 40–46. [吕耀怀。"论全球化时代的信息伦理"。*现代国际关系* 2002 (12), 頁 40–46。]

Lynch, Daniel C. *After the Propaganda State: Media, Politics, and "Thought Work" in Reformed China*. Stanford, CA: Stanford University Press, 1999.

———. "International 'Decentering' and Democratization: The Case of Thailand." *International Studies Quarterly* 48, June 2004, 339–62.

———. "Taiwan's Democratization and the Rise of Taiwanese Nationalism as Socialization to Global Culture." *Pacific Affairs*, Winter 2002–2003, 557–74.

———. "Taiwan's Self-Conscious Nation-Building Project." *Asian Survey* 44(4), July–August 2004, 513–33.

Ma Chih-su. "'Ziyou Zhongguo' banyan de jiaose" ("The Role Played by *Free China Fortnightly*"). *Lishi Yuekan (Historical Monthly)* May 2002, 92–99. [馬之驌。「『自由中國』扮演的角色」。*歷史月刊*, 2002 年 5 月, 頁 92–99。]

Ma Ling. "Interview with Yao Youzhi." *Ta Kung Pao*, May 3, 1999, A4. Translated in *FBISDCR*, May 17, 1999.

Mann, Michael. *The Sources of Social Power, Vol. 1: A History of Power from the Beginning to AD 1760*. Cambridge, UK: Cambridge University Press, 1986.

Mao Yushi. "Liberalism, Equal Status, and Human Rights." *Journal of Democracy* 9 (4), 1998, 20–23.

Mao Zhongwei. "Taiwan Independence Elements Assemble in Taiwan to Clamor for 'Taiwan Independence.'" *Jiefangjun Bao*, March 25, 2002. Translated in *FBISDCR*, April 24, 2002.

Marisa Chimprabha. "Minister: ASEAN 'Non-Interference' Policy Needs Review." *The Nation*, June 13, 1998. Reprinted in *FBISDREA*, June 17, 1998.

———. "UN Envoy Cites Climate of Fear." *The Nation*, May 28, 2003. <http://www.nationmultimedia.com>.

McCargo, Duncan. *Chamlong Srimuang and the New Thai Politics*. London: C. Hurst & Co., 1997.

———. "Introduction: Understanding Political Reform in Thailand." In Duncan McCargo, ed., *Reforming Thai Politics*. Copenhagen: Nordic Institute of Asian Studies, 2002, 1–18.

McCullough, Erskine. "King's 'Dramatic Intervention' Ends Crisis." Agence France-Presse, June 10, 1992. Reprinted in *FBISDREA*, June 11, 1992, 47.

Meisner, Maurice J. *Mao's China and After*, 3rd ed. New York: Simon and Schuster, 1999.

"Mei you gaige jiu mei you qiantu" ("No Future Without Reform"). *Meilidao (Formosa)* 1(3), October 1979, 6–7. [「沒有改革就沒有前途」。*美麗島* 1 (3), 1979 年 10 月, 頁 6–7。]

Meyer, John W. "The Changing Cultural Content of the Nation-State: A World Society Perspective." In George Steinmetz, ed., *State/Culture: State*

Formation After the Cultural Turn. Ithaca, NY: Cornell University Press, 1999, 123–43.

———. "Globalization, National Culture, and the Future of the World Polity," Wei Lun Lecture, Chinese University of Hong Kong, November 28, 2001.

———. "The World Polity and the Authority of the Nation State." In Albert Bergesen, ed., *Studies of the Modern World-System*. New York: Academic Press, 1980, 109–37.

Meyer, John W., George M. Thomas, and Francisco O. Ramirez. "World Society and the Nation-State." *American Journal of Sociology* 103(1), 1997, 144–81.

"Minzhu, fazhi, yu hefaxing weiji" ("Democracy, Rule of Law, and Legitimacy Crisis"). *Meilidao (Formosa)* 1(3), October 1979, 4–8. [「民主、法治、與合法性危機」。*美麗島* 1(3), 1979 年 10 月, 頁 4–8。]

"Minzhu wansui" ("Long Live Democracy"). *Meilidao (Formosa)* 1(1), August 1979, 4–9. [「民主萬歲」。*美麗島* 1(1), 1979 年 8 月, 頁 4–9。]

Moore, Barrington, Jr. *Social Origins of Dictatorship and Democracy: Lord and Peasant in the Making of the Modern World*. Boston: Beacon Press, 1966.

Morell, David. *Power and Parliament in Thailand: The Futile Challenge, 1968–1971*. Ph.D. dissertation, Princeton University (2 volumes), 1974.

———. "Thailand: Military Checkmate." *Asian Survey* 12(2), 1972, 156–67.

Morell, David and Chai-anan Samudavanija. *Political Conflict in Thailand: Reform, Reaction, Revolution*. Cambridge, MA: Oelgeschlager, Gunn, and Hain, 1981.

"More on US Ambassador to PRC." Agence France-Presse, May 9, 1999. Reprinted in *FBISDCR*, May 10, 1999.

Mudie, Luisetta. "PRC Trying to Rein In Xenophobia After NATO Attack." Agence France-Presse, May 9, 1999. Reprinted in *FBISDCR*, May 10, 1999.

Mulder, Niels. *Inside Thai Society: Interpretations of Everyday Life*. Amsterdam: The Pepin Press, 1996.

Munck, Gerardo L. "The Regime Question: Theory-Building in Democracy Studies." *World Politics* 54(1), October 2001, 119–44.

Murashima, Eiji. "The Origin of Modern Official State Ideology in Thailand." *Journal of Southeast Asian Studies* 19(1), March 1988, 80–96.

Naruemon Thabchumpon. "NGOs and Grassroots Participation in the Political Reform Process." In Duncan McCargo, ed., *Reforming Thai Politics*. Copenhagen: Nordic Institute of Asian Studies, 2002, 183–99.

Nathan, Andrew J. *Chinese Democracy*. Berkeley, CA: University of California Press, 1985.

"National Letdown in the Making." *Bangkok Post*, April 6, 1992, 4. Reprinted in *FBISDREA*, April 6, 1992, 63.

Ni Shixiong and Wang Yiwei. "Shilun guoji guanxi minzhuhua" ("On Democratization of International Relations"). *Guoji Wenti Yanjiu (International Studies)* 2002(3), 22–26. [倪世雄王义桅。"试论国际关系民主化"。*国际问题研究* 2002(3), 页 22–26。]

"No Foreign or Indigenous Dogmatism: China Should Have Its Own Definition of 'Democracy.'" *Ta Kung Pao*, September 11, 2002. Translated in *FBISDCR*, November 7, 2002.

Nophakhun Limsamanphun. "Comment." *The Nation*, June 16, 1992, A6. Reprinted in *FBISDREA*, June 16, 1992, 37–38.

———. "Watchdog: An Anatomy of the Prime Minister's Management Style." *The Nation*, March 20, 2005. <http://www.nationmultimedia.com>.

"Now, There Is No-Win Situation in the Country," *The Nation*, June 10, 1994, A6. Reprinted in *FBISDREA*, June 10, 1994, 53–54.

Nutsara Sawatsawang. "Thailand Calls for More Freedom for People in ASEAN." *Bangkok Post*, December 16, 1997, 4. Reprinted in *FBISDREA*, December 18, 1997.

O'Brien, Kevin J. "Villagers, Elections, and Citizenship in Contemporary China." *Modern China* 27(4), October 2001, 407–35.

O'Donnell, Guillermo. "In Partial Defense of an Evanescent 'Paradigm.'" *Journal of Democracy* 13(3), 2002, 6–12.

O'Donnell, Guillermo and Philippe C. Schmitter. *Transitions from Authoritarian Rule: Tentative Conclusions About Uncertain Democracies*. Foreword by Abraham F. Lowenthal. Baltimore, MD: The Johns Hopkins University Press, 1986.

"Official's Move to China Sparks Security Concerns." *Taipei Times*, May 17, 2002. <http://www.taipeitimes.com>.

Oksenberg, Michel and Steven Goldstein. "The Chinese Political Spectrum." *Problems of Communism* 23, March–April 1974, 1–13.

"Opposition on Government's Political Reform Drive." *The Nation*, August 9, 1995, A1. Reprinted in *FBISDREA*, August 10, 1995, 64–65.

Osiander, Andreas. "Sovereignty, International Relations, and the Westphalian Myth." *International Organization* 55(2), June 2001, 251–87.

"Overhauling Thai Politics Towards Reforms." *Krungthep Thurakit*, June 6, 1994, 2. Translated in *FBISDREA*, June 7, 1994, 36.

"Pak Mun Debacle Due to Communications Gap." *Bangkok Post*, March 9, 1993, 4. Reprinted in *FBISDREA*, March 9, 1993, 48–49.

Pan, Philip P. "A Study Group Is Crushed in China's Grip." *Washington Post*, April 23, 2004, A01.

Pan Zhongqi, "Baquan de kunjing" ("The Dilemma of Hegemony"). *Meiguo Yanjiu (American Studies Quarterly)* 17(3), 2003, 52–64. [潘忠岐。"霸权的困境"。美国研究, 2003, 17(3), 頁 52–64。]

Pasuk Phongpaichit and Chris Baker. "Power in Transition: Thailand in the 1990s." In Kevin Hewison, ed., *Political Change in Thailand: Democracy and Participation*. London: Routledge, 1997, 21–41.

———. *Thailand: Economy and Politics*. Oxford: Oxford University Press, 1995.

Pei, Minxin. "Rights and Resistance: The Changing Contexts of the Dissident Movement." In Elizabeth J. Perry and Mark Selden, eds., *Chinese Society: Change, Conflict, and Resistance*. London: Routledge, 2000, 20–40.

Peng Ming-min. *A Taste of Freedom*. New York: Holt, Rinehart, and Winston, 1972.

Perrin, Andrew. "The Thaksin Effect." *Time*, October 27, 2003. <http://www.time.com>.

Phaisan Sicharatchanya. "Dirty Politics Is Eroding the Faith of the Public." *The Sunday Post*, May 23, 1993, 22. Reprinted in *FBISDREA*, May 25, 1993, 49–50.

Phanrawi Tansuphaphon and Nutsara Sawatsawang. "Thailand Welcomes ASEAN Shift on Openness." *Bangkok Post*, July 25, 1998. Reprinted in *FBIS-DREA*, July 28, 1998.

Phillips, Steven. "Between Assimilation and Independence: Taiwanese Political Aspirations Under Nationalist Chinese Rule, 1945–1948." In Murray A. Rubinstein, ed., *Taiwan: A New History*. Armonk, NY: M.E. Sharpe, 1999, 275–319.

"Plan to Restrict Movement of High-Tech Workers Seen as Exercise in Futility." *Taipei Times*, April 19, 2002. <http://www.taipeitimes.com>.

"PM's Declaration: Democracy Is Not My Goal." *The Nation*, December 11, 2003. <http://nationmultimedia.com>.

"PM Slams 'Anarchists.'" *The Nation*, December 25, 2002. <http://www.nationmultimedia.com>.

"PM Slams UN Envoy as Biased." *The Nation*, May 29, 2003. <http://www.nationmultimedia.com>.

"PM's Rating Soars After Tsunami Hit." *Bangkok Post*, January 5, 2005. <http://www. bangkokpost.com>.

"PM Vows to Resolve Pak Mool Crisis His Way." *The Nation*, December 19, 2002. <http://www.nationmultimedia.com>.

"Political Reform: A Serious Question of Sincerity." *The Nation*, November 15, 1995, A4. Reprinted in *FBISDREA*, November 15, 1995, 75–76.

"Political Reform Only Real Way to Achieve Maturity." *Bangkok Post*, June 21, 1995, 4. Reprinted in *FBISDREA*, June 21, 1995, 68–69.

Pollack, Jonathan D. "More than Bombing Roils the Waters of Sino-US Relations." *Los Angeles Times*, May 11, 1999. <www.latimes.com>.

"PollWatch Submits Suggestions for Fair Elections." *The Nation*, June 21, 1992, A1. Reprinted in *FBISDREA*, June 23, 1992, 55–56.

Pomeranz, Kenneth. *The Great Divergence: China, Europe, and the Making of the Modern World Economy*, Revised ed. Princeton, NJ: Princeton University Press, 2001.

Prawase Wasi. "An Overview of Political Reform." In Duncan McCargo, ed., *Reforming Thai Politics*. Copenhagen: Nordic Institute of Asian Studies, 2002, 21–27.

"PRC Officials View New Role Played by Internet." Xinhua News Agency, March 8, 2001. Reprinted in *FBISDCR*, March 12, 2001.

"PRC Says Party Groups Not to Affect Taiwan Companies." Xinhua, December 26, 2001. Reprinted in *FBISDCR*, December 27, 2001.

"PRC's Xinjiang Anti-Crime Campaign Targets Muslim Separatists." Agence France-Presse, April 27, 2001. Reprinted in *FBISDCR*, April 30, 2001.

Pridi Banomyong. *Pridi by Pridi: Selected Writings on Life, Politics, and Economy*. Translated and Introduced by Chris Baker and Pasuk Phongpaichit. Chiang Mai, Thailand: Silkworm Books, 2000.

"Prime Minister Addresses Nation." Bangkok Army Television Channel 5, May 8, 1992. Translated in *FBISDREA*, May 11, 1992, 43–45.

"The Principle of the Obsolete Politicians." *Krungthep Thurakit*, June 10, 1994, 2. Translated in *FBISDREA*, June 13, 1994, 52–53.

"Pro-Democracy MPs Continue Protest." *The Nation*, April 15, 1992, A1–A2. Reprinted in *FBISDREA*, April 15, 1992, 49–50.

"Professional Leadership Needed for State Firms." *The Nation*, July 22, 1992, A6. Reprinted in *FBISDREA*, July 1992, 47–48.

"A Program for Education in Patriotism." Xinhua, September 4, 1994. Translated in *FBISDCR*, November 12, 1995.

Prudhisan Jumbala. "Thailand: Constitutional Form Amidst Economic Crisis." In *Southeast Asian Affairs 1998*. Singapore: Institute of Southeast Asian Studies, 1998, 265–91.

Przeworski, Adam, Michael E. Alvarez, Jose Antonio Cheibub, and Fernando Limongi. *Democracy and Development: Political Institutions and Well-Being in the World, 1950–1990*. Cambridge, UK: Cambridge University Press, 2000.

Putnam, Robert D. *Making Democracy Work: Civic Traditions in Modern Italy*. Princeton, NJ: Princeton University Press, 1993.

"*Renmin Ribao (People's Daily)* Commentator on Embassy Bombing." *Renmin Ribao (People's Daily)*, May 9, 1999. Translated in *FBISDCR*, May 11, 1999.

"*Renmin Ribao (People's Daily)* Condemns 'Pro-Democracy' Elements." Xinhua News Service, May 17, 1999. Reprinted in *FBISDCR*, May 18, 1999.

"*Renmin Ribao (People's Daily)* Editorial: Build Our Motherland into an Even Better Country." Xinhua, September 30, 1996. Translated in *FBISDCR*, October 1, 1996.

Ren Zhongping. "On Patriotism, Collectivism, and Socialism." *Renmin Ribao (People's Daily)*, June 28, 2000. Translated in *FBISDCR*, July 31, 2000.

Reynolds, Craig J. "Introduction: National Identity and Its Defenders." In Craig J. Reynolds, ed., *National Identity and Its Defenders: Thailand, 1939–1989*. Chiang Mai, Thailand: Silkworm Books, 1991, 13–29.

Reynolds, Frank E. "Legitimation and Rebellion: Thailand's Civic Religion and the Student Uprising of October 1973." In Bardwell L. Smith, ed., *Religion and Legitimation of Power in Thailand, Laos, and Burma*. Chambersberg, PA: Anima Books, 1978, 134–46.

"Rhetoric, Military Manoeuvres Reflect Growing Chinese Angst Over Taiwan." *Channel News Asia*, July 20, 2004. <http://www.channelnewsasia.com/stories/afp_asiapacific /view/96550/1/.html>. Retrieved August 2, 2004.

Rice, Edward E. *Mao's Way*. Berkeley, CA: University of California Press, 1974.

Rigger, Shelley. *From Opposition to Power: Taiwan's Democratic Progressive Party*. Boulder, CO: Lynne Rienner, 2001.

Risse, Thomas and Kathryn Sikkink, eds. *The Power of Human Rights: International Norms and Domestic Change*. Cambridge, UK: Cambridge University Press, 1999.

Robinson, William. *Promoting Polyarchy: Globalization, US Intervention, and Hegemony.* Cambridge, UK: Cambridge University Press, 1996.

Rodan, Garry, ed. *Political Oppositions in Industrializing Asia.* New York: Routledge, 1996.

Rotberg, Robert I. "Prospects for a Democratic Burma," In Robert I. Rotberg, ed., *Burma: Prospects for a Democratic Future.* Washington, DC: The Brookings Institution Press, 1998, 1–7.

Rubinstein, Murray A. "Political Taiwanization and Pragmatic Diplomacy: The Eras of Chiang Ching-kuo and Lee Teng-hui, 1971–1994." In Murray A. Rubinstein, ed., *Taiwan: A New History.* Armonk, NY: M.E. Sharpe, 1999, 436–80.

Seksan Prasertkul. "The Transformation of the Thai State and Economic Change, 1855–1945." Ph.D. dissertation, Cornell University, 1989.

"Senior Academic on Political Development" (interview with Seksan Prasoetkun). *Siam Rat,* June 11, 1994, 3. Translated in *FBISDREA,* August 16, 1994, 80–81.

Shambaugh, David. "China's International Relations Think Tanks: Evolving Structure and Process." *The China Quarterly,* September 2002, 575–96.

"Shameful for ASEAN to Embrace Burma." *The Sunday Nation,* June 1, 1997, A4. Reprinted in *FBISDREA,* June 3, 1997.

Shan Min. "What Is the United States Intending to Do with Its China Security Strategy?" *Liaowang (Outlook),* April 30, 2001, 31. Translated in *FBISDCR,* May 14, 2001.

Shari, Michael. "Thaksin's Thailand." *Business Week,* July 28, 2003. <http://www.businessweek.com>.

Shen Qurong. "Wenming duihua de guoji guanxi yihan" ("Dialogue Across Cultures: Implications for International Relations"). *Xiandai Guoji Guanxi (Contemporary International Relations)* 2001 (10), 24–30. [谌取荣。"文明对话的国际关系意含"。现代国际关系 2001(10)，頁 24–30。]

Shi Aiguo. "'Minzhu heping lun' pouxi" ("An Analysis of the 'Democratic Peace' Thesis"). *Xiandai Guoji Guanxi (Contemporary International Relations)* 2002 (9), 1–6. [施爱国。"'民主和平论'剖析"。现代国际关系 2002 (9)，頁 1–6。]

Shih Cheng-feng. "Taiwan minzuzhuyi de jiexi: zhengzhi mianxiang de sange jingzheng tujing" ("Explanations of Taiwanese Nationalism: Three Competing Political Directions"). In Chang Yen-hsien, Tseng Chiu-mei, and Chen Chao-hai, eds., *"Maixiang 21 shiji de taiwan minzu yu guojia" lunwenji* ("*Collected Essays on 'the Taiwanese Nation and State's March to the 21st Century'*"). Taipei: Wu Sanlian Jijinhui, 2002, 325–43. [施正鋒。"台灣民族主義的解析——政治面相的三個競爭途徑"。張炎憲、曾秋美、陳朝海編。「邁向 21 世紀的台灣民族與國家」論文集。(台北 : 吳三連基金會，2002)，頁 325–43。]

Shih Chun-yu. "Coordination Between New Guidelines in the East and New Concept in the West." *Ta Kung Pao,* May 1, 1999, A4. Translated in *FBISDCR,* May 3, 1999.

Shih Ming. *Taiwan bu shi Zhongguo de yibufen (Taiwan is Not a Part of China).* Taiwan: Qianwei Chubanshe, 1992. [史明。台灣不是中國的一部分。台灣 : 前衛出版社，1992。]

Shi Yinhong. "Geju, chaoliu, shidai tezheng" ("The Situation, Trends, and Special Contemporary Characteristics"). *Xiandai Guoji Guanxi* (*Contemporary International Relations*) 2002 (7), 8–10. [时殷弘。"格局・潮流・时代特征"。现代国际关系, 2002 (7), 頁 8–10。]

Shu, Wei-der. "Who Joined the Clandestine Political Organization?" In Stephane Corcuff, ed., *Memories of the Future: National Identity Issues and the Search for a New Taiwan*. Armonk, NY: M.E. Sharpe, 2002, 47–69.

Sirikul Bunnag and Yuwadee Tunyasiri. "King Approves New Constitution." *Bangkok Post*, October 12, 1997, 1. Reprinted in *FBISDREA*, October 1997.

S. J. "Introduction." In Sulak Sivaraksa, *Powers That Be: Pridi Banomyong Through the Rise and Fall of Thai Democracy* (Translated and Introduced by S. J.). Bangkok: Committees on the Project for the National Celebration on the Occasion of the Centennial Anniversary of Pridi Banomyong, Senior Statesman, 1999, 1–11.

"Social Cost of Development." *Bangkok Post*, April 15, 1992, 4. Reprinted in *FBISDREA*, April 15, 1992, 51–52.

Somchai Meesane and Supawadee Susanpoolthong. "Minister Sees Communist Plot Behind Draft Charter." *Bangkok Post*, August 24, 1997, 1. Reprinted in *FBISDREA*, August 27, 1997.

Song Yimin. "2010 nian qian wo guo zai shijie shang mianlin de jiyu yu tiaozhan" ("Opportunities and Challenges That China Will Face in the World Before 2010"). *Guoji Wenti Yanjiu* (*International Studies*) 2000 (3), 1–6. [宋以敏。"2010年前我国在世界上面临的机遇与挑战"。国际问题研究 2000(3), 頁 1–6。]

Stainton, Michael. "The Politics of Taiwan's Aboriginal Origins." In Murray A. Rubinstein, ed., *Taiwan: A New History*. Armonk, NY: M.E. Sharpe, 1999, 27–44.

"Student Body Hands Out Manual on Possible Coup." *Bangkok Post*, June 8, 1992, 3. Reprinted in *FBISDREA*, June 9, 1992, 54.

"Suchinda Addresses Closing." Bangkok Thai Color Television, May 7, 1992. Translated in *FBISDREA*, May 7, 1992, 36.

"Suchinda on Religious Belief to Well-Wishers." Bangkok Radio Thailand Network, May 8, 1992. Translated in *FBISDREA*, May 12, 1992, 49.

"Suchinda's Near Impossible Task of Reviving Confidence." *Bangkok Post*, May 7, 1992, 2.

Sulak Sivaraksa. "Buddhism and Human Rights in Siam." In Sulak Sivaraksa, ed., *Socially Engaged Buddhism for the New Millennium*. Bangkok: Sathirakoses-Nagapradipa Foundation and Foundation for Children, 1999, 195–212.

―――. "The Crisis of Siamese Identity." In Craig J. Reynolds, ed., *National Identity and Its Defenders: Thailand, 1939–1989*. Chiang Mai, Thailand: Silkworm Books, 1991, 41–58.

―――. *Loyalty Demands Dissent: Autobiography of a Socially Engaged Buddhist*. Berkeley, CA: Parallax Press, and Bangkok: Thai Inter-Religious Commission for Development, 1998.

————. *Powers That Be: Pridi Banomyong Through the Rise and Fall of Thai Democracy*. Translated and Introduced by S. J. Bangkok: Committees on the Project for the National Celebration on the Occasion of the Centennial Anniversary of Pridi Banomyong, Senior Statesman, 1999.

Sunait Chutintaranond and Than Tun. *On Both Sides of the Tenasserim Range: History of Siamese-Burmese Relations*. Bangkok: Chulalongkorn University Institute of Asian Studies, 1995.

Sun Chih. "Making Political Civilization One of the Objects of Development." *Ta Kung Pao*, September 5, 2002, A2. Translated in *FBISDCR*, September 9, 2002.

Sun Ta-ch'uan. "Jiafeng zhong de zuqun jiangou: fan yuanzhumin yishi yu taiwan zuqun wenti de hudong" ("Ethnicity Construction in a Crevice: The Mutual Interplay Between Pan-Aboriginal Consciousness and Taiwan's Ethnic Problems"). In Chang Yen-hsien, Chen Mei-jung, and Lee Chung-kuang, eds., *Taiwan jinbainianshi lunwenji* (*Collected Essays on Taiwan's Recent 100 Years of History*). Taipei: Wu Sanlian Jijinhui, 1996, 353–75. [孫大川。「夾縫中的族群建構——泛原住民意識與 台灣族群問題的互動」。張炎憲、陳美蓉、黎中光編。*台灣近百年史論文集*。(台北：吳三連基金 會, 1996), 頁 353–75。]

Sun Yat-sen. *San Min Chu I: The Three Principles of the People*, With two supplementary chapters by Chiang Kai-shek. Taipei: Government Information Office, 1996.

Sun Zhaozhen. "2001 Saw Ongoing Increase in Economic and Trade Interdependence Between Mainland China and Taiwan." Zhongguo Xinwen She, February 3, 2002. Translated in *FBISDCR*, February 5, 2002.

Supara Janchitfah. "Enemies of the State?" *Bangkok Post*, January 5, 2003 <http://www.bangkokpost.com>.

Supawadee Susanpoolthong and Ampa Santimetaneedol. "Thai Government Must Support Draft to Head Off 'Uprising.'" *Bangkok Post*, August 1, 1997, 2. Reprinted in *FBISDREA*, August 4, 1997.

Surin Maisrikrod. "Joining the Values Debate: The Peculiar Case of Thailand." *Sojourn* 14(2), October 1999, 402–13.

Surin Pitsuwan. "The Role of Human Rights in Thailand's Foreign Policy." Speech delivered at the seminar on "Promotion and Protection of Human Rights by Human Rights Commissions," Germany, October 2, 1998. <http://www.thaiembdc.org/pressctr/statemnt/others/fm_hr1098.htm>. Retrieved November 11, 2003.

"Surin Sees Benefits in Intervention Policy." *The Nation*, June 27, 1998. Reprinted in *FBISDREA*, June 30, 1998.

Suthichai Yun. "92: Beyond Soul-Searching." *The Nation*, January 1, 1992, A1. Reprinted in *FBISDREA*, January 3, 1992, 66–67.

————. "Chuan Urged to Set Vision, Agenda for Nation." *The Nation*, November 30, 1992, A1. Reprinted in *FBISDREA*, December 2, 1992, 62–63.

"'Taidu yundong' de mishi yu yumei" ("Ignorance and Misleadingness of the Taiwan Independence Movement"). *Zhongguo Luntan* (*The China Tribune*)

1(11), March 10, 1976, 1. [「『台獨運動』的迷失與愚昧」。*中國論壇* 1(11), 1976 年 3 月 10 日,頁 1。]

"Taiwan Businesses in PRC Discover Political Risks." Central News Agency (Taiwan), December 30, 2001. Reprinted in *FBISDCR*, December 31, 2001.

"Taiwan Businesses Invest More on Chinese Mainland." Xinhua, April 4, 2002. Reprinted in *FBISDCR*, April 5, 2002.

"Taiwan Cabinet Fund to Withdraw Investment in PRC-Based Semiconductor Firm." Agence France-Presse, April 18, 2002. Reprinted in *FBISDCR*, April 19, 2002.

"Taiwan-China Trade Up 33.1% in 2004." Agence France-Presse, March 1, 2005. <http://taiwansecurity.org/AFP/2005/AFP-020305.htm>. Retrieved July 24, 2005.

"Taiwan Eases Controls on PRC-Bound Investment." Agence France-Presse, August 26, 2001. Reprinted in *FBISDCR*, August 27, 2001.

"Taiwanese Workers March Against Rising Unemployment in May Day Parade." Agence France-Presse, May 1, 2002. Reprinted in *FBISDCR*, May 2, 2002.

"Taiwan's Cabinet Decides to Ease Half-Century Ban on Chinese Investments." Agence France-Presse, March 27, 2002. Reprinted in *FBISDCR*, March 28, 2002.

"Taiwan's First Half Investment in China up 68 Percent Despite Tension." *Channel News Asia*, July 21, 2004. <http://www.channelnewsasia.com/stories/afp_asiapacific_business/ view/96791/1/.html>. Retrieved July 24, 2005.

"Taiwan's Unemployment Rate Hits 4.09 Percent." *Forbes*, February 25, 2005. <http://www.forbes.com/work/feeds/ap/2005/02/25/ap1848692.html>. Retrieved July 24, 2005.

"Taiwan Warned of Courting Disaster." *Taipei Times*, March 27, 2005. <http://www.taipeitimes.com>.

Tambiah, S. J. "Sangha and Polity in Modern Thailand: An Overview." In Bardwell L. Smith, ed., *Religion and Legitimation of Power in Thailand, Laos, and Burma*. Chambersberg, PA: Anima Books, 1978, 111–33.

Tang Runhua. "The True Face of the West's 'Press Freedom.'" Xinhua, June 3, 1999. Translated in *FBISDCR*, June 7, 1999.

Tang Tianri. "The Trend Toward Multipolarity of the World Is Irresistible." *Liaowang (Outlook)*, October 1, 2001, 41. Translated in *FBISDCR*, October 15, 2001.

Taylor, Kenneth W. "The Early Kingdoms." In Nicholas Tarling, ed., *The Cambridge History of Southeast Asia, Volume One, Part One: From Early Times to c. 1500*. Cambridge, UK: Cambridge University Press, 1999, 168–73.

Teschke, Benno. *The Myth of 1648: Class, Geopolitics and the Making of Modern International Relations*. London: Verso, 2003.

"Thailand Supports ASEAN Commission on Human Rights." *The Nation*, May 27, 1998. Reprinted in *FBISDREA*, May 29, 1998.

Thak Chaloemtiarana. *Thailand: The Politics of Despotic Paternalism*. Bangkok: The Social Science Association of Thailand, Thai Khadi Institute, Thammasat University, 1979.

"Thaksin's 'War on Dark Influences.'" *Asia-Pacific Business*, May 30, 2003. <http://www.asiapacificbusiness.ca>.

"Thaksin Taught the Value of Criticism." *The Nation*, December 5, 2003. <http://www.nationmultimedia.com>.

Thongchai Winichakul. *Siam Mapped: A History of the Geo-Body of a Nation.* Honolulu: University of Hawaii Press, 1994.

Thirayuth Boonmi. "Good Governance: A Strategy to Restore Thailand" (edited and translated by Savitri Gadavanij). In Duncan McCargo, ed., *Reforming Thai Politics*. Copenhagen: Nordic Institute of Asian Studies, 2002, 29–35.

"Thousands Rally to Demand New Constitution." *The Nation*, June 9, 1994, A1. Reprinted in *FBISDREA*, June 9, 1994, 52–53.

"Tibetan Monks Suffer China Patriotism Campaign." Agence France-Presse, August 1, 1997. Reprinted in *FBISDCR*, August 25, 1997.

Tien, Hong-Mao. *The Great Transformation: Political and Social Change in the Republic of China*. Stanford, CA: Stanford University Press, 1989.

T'ien Hsin. "'Waishengren' zhiyouzhuyizhe dui 'taiwan qiantu' de taidu" ("Liberal 'Mainlanders' Attitudes Towards Taiwan's Future"). In Chang Yen-hsien, Chen Mei-jung, and Lee Chung-kuang, eds., *Taiwan jinbainianshi lunwenji (Collected Essays on Taiwan's Recent 100 Years of History)*. Taipei: Wu Sanlian Jijinhui, 1996, 331–51. [田欣。『外省人』自由主義者對『台灣前途』的態度」。張炎憲、陳美蓉、黎中光編。*台灣近百年史論文集*。(台北 : 吳三連基金會, 1996), 頁331–51。]

"Time to Focus on How to Deal with the Military." *The Nation*, June 19, 1992, A6. Reprinted in *FBISDREA*, June 1992, 49–50.

Tkacik, John J., Jr. "China's 'S & M' Journal Goes Too Far on Korea." *Asia Times*, September 2, 2004. <http://www.atimes.com/atimes/China/FI02Ad06.html>. Retrieved June 9, 2005.

"To Grasp In-Depth Important Thinking of 'Three Represents.'" Xinhua, July 20, 2003. Reprinted in *FBISDCR*, July 21, 2003.

"Trouble Continues Under Chen Shui-bian." *China Daily* (Internet ed.), May 1, 2002. <http://www.chinadaily.com.cn>.

Tung Fang-yuan. "Lun zhanglao jiaohui yu taiwan de xiandaihua." In Chang Yen-hsien, Chen Mei-jung, and Lee Chung-kuang, eds., *Taiwan jinbainianshi lunwenji (Collected Essays on Taiwan's Recent 100 Years of History")*. Taipei: Wu Sanlian Jijinhui, 1996, 207–11. [董芳苑。「論長老教會與台灣的現代化」。張炎憲、陳美蓉、黎中光編。*台灣近百年史論文集*。(台北 : 吳三連基金會, 1996), 頁207–11。]

"An Unforgivable Betrayal." *The Nation*, April 6, 1992, A8. Reprinted in *FBISDREA*, April 6, 1992, 64.

Unger, Jonathan, ed. *Chinese Nationalism*. Armonk, NY: M.E. Sharpe, 1996.

"Unswervingly Promote Democracy at Rural Grassroots Levels." *Renmin Ribao (People's Daily)*, August 19, 2002. Translated in *FBISDCR*, August 22, 2002.

"US Business Group Says Taiwan Risks Making Itself Irrelevant." *Taipei Times*, May 8, 2002. <http://www.taipeitimes.com>.

"US Criticism of China's Human Rights Record Reveals Cold War Mentality." Xinhua, March 31, 2004. Reprinted in *FBISDCR*, March 31, 2004.

Van Praagh, David. *Thailand's Struggle for Democracy: The Life and Times of M.R. Seni Pramoj*. New York: Holmes and Meier, 1996.

Vasana Chinvarakorn. "Remembering a Servant of Buddha." *Seeds of Peace* 19(3), September–December 2003, 31–33.

Veera Prateepchaikul. "Grouping Puts Its Reputation on the Line." *Bangkok Post*, June 3, 1997, 11. Reprinted in *FBISDREA*, June 5, 1997.

"Veteran Diplomat Writes Article Urging Jiang Zemin for Political Reform." *Sing Tao Jih Pao*, February 12, 2000. Translated in *FBISDCR*, February 16, 2000.

"Vice-premier Qian Qichen on Cross-strait Negotiations." *People's Daily*, January 16, 2003. <http://english.people.com.cn/ 200301/16/eng20030116_110195. shtml>. Retrieved July 18, 2004.

Visalo, Bhikkhu. "Buddhism for the Next Century: Toward Renewing a Moral Thai Society." In Sulak Sivaraksa, ed., *Socially Engaged Buddhism for the New Millennium*. Bangkok: Sathirakoses-Nagapradipa Foundation and Foundation for Children, 1999, 235–52.

Voice of the Asia-Pacific Human Rights Network. "Thailand's National Human Rights Commission." <http://www.hrdc.net/sahrde>.

Wachman, Alan M. *Taiwan: National Identity and Democratization*. Armonk, NY: M.E. Sharpe, 1994.

Wang Er-min. "Xihua wenti de huisi" ("Looking Back on the Westernization Question"). *Zhongguo Luntan (The China Tribune)* 2(9), August 10, 1976, 42. [王爾敏。「西化問題的迴思」。中國論壇, 1976 年 8 月 10日, 頁 42。]

Wang Jinfu and Chen Binhua. "A New Chapter in Democratic Politics." Xinhua News Agency, October 20, 2002. Translated in *FBISDCR*, October 23, 2002.

Wang Jisi. "Lue lun dangqian shijie de zhengzhi tezheng" ("Special Political Characteristics of the Contemporary World"). *Xiandai Guoji Guanxi (Contemporary International Relations)* 2002 (7), pp. 5–8. [王缉思。"略论当前世界的政治特征"。现代国际关系 2002(7), 頁 5–8。]

———. "Meiguo baquan de luoji" ("The Logic of American Hegemony"). *Meiguo Yanjiu (American Studies Quarterly)* 17(3), 2003, 7–29. [王缉思。"美国霸权的逻辑"。美国研究, 2003, 17(3), 頁 7–29。]

Wang Leiming. "Cults Endanger National Security." Xinhua, September 27, 2000. Translated in *FBISDCR*, October 12, 2000.

Wang Shaoguang. "The Social and Political Implications of China's WTO Membership." *Journal of Contemporary China* 9(25), 2000, 373–405.

Wang Shih-liang. "Ri ren zai Tai zhimindi tizhi zhi dianding" ("Establishment of the Japanese Colonial System in Taiwan"). *Meilidao (Formosa)* 1(1), August 1979, 94–95. [王詩琅。「日人在台殖民地體制之奠定 美麗島 1(1), 1979 年 8月, 頁 94–95。]

Wang Sirui. "Zhongguo jingji zengzhang yu zhengzhi gaige" ("Economic Growth and Political Reform"). *Zhanlue yu Guanli (Strategy and Management)* 2001 (3), 71–80. [王思睿。"中国经济增长与政治改革"。战略与管理, 2001 (3), 頁 71–80。]

Wang T'ai-sheng. "Bainian lai taiwan falu de xifanghua" ("The Westernization of Taiwanese Law During the Past 100 Years"). In Chang Yenhsien, Chen Mei-jung, and Lee Chung-kuang, eds., *Taiwan jinbainianshi lunwenji (Collected Essays on Taiwan's Recent 100 Years of History)*. Taipei: Wu Sanlian Jijinhui, 1996, 377–97. [王泰升。「百年來台灣法律的西方化」。張炎憲、陳美蓉、黎中光編。*台灣近百年史論文集*。(台北 : 吳三連基金會，1996)，頁 377–97。]

Wang Tianxi. "End-of-century War." *Renmin Ribao (People's Daily)*, April 21, 1999, 6. Translated in *FBISDCR*, April 22, 1999.

Wang T'u-fa. "Yongxu fazhan de chanye zhengce yu guotu guihua" ("Industrial Policy and National Land-Use Planning for Sustainable Development"). In Chang Yen-hsien, Tseng Chiu-mei, and Chen Chao-hai, eds., *"Maixiang 21 shiji de taiwan minzu yu guojia" lunwenji (Collected Essays on 'the Taiwanese Nation and State's March to the 21st Century'")*. Taipei: Wu Sanlian Jijinhui, 2002, 107–24. [王塗發。「永續發展的產業政策與國土規劃」。張炎憲、曾秋美、陳朝海編。「邁向21世紀的台灣民族與國家」論文集。台北: 吳三連基金會，2002)，頁 107–24。]

Wang Xialin. "Building Socialist Political Civilization and Promoting All-Round Social Progress." *Renmin Ribao (People's Daily)* (English-language Internet ed.), April 28, 2003. Reprinted in *FBISDCR*, April 28, 2003.

Wang Xiaode. "Guanyu 'Meiguohua' yu quan qiu duoyuan wenhua fazhan de sikao" ("Thoughts on Americanization and Global Multicultural Development"). *Meiguo Yanjiu (American Studies Quarterly)* 17(3), 2003, 87–104. [王晓德。"关于 '美国化'与全球多元文化发展的思考"。美国研究,2003, 17(3)，頁 87–104。]

Wang Xiaodong. "Dangdai Zhongguo minzuzhuyi lun" ("On Contemporary Chinese Nationalism"). *Zhanlue yu Guanli (Strategy and Management)* 2000 (5), 69–82. [王小东。"当代中国民族主义论"。战略与管理2000(5)，頁 69–82。]

Wang Xingfang. "Qian tan renquan baozhang yu renquan waijiao" ("A Preliminary Analysis of Human Rights Protection and Human Rights Diplomacy"). *Guoji Wenti Yanjiu (International Studies)* 2000 (2), 15–19. [王杏芳。"浅谈人权保障与人权外交"。国际问题研究, 2000(2)，頁 15–19。]

Wang Xinhong. "Autonomous Regional Party Committee Convenes Regional Teleconference." *Xinjiang Ribao*, December 9, 2001. Translated in *FBISDCR*, January 7, 2002.

Wang Yi. "Quanqiuhua Beijing xia de duojihua jincheng" ("Globalization and the Process of Multipolarization"). *Guoji Wenti Yanjiu (International Studies)* 2000 (6), 1–6. [王毅。"全球化背景下的多极化进程"。国际问题研究2000(6)，頁 1–6。]

Wang Zhenyao. "Zhongguo de cunmin zizhi yu minzhuhua fazhan daolu" ("The Autonomy of Chinese Villagers and the Road of Democratization"). *Zhanlue yu Guanli (Strategy and Management)* 2000 (2), 99–105. [王振耀。"中国的村民自治与民主化发展道路"。战略与管理, 2000(2)，頁 99–105。]

Wang Zhijun. "'Hou lingtu shidai' yu diyuan zhanlue de shanbian" ("The 'Post-Territorial Era' and the Evolution of Geopolitical Strategy").

Xiandai Guoji Guanxi (*Contemporary International Relations*), 2000 (5), 32–35. [王志军。"'后领土时代'与地缘战略的嬗变"。*现代国际关系*, 2000(5), 頁 32–35。]

Wang Zhi. "Why Not Drink the Water in Close Vicinity to Quench Burning Thirst?" *Renmin Ribao* (*People's Daily*), April 30, 2002. Translated in *FBIS-DCR*, May 2, 2002.

Weigle, Marcia and Jim Butterfield. "Civil Society in Reforming Communist Regimes: The Logic of Emergence." *Comparative Politics* 25, October 1992, 1–23.

Whitehead, Laurence. "Three International Dimensions of Democratization." In Laurence Whitehead, ed., *The International Dimensions of Democratization*. Oxford: Oxford University Press, 1996, 3–25.

"Why Dalai Tells Wild Lies." Zhongguo Xinwen She, June 30, 2000. Translated in *FBISDCR*, July 7, 2000.

Wichit Chaitrong and Watcharapong Thongrung. "Thailand's Future: Another Crisis Is Looming." *The Nation*, November 28, 2004. <http://www.nationmultimedia.com>.

Wight, Martin. *International Theory: The Three Traditions* [Wight's essays from the 1950s], Gabriele Wight and Brian Porter, eds. New York: Holmes and Meier, 1992.

Wills, John E., Jr. "The Seventeenth-Century Transformation: Taiwan Under the Dutch and the Cheng Regime." In Murray A. Rubinstein, ed., *Taiwan: A New History*. Armonk, NY: M.E. Sharpe, 1999, 84–106.

Winckler, Edwin A. and Susan Greenhalgh, eds. *Contending Approaches to the Political Economy of Taiwan*. Armonk, NY: M.E. Sharpe, 1988.

Wittrock, Bjorn. "Modernity: One, None, or Many? European Origins and Modernity as a Global Condition." *Daedalus: Journal of the American Academy of Arts and Sciences* 129(1), Winter 2000, 47–48.

"Women dui 'Meilidao shijian' de yixie ganxiang" ("A Few of Our Thoughts on the 'Formosa Incident'"). *Zhongguo Luntan* (*The China Tribune*) 9(6), December 25, 1979, 2. [「我們對『美麗島事件』的一些感想」。*中國論壇* 9(6), 1979 年 12 月 25 日, 頁 2。]

Wood, Alan T. *Asian Democracy in World History*. New York: Routledge, 2004.

World United Formosans for Independence. <http://www.wufi.org>.

Wright, Teresa. "The China Democracy Party and the Politics of Protest in the 1980s–1990s." *The China Quarterly*, December 2002, 906–26.

Wu Jing. "China's Largest Human Rights Website Opens in Beijing." Xinhua, January 22, 2002. Reprinted in *FBISDCR*, January 23, 2002.

Wu, Lilian. "Businesses Dissatisfied with Government's Mainland Policy." Central News Agency (Taiwan), April 25, 2002. Reprinted in *FBISDCR*, April 26, 2002.

———. "Government to Improve Help for Taiwan Businessmen in Mainland." Central News Agency (Taiwan), February 22, 2002. Reprinted in *FBISDCR*, February 25, 2002.

————. "Kinmen Schools to Accept Children of Taiwan Businesspeople on Mainland." Central News Agency (Taiwan), April 2, 2002. Reprinted in *FBISDCR*, April 3, 2002.

————. "Legislative VP Says Direct Cross-Strait Transport Crucial for Taiwan." Central News Agency (Taiwan), April 28, 2002. Reprinted in *FBISDCR*, April 29, 2002.

————. "No Taiwan Businessmen on Mainland Have Joined CCP." Central News Agency, December 20, 2001. Reprinted in *FBISDCR*, December 21, 2001.

————. "NSC Will Not Register High-Tech Personnel in Taiwan," Central News Agency (Taiwan), April 15, 2002. Reprinted in *FBISDCR*, April 16, 2002.

————. "TSU Promoting Taiwan as National Title." Central News Agency (Taiwan), April 23, 2002. Reprinted in *FBISDCR*, April 24, 2002.

Wu Nai-te and Ch'en Ming-tung. "Zhengquan zhuanyi he jingying liudong: Taiwan difang zhengzhi jingying de lishi xingcheng" ("Transformations in Political Power and the Circulation of Elites: The Historical Formation of Taiwan's Local Political Elites"). In Chang Yen-hsien, Lee Hsiao-feng, and Tai Pao-cun, eds., *Taiwan shi lunwen jingxuan* (*Selected Essays on Taiwanese History*). Taipei: Yushan She, 1996, 351–85. [吳乃德 、 陳明通。「政權轉移和菁英流動: 台灣地方政治菁英的歷史 形成」。 張炎憲、李筱峯、戴寶村編。*台灣史論文精選*。(台北: 玉山社, 1996), 頁 351–85。]

Wu, Sofia. "MAC to Review Legal Issues Regarding Cross-Strait Marriages." Central News Agency (Taiwan), April 22, 2002. Reprinted in *FBISDCR*, April 23, 2002.

————. "More than 10,000 Taiwan Students Studying in Mainland China." Central News Agency (Taiwan), August 4, 2001. Reprinted in *FBISDCR*, August 6, 2001.

————. "President Credits Latest Taiwan Cultural Boom to Democratization." Central News Agency (Taiwan), April 18, 2002. Reprinted in *FBISDCR*, April 19, 2002.

————. "Pro-Taiwan Activists to Promote Use of 'Taiwan' in Group Names." Central News Agency (Taiwan), April 23, 2002. Reprinted in *FBISDCR*, April 24, 2002.

————. "Talent Control Would Tarnish Democratic Taiwan: Nobel Laureate." Central News Agency (Taiwan), April 22, 2002. Reprinted in *FBISDCR*, April 23, 2002.

Wu Yuan. "At the Foot of Mount Yangming: Lee Teng-hui Calls for Removal of 'Minister of Education.'" *Ta Kung Pao*, January 10, 2002. Translated in *FBISDCR*, January 15, 2002.

Wyatt, David K. "Contextual Arguments for the Authenticity of the Ramkhamhaeng Inscription." In David K. Wyatt, ed., *Studies in Thai History*. Chiang Mai, Thailand: Silkworm Books, 1994, 48–58.

————. "Education and the Modernization of Thai Society." In David K. Wyatt, ed., *Studies in Thai History*. Chiang Mai, Thailand: Silkworm Books, 1994, 219–44.

————. "Interpreting the History of the Fifth Reign." In David K. Wyatt, ed., *Studies in Thai History*. Chiang Mai, Thailand: Silkworm Books, 1994, 267–72.

————. "King Chulalongkorn the Great: Founder of Modern Thailand." In David K. Wyatt, ed., *Studies in Thai History*. Chiang Mai, Thailand: Silkworm Books, 1994, 273–84.

————. "The 'Subtle Revolution' of King Rama I of Siam." In David K. Wyatt, ed., *Studies in Thai History*. Chiang Mai, Thailand: Silkworm Books, 1994, 131–72.

————. *Thailand: A Short History*. New Haven, CT: Yale University Press, 1982.

Xiao Gongqin. "Hou quanneng tizhi yu 21 shiji Zhongguo de zhengzhi fazhan" ("The Post-Totalitarian System and China's 21st Century Political Development"). *Zhanlue yu Guanli* (Strategy and Management) 2000 (6), 1–8. [萧功秦。"后全能体制与21世纪中国的政治发展"。战略与管理2000(6), 页 1–8。]

————. "Shixi Zhong Mei zhengzhi wenhua zhangli") ("An Analysis of the Tension Between Chinese and American Political Cultures"). *Zhanlue yu Guanli* (*Strategy and Management*) 2001 (2), 39–46. [萧功秦。"试析中美政治文化张力"。战略与管理, 2001 (2) 页 39–46。]

Xiao Ping. "China Can Have Its Own Road to Democratic Politics." *Ta Kung Pao*, August 27, 2001. Translated in *FBISDCR*, November 1, 2001.

Xie Hong. "On Democracy, Freedom, and Human Rights." *Renmin Ribao* (*People's Daily*), December 5, 2000, 9. Translated in *FBISDCR*, December 13, 2000.

Xing Benxi. "On Marxism and Deng Xiaoping Theory." *Renmin Ribao* (*People's Daily*), August 17, 2000, 9. Translated in *FBISDCR*, August 30, 2000.

"Xinhua Reports on Internet Bringing Major Changes to China." Xinhua News Agency, October 19, 2002. Reprinted in *FBISDCR*, October 21, 2002.

"Xinjiang Mobilizes the Whole People to Launch Anti-Separatism Struggle in the Ideological Field." Zhongguo Xinwen She, February 1, 2002. Translated in *FBISDCR*, February 4, 2002.

Xin Wen. "Methods Used by 'Falungong' to Trample on Human Nature, Infringe on Human Rights." Xinhua, June 12, 2000. Translated in *FBISDCR*, July 10, 2000.

Xi Xin. "Why So Many Taiwan Think Tanks?" *Wen Wei Po*, January 6, 2002. Translated in *FBISDCR*, January 22, 2002.

Xu Xianglin. "Yi zhengzhi wending wei jichu de Zhongguo jianjin zhengzhi gaige" ("The Step-by-Step Political Reform of China Based on Political Stability"). *Zhanlue yu Guanli* (*Strategy and Management*) 2000 (5), 16–26. [徐湘林。"以政治稳定为基础的中国渐进政治改革"。战略与管理2000(5) 页 16–26。]

Yang Cheng. "Lun quanqiu zhili zhong de dazhong chuanbo xiaoying" ("On the Global Mass Communication Effect in Global Governance"). *Xiandai Guoji Guanxi* (*Contemporary International Relations*) 2002 (10), 41–45. [杨成。"论全球治理中的大众传播效益"。现代国际关系, 2002(10), 页 41–45。]

Yang Jianping. "Fazhi minzhu: houfa guojia de zhengzhi xuanze" ("Democracy Under Law: A Political Choice for Developing Countries"). *Zhanlue yu Guanli (Strategy and Management)* 2001 (6), 86–92. [杨建平。"法治民主：后发国家的政治选择"。战略与管理, 2001(6), 頁 86–92.]

Yang Yang. "Qian xi wenhua zai guoji guanxi zhong de zuoyong" ("The Role of Culture in International Relations"). *Xiandai Guoji Guanxi (Contemporary International Relations)* 2002 (4), 38–42. [杨阳。"浅析文化在国际关系中的作用"。现代国际关系, 2002(4), 頁 38–42。]

Yang Yonghong. "Meiguo baquanzhuyi de xin fazhan" ("The Latest Development of US Hegemonism"). *Guoji Wenti Yanjiu* (International Studies) 1999 (4), 6–8. [杨永红。"美国霸权主义的新发展"。国际问题研究, 1999 (4), 頁 6–8。]

Yan Xuetong. "Lishi de jixu: lengzhan hou de zhuyao guoji zhengzhi maodun" ("The Extension of History: Main International Political Contradictions After the Cold War"). *Xiandai Guoji Guanxi (Contemporary International Relations)*, 2000 (6), 1–12. [阎学通。"历史的继续: 冷战后的主要国际政治矛盾"。现代国际关系, 2000(6), 頁 1–12。]

Yeh, Benjamin. "Taiwan Mulls Importing Water from China." Agence France-Presse, April 24, 2002. Reprinted in *FBISDC*, April 25, 2002.

"'Yes' Vote Paves Way for New Era." *The Sunday Nation*, September 28, 1997, A1. Reprinted in *FBISDREA*, September 30, 1997.

Yindee Lertcharoenchok. "Rights Activists Urge Review of Relations with Burma." *The Nation*, May 15, 1997, A6. Reprinted in *FBISDREA*, May 16, 1997.

"Ying bu rongxu tiaobo suowei 'Taiwanren yu Daluren' de ganqing" ("We Should Not Permit Incitement of the So-Called 'Taiwanese and Mainlander' Sentiment"). *Xiandai Zhengzhi (Modern Politics)* 7(2), August 20, 1960, 2. [「應不容許挑撥所謂『台灣人與大陸人』的感情」。现代政治, 1960 年 8 月 20 日, 頁 2。]

Yiu, Cody. "New CTS Manager Fends Off Harsh Attacks." *Taipei Times*, June 28, 2004, 3. <http://www.taipeitimes.com/News/taiwan/archives/2004/06/28/2003176838>. Retrieved July 12, 2005.

You Ch'ing. "Lun dikangquan" ("On the Right to Resist"). *Meilidao (Formosa)* 1(2), September 1979, 79–82. [尤清。「論抵抗權」。美麗島 1 (2), 1979 年 9 月, 頁 79–82。]

Yue Yan and Zhen Hai. "The Most Extensive Practice of Socialist Democracy." *Renmin Ribao (People's Daily)*, December 24, 1997. Translated in *FBISDCR*, December 29, 1997.

Yuwadee Tunyasiri. "Essay Competition for the Poor to Carry On." *Bangkok Post*, November 4, 2003. <http://www.bangkokpost.com>.

———. "PM Denies Trying to Cut NGO Funding." *Bangkok Post*, May 10, 2003. <http://www.bangkokpost.com>.

———. "Thaksin Urges City Hall, Organizers to Reach Compromise." *Bangkok Post*, October 4, 2003, 2.

Yu Xilai. "21 shiji Zhongguo xiandaihua yicheng (shang)" ("Agenda of China's Modernization in the 21st Century—Part 1"). *Zhanlue yu Guanli (Strategy and Management)* 2001 (2), 67–77. [喻希来。"21世纪中国现代化议程(上)"。战略与管理, 2001(2), 頁 67–77。]

————. "21 shiji Zhongguo xiandaihua yicheng (xia)" ("Agenda of China's modernization in the 21st Century—Part 2"). *Zhanlue yu Guanli (Strategy and Management)* 2001 (4), 1–12. [喻希来。"21世纪中国现代化议程(下)"。*战略与管理*, 2001 (4), 頁 1–12.]

————. "Guoji zhengyi yu guoji minzhu" ("International Justice and International Democracy"). *Zhanlue yu Guanli (Strategy and Management)* 2003 (5), 49–64. [喻希来。"国际正义与国际民主"。*战略与管理* 2003(1), 頁 61–75。]

————. "Shijie wenming zhong de Zhongguo wenhua" ("Chinese Culture in World Civilization"). *Zhanlue yu Guanli (Strategy and Management)* 2001 (1), 61–75. [喻希来。"世界文明中的中国文化"。*战略与管理* 2003(5), 頁 49–64。]

"Zai Meiguo chengren Zhonggong de zhenhan zhong kaizhan xinju" ("After the Shock of US Recognition of the Chinese Communists, Open up New a Situation"). *Zhongguo Luntan (The China Tribune)* 7(6), December 25, 1978, 1. [「在美國承認中共的震撼中開展新局」。*中國論壇* 7(6), 1978 年 12 月 25 日, 頁 1。]

Zhang Ji and Li Hui. "Leng zhan hou guoji zhengzhi zhong de wenhua chongtu" ("Cultural Conflicts in International Politics After the Cold War"). *Xiandai Guoji Guanxi (Contemporary International Relations)* 2002 (4), 43–48. [张骥 李 辉。"冷战后国际政治中的文化冲突"。*现代国际关系*, 2002(4), 頁 43–48。]

Zhang Li and Bai Jie. "Hulianwang de fazhan dui guoji guanxi de yingxiang" ("Impacts of Internet Development on International Relations"). *Xiandai Guoji Guanxi (Contemporary International Relations)* 2000 (11), 12–16. [张力、白洁。"互联网的发展对国际关系的影响"。*现代国际关系*, 2000(11), 頁 12–16。]

Zhang Minqian. "Quanqiuhua yu Meiguo de zhanlue" ("Globalization and the US Strategy"). *Xiandai Guoji Guanxi (Contemporary International Relations)*, 2000(6), 28–31. [张敏谦。"全球化与美国的战略"。*现代国际关系*, 2000(6), 頁 28–31。]

Zhang Shenjun. "Quan qiu jiegou chongtu yu Meiguo baquan de hefaxing weiji" ("Global Structural Conflict and the Legitimacy Crisis of American Hegemony"). *Meiguo Yanjiu (American Studies Quarterly)* 17(3), 2003, 30–41. [张 胜军。"全球结构冲突与美国霸权的合法性危机"。*美国研究*, 2003, 17(3), 頁 30–41。]

Zhang Sutang and Wu Yilong. "Li Peng Visits Fujian, Urges People's Congresses to Contribute to Building Political Civilization." Xinhua News Service, December 17, 2002. Translated in *FBISDCR*, December 19, 2002.

Zhang Tiegang. "A New Milestone in Sino-Russian Relations." *Liaowang (Outlook)*, July 23, 2001. Translated in *FBISDCR*, August 15, 2001.

Zhang Wenmu. "Zhongguo guojia anquan zhexue" ("China's Philosophy of National Security"). *Zhanlue yu Guanli (Strategy and Management)*, 2000 (1), 24–32. [张文木。"中国国家安全哲学"。*战略与管理*, 2000 (1), 頁 24–32。]

Zhang Yan. "Xinxi shidai de diyuan zhengzhi yu 'kejiquan'" ("Geopolitics in the Information Age and 'Sci-Tech Power'"). *Xiandai Guoji Guanxi (Contemporary International Relations)* 2001 (7), 18–23. [张妍。"信息时代的地缘政治与治与"。*现代国际关系*, 2001(7), 頁 18–23。]

Zhang Zhengdong. "NATO's Hegemonic Logic." *Liaowang (Outlook)*, April 26, 1999. Translated in *FBISDCR*, April 26, 1999.

Zhang Zhengdong and Yuan Bingzhong. "Tentative Analysis of NATO's New Strategic Concept." Xinhua News Service, April 26, 1999. Translated in *FBIS-DCR*, May 3, 1999.

Zhan Jiafeng and Zhang Jinrong. "Keji geming yu diyuan zhengzhi lilun de yanbian" ("Sci-Tech Revolution and the Evolution of Geopolitics"). *Xiandai Guoji Guanxi* (*Contemporary International Relations*) 2001 (6), 31–35. [詹家峰、张金荣。"科技革命与地缘政治理论的演变"。现代国际关系, 2001 (6), 頁 31–35。]

Zhao, Suisheng, ed. *China and Democracy: Reconsidering the Prospects for a Democratic China*. New York: Routledge, 2000.

———. "Chinese Nationalism and Its International Orientations." *Political Science Quarterly* 115(1), Spring 2000, 1–33.

Zheng Hangsheng. "Drawing a Line of Demarcation Between Socialist Democracy and Congressional Democracy of the West." *Renmin Ribao* (*People's Daily*), July 11, 1996. Translated in *FBISDCR*, July 22, 1996.

Zheng Yongnian. "Zhengzhi gaige yu Zhongguo guojia jianshe" ("Political Reform and State Building in China"). *Zhanlue yu Guanli* (*Strategy and Management*) 2001 (2), 1–11. [郑永年。"政治改革与中国国家建设"。战略与管理, 2001(2) 頁 1–11。]

Zhou Xirong. "On Socialist Democracy." *Renmin Ribao* (*People's Daily*), April 16, 1995, 9. Translated in *FBISDCR*, June 13, 1996.

Zhu Huaying. "Seminar on WTO and Cross-Strait Economic and Trade Ties Held in Beijing." Xinhua, January 8, 2002. Translated in *FBISDCR*, January 10, 2002.

Zittrain, Jonathan and Benjamin Edelman. "Empirical Analysis of Internet Filtering in China." Berkman Center for Internet and Society, Harvard Law School. <http://cyber.law.harvard.edu/filtering/china/>. Retrieved May 19, 2004.

Zweig, David. *Internationalizing China: Domestic Interests and Global Linkages*. Ithaca, NY: Cornell University Press, 2002.

CHARACTER LIST

Aihua 矮化
Badao 霸道
Baquan xintai 霸權心態
Beiqing 悲情
Bentu 本土
Benzhi 本質
Biaodaquan 表達權
Boai 博愛
Bu yao dang tou 不要當頭
Chengshou 成熟
Chongsu 重鑄
Chuanshengtong 傳聲筒
Chuli weiyuanhui 處理委員會
Daijipai 待機派
Dangwai 黨外
Datong 大同
Datongxiaoyi 大同小異
Daxue Zazhi 大學雜誌
Da Zhongguo Minzuzhuyi
　　大中國民族主義
Ding tianxia guannian 定天下觀念
Dongfangren 東方人
Duojihua shidai 多極化時代
Ezhi 扼制
Fazhi minzhu 法治民主
Fuyong 附庸
Genben liyi 根本利益
Gongde 公德
Gongjuhua 工具化
Guilu 規律
Guojia danwei zhenshi gan
　　國家單位真實感

Guoji gonggong lingyu 國際公共領域
Guojia jianshe 國家建設
Guoji minzhu 國際民主
Guoji siyu 國際私域
Guoji ziyou 國際自由
Guomin guojia 國民國家
Haiquan lilun 海權理論
Han minzu 漢民族
Hao zhan 好戰
Heping yu fazhan 和平與發展
Huangminhua 皇民化
Jiayi paichi 加以排斥
Jiegui xiangqia 結軌相洽
Jinsi yongheng de zhuti 近似永恆的主題
Li 理
Liang guo liang fu 兩國兩府
Liliang zhongxin 力量中心
Ling qi lu zao 另起爐灶
Lizu Taiwan, xionghuai dalu, fangyan
　　shijie 立足台灣, 胸懷大陸, 放眼世界
Mao Gong 毛共
Mei ba 美霸
Miulun he guailun 謬論和怪論
Neidi yanchang 內地延長
Nuezheng 虐政
Nuhua 奴化
Qin Mei 親美
Quanqiu 全球
Quanqiu zhili 全球治理
Ren 仁
Renquan 人權
Renquan xuanyan 人權宣言

Renshi Taiwan 認識台灣
Rentong fanwei 認同範圍
Shendu 身督
Shifan zuoyong 示範作用
Shijie de duoyangxing 世界的多樣性
Shijie ge guo ronghe 世界各國融合
Shijie gongmin 世界公民
Shuchu minzhu 輸出民主
Taijian 台奸
Taiwan Bihui 台灣筆會
Taiwan duli jianguo lianmeng
　　台灣獨立建國聯盟
Taiwan duli lianhehui 台灣獨立聯合會
Taiwan Gongheguo 台灣共和國
Taiwan minzu 台灣民族
Taiwan qingnian 台灣青年
Taiwan shi Taiwanren de Taiwan
　　台灣是台灣人的台灣
Taiwan Wenhua Xiehui 台灣文化協會
Taiwan zhuti de wenti 台灣主體的問題
Taiwan zhutiguan 台灣主體觀
Taiwan zijiu xuanyan 台灣自救宣言
Tianxia 天下
Tiyong 體用
Waisheng zhu 外省豬
Wangdao 王道
Wenhua chanpin 文化產品
Wenhua qiangquan 文化強權
Wenhua rentong 文化認同
Wenming zaizao 文明再造
Wenxing 文星
Xiangtu wenxue 鄉土文學
Xianshi 現實
Xin 信
Xin er duli de guojia 新而獨立的國家

Xingxiang de youshi 形象的優勢
Xin Taiwanren 新台灣人
Yanlun yilu 言論一律
Ya wenming 亞文明
Yazhou de jia 亞洲的家
Yeman 野蠻
Yi 義
Yiban zhengyi 一般正義
Yiduan 異端
Yi min bi guan 以民迫官
Yindao 引導
Yi shang wei zheng 以商圍政
Yitihua 一體化
You panluan yitu 有叛亂意圖
Youyuegan huo bingtai 優越感或病態
Youzhi 幼稚
Zai Taiwan de Zhongguo wenxue
　　在台灣的中國文學
Zaiti 載體
Zhanglao Jiaohui 長老教會
Zhi 智
Zhina 支那
Zhonghua Kuomintang 中華國民黨
Zhonghua Minguo 中華民國
Zhonghua Taiwan Minzhuguo
　　中華台灣民主國
Zhonghua wenhua fuxing yundong
　　中華文化復興運動
Zhongyuan 中原
Zijue 自決
Ziyou Zhongguo 自由中國
Zi wenming 子文明
Ziwo wanshan 自我完善
Zonghe guoli 綜合國力
Zuqun 族群

INDEX

A

American hegemonism, 4, 15, 90, 108, 206
Anglo-Saxon sense of superiority, 98
Anti-Money Laundering Office (AMLO), 84
APEC summit, in Thailand, 1, 2, 84; anti-Western style democracy, 5, 14; classifying theories of, 5; domestic level dynamics, 5; conventional and conservative "pluralist" approaches, 9; critical theory, 7; democratic liberties, 4, 192; future of, 207–15; global culture, 8, 10–11; international demonstration effects, 6; NGO activism, 3; structuralist bias, 10; theorists, views of; Carothers, Thomas, 6, 219–220; Cox, Robert, 7; Finnemore, Martha, 9–10; Gilley, Bruce, 7–8; Huntington, Samuel, 6, 95; Robinson, William, 6–7, 50, 141; Whitehead, Laurence, 6; world polity theory, 8; ascending solidarism, 9; and international NGOs, 10
Asian democratization, 3, 5, 20
Asian economic meltdown, 46, 57, 68, 86, 88
Asian values, 14, 70; movement, 45
Association of Southeast Asian Nations (ASEAN), 73–74, 75–76, see also Thai political spectrum

B

Banyat Bantadtan, 3

C

Chakri dynasty, 27, 36
Chamlong Srimuang, 34–36, 38, 41, 54–57, 60, 64, 85, 86
Chen Shui-bian, 174, 180, 181, 182, 185, 197, 198, 202
Chiang Kai-shek's nationalism, 121
China Human Rights Research Association (CHRRA), 111, 112, 115
China, recentering of; diplomatic issues of, 145–147; economic development, of China, 144
Chinese Communist Party (CCP), 4, 14–17; aversion to decentering, 88, 207, 227; Chinese elites, role of, 89, 91–92, 232, see also intellectual cross-currents, in CCP; cosmopolitan global order, emergence of, 91; hegemonism and democracy-promotion, 95–102, 233; and American culture, 98–99, 102; American military intervention, 106–107; growth of, 97; opposition to US, 95–96; Wang Jisi, views of, 96–98, 142; Western democracy promotion, features of, 100–101; and human rights, 109–111; and international democratization, 140–144; and the Internet, 243; cultural flow through, 127–129; public opinion, posting of, 127; users of, 126; Kosovo crisis, 102–109, 140; Beijing Massacre, 102, 108; Sino-US relations, 102–104; and multipolarization, 140–144; Zhang

**EAST-WEST CENTER SERIES
ON CONTEMPORARY ISSUES
IN ASIA AND THE PACIFIC**